ASSAULT ON NORMANDY

ASSAULT ON NORMANDY

First-Person Accounts from the Sea Services

Edited by Paul Stillwell

NAVAL INSTITUTE PRESS / ANNAPOLIS, MARYLAND

© 1994
by the United States Naval Institute
Annapolis, Maryland

Library of Congress Cataloging-in-Publication Data

Assault on Normandy: first-person accounts from the sea services/
    edited by Paul Stillwell.
        p.   cm.
    Includes bibliographical references and index.
    ISBN 1-55750-781-3
    1. World War, 1939–1945—Campaigns—France—Normandy. 2. World
War, 1939–1945—Naval operations, American.   3. World War,
1939–1945—Personal narratives, American.   I. Stillwell, Paul,
1944–
D762.N67A87   1994
940.54′2142—dc20   93-49791
                                                                            CIP

Printed in the United States of America on acid-free paper ⊗

3 5 7 9 8 6 4 2

First printing

CONTENTS

PREFACE   ix

THE MEMORY OF DEPARTED SHIPMATES   1
By Commander Hans E. Bergner, U.S. Naval Reserve (Retired)

DISASTER AT DIEPPE, SUCCESS AT NORMANDY   9
By Rear Admiral Elliott B. Strauss, U.S. Navy (Retired)

STRATEGY AND SECRECY   14
By George M. Elsey

ADMIRAL STARK'S ROLE   19
By Rear Admiral Neil K. Dietrich, U.S. Navy (Retired)

ADMIRAL RAMSAY AND I   23
By Admiral Alan G. Kirk, U.S. Navy (Retired)

ULTRA WARNINGS   29
By McGeorge Bundy

GERMAN NAVAL OPERATIONS ON D-DAY   33
By Vice Admiral Friedrich Ruge, Federal German Navy (Retired)

EXERCISE TIGER—SCREAMS OF AGONY   41
By Eugene E. Eckstam, M.D.

STRIPE FIVE AND YOU'RE OUT   46
By Admiral Alfred C. Richmond, U.S. Coast Guard (Retired)

IKE REMEMBERED ME   50
By Vice Admiral John D. Bulkeley, U.S. Navy (Retired)

CLOSE-IN SUPPORT AT OMAHA BEACH   57
By Vice Admiral Lorenzo S. Sabin, U.S. Navy (Retired)

TRAFFIC COP   64
By Captain Richard H. Crook Jr., U.S. Naval Reserve (Retired)

DD SPELLED DISASTER   68
By Dean L. Rockwell

LANDING THE BIG RED ONE   72
By Robert E. Adams

MY ONLY JOB WAS TO STAY ALIVE   76
By Lieutenant Commander Paul S. Fauks, U.S. Navy (Retired)

SURVIVING THE LONDON BLITZ—AND MEETING A HUSBAND   83
By Barbara Clare Fauks

NOIC UTAH   86
By Commodore James E. Arnold, U.S. Naval Reserve

COMBAT DEMOLITION UNIT   93
By Orval W. Wakefield

THE BEST SEAT FOR A REALLY BIG SHOW   98
By Captain John R. Blackburn, U.S. Navy (Retired)

MAKE LOVE *AND* WAR   106
By Rear Admiral F. Julian Becton, U.S. Navy (Retired)

DREAD OF THE UNKNOWN   112
By Lieutenant Davis C. Howes, U.S. Naval Reserve (Retired)

SHIPWRECKED IN THE CHANNEL   119
By Lieutenant General Orwin C. Talbott, U.S. Army (Retired)

BROKEN SHIP, BROKEN BODY   125
By William D. Branstrator

GETTING THE TROOPS 'OVER THERE'   131
By John L. Horton

SUB-ORDINARY SEAMAN   136
By Richard A. Freed

LIBERTY SHIP SIGNALMAN   142
By Cornelius A. "Pete" Burke

WHEN SEVENS WEREN'T LUCKY   148
By Father Patrick W. Kemp

DESIGNING THE LST   154
By John C. Niedermair

CIVILIANS IN UNIFORM   159
By Walter Trombold

THE HAZARDS OF LONDON (AND NORMANDY)   165
By Commander Allen Pace, U.S. Naval Reserve (Retired)

MULBERRIES AND GOOSEBERRIES   170
By Rear Admiral Edward Ellsberg, U.S. Naval Reserve (Retired)

BATTLESHIP COMMANDER   182
By Vice Admiral Carleton F. Bryant, U.S. Navy (Retired)

A STRANGE PLACE FOR A MARINE   188
By Irvin Airey

THE CAPTURE OF CHERBOURG   194
By Captain Quentin R. Walsh, U.S. Coast Guard (Retired)

THE NON-AMPHIBIOUS SWAN OF CHERBOURG   203
By Rear Admiral George W. Bauernschmidt, Supply Corps, U.S. Navy (Retired)

SUBMARINES AND BUZZ-BOMB LAUNCHERS   210
By Rear Admiral James R. Reedy, U.S. Navy (Retired)

A WARM WELCOME IN SOUTHERN FRANCE   217
By Admiral H. Kent Hewitt, U.S. Navy (Retired)

THE DEATH OF ADMIRAL MOON   225
By Captain John A Moreno, U.S. Navy (Retired)

DOG TAGS AND DIRTY BEANS   231
By Commander Albert K. Murray, U.S. Naval Reserve (Retired)

BEACH JUMPERS DON'T REALLY JUMP   235
By Captain Douglas Fairbanks Jr., U.S. Naval Reserve (Retired)

SURFACE ACTION AT POINT-BLANK RANGE   242
By Vice Admiral John D. Bulkeley, U.S. Navy (Retired)

THE ALSOS MISSION   249
By Rear Admiral Albert G. Mumma, U.S. Navy (Retired)

A DIFFERENT KIND OF UNIFORM   257
By Rex Barney

GAMBLING FOR DRAMAMINE   262
By Lieutenant Colonel James H. Skidmore, U.S. Army Reserve (Retired)

THREE FACES   268
By Robert Lee

A SENSE OF DUTY TO THE FATHERLAND   272
By Hans J. Degelow

MOVING INTO GERMANY   278
By Rear Admiral Donald J. MacDonald, U.S. Navy (Retired)

ACROSS THE RHINE   283
By Lieutenant Norris Houghton, U.S. Naval Reserve

SURRENDER!   289
By Captain Harry C. Butcher, U.S. Naval Reserve

GLOSSARY   293

SOURCES OF ARTICLES   295

ACKNOWLEDGMENTS   297

INDEX   301

PREFACE

On June 6, 1969, the twenty-fifth anniversary of the Allied invasion of Normandy, I had a date with a local schoolteacher to see a movie in downtown Long Beach, California. It was Darryl Zanuck's epic *The Longest Day*, a dramatization of the events of D-Day. The picture provided a tunnel through time, because the story it depicted was at considerable odds with what we in the navy were experiencing twenty-five years afterward.

Only a couple of months returned from the Western Pacific, I was serving that June in the crew of the battleship *New Jersey*. Already I'd heard of plans for American forces to be returned home from Vietnam. I was incredulous, because the job there was not yet done. Ironically, those of us who had been in ships off the coast of Vietnam were as far removed as we could be from a sense of the eroding national will for a war in Southeast Asia. It was only years later, when I saw TV tapes of the 1968 Democratic national convention, that I had a sense of the way in which the national mood had become ever more ugly and antiwar at the end of the Sixties.

On that June night the problems of Vietnam faded away for three hours as the characters on the screen showed the audience a different time—one when national sacrifice was commonplace, expected, and made ungrudgingly. Hitler's forces held sway in much of Europe, and the time for liberation had come. Restoration of freedom was a goal that united the country. Men and women of the U.S. military services were treated warmly by their fellow citizens.

In the film, paratroopers stepped out into the darkness, not knowing if they would be alive or dead when they reached the ground. Commandos lurked near a railroad bridge to perform acts of sabotage. Soldiers on board ship shot craps, knowing that a far larger gamble was coming with the next dawn. Glider pilots went up in flimsy craft that all too often had an unhappy fate ahead. Soldiers clambered out of landing craft onto a hostile shore—particularly at Omaha Beach—and faced a withering fire from German machine guns, mortars, and 88-millimeter guns.

On the other side, the German soldiers and the French civilians reacted—in their separate ways—as the invasion came at long last. France had been a captive of the Germans since the spring of 1940, and now the hour of reckoning had come. Hitler and his minions were to be on the defensive thenceforth.

As the movie unfolded, viewers could see that the invasion of Normandy had not been a certain success from the start. It was a collection of risks, actions, and circumstances that eventually led to victory. Men made it happen. The show was dramatic, yet there was something unsatisfying about *The Longest Day*, particularly when viewed through navy eyes. The problem was that those flickering black-and-white images on the screen made it seem that the naval and maritime forces involved were only appendages, only footnotes, as it were, in the telling of the story. In a three-hour movie, only about ten or fifteen minutes were devoted to the naval aspects.

In fact, however, the sea services were indispensable in the campaign to recapture France and the other occupied European nations. Ships—U.S. Navy, Coast Guard, merchant marine, and foreign vessels—formed a moving bridge across the Atlantic. They carried the men and they carried the materials of war. Landing craft put the soldiers onto the far shore, and bombardment ships provided essential gunfire support to the troops. Even after the initial days of assault, ships continued to disgorge huge quantities of ammunition, food, fuel, equipment, and supplies to keep the armies going toward Germany.

The navy was also in the Mediterranean in August 1944 as it landed still more soldiers in southern France so they could join forces with their brethren in Normandy and effect a pincer movement. Navy landing craft enabled thousands of soldiers to cross the Rhine River.

In many ways that movie typifies the focus of histories of the operation. For the most part, the telling of the story of D-Day and the capture of France has begun at the beach and moved inland. But the experiences of the men on the water deserve their day as well. Probably the best overall volume on the role of the U.S. Navy in the campaign is Samuel Eliot Morison's *The Invasion of France and Germany: 1944–1945* (Little,

Brown, 1957), which covers Normandy, the assault on southern France, and the crossing of the Rhine in Germany. It is an operational view, providing a comprehensive picture of both strategy and tactics.

On a more personal level, two valuable memoirs of the navy side are Edward Ellsberg's *The Far Shore* (Dodd, Mead, and Company, 1960) and John Mason Brown's *Many a Watchful Night* (McGraw-Hill, 1944). Each necessarily focuses on the author's personal experiences and relates them to the larger whole. Both are recommended reading, but there is still more to be told about the lives of individuals.

The collection that follows is an attempt to relate the naval and maritime story through a series of first-person accounts that represent the experiences of people from much larger groups. These firsthand narratives capture the drama, the sense of sacrifice that were characteristic of the period, particularly the impact of the operation on individuals. It is the human story.

Implicit in many of these accounts is teamwork, the bond that forms among shipmates as they face shared dangers. The narrators that follow come from a variety of sea service vessels and communities: battleships, destroyers, cruisers, landing ships, patrol craft, PT boats, minesweepers, troop transports, cargo ships, landing craft, naval aviation, beach battalions, combat demolition units, beach jumpers, planners, medical personnel, combat artists, ship designers, naval engineers, naval armed guards, merchant mariners, the U.S. Coast Guard, and the U.S. Marine Corps. The relatively large number of narratives from LST men is indicative of the vital role those ugly ships played in the success of the landings at Normandy and southern France.

The book also includes a few stories by soldiers to describe the campaign of movement from the Normandy beachhead to the Rhine. These men represent the hundreds of thousands who crossed the Atlantic by ship so they could fight ashore and ensure the defeat of Nazi Germany.

The men in this book—both Germans and Americans—range from the admirals in command to those facing enemy fire directly. One woman completes the collection because she is representative of still another group—those who became war brides after meeting American servicemen.

The gathering of these stories has been a fascinating process, particularly because of the opportunity to meet and talk with such a diverse group of participants. Some of these chapters are from previously published accounts and some from unpublished manuscripts. About two-thirds of these narratives are from individuals who told their stories through interviews, either by telephone or in person.

Vice Admiral John D. Bulkeley is one of several navy

men who were particularly eager to cooperate because of the feeling that their service's contribution to Normandy has not been adequately told to most Americans. Bulkeley, who fits the category of living legend, has a home in Silver Spring, Maryland, that should also be classified as a museum. History is everywhere. On a hook hangs a battered khaki cap that dates from his PT boat days in 1942. Nearby is a model of a PT boat with the tiny tan figure of movie character ET sitting proudly in the cockpit. On the wall are framed photos of President Franklin D. Roosevelt and King George VI. Near the door is the brass casing from a powder charge used in shooting a 5-inch projectile at German corvettes off the south of France. In the basement is a replica of Admiral Bulkeley's PT boat bunk.

Another contributor, Douglas Fairbanks Jr., lives in New York. His office in Manhattan is also replete with photos and souvenirs. His wartime helmet is there, as are a death mask of Napoleon and hundreds of photos documenting a career in the movies and theater. His ties with the British are evident, including photos of members of the British royal family that Fairbanks has known.

On the Eastern Shore of Maryland, Coast Guard Captain Quentin Walsh and his wife, Mary Ann, live in a farmhouse built in the eighteenth century. It has gabled windows, and the ends of the roof are adorned by twin chimneys. The home displays photos from Normandy and also a brass model of a harpoon-shooting gun, for Captain Walsh was part of a whaling expedition in the late 1930s. The couple's wedding album recalls the time in 1943 when they pushed up their marriage date so Walsh could hurry to Britain for the assignments that led eventually to D-Day. During the honeymoon in New York, their hotel windows were perpetually open in the heat of summer. The tramp of soldiers' feet and calls of cadence reaching the room were an all-too-present reminder of the overseas duty that lay ahead.

In another farmhouse, this one in western Missouri, Lieutenant Colonel Jim Skidmore recalls his army days while seated in a living room gracefully decorated by his wife, Phyllis. He is an innately modest man, and as he tells of his exploits, Phyllis reminds him of achievements worth putting on the record. Along with the modesty comes a sense of humor, so that a twinkle often shines in Skidmore's eye as a memory replays itself.

Across the state, in a suburban ranch house outside St. Louis, Paul and Barbara Fauks describe their meeting in a London subway in 1944. I first came to know the couple in 1972 when Paul and I were both working for the St. Louis Cardinals. This friendly man and I soon discovered that we had mutual interests in baseball and the navy. Two decades later, his sea stories are worth listening to once again—this time with a tape recorder nearby. As Barbara tells her story, it is in the British accent she grew up with and retains to this day.

In an elegant neighborhood in northwest Washington, D.C., lives Rear Admiral Donald MacDonald, who earned a chestful of medals as a destroyer skipper in the desperate Solomons campaign in mid-World War II. His den is also adorned with a collection of photos, including autographed pictures from the naval leaders of the 1940s. There are mementos as well from his time as skipper of the presidential yacht for Harry Truman. A sideboard has another reminder of the war. Inherited from his mother are three black-and-white photos in frames that are hinged together. They show MacDonald and his two brothers in uniform. Such service by brothers was commonplace during the war; uncommon was the fact that one of MacDonald's brothers flew with Charles Lindbergh during operations in the South Pacific.

Also in an exclusive area of Washington is Rear Admiral Elliott Strauss, who graduated from the Naval Academy in 1923. He relaxes in a den adorned with a signed photo of Lord Mountbatten, whom he served so many years ago. Effortlessly, the ninety-year-old admiral rolls away the years and recalls his repeated tours of duty in Great Britain. He also explains, with considerable pleasure, that his era was the best time to have been a naval officer; things have gone downhill since then, he says.

Rear Admiral George Bauernschmidt, who graduated from the academy a year before Strauss, lives in an apartment in Annapolis and has a puckish sense of humor. He explains, for instance, that he knew his classmate Hyman Rickover "before he became a genius." He also remembers that Supply Corps officers were second-class citizens for many years, dominated by the philosophies imparted by the line. Since he was a line officer himself before color blindness sent him to supply, he did not accept gently the lot handed him by circumstance.

North of Baltimore, in a suburb far removed from the hostile streets he once patrolled as a policeman, Irvin Airey pulls out the cruise book he received on board the battleship *Arkansas*. The pride of serving in the Marine Corps is still with him. Then he goes to a den and points out the awards earned during his police work; he recalls that duty as being more dangerous than service in World War II. Several weeks later, at the Naval Academy, Admiral William Crowe, former Chairman of the Joint Chiefs of Staff, reads the words of Airey and others who served at sea during the war. In the background a symphony orchestra plays Richard Rodgers's stirring "Victory at Sea" composition. The combination of words and music moves the audience, evoking images of that war half a century earlier.

Rear Admiral Al Mumma, the type of individual who is in charge of whatever he is involved in, welcomes me to a beautiful home in a golf-course community in New Hampshire. The setting, amid green forests and New England lakes, is idyllic. As a naval engineer, he has had a hand in any number of ship designs. Now he tells me that he has helped design the house as well. Its picture windows afford vistas of the scenery beyond. He pauses when pointing out a framed picture of Admiral Arleigh Burke, the CNO whom Mumma served when he was Chief of the Bureau of Ships. He recalls the time the childless Burke turned to Carmen Mumma and said, "I suppose you're one of those SOGPIPs. That's a silly old grandmother, pictures in purse."

At a symposium in San Antonio on the subject of the Pacific War, the noted wartime submariner Slade Cutter introduces a friend, Rear Admiral Sunshine Jim Reedy. The admiral, now outfitted with a gray goatee and walking with a cane, reports that he was the wartime skipper of Joseph P. Kennedy Jr., brother of the future president. His account of their time together, delivered with considerable energy, is a lively one.

In an apartment in Bloomington, Minnesota, Bob Lee points to a model of an army antiaircraft vehicle and relates stories that have been buried deep within his memory—some because they have been too painful to think about very often. He says that he has not even shared some of these memories with his wife, Helen. Not all the wounds of war are physical ones.

Father Patrick Kemp takes a break from packing up the possessions he has accumulated in a career of service in the church. Just a few days before leaving the rectory behind his parish church in Bowie, Maryland, he is surrounded by books, photos, his stamp collection, and cartons of things that have come off shelves and out of closets. Later, after a move to a retirement apartment in Annapolis, Kemp brings out an album filled with fifty-year-old photos. Included are tiny black-and-white shots of the family that befriended him in western England before he headed off to the invasion of France.

Rex Barney, once a pitcher for the Brooklyn Dodgers and now a public address announcer for the Baltimore Orioles, pauses after signing autographs for fans who have gathered at an Annapolis shopping center. The book he is signing this evening contains such vivid descriptions of a soldier's life that a chapter is well worth including here, along with the stories of the navy men.

Another army man, Lieutenant General Orwin Talbott, lives in a spacious Annapolis home, across the Severn River from the Naval Academy. He is extremely well organized, with the result that his story of having to abandon ship is delivered so smoothly that he almost seems to be reading from a script. Even in sport shirt and slacks, his presence is a commanding one.

In a prosperous suburb west of Milwaukee, a former German naval officer, Hans Degelow, seems more patriotic about the United States than many people who were born here. Yet there is still a fierce pride about his service on behalf of Germany—and wistful thoughts as he remembers his many Naval Academy classmates who went into U-boats and perished. He brings out hundreds of photos; the negatives were once buried in a backyard in Germany to protect them from the advancing Russians. He opens the pages of a notebook he kept at the Naval Academy, written in a now-outmoded German script and illustrated with colorful drawings. His German heritage will remain an important part of him as long as he lives.

A formal parlor from long ago provides the setting in which Rear Admiral Julian Becton describes his naval service. He and his family live in a turn-of-the-century mansion on Philadelphia's Main Line. The pictures and mementos are instant transports to a past of elegant living when the house was doubtless operated by a bevy of servants. The yipping of a passel of nervous dogs seems somehow incongruous in this stately setting. Becton and his wife, Betty, are invariably gracious, and Betty's brother, Dick Reuss, provides a tour of the mansion's basement, which houses what is undoubtedly among the finest private collections of railroad memorabilia in the country.

I encounter George Elsey at the army's Fort Myer, adjacent to the Arlington National Cemetery. We are there for the funeral of a mutual friend, naval historian Roger Pineau. Tall, slim, and urbane, Elsey brings forth recollections of his departed friend. Pineau specialized as a Japanese linguist and served in that capacity for Samuel Eliot Morison's naval history. Thus, as he comes to the end of his remarks, Elsey turns toward Pineau's remains, renders a naval salute, and says, "Sayonara, Roger." It is the perfect gesture of farewell for a navy man who knew the Japanese well. Elsey, as with the other contributors to this volume, has reached a point in life at which he finds himself too often attending the funerals of friends.

Other contributors are voices through the telephone wire, occasionally cautious, at first, about being tape-recorded. But the hesitation and self-consciousness evaporate quickly. After all, how often does an old sailor have a willing audience for sea stories? The tales unfold: waves pound, soldiers are seasick, German and American guns fire, hundreds and hundreds of airplanes fly overhead, troops land, sailors and shipmates are wounded and killed, and the Allies move on toward eventual victory. The seventy-year-old storyteller becomes twenty for an hour. It is 1944 again.

THE MEMORY OF DEPARTED SHIPMATES

By Commander Hans E. Bergner, U.S. Naval Reserve (Retired)

On the night of June 4, 1944, the *LST-282* pushed her stubby bow into the waves of the English Channel as she headed toward Normandy. After months of planning and training, we in her crew were part of a vast armada preparing to strike the first blow in the liberation of France. My thoughts that night were less about making history than they were about survival. As I lay in my bunk, thinking about what was ahead, I said a few more prayers than I normally did.

In fact, the weather was so rough that the invasion was postponed for a day. And so it was that the crew's sense of anxiety was stretched still further. On the night of June 5, we set out once more to embark on the invasion. That night, when it came time to pray, I told the Lord that everything I had said the night before still applied.

The *LST-282* was commanded by Lieutenant Lawrence Gilbert and also served as the flagship of LST Group 29, Flotilla 10, with Commander J. C. Guillot as group commander. When we went to Normandy in June of 1944, Commander Guillot was on board with his staff and he also served as officer in tactical command of our convoy of minesweepers, five LSTs, two rescue tugboats, and two destroyers. Each LST towed a large rhino barge, onto which our cargo was to be off-loaded just off the beach. Thus, behind the brave minesweepers, we were to be the first ship of the first convoy to Utah Beach.

At 2:42 A.M. on D-Day we anchored off Utah Beach. We had something brand new on board for this operation—an amazing aid to navigation known as Loran. It gave us precise bearings and ranges on two different transmitting stations, so we could accurately fix the position of the transport area. After we followed the minesweepers in and anchored, then the transports anchored in relation to the *LST-282*. We also carried demolition teams to destroy beach obstacles; they shoved off for the beach in our LCVPs at 2:46. Two of our six boats were swamped on the beach, but the officers and crews were recovered.

Then it came time to load the bulk of our troops in LCMs from the transports so they could go ashore at H-hour. There were some good-sized swells heading in toward the beach. It was still dark as the troops climbed down the debarkation nets on the ship's sides. I recall seeing the swells bring the landing craft up to meet the descending soldiers. It was tricky, forcing the soldiers to jump in at just the right time. They had to be pretty nimble to avoid serious injury.

One of the soldiers that we carried to Normandy was a man named Werner Kleeman, a Jewish man who had escaped from a concentration camp in Germany. I learned of this later when I saw him being interviewed on television by Tom Brokaw on the occasion of the forty-fifth anniversary of the invasion. After his escape, he went initially to England, then to the United States, where he later enlisted in the army. He was assigned to a communication unit of the 4th Infantry Division. As he told Brokaw, a photographer assigned to one of their units wanted to let the headquarters in England know that everything had gone well. When the ship was about six miles offshore, we unloaded army cargo onto our rhino barge. After the soldiers got onto the barge, this man took a photo with his camera pointed back toward our bow.

As Kleeman explained, since the photographer didn't want to break radio silence on D-Day, he tied the negative for this picture onto the leg of a carrier pigeon that was supposed to fly back to England. The next thing they knew of the photo came about four to six weeks later. The Allies had taken Cherbourg, including capture of a German headquarters unit. On the desk of one of the officers was a German newspaper with that picture printed on the front page. The hull number of our ship—282—was clearly visible in the photo. Underneath the photo was a caption explaining that the carrier pigeon became exhausted and fell behind German lines. It didn't make it to England, so the Germans developed the film and sent the picture to the newspaper. The caption further said that the barge onto which the LST unloaded hadn't made it ashore

The *LST-282* discharges a Jeep onto an LCT for the final trip to the invasion beach at Normandy. (*Navy photo in the National Archives: 80-G-253137*)

because it had been destroyed by German artillery. This was not true, because Kleeman has told me that none of the 4th Division equipment from our ship was lost.

The *LST-282* was set up as a hospital ship, providing initial medical care to wounded personnel and then transporting them back to England. As I remember, we had three surgeons and twenty-four pharmacist's mates on board for the invasion. The bulkheads on the sides of the ship's tank deck were equipped to mount litters. The wardroom was set up to handle the most serious cases of surgery. We started getting some of the wounded from Utah Beach, but then we moved and began receiving casualties from Omaha too because the fighting was much fiercer there. All types of craft brought them to the *LST-282*.

I didn't see the action ashore, but I saw the results. The soldiers' uniforms were impregnated with a chemical to protect against poison gas. Before sending the wounded below to the tank deck, medical personnel on the main deck cut off the uniforms from the soldiers and piled them on the fantail. The sun shone on that stack, and the odor produced by the combination of blood and chemicals was most unpleasant. I didn't go back there anymore. The next day we went to England

and unloaded our human cargo at Southampton.

On about D+3 we carried a load of Sherman tanks to Omaha Beach. These were among the first to cross the English Channel, because the army had an urgent need for them ashore. When we were on the beach we could hear the big guns inland and knew the tanks would soon be headed there as well. Once we beached the ship, we had to wait a few hours for the tide to go out so we would be able to put the tanks onto dry land. For the evening meal the skipper directed the cooks to fry pork chops for the army boys. He wanted them to go into battle with a good meal under their belts.

When we returned to England on that trip, we carried wounded German prisoners along with the Americans. Since my parents had come from Germany and I spoke German, I was able to serve as interpreter when the doctors needed to ask questions of the wounded prisoners. We had one hard-boiled SS trooper, a sergeant, who had popped up out of a burning tank. Once on board the LST he said he didn't want his dressings changed. He had apparently been in a dazed condition when he was captured, and the British had applied the initial battle dressings. All we could see were his eyes, but it was time to change the bandages. He didn't want our doctors to do it, because he assumed they would kill him. I convinced him that the doctors would not harm him and that we were not the type of people that he had been told we were.

Then he asked, "Do you, as an officer, think I did my duty?" He explained that the heat inside the tank forced him out and that the British had grabbed him while his uniform was on fire. It seemed to me that he wanted some sort of reassurance that he could still go to a "military heaven" after being captured alive. When I told him that I thought he had probably done about as much as any human being could under those circumstances, he said something that I will never forget: "Well, those were British; I knew they weren't Russian. If they had been Russian—even if they had cut me into a million pieces, every one of my pieces would have fought on." That gives you an idea of the hatred that was part of the indoctrination the German SS troopers received.

Fortunately, the *LST-282* was relatively safe from enemy fire during its stay off the Normandy beachhead. Enemy shore batteries had been a big concern to us beforehand. We wouldn't have been in range of anything except the largest guns, but the Allies knew that the Germans had them on Pointe du Hoc, on the

bluff between Omaha and Utah. Rangers under Lieutenant Colonel James Rudder were assigned to scale those cliffs and silence the guns. They met a lot of opposition, being fired down upon by machine guns from the top. But when the soldiers finally scaled the cliffs, they discovered that the Germans had moved the big guns elsewhere. If those guns had still been in place, we probably would have been fired on.

The several trips we had made safely between the beachheads and England following the invasion had given me a sense of confidence that I could withstand another operation. After Normandy, we went to the Mediterranean so the ship could take part in the invasion of southern France. We knew that this time we would be beaching on D-Day itself. When we were loading north of Naples, I talked to my close friend and roommate who was the ship's gunnery officer, Peter Hughes. I said, "Pete, I feel quite different about this one. I'm not as concerned."

He turned to me and said, "You know, it's strange you should say that. I really wasn't so afraid in Normandy, but this time I have a bad feeling."

It appeared that we would have an easy day of it on August 15. We waited offshore after watching the

The tank decks of LSTs had brackets in the bulkheads to carry stretchers. Shown here is the *LST-281*. Bergner's ship used a similar arrangement to carry Bill Branstrator, whose article appears later in the book, from France to England for further medical treatment. (*Navy photo in the National Archives: 80-G-257903*)

The burned-out hulk of the *LST-282* smolders off the beach at Cape Dramont in southern France. (*Navy photo in the National Archives: 80-G-362809*)

H-hour bombing of the beach and saw our LCVPs return safely after landing assault forces on Green Beach. We saw no enemy planes. With our binoculars we could see resort homes and the hills behind them. In a sense, we sunbathed on the Riviera that day as the ship circled and waited in the transport area for our turn to go in. Our turn came late because there was no immediate requirement for the primary cargo we were carrying: 155-millimeter Long Tom artillery pieces of the 36th Infantry Division. The main deck and tank deck of the *LST-282* were jam-packed with those guns and their trailers full of ammunition.

We didn't get the word to the beach until about nine o'clock in the evening, after the sun had gone down. We were about three-quarters of a mile from Green Beach. I was on the forecastle, standing on a raised gun tub. My duty was to handle the sound-powered telephones on the forward battery of 20-millimeter and 40-millimeter antiaircraft guns. Hughes, on the conning tower, was on the other end of the phones.

We spotted two planes coming in from over the land, far away off the starboard bow. We were talking back and forth about what the planes might be. Suddenly, there were three planes instead of two, and the third one appeared smaller and, we assumed, farther away. The reason it looked farther away was that it was not a plane but a small radio-controlled glider bomb. It had been launched unseen from a Dornier 215. It headed initially toward the transport area, then turned at a right angle and dived right onto the *LST-282*. We got a few shots off with the ship's guns, but they were well astern of this bomb that was

probably moving at several hundred miles an hour.

It hit right in front of our ship's wheelhouse and went into the main engine room, where it exploded. Hughes, the gunnery officer, was killed instantly, blown from the conn down onto the main deck. My own first conscious memory is of being on the main deck rather than on the elevated gun tubs. Whether I was knocked down by the concussion or jumped because of fear, I don't really know. I looked back at the conn and could see that it was all crumpled. There was no sign of life. Flames were starting up. The next ten to twenty minutes were terrible. The Long Tom artillery ammunition began cooking off and exploding, as did the ammunition in the ship's own magazines.

There never was any formal order to abandon ship, but people saw the obvious and jumped overboard. I tried to warn some soldiers to stay on board, because we had been taught in midshipman school not to leave the ship until directed because conditions might be even worse in the water. But soldiers get nervous on board ship, where there are no foxholes, so they said to me, "F__ you," and off they went.

The first lieutenant had the bow doors halfway open when the bomb hit and all power failed. The bow ramp was still closed, and all the troops manning their vehicles on the tank deck would have been trapped. The rear cables of a large cargo elevator on the main deck were parted, however, causing the rear portion of the elevator to fall onto trucks in the tank deck. That formed a ramp from the tank deck to the main deck. Many injured soldiers, some with their uniforms on fire, scrambled up that ramp to safety. It was similar to the way red ants escape from an ant hole when someone pours in gasoline.

By now the ship had moved to within about half a mile of the beach. Lieutenant Gilbert, the skipper, got the Navy Cross for his actions that night, and he deserved it. He ordered hard left rudder, which kept the exploding *LST-282* from moving in among the LSTs already lined up on the beach. As it was, we careened off to port, and eventually ran aground on some rocks in front of a beautiful resort home.

In addition to his ship handling, the skipper rescued a signalman, George Heckman, who had a badly broken leg. He carried Heckman down three flights from the bridge to the water's edge, and there someone else took over and began pulling him ashore. Then the captain went back and got the engineer officer, Edward Durkee, who was unconscious and had a back full of shrapnel. The captain secured him by his life belt to the rudder post. Both were later recovered in an unconscious condition by rescue craft. The skipper himself had been wounded severely in one arm, so he did those rescues with one arm.

The last people who left the ship swam ahead, trying to beat the hulk ashore. The engines had stopped running as soon as the bomb exploded, but momentum continued to carry the ship toward shore. I myself finally jumped off the port bow. I think I let myself down to the anchor so I wouldn't have to jump so far. In midshipman school I was a non-swimmer and had to go to swimming class when the other guys went to physical education. All I had learned during my youth in the Texas hill country was dog paddling in various creeks. But I beat that LST ashore. I had an inflatable life belt around my waist, and it worked well. The army had criticized those belts after so many men were lost in Exercise Tiger, claiming that men were pitched forward, forcing their faces into the water. I have to say that my life belt was effective when it came to the test.

When we got ashore, we got behind a large rock on the beach. As the ship got closer, the good swimmers went out and helped the wounded men get ashore. We dragged them behind the rock because we were afraid the exploding ammunition might send shrapnel onto us. Eventually, when we couldn't find any more shipmates or army men, we went up a road to Green Beach. Others, in the water astern of the ship, were rescued by boats from the other ships in the area.

We boarded a sister LST and backed off that night. At that point I panicked and began having what might be called hallucinations. I wanted to get off and go back to my own ship, worried that Pete Hughes might still be alive and I could save him. I calmed down when a shipmate said he had seen Pete lifeless on the deck. It was a horrible night for many of us. Our ship was still burning and, I have been told, smoldered for several days. In those hours afterward I didn't want to look at

In 1984 Bergner poses on the rocky shore where the *LST-282* came to rest forty years earlier. (*Courtesy Gladys Bergner*)

Bergner came across this burned, rusted piece of mooring cable from his ship when he visited southern France in 1984. (*Courtesy Gladys Bergner*)

the *LST-282*, but somehow I kept doing so.

For many years after that I certainly had no wish to set foot on that beach again. But then, in 1984, the various nations that had been involved in the Normandy D-Day got together to observe the fortieth anniversary. In June of that year I watched the celebrations on television with such great interest that my wife, Gladys, encouraged me to go to Europe that fall. I visited some cousins in Germany and also went back to the beaches at Normandy and southern France. I stayed overnight at Nice and then got oriented by going to the American consulate there. I learned from people there where our landing site, Green Beach, near Saint-Raphaël, had been in 1944. I wasn't on time for a bus from Saint-Raphaël to the area, so I followed my cardiologist's advice about walking and set out on the four-mile trip to the beach at Cape Dramont.

After a while the coastline looked very familiar. I tried to question a French lady washing a car, and I frightened her because she couldn't understand English. Fortunately, she summoned her husband, who could. I inquired about the ship that was bombed and burned, and he told me that the abandoned ship had been on the rocks for many years. After they opened a bottle of wine to celebrate my return, he drove me to the exact spot where the *LST-282* had ended her last voyage so many years earlier. I identified it myself by finding the big rock that we had moved behind when the ship was still exploding.

The Frenchman left me there—alone. I was carrying with me a photo of the LST that someone had taken the day after the ship was hit. In the background of the photo was a beautiful resort home. It was still there in 1984, so I decided to find the exact spot from which thepicture had been taken, then take one of my own.

As I climbed around in the boulders on the beach, I stopped at one point to rest. I looked down and I saw a coiled wire cable, hollow in the center. I recognized it as the core of what had been a piece of 6-inch wire rope, the type used as a bow line for LSTs. I knew it could not have come from a merchant ship because along that coast there are no piers for a ship of any size to moor. The luxury liners must anchor offshore and transport their passengers ashore in smaller vessels. The remaining strands of wire showed evidence of burning and many years of rusting. I knew it had to be a portion of the bow hawser off the *LST-282*. Someone had evidently hidden it among the rocks. He probably planned to come back and get it later but never did.

As I sat there and remembered the terrible things that had happened that night, I began crying. I have seldom felt so alone or so strange, because I was there for people whose lives had ended forty years earlier. I wished for my wife or a shipmate—someone—to share the moment. I called Gladys that night and told her I had just experienced one of the most stirring days of my life.

HANS ERICH BERGNER (1922–1993) received his bachelor's degree in history and government from Southwestern University, Georgetown, Texas, in 1943. He subsequently received a master's degree in administrative education from Southwest Texas State University in San Marcos. He took V-7 officer training at Columbia University in New York and was commissioned an ensign in the Naval Reserve in November 1943. After his service as assistant gunnery officer in the *LST-282*, he served in the *LST-1043* in the Pacific, finishing as commanding officer. The war ended before the ship could get into combat. After his release from active duty in April 1946, he entered the field of education, spending seventeen years in the school system in Comfort, Texas. He was a teacher, bus driver, coach, principal, and superintendent. From 1964 until his retirement in 1977 he was superintendent of schools in Fredericksburg, Texas. He completed twenty-one years of Naval Reserve duty in 1964 and qualified for retirement as a commander. Among his reserve duty was service as an instructor at Reserve Officer Candidate School at Long Beach and Newport in the 1950s. After retirement Commander Bergner lived in Fredericksburg, where he was a German-speaking volunteer docent in the *Vereins Kirche* (Society Church) Museum. He died on October 15, 1993, a few months after the interviews for this chapter. (*Courtesy Hans E. Bergner*)

The late Commander Bergner's story encapsulates a number of themes of this book: the invasion of Normandy, the invasion of southern France, the contributions of the navy, the vital role of LSTs, the tragedy of war, and the lasting bond that develops among shipmates. We also need to look at the bigger picture.

The reason that Bergner and all those LSTs were there was that the Axis war machine occupied much of Europe. The watershed period was the spring of 1940. War had broken out in Poland in September 1939, but for the next several months the Continent was involved in what was known as "phony war." In the spring all of that changed, and in rapid order France, Scandinavia, and the Low Countries fell. In just over half a year, Germany had moved to the Atlantic—something it wasn't able to achieve in the four years of World War I.

England itself was threatened with invasion in the autumn of 1940, but the threat never materialized—in part because of the heroic Battle of Britain and in part because German Chancellor Adolf Hitler wasn't able to muster the necessary amphibious strength to ferry his troops across the English Channel for an invasion. Frustrated, Germany invaded Russia instead in the spring of 1941 and got itself involved in a two-front war.

From that point onward, the return to the European continent became one of the foremost strategic goals of the Allies. The pressure was particularly acute from Soviet Premier Joseph Stalin, who wanted the Germans distracted on the Western Front so they would not be so relentless in their fighting on the Eastern Front. Britain, however, was reluctant. The British had long memories of the stalemate trench warfare of 1914–18 and shorter memories of escaping by the skin of their teeth when they evacuated their expeditionary forces from the beaches of Dunkirk as France was falling in 1940.

A key relationship was that of the Americans and the British. Like the Soviets, the Americans were also interested in building up toward an invasion. Prime Minister Winston Churchill shook things up when he appointed Lord Louis Mountbatten, part of the royal family, Chief of Combined Operations, with an eye toward exploring options for the return of Allied power to the Continent. One of the first such ventures was at Dieppe, France, in the summer of 1942. The Allies learned many lessons from that operation; probably the foremost one was that the Allied amphibious capability was not yet ready for prime time. And thus it was that the major invasion of 1942 was against relatively light opposition in North Africa rather than against the Axis first team in France.

The next several chapters explore the developing relationship between the British and their former colonists across the Atlantic as D-Day approached and was executed.

Finally, it is worth mentioning just what the term D-Day means. Essentially, it is shorthand for Day-Day, the day on which the invasion was to take place, just as H hour stands for the time at which the first wave was to hit the beach. In the many months of planning

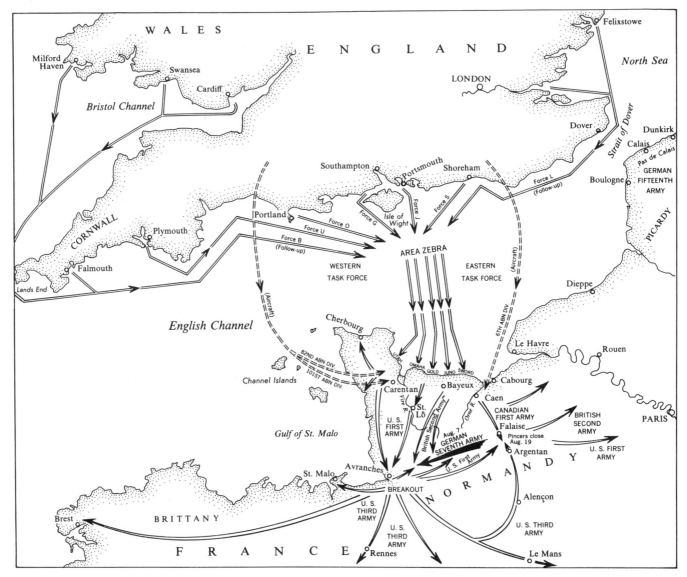

(*Courtesy Dr. E. B. Potter*)

that went into the operation, the exact date would not be known precisely. Thus, in the planning documents it was referred to merely as D-Day, and that served as a benchmark from which to measure time either backward or forward. Referring to events that were to precede the invasion date, such as moving troops to the debarkation ports, it might be D-5. When referring to post-invasion events, such as the delivery of a resupply of certain types of ammunition, it might be D+3. With this system there was no need during the planning phase to specify a certain date, which was just as well, because the undertaking was so enormous that flexibility was an essential component of the preparation.

DISASTER AT DIEPPE, SUCCESS AT NORMANDY

By Rear Admiral Elliott B. Strauss, U.S. Navy (Retired)

In 1942 I was introduced to Admiral Dickie Mountbatten shortly after he had become Chief of Combined Operations. Prime Minister Winston Churchill felt that this business of interservice work, especially amphibious operations, was very important. Although Mountbatten's substantive rank was still captain, he was made a vice admiral, a lieutenant general, and an air marshal, all at the same time.

A little later he asked Admiral Harold Stark, Commander U.S. Naval Forces in Europe, to have a U.S. naval officer attached to his staff. Stark assigned me, and Mountbatten was kind enough to say, "I was hoping maybe I'd get you." So I became the first American officer on his Combined Operations staff. I expected to be a sort of liaison officer, but I found out that I was completely integrated into the staff, and as other American officers came on, they were too. We were given just the same jobs as the British officers were in planning raids and that type of thing.

Mountbatten was accused of being a little bit like OSS, the American Office of Strategic Services, forerunner of the CIA. In Mountbatten's case, people always said OSS stood for "Oh, so social"; and there were a number of people you might say were social celebrities. But they were all able. It was a hardworking staff, and as I think everybody knows, the commandos, who were in specially constructed battalions, were a part of Lord Louis's command. They were organized and trained to do particular types of actions.

I shared a desk for a while with a commander called Red Ryder. He was R. E. D. Ryder, and he was the man who in March 1942 used a team of commandos to take the *Campbeltown* into Saint-Nazaire, France, and disable a dry dock the Germans might have used for the *Tirpitz*. From knowing Ryder and other bona fide heroes, I decided that these were irreplaceable men, but they must be "oddballs" to do their exploits. Ryder, in spite of being a hero, was not promoted to captain. He retired and was later elected to Parliament.

Mountbatten was the sort of commander who used

Admiral Lord Louis Mountbatten inspects commando troops. As Chief of Combined Operations, he was responsible for preparing British forces for amphibious warfare. (*Imperial War Museum*)

his staff and knew all about them. He wasn't the sort of boss who had little contact with those people down below. I saw quite a lot of him, officially and socially. I was there with him for about eighteen months, until he left to go to India, and he asked me if I'd like to go also. But I hadn't had any sea duty during the war, and I couldn't look people in the face if I didn't. So I had to decline, although that would have been an interesting job. But I kept up with him through the years, and I would say that we really became friends. He was godfather to my youngest son.

During Mountbatten's time in Combined Operations, the prospect of the invasion of France came up increasingly. At one point he arranged an initial

9

planning conference at Largs in Scotland, and he called in the people who very possibly might have been the commanders for an invasion. As it worked out, none of the senior people who were there did end up in the invasion command. The idea was where the invasion should take place; when and how it should be done. My boss, Captain Jock Hughes-Hallett, was there. I can remember his reaction when somebody said, "We should go to the area near Cherbourg, but there are no harbors there."

Hughes-Hallett said, "Then if there are no harbors, we shall have to build one." That was the origin of the idea of the artificial harbor, which was actually done for the invasion of Normandy. (Incidentally, he was known as "Hughes-Hitler," which I think was rather unfair, although he was very austere and he never married.)

Another officer on the staff was a British lieutenant commander named Ackroyd Norman Palliser Costobadie. Hughes-Hallett got ahold of him one day and said, "Costobadie, I want you to make me an outline plan for so and so and have it ready by four o'clock this afternoon."

Costobadie said, "Captain, I'll try to do it, but commander so-and-so had me up until four o'clock this morning, and I'm not in very good shape."

Hughes-Hallett said, "Costobadie, I don't care how you spend your evenings. I want that report by four o'clock in the afternoon," which was, I'm afraid, rather typical of him. But I liked him and we got along well. One of the things he did was make an effort to see how the Royal Navy handled the men in the transports. So he put on a private's uniform and went aboard a transport to check on this. It's sort of the initiative he had; in other words, he wanted to know firsthand, and I give him full marks for that.

The first real venture that Combined Operations made was an amphibious raid on Dieppe, France, on August 19, 1942. Prime Minister Churchill had decided that some fairly large effort should be made because the war had become so stagnant by then. Another thought was that the Canadians had been in England for some time and were restless. So a plan was conceived to land on Dieppe and try to take prisoners, destroy the batteries, and test the ability to land on an enemy coast. A subsidiary aim was to try to capture a German radar.

A plan was made in Combined Operations, but then the Canadians were called in—the actual landing force—because it was a principle that the people who did the operation would make the plan that obtained. Combined Operations felt that to go in directly across the beach was probably not feasible; they should attack from the flanks. But the Canadians felt that they could do a direct assault. A compromise was made that was a combination of a flanking movement and a direct assault.

The brigade was commanded by Major General John Hamilton Roberts, Commander Second Canadian Division, and there were also assorted units from other parts of the British Empire. The surprise element was a combination of landing ships, which carried landing craft and craft which went directly across from the Portsmouth area. The support was seven "Hunt"-class destroyers and one Polish destroyer. A "Hunt"-class destroyer didn't even measure up to the destroyer escorts in our navy. It had 4-inch guns with step-by-step fire control. The units arrived there on time for the most part—there were two that didn't—and effected surprise. So for the first hour or so, there were no German planes up.

I went along as an observer on behalf of Combined Operations. I was in the "Hunt"-class destroyer called the *Bleasdale*, which was to give fire support and make smoke. When the Canadian troops started ashore they had a hard time, because some of them landed in too-deep water. The beach was shingle, and when the tanks got ashore, the tracks rotated on the shingle, and they had difficulty getting off the beach. Then, eventually, in an hour or so, the German planes started coming over, and the British planes came over from England. But the fighters could only stay a very short time, so they had to come over in waves, really.

From a naval standpoint, I think you could say the raid was a success. The air battle was a success, considering the limitation of the numbers available and the flying range of the planes. From the military side it was almost a fiasco, because a great many of the Canadian troops were killed and many more were captured. One of the few successes was on the one flank. A commando under Lieutenant Colonel Lord Lovat got up and silenced one of the 5.9-inch guns. The other one was never silenced. Captain Hughes-Hallett was the naval commander for the operation, and I heard him say afterwards that he had read in accounts of battles that the decks ran with blood. He said, "I never expected actually to see that, but on this raid I did. The decks were running with blood."

We took on board a great many people: troops who had escaped from the beaches and some aviators who were shot down. I saw one British Spitfire fighter shot down by our own antiaircraft fire in the latter's enthusiasm. This is not a rare occurrence at all. I sometimes thought of trying for a doctorate on the amount of casualties that in any war one inflicts on its own side. I mean, at a wild, uninformed guess, this could run between 10 and 15 percent.

One of the "Hunt"-class destroyers, the *Berkeley*, got a direct bomb hit and was broken in two and had to be sunk by torpedo fire from one of the other destroyers. An American army colonel, Loren B. Hillsinger, was on Mountbatten's staff; he was in the *Berkeley* and lost a foot in the action. (He later wound up having several

This German photograph was taken at low water—probably on August 20, 1942, the day after the raid on Dieppe. Shown on the beach where the Allies were overwhelmed by the enemy are a number of abandoned tanks and landing craft. (*Naval Institute Collection*)

operations and lost more and more of the leg each time.) The destroyers got in so close to the beach that one of my main worries was that we would go aground, because the ship didn't pay too much attention to soundings. There were no leadsmen, and the depth finder in the *Bleasdale* went out very early in the game. They were in so close that they were subject to gunfire and rifle fire from the shore. As for me, I don't believe anybody who says that he was not frightened.

There were no particular recriminations afterward over the capture and death of so many Canadian soldiers on the beach at Dieppe. I think the effort was considered worthwhile. That I question, because I think that some of the lessons we learned from it were wrong lessons. For example, one of the lessons they thought they had learned was that you could keep attack transports off an enemy coast only long enough to drop one relay of boats. Well, we learned in the Pacific that with adequate air support, you could keep a transport there all day, or even longer.

One legitimate lesson was that bombardment by 4-inch guns was not heavy enough to make the defenders keep their heads down. In the Pacific and at Normandy, major-caliber guns were used with more success. I suppose the most useful lesson from Dieppe was that the Allies were still a long way from being able to mount a major invasion of the European continent.

After the invasion of North Africa and other events of the war, I left Combined Operations at the time that Admiral Mountbatten left. I was then transferred to the planning staff of Admiral Sir Charles Little, Royal Navy, who was a potential naval commander for the invasion of Normandy. He was detached and sent down to the Mediterranean before the invasion, but at that time General Sir Frederick Morgan was assigned as COSSAC, which stood for Chief of Staff of the Supreme Allied Commander. He was in charge of the planning for the invasion of Normandy, and his whole setup was directed to that end.

His headquarters was in Norfolk House in London, and my little planning group under Captain Lyman Thackrey was the U.S. component of the naval staff for the invasion. This involved forces planning: for instance, things like ambulance LSTs and beach gradients and force composition. The planning effort was really the forerunner of Neptune, which was a code name for the naval part of the invasion of Normandy. Our job was to write some of the detailed plans and the overall plans for that operation.

Before the invasion the staffs moved to Southwick Park, which was just north of Portsmouth. The Norfolk House phase was, of course, before the overall commander was even appointed. The discussion then was whether General George Marshall or General Dwight

Eisenhower would be the supreme allied commander for the invasion; Eisenhower, of course, was named. The British naval commander was Vice Admiral Sir Philip Vian, and the American section was commanded by Rear Admiral Alan Kirk.

At Southwick Park the planning went on really as before. The thought then was that General Morgan would be the chief of staff to whomever was appointed supreme allied commander, and, as it turned out, General Eisenhower wanted an American, Lieutenant General Walter Bedell Smith, for his chief of staff instead. It was successful, but in some ways I feel that it might have been a mistake. It would have been logical to have an American as supreme allied commander and a British chief of staff.

I asked General Morgan if, when the invasion came, he would get command of an army corps and take it over. He said, "No, they're going to keep me here as a hostage because if the plans go all right, well, I'll be all right. If something goes wrong, they want me right here to put the blame on." So he was kept on as deputy chief of staff to the supreme allied commander. I think that General Morgan has never got sufficient credit for the part he played in the invasion. Later on, when we were in Southwick Park, and actually just before I was detached to go back to the United States and get an assignment at sea, I went to see him and said, "I'm leaving, General, and I'd like to call on you and pay my respects."

He was living in a tent in Southwick Park. He said, "Don't bother about the respects. I have just been given a bottle of whiskey. You come down this evening, and we'll see what we can do about killing it." So I had a long session with him in his tent, and I must have been very naive because he said, "You know, this war will be over pretty soon. The young fellows can go back and raise families and get jobs. We middle-aged ones, for the rest of our lives we're going to be wound up in trying to do something about the threat of Russia. That's going to be our job. They will be trying to take over the world, and we've got to do something about it."

Well, I thought these were our gallant allies, and it had never occurred to me that what he said was true. But General Morgan was one of the first people to be aware of that and to try to tell people what was going to happen.

As for the American naval commander, I'd known Alan Kirk since he was a lieutenant commander. As a matter of fact, his mother-in-law had introduced my mother and father to one another. Kirk told me that his appointment as the naval commander for the U.S. section of the invasion was made rather against the wishes of Admiral Ernest King, the Chief of Naval Operations. There was enough political power behind it so that he got the job; I believe Dean Acheson, later

the secretary of state, was his backer. But Kirk was in the position that if his foot slipped at all, he might well be taken out of it. He walked much more tenderly than he would have if it had been a clear-cut appointment.

He was kept a rear admiral the whole time, as I remember, and his opposite number, Philip Vian, was a vice admiral. When I left Mountbatten's staff, I was assigned to Admiral Kirk's staff, but really had no function because I was almost immediately transferred to the staff of Admiral Bertram Ramsay, the overall naval commander. I was the plans officer under Thackrey, who was the chief of our little group.

Of course, the actual operational planning was done by Kirk's people; we just did the part that depended on Admiral Ramsay. One time, for instance, the lines of demarcation between the beaches were laid out east and west. Admiral Kirk sent for me and said that the U.S. Navy planners would like to have the lines made normal to the beach, because they felt that the craft would have to cross from one sector to the other with these east and west lines. I went to see Admiral Vian and his staff, which I think was still in Norfolk House, and I said, "Admiral Kirk thinks it might be better to have these lines normal to the beach," and told him why.

He said, "You Yanks want everything. No, I won't do it. They're going to stay where they are." Well, that was the answer. Why, I don't know, but that was the sort of thing, among the many things, that we had to do.

One of the issues in our planning was the question of the best time for the invasion. One story from the very early phases of it was that Churchill had a group around him and said, "Does anybody here know when the Norman invasion—William the Conqueror's—when that took place?"

Some idiot said, "1066." But the answer was that it was in late September. But early on they decided to do it within very close limits of factors such as moonlight and tides. Of course, the big decisions were things like the artificial harbors—how to construct them, how to take them over—doing away with the beach obstacles, and then the logistics afterwards.

As everyone knows, the date of the actual invasion was touch and go on account of the weather, and General Eisenhower had a lot of courage when he decided to go ahead with it. After the first landings, of course, we were very anxious for news in the headquarters at Southwick Park. The first reports that came back were encouraging, because our Utah Beach operation went very smoothly. There were very few casualties, and the three British beaches went very well. The real fighting was on Omaha Beach. Some of the British members of Ramsay's staff more or less asked, "What's holding you Yanks up? Why can't you go? Everybody else has gone inland." The answer was that the bulk of the fighting was taking place on Omaha Beach.

On June 8 a group of us went over to France to observe the invasion beaches from offshore. I visited Omaha and Utah, where the troops had pretty much moved inland, and the only threat was from dropped mines. There were some German aircraft coming along the beaches, and there was antiaircraft fire trying to stop them. Otherwise, it was pretty quiet. During the time we lay off the beach, Commander Eugene Carusi, one of the beachmasters, received a .30-caliber bullet through the top of one lung, but survived. Gene was a friend of mine from Washington. He was a Naval Academy graduate, had resigned, but came back as a reserve for the war.

Our trip was in a small Coast Guard cutter, the *Long Island*, that ferried people back and forth. Cross-Channel communications had by then been established, and quite a number of observers were going over. I remember hearing that one of them was a naval officer who was going to go over in one of the cross-Channel steamers. A transport officer said to him, "Would you mind if a marine captain so-and-so shared your cabin?"

The naval officer said to him, "I make it an invariable rule never to share a cabin with a stranger of my own sex. No, I want to go alone." And he did.

ELLIOTT BOWMAN STRAUSS (1903–), son of Admiral Joseph Strauss, graduated from the Naval Academy in 1923 and served as a junior officer in the *Concord*, *Hannibal*, *Arkansas*, *Toucey*, *Blakeley*, and *Manley*. Prior to World War II he was on the staff of Commander Atlantic Squadron and navigator of the *Nashville*. He commanded the destroyer *Brooks* during Neutrality Patrol operations in 1940–41. He had a number of tours of duty involving Great Britain, including service as assistant naval attaché in the mid-1930s, naval observer in London, staff work for amphibious operations in Europe and North Africa during the war, and postwar study at the Imperial Defence College. In 1944–45 he commanded the attack transport *Charles Carroll*. After the war, Strauss had duty in connection with the formation of the United Nations and served as first commanding officer of the cruiser *Fresno*. Subsequent duties included OpNav, command of Destroyer Flotilla Six, and as part of the U.S. mission to NATO. After retirement in 1953 he remained in Paris as Staff Assistant Secretary of Defense for International Security Affairs. Later, he worked for Bucknell University and the Agency for International Development. Admiral Strauss, who is chairman of the Naval Historical Foundation, lives in Washington, D.C. (*Courtesy Rear Admiral Elliott B. Strauss*)

STRATEGY AND SECRECY

By George M. Elsey

From the time of the American–British Commonwealth strategy talks in 1941, months before Pearl Harbor, the United States and Great Britain were in agreement that the enemy to defeat first was Germany. American planners assumed this would mean a return in force to the Continent and that the attack should be directly across the English Channel. The British, remembering Dunkirk, were not so sure. Their bitter memories were supplemented by carefully assembled information on Operation Sea Lion. The Germans had failed to mount an invasion of England in 1940 for good reason: they controlled neither the Channel nor the skies above it. They were woefully lacking in sea transport, and they had no special craft fit for across-the-beach landings.

When Prime Minister Winston Churchill and the British Chiefs of Staff visited Washington three weeks after Pearl Harbor, they found some Americans already talking of an invasion. The British were quick to point out that we had all the problems the Germans had had earlier. There was, however, one difference. When difficulties had appeared for Sea Lion, Hitler had lost interest and turned eastward to launch the Russian attack. Our leaders were of a different mind. They had an impelling desire to do prompt battle in the West. The prime minister came back to Washington in June 1942 to explore the possibilities.

My first personal impressions were of the vigor of the little man, always with a sheaf of dispatches in hand, shuttling back and forth between his bedroom, Harry Hopkins's tiny office, and the president's study— all on the second floor of the White House. But the president and the prime minister could not make resources match desire. Not only did we lack air and sea control, the Germans had such mastery of all ports that an open-beach landing would be required. We were as unprepared in 1942 as they had been in 1940. Our navy had established a "Triple A" priority in April 1942 for beaching and landing craft, but actual production had scarcely begun. It was late July before there was an agreement on a first step—Operation Torch, the landing in Morocco and Algeria in November.

When our Joint Chiefs of Staff grudgingly accepted Torch, much of their reluctance was due to their belief that it would become a quicksand, sucking them into an extended Mediterranean campaign. The Casablanca Conference of January 1943 confirmed their fears. President Roosevelt returned to the White House from Morocco in high spirits. He had a great sense of history, and he was elated that he had just made history on several counts: he was the first president to fly while in office; his persuasion had brought Frenchmen Henri Giraud and Charles de Gaulle together—so *he* thought; and he and Winston had a winning team. But our army planners were despondent. They were certain that the agreements extracted by the British at Casablanca for a summer invasion of Sicily committed us to at least a year of further Mediterranean adventures.

Through the fretful spring of 1943, the U.S. Navy was largely silent on these matters. As I briefed President Roosevelt, Admiral William D. Leahy, and Harry Hopkins in the White House Map Room—secreted on the ground floor of the mansion—and listened to their lengthy analyses of cables flowing in from Churchill, Soviet Marshal Joseph Stalin, and theater commanders, it was clear to me, not only by formal decision of our Joint Chiefs of Staff but by the Commander in Chief's strongly expressed personal conviction, that Europe was the army's baby.

The navy had two lusty problem children of its own: the Pacific and German U-boats. A delay in the main assault on Europe was not unwelcome to the navy. Admiral Ernest J. King's planners were painfully aware of shipping requirements. From their point of view, scarce steel, labor, and machinery were better devoted to convoy escorts and subchasers than to building an inventory of amphibious craft in the United Kingdom that would not be required until some highly uncertain date in the future. And such craft as were built, the navy felt, should go to Admiral Chester W. Nimitz, who had immediate use for them in the Pacific.

Churchill came back to the White House in May 1943. He haunted our Map Room—especially in the late-night hours—and he irked the president by learning the news from the president's own staff sooner than FDR himself. Churchill was elated to be the one to grab

Prime Minister Winston Churchill visits his beloved Royal Navy. He served as First Lord of the Admiralty in World War I and World War II. He is shown here with Vice Admiral Bruce Fraser. (*Ministry of Defence*)

from my hand and wave aloft in White House corridors General Dwight Eisenhower's victory message when German resistance ended in Tunisia on May 13. He was positively jubilant at the progress of the antisubmarine campaign. Each day he was with us, one round black pin came down from our chart of the Atlantic, meaning one less U-boat. Some days two, and on one memorable day three, pins were plucked.

Churchill was confident—and he was proven correct in the following weeks—that the tide had turned in the Battle of the Atlantic. Wherever and whenever the main thrust against Germany was to take place, there was no longer any doubt that sea-lanes could be kept open by the British and American navies to move all required personnel and supplies for an invasion, in addition to meeting continuing requirements in the Mediterranean and ever-mounting shipping require-

ments for the support of the Russians.

The prime minister's obvious enthusiasm for continued and expanded Mediterranean operations deepened American suspicions as to British long-range intentions. Furthermore, just at this moment, planners in London gave birth to a paper stating that eighty-five hundred landing ships and craft would be required for a cross-Channel assault in 1944. Admiral King knew that production rates made it impossible to build this volume. He concluded that the British had no intentions of a cross-Channel attack and had proposed this preposterous requirement as a way of sinking the whole idea.

British advocacy of a Mediterranean strategy now won some unexpected allies. As the spring of 1943 wore on, the senior U.S. naval representatives on the Joint War Plans Committee concluded that perhaps the British were right in advocating that Allied emphasis remain in the Mediterranean. Not nearly as much shipping would be required. While it was not frankly expressed, implicit in their position was the belief that the Pacific would be the beneficiary in such a switch in strategic plans. The navy's heresy from the established American point of view was short-lived. By the time this paper reached the Joint Chiefs of Staff for formal decision, Admiral King had been persuaded to rally behind General George C. Marshall.

When Roosevelt, Churchill, and the Combined Chiefs assembled in Quebec in August, the Americans were unanimous in advocating Operation Overlord for the spring of 1944. I was at Quebec, and I know with what relief and confidence the president and our chiefs returned to Washington in the certain belief they had won from the British a firm commitment to a cross-Channel invasion in May 1944.

With that decision solid, our navy buckled down to what it thought would be its principal task for Operation Neptune, as the naval operations within Overlord were now named. That was to ensure an adequate supply of transports and the special types of amphibious craft for such a landing. Production schedules were revised again and craft were reallocated from the Pacific. Unlike any Pacific invasion or Morocco or Sicily, however, the U.S. Navy was expected to have no responsibility for gunfire support and only a minor supplementary role to the Royal Navy in antisubmarine warfare, antitorpedo boat warfare, and minesweeping.

Ship production obviously was but part of the problem; organizing bases and training amphibious crews were also high priority requirements. Rear Admiral John L. Hall, as a veteran of the Moroccan and Sicilian landings, went up to England from the Mediterranean to mold an effective force out of the thousands of young naval recruits—many fresh from boot camp in the States—who arrived weekly during the winter. Assigned to London to represent historian Samuel

At the Quebec conference in August 1943, the Allied leaders made a commitment to a cross-Channel invasion of France the following spring. Seated in this picture from the conference are President Franklin D. Roosevelt and the Earl of Athlone, Governor General of Canada. Standing are Canadian Prime Minister William MacKenzie King and British Prime Minister Winston Churchill. (*U.S. Army photo in the National Archives: SC 178020*)

Eliot Morison, I joined some hundreds of these young men in a stormy March crossing on board the *Queen Mary*, and I can testify to their—and my—greenness.

Rear Admiral John Wilkes, whose ungainly title of Commander Landing Craft and Bases Europe was apt to distract one's attention from the importance of his task, set up shop at Plymouth, not far from the bowling green on which Sir Francis Drake had finished his game while excited spectators warned him that the Spanish Armada was in sight. With Drake-like composure, Admiral Wilkes supervised the hectic establishment of temporary bases in coves and inlets all along the Cornish and Devon coasts, and exercised new craft and newer crews relentlessly.

There was nothing unusual about such building and training, but our senior naval officers found their role in planning the great operation to be uniquely restricted. All decisions as to the place, the timing, and the scale of the assault were in the hands of others. The American naval role was expected to be so limited that only two American naval officers were assigned to Lieutenant General Frederick Morgan, the British officer directing the Anglo-American team planning Overlord. On the other hand, General Eisenhower's decision to expand from a three-division to a five-division assault, reached soon after he assumed com-

mand in January 1944, had immediate and major implications for our navy.

In the first place, the Royal Navy no longer could provide adequate fire support for an assault on five beaches instead of three. Dieppe and Sicily had proved the need for overwhelming naval gunfire, a lesson not lost on Rear Admiral Alan Kirk, who also had recently arrived from the Mediterranean to head the U.S. naval contingent. Admiral Kirk was not shy in expressing his concern to Admiral Sir Bertram Ramsay, Royal Navy, who was to be the Allied Naval Commander in Chief, and he also began a series of appeals to Admiral King in Washington that became increasingly strident as the weeks passed. Adding to Kirk's irritation at not receiving what he regarded as adequate understanding of his problem was his conviction that the British were holding entirely too many aircraft carriers, battleships, and cruisers in reserve at Scapa Flow.

The Americans, having no memory of the Anglo-German Battle of Jutland in 1916, never did understand why the British were so intimidated by the remnants of the German fleet. King shared Kirk's cynical attitude and delayed allocating three battleships, two heavy cruisers, and twenty-two destroyers until it was apparent the British were adamant. It was mid-April before Kirk knew what fire-support ships he would have.

What about sea lift for the newly added American assault division slated to land on the Cotentin Peninsula, on the beach called Utah? Where were those ships coming from? And where were the LSTs for the new British beach? The British were building none themselves. We had to provide them all, and there were no spare LSTs anywhere. The Anzio landings in Italy had chewed up more shipping than expected. The whimsical addition of a landing in southern France, Operation Anvil, to coincide with Overlord, promised so offhandedly to Stalin by Roosevelt and Churchill at the Teheran Conference the preceding November, was an albatross around the necks of those responsible for allocating shipping. There seemed to be no solution except to postpone both invasions. Overlord was put over from May to June and Anvil from May to July. By that time, barring unexpected tragedies, the additional production from American shipyards would make up the requirements, but there would be no LSTs to spare.

The postponement had a number of ramifications, not all of them foreseeable. German Field Marshal Erwin Rommel had arrived in France at Christmastime 1943. Wisely counseled by his naval adviser, Vice Admiral Friedrich Ruge, he was driving with relentless vigor to improve French coastal defenses, particularly in the Bay of the Seine. He could add little by way of big guns, however. Despite his most diligent efforts, he was able to persuade the German navy to release only two large batteries of four guns each for this area.

Mines were another matter. In the space of four months, four million land mines were laid along the coast behind possible landing beaches. Rommel had no success, however, in convincing the German navy to replenish the mid-Channel minefields laid in 1942 and 1943, and—to the good fortune of the Allies—no additional mines were laid in the Bay of the Seine prior to the landings.

Rommel's great success was in taking full advantage of the extraordinary beach-and-tide conditions. Beginning in March, he began studding the beaches with thousands of steel, cement, and wooden obstacles, many of them with mines attached. Each week's postponement of the invasion was to mean a more difficult initial assault.

The rapid spread of obstacles on the invasion beaches was not only a threat, it also became a key factor in determining the date of the assault. The army had wanted to land at high tide so that troops would not be exposed on the broad, flat beaches. But now, boats would have to discharge seaward of the obstacles and the landings would have to be at low tide or soon thereafter. The army insisted that the Channel crossing should be in darkness—for secrecy. But the navy needed daylight for coastal bombardment and for accurate pilotage into the beaches. On which days would low tide coincide with first light? Juggling these and many other factors, General Eisenhower chose June 5 as D-Day.

It would be misleading to say that the final weeks before the invasion passed without incident, but it can be said that the navy's role unfolded remarkably close to plan. Except for two LSTs sunk and a third damaged by German torpedo boats in late April during a landing exercise of Rear Admiral Don Moon's Utah force on the south coast of England, the German navy was nowhere a menace. As I traveled from base to base, I heard rumors of LCTs captured by German torpedo boats and taken to France. The stories kept sailors and junior officers nervously alert on every exercise, but it never happened. U-boats were still in the North Sea and in the Atlantic in strength, but none tried to enter the Channel.

I was by now on board the USS *Ancon*, Admiral Hall's flagship for Omaha. Here I found that our greatest anxiety was the speed with which the beaches in the target area were being covered with obstacles. Could lanes be opened through the maze of obstacles fast enough after the first wave touched down in order for succeeding waves to land before obstacles were covered by the onrushing tide? If not, then indeed the defenders might, just might, turn the landings into a bloody shambles. This was clearly Rommel's intent—to stop the invasion right on the beaches. Each day's "take" of photoreconnaissance planes brought new concerns. Photo interpreters focused their tired eyes so long on familiar scenes that a colleague on the *Ancon* assured me solemnly that he could recognize the horses commandeered from local farmers being used to drag obstacles into place on Omaha.

Inevitably, the question arose: Have the Germans discovered our plans?

The success of Overlord has become so much a part of our consciousness that it is hard to recall the uncertainty, secrecy, suspense, and suspicion that marked the end of May. Yet, unless we remember the mounting tensions in

First Lieutenant Albert Lanker, a P-38 pilot for the Army Air Forces, took this photo on a low pass over the beach on May 6, one month before D-Day. These are timber ramps designed to rip open landing craft. German soldiers on the beach run for cover as Lanker buzzes over them. (*U.S. Air Force*)

Rear Admiral John Hall, left, looks on as Lieutenant (junior grade) W. C. Kiesel gives King George VI a tour of the flagship *Ancon*'s photo lab. At right are the ship's skipper, Commander Meade S. Pearson, and Rear Admiral Alan Kirk. (*Naval Historical Center: AGC-4 No. 5019*)

our own ships and camps and squadrons, we are missing an essential element in the history of the greatest of all invasions. Each day the great overriding question loomed larger in our minds: Had the Germans found out? The army was inclined to think not. It was watching German troops in the Pas-de-Calais and was reassured that none were being shifted toward the assault area. The navy,

focusing its attention on the target beaches, was more worried.

It would, we thought, be a miracle if the secret had not leaked. Tens of thousands of operation orders were being distributed. The Hydrographic Office had released 350,000 charts and publications to American ships and craft. Vivid, detailed, panoramic scenes of beaches had been painted by Naval Reserve Lieutenant Fred Wight, a Cape Cod artist, and they had been duplicated by the hundreds. Still, it was all scrupulously guarded. When the British distributed charts of the Bay of the Seine by mistake to a number of commercial tugs, with characteristic aplomb they quickly printed charts of Boulogne stamped "Top Secret" and gave those out.

Only if one were designated a Bigot—the awkward code name for a person who had the proper security clearance and had a "need to know"—was he entitled to be told the date and the hour and the place. We were so security minded that when King George VI visited the *Ancon* on May 25 at Portland, and asked what lay behind closely drawn curtains in our intelligence center, the very junior officer stationed with me answered, "Very secret information, Sire," and remained motionless before the curtains. The king took the hint and moved on. An angry captain demanded of my companion some minutes later why he had been so rude to the king. He received the entirely correct answer: "Sir, nobody told me he was a Bigot."

GEORGE MCKEE ELSEY (1918–) graduated from Princeton University in 1939 with a bachelor's degree and received a master's degree in history from Harvard the following year. In 1941 he was commissioned a Naval Reserve officer and joined the staff in the White House Map Room shortly after U.S. entry into World War II. In preparation for and during the invasion of Normandy, he was on temporary duty in England and France representing historian Samuel Eliot Morison. He later assisted in preparing *The Invasion of France and Germany, 1944–1945*, one of Morison's fifteen-volume series on U.S. naval operations in the war. Returning to inactive duty in 1947 with the rank of commander, Mr. Elsey joined the staff of President Harry S Truman and remained at the White House throughout that administration. Mr. Elsey began a long association with the American Red Cross in 1953. He served as its president from 1970 to 1983 and still remains an active consultant. In addition to membership on the boards of several business corporations, he has been active in educational and cultural organizations. He is currently president of the White House Historical Association and a trustee of the National Geographic Society. Mr. Elsey is a resident of Washington, D.C. (*Courtesy George M. Elsey*)

ADMIRAL STARK'S ROLE

By Rear Admiral Neil K. Dietrich, U.S. Navy (Retired)

In early 1942, in the wake of the Japanese attack on Pearl Harbor, Admiral Harold R. Stark was relieved as Chief of Naval Operations and sent to London, where he became Commander U.S. Naval Forces in Europe. A year and a half later, in the fall of 1943, I arrived in London and reported to Admiral Stark's staff. The war at this stage was not a happy one, and, of course, it was still some time before the invasion. I don't want to imply that war is ever a happy occasion, but there are some occasions that are happier than others. We weren't yet winning.

Immediately upon reporting to Admiral Stark I was told that my assignment would be as assistant to Commodore Howard A. Flanigan. He was a very well-known and exceedingly able officer who had retired in 1936 and then had returned to active duty with the coming of the war. Because of his familiarity with shipping and because of his ability, he was ordered to Europe, where his first duties were in charge of the shipping responsibilities for Admiral Stark.

When he started in the job in 1942, Admiral Stark had no operational command in Europe, and his staff was largely one for diplomatic purposes. But he did have a section of his staff charged with the responsibility for American convoys. Without the convoys arriving from the United States with supplies—oil, food, and other necessities—Great Britain would hardly have lasted more than a matter of weeks. There were times in which the supply level in the British Isles was frighteningly low.

Within the European theater in the fall of 1943, Admiral Stark was beginning to gather together an operational staff—a larger staff of officers than he had had previously—because the invasion of Europe had been scheduled for May of 1944. He needed these additional people to handle the responsibilities he would have when U.S. naval support forces and personnel began to arrive in England.

One of Admiral Stark's particular responsibilities throughout his time in London was in a pseudo-diplomatic status. He had a very friendly, very intimate contact with the American ambassador, John G. Winant. He assisted Mr. Winant in conferences of the highest

Admiral Harold R. Stark, Commander U.S. Naval Forces in Europe, arrived in London after having been Chief of Naval Operations during the Japanese attack on Pearl Harbor. (*Painting by navy combat artist Dwight C. Shepler*)

order in regard to the conduct of the war itself and recommendations that were made to President Roosevelt and others within the U.S. government. One of these responsibilities was for postwar planning—the arrangements and exchange of ideas with the British and other Allies. At that time I would say the status of the postwar plans was more than nebulous but considerably less than concrete. Much depended on how the rest of the war proceeded and the conditions, if any, under which Germany eventually surrendered.

Ambassador Winant leaned very heavily on Admiral Stark, not only for his naval and military advice but also for his judgment, knowledge of the English, knowledge of the world situation, and vast experience over a long period of naval service. Admiral Stark actually reached the mandatory retirement age of sixty-four in November 1944 but was continued on active duty by the direction of the president. Admiral Stark and the war effort benefited from his service with the Royal Navy in World War I, when he had been on duty in London on the staff of Admiral William S. Sims. This had given him personal contact with many of the individuals who later became senior officers in the Royal Navy and even with the future King George VI, who had been a junior naval officer in World War I.

I think it would be correct to say that Admiral Stark had a personal friendship with the king at that time. He could ask to see the king on a matter he considered particularly important. This, of course, was not often done. Admiral Stark and Prime Minister Churchill saw each other often, another example of the unique position he had in the American military setup in England. Except possibly for General Eisenhower, he had more direct access to the civilian authorities of England than any other officer of any service who was there.

Admiral Stark and General Eisenhower, incidentally, were very close, on the basis of friendship and mutual respect. When Admiral Stark wished to see or speak with General Eisenhower directly, there was never any question but what he could do so. Likewise, on frequent occasions General Eisenhower would communicate directly with Admiral Stark, who, on the basis of his age, his seniority, his competence, and his

Howard Flanigan, shown here as a rear admiral, had retired from the navy and gone on to succeed in organizing the New York World's Fair of 1939–40. His administrative ability and driving personality made him an asset on Stark's staff. (*Naval Historical Center: S-008-E*)

In March 1944 Admiral Stark poses in London with the U.S. ambassador to Great Britain, John G. Winant. (*Navy photo in the National Archives: 80-G-58820*)

experience, was recognized in the military group as being an elder statesman.

As we moved forward with plans and preparations for the invasion, Admiral Stark's assignment was extremely involved and difficult. Although he was always kept informed, he was left very little time to give personal supervision to the operational details of his command. These activities were expanding at a tremendous rate, rising almost like a cloud from an atomic explosion. For example, in accordance with our arrangements with the British, we began to build and open amphibious bases on the south coast of England—Falmouth, Torquay, Dartmouth, Salcombe—and a headquarters base for supplies at Exeter. At Exeter a large golf course was being taken over. I went there on an inspection trip on behalf of Admiral Stark and could see tears pouring down the cheeks of the local golf enthusiasts. This was a necessary sacrifice to the war, but a real tragedy for any golfer.

Events moved rapidly forward, and more and more of the top commanders arrived, including Rear Admiral Alan Kirk, Rear Admiral John Hall, and Rear Admiral Don Moon. American personnel were pouring into England in vast quantities, something around a million and a half altogether. When you include all of the bases, all of the ports, all of the camps—and the training that was going on in the island—the fact that the Germans didn't do more to disrupt things was remarkable. We know that the Germans knew a great deal, both from air observation and from the agents they had in England. But how they applied their knowledge was another matter.

They did not attack the ports to any great degree, which is something that still remains a mystery. They dedicated their rockets and bombing in a large part upon certain large cities. If the same bombs and rockets had been concentrated on the ports of England, it might have been an entirely different story. The last week or ten days preceding the invasion all the ports of England were jammed with ships that had to be there for supplies and for the loading of men and material and equipment. As I recall from memory, there was only one really serious bombing raid upon any of the eastern and southern ports of England in the last ten days.

During that period of buildup, we had one of the most beautiful springs ever known in England, but little luxury to enjoy it. In London we were swamped with the details of work, trying to screen all the requests for necessary items and men, and the planning for the establishment of American bases in France once our forces were ashore. One item I remember in particular was certain equipment required for minesweepers. They were to precede the advance of the Allied forces toward Normandy, and at almost the last moment, during the last week, certain items were found to be in short supply. We requested the items by telephone from the United States, and they were flown over to arrive just before the invasion. This was the type of emergency that seemed to develop almost hourly as the deadline came on with ever greater rapidity.

Within the headquarters of Admiral Stark we set up an operations room. It was established with the greatest of secrecy under the supervision of a few who knew all the plans and who actually knew the date. I was outside of London on several emergency tours of inspection and saw the army forces moving south—the tanks, the infantry, the motorized equipment. It was an amazing sight; you would have had to see it to believe that so many people could be moved and kept under control and fed and morale maintained—all the while maintaining tight security.

During the first week in June, certain members of the staff were sleeping in the operations room. We were there when the invasion was postponed on account of weather, when the date was reset, and when it actually took place. I was not with the invasion forces; I wish I could have been. I was, however, on the job in London, where we were set to receive any requests in which Admiral Stark could give assistance to the operating forces that were actually conducting the invasion.

On the morning when the church bells began to ring at dawn, we knew then that the news had been received and made public. That first day we were getting varied messages. There was great confusion, as is always so on the battlefield. Toward the end of the day a few stragglers from damaged ships began to show up in London. On the second day, the commanding officer of a destroyer that had been sunk appeared in our headquarters and gave us an eyewitness account of how he saw things from his ship. That gave us a little closer touch. About the fourth or fifth day, Commodore Flanigan—being a man of action—decided he wanted to see the invasion scene himself, and I went with him to the far shore. We landed, saw the beaches, talked to U.S. naval personnel over there, saw their problems, and found out directly several things that we could do to be of assistance. At long last, we saw the reality that had come from all our planning and preparation.

NEIL KITTRELL DIETRICH (1901–1982) graduated from the Naval Academy in 1923 and served in the battleship *Colorado*, the destroyers *Wood* and *Greer*, the carrier *Langley*, the cruiser *Marblehead*, and two tours as an instructor at the Naval Academy. In the late 1930s he served on the staffs of Commander Battleships and Commander Battle Force. He was commanding officer of the destroyer *Lamson*, then served in the Bureau of Navigation in Washington. Dietrich was the first executive officer of the battleship *Alabama* in 1942–43, then reported to Admiral Harold Stark's staff in London. On returning to Washington, he served as flag secretary for Fleet Admiral Ernest J. King and later administrative aide for Fleet Admiral Chester Nimitz. He commanded the cruiser *Houston*, then became chief of staff to Commander Battleships-Cruisers Atlantic Fleet. Later he was chief of staff to Commander Sixth Task Fleet in the Mediterranean, then executive assistant to the Chief of Naval Operations, Admiral Forrest Sherman. As a flag officer, Admiral Dietrich was Commander Destroyer Flotilla Two, U.S. naval attaché to Great Britain, Deputy Commander of the Military Sea Transportation Service, Commander Mine Force Atlantic Fleet, and Commander Fourteenth Naval District. He retired from active duty in 1958 and joined the Hazeltine Corporation as vice president. (*Navy photo in the National Archives: 80-G-46757*)

ADMIRAL RAMSAY AND I

By Admiral Alan G. Kirk, U.S. Navy (Retired)

In early November 1943 I got my Normandy staff together and proceeded to London. I had an early meeting with Admiral Harold Stark, Commander U.S. Naval Forces in Europe. I was given to understand that the naval planners in Norfolk House had become something of an irritation to Admiral Stark. It was expected that my staff would supersede and displace these other naval planners who were in Norfolk House with Admiral Sir Bertram Ramsay, Royal Navy, who was the overall naval commander of the invasion force. So I realized there was a troubled atmosphere and I would have to play my hand carefully, with cards close to the chest.

We had a slight arm's-length position vis-à-vis Admiral Stark, who perhaps quite reasonably felt that he was the person who should command the American side of the invasion and not somebody else who had just come up from a lower echelon. Then we had this friction between the planners in Norfolk House and Admiral Stark's chief of staff. We had also to play a double hand: the operation to assume control of France, yet at the same time to go ahead with the long-range planning for Normandy, which had been chosen as the site for the invasion. There were always little undercurrents running around. I was surprised. I suppose that's what happens in big war commands, just as I suppose it happens in big business organizations where people look for advancement and more power for themselves. Frankly, I was really upset and annoyed that Admiral Stark had allowed it to exist.

Then we had to make contact with Admiral Ramsay. Here is where I was really a little less than diplomatic, shall we say. Recalling our very friendly relationship in terms of golf games the year before, when we were involved in operations in the Mediterranean, I suggested we have lunch—which he declined. He didn't think he could lunch with me now. Then I thought to myself, I made a mistake. I really should have gone over formally and reported to him as the American naval commander under him; he was to be the Allied Naval Commander of the Expeditionary Force for the Invasion of Europe. So, with good grace I accepted his excuse for not being able to lunch and hightailed it over to see him right away.

At this stage it was not contemplated that the American navy should do very much in the invasion of Normandy. The plan called for three British landings on the west of the Seine River—actually the Orne that flows into the sea at Quistran. Then we would have just one landing, what later became Omaha Beach. I was expected by Ramsay and his chief of staff, George Creasy, to be adviser on this staff for American naval operations; the actual task group of Americans that landed was to be under Admiral Ramsay completely. That wasn't to my taste, and I was certain that we would have to do more than land on one beach. I was sure that the American side would insist on fuller participation, and eventually the U.S. Navy would have to send a good many more forces than they had originally outlined for it.

Then I went to see Admiral Andrew Cunningham, who had come back from Washington, where he had been the British representative on the Combined Chiefs of Staff. He was an old friend of mine. He was very cheerful, very nice, very kind and said, "Of course, you'll be with Admiral Ramsay in a big bomb shelter on the south coast of England."

I said, "Oh, no, I don't expect to be there at all. I expect to be on my flagship off the coast of Normandy." This was perhaps a little pert on my part because at that time there was only one beach assigned to the U.S. forces. He smiled indulgently and let it go at that. Actually, of course, it turned out that I insisted and presented the case.

Before Christmas, Field Marshal Bernard Montgomery was nominated to be the principal military commander. He came back to England from the Mediterranean. He examined the Normandy plan with care and saw that it was not going to be satisfactory. "This is not strong enough. We haven't got enough troops, weight of metal, and weight of armor. The port of Cherbourg is vital to the further support of the American armies in France and to some extent of the British armies too. The port of Cherbourg has got to be captured as quickly as possible." To do that it was necessary to make a further landing to the westward in the Bay of

Admiral of the Fleet Bertram Ramsay, center, receives a briefing in March 1944 from Captain P. L. Mather on board the *Ancon*, flagship for Omaha Beach. Admiral Kirk, officially subordinate to Ramsay, is at right. (*Navy photo in the National Archives: 80-G-219976*)

the Seine, to cross the Cherbourg Peninsula at its base and cut off the Germans north of the line and resist reinforcements coming from the south of that line, and then proceed to assault and take Cherbourg as quickly as possible.

That modification was forced upon the authorities; I put it that way on purpose—forced upon the authorities. Then the question came up from my angle as the American naval officer in charge of the Western Task Force of the invasion: Could we make a successful landing on the Cotentin Peninsula? The Cherbourg Peninsula? I agreed it could be done, but, of course, that would call for more naval forces, not only men-of-war but also LSTs and LCIs and all the various ferries and whatnot we were organizing for that port, as well as the artificial harbor.

Well, it was then agreed there would be a second American front. Admiral Ramsay's staff greeted that with, I'd say, less than a cheerful attitude, because they saw at once that I had been correct in my earlier insistence that I would have to be afloat off the beaches with two task groups, exercising my command over them, instead of down in a bunker on the south coast of England. It was a very logical thing to do. The more closely you examined the problem, the more reasonable it seemed to be. Then, of course, in Washington it was necessary to assemble the extra troops for that: men who had some amphibious training and some of the landing craft, and for me the gunfire-support vessels necessary for the operation.

General Dwight Eisenhower was appointed as supreme commander in January 1944. I had known him in London, in Sicily, in Washington, and I knew

Lieutenant General Walter Bedell Smith, his chief of staff. Major General George Patton came over. He was put in cotton wool out of sight because they didn't want anybody to know that he was going to be in the battle because all the Germans thought he was a Sherman and a Sheridan combined in one. We wanted to keep it dark that he was there. He was also in a rather dubious position after that incident in the hospital when he slapped some wounded soldier in bed and said he was a coward. Well, that was smoothed over.

My staff and I then ran into a situation that was most difficult. The whole war college system of training for our navy always gave broad directives from the top to the principal commanders, who worked out their plans and submitted them to the topside fellow for approval and then passed it downward. Each fellow then did the details with his staff. Well, the British didn't do that. All the planning was done in Norfolk House by Admiral Ramsay and his staff in the minutest detail. These orders would come to me and would have to be sent down the line. It was really quite a mental adjustment. It didn't bother the naval reserves; hell, they'd never had another system of training, but it did bother the regular navy officers, especially those who'd been trained and brought up not just in a war college doctrinaire way but had seen those things actually carried out in all the peacetime maneuvers of the fleet and also all the operations of the war until this.

It was really quite a problem. My staff officers would from time to time make comments: "We could do it better this way or that way," and these were never accepted by Admiral Ramsay's staff. In fact, we got some rather tough little comments back, directed at me for allowing these younger officers in their turn to speak out against the voice of the commander in chief. It got to be a little touchy, a little bit awkward.

The British Admiralty has always controlled the operations of their fleets in home waters. They controlled the 1916 Battle of Jutland from the Admiralty in a great sense. The famous PQ-17 convoy to Murmansk in 1942 was controlled from the Admiralty. It was the Admiralty that ordered away all the escort ships, including the division of light cruisers and destroyers. The search for the *Bismarck* in 1941 was controlled by the Admiralty. Mr. Churchill interfered in all theaters of war with his ideas. Even in Burma they started to interfere, but General William Slim repudiated them and slapped them back.

As the planning progressed, there was considerable concern on our side about the German E-boats known to be in Cherbourg Harbor. They were pretty active, dashing out and around in the sea-lanes of the Channel itself. They appeared to be practically the only naval menace to our flank, the western section. We got to thinking about these E-boats. We knew they were in shelters inside Cherbourg Harbor. We had the battleship *Nevada* with her new 14-inch guns. After Pearl Harbor she had been rebuilt and had these marvelous 14-inch guns with the long-range, the high-angle, fire.

I proposed that we take the *Nevada* out to sea off Cherbourg, give her a heavy screen of destroyers against possible submarine attack, give her adequate fighter cover, which was perfectly simple to do, and have her go out on one bright sunny day with what we call "airplane spot"—putting a trained naval spotter for gunfire in different planes to watch where the shots fell in Cherbourg Harbor and tell the ship what to do to correct the range or the deflection to hit the target. My staff and I worked this out. We felt that a moderate amount of ammunition could be expended on that and might really do quite a bit of damage to these nests where the E-boats were sheltered in the night.

Well, it caused quite a bit of furor because this paper got in the hands of my friend General Bedell Smith before it got to Admiral Ramsay. Our meeting was rather a heated occasion in which the British admiral threw the idea out of the window and only by the grace of God was it possible for me to say really that the proposal had gone forward more directly into the Supreme Allied Commander's hands than normally would have been the case. Ramsay would have returned it to me with disapproval, or whatever he wanted to say, but probably would not have forwarded it at all to Eisenhower. It would not be wholly truthful not to confess that steps were taken to make sure this got into the hands of the chief of staff of General Eisenhower before the British admiral who had become very testy and very difficult about the American effort. In any case, it was called off. We didn't do it.

I and my staff found the differences in the British and American approaches to naval command a very complicating feature in dealing with Ramsay and his staff. The Normandy operation, the landing, became in the eyes of the British what they termed a set piece. In other words, no initiative was possible. It was like a fireworks display. You set off a little wick at a certain point and certain things begin to burn, lights go off, and whatnot. That was their idea of what this was to be—a somewhat formalized affair.

I always had maintained that the resourcefulness of the American man—man or boy—was such a great asset that if we wanted to take a certain hill or a certain beach or a certain landing place, we should say, "This is what we think is the best way from our studies. When you get there, if you should find it different from that, disregard the 'how.' You know what you're supposed to do and why you are supposed to do it, and you do it!" That is what they did in Normandy, in Sicily, what the army did all through France and the whole campaign in western Europe. It was the initiative of the American soldier or sailor. His resourcefulness was an asset which we have and have had, and I hope we always will have.

In late April 1944 I went down to Plymouth and hoisted my flag in the *Augusta*, took my staff down there, and we set up the headquarters command. Then I went to see Admiral Ramsay at his headquarters near Southampton, near Eisenhower's own headquarters, and made final preparations. I think that it was obvious that things were going all right. The whole southern end of England was literally stuffed with the American army coming down from their training centers—with all their equipment—across the lanes and highways. A bulldozer very often had to go ahead and widen the roads here and there, but the British took it very nicely. There was never any complaint about that.

After a day's delay because of weather, I sailed on the *Augusta* on the afternoon of Monday, June 5, heading eastward to the Isle of Wight, where there was the big circle we called Piccadilly Circus. All the shipping arrived and fanned out in five lanes—three British and two American—for the coast of France. The *Augusta* turned south, west of south, into our channel heading for Omaha Beach.

At dawn on June 6 the *Augusta* was almost in a position to fire her share of the bombardment of the beaches. The naval gunfire began on schedule. Curiously enough, my own reaction as we neared H-hour and began firing from the *Augusta* and all the other ships was one of letdown. I couldn't say it was disappointment, but there was no heavy German gunfire against the ships, against the transports. The point I make is that we had devoted quite a lot of attention to areas where we thought the Germans had heavy guns in the naval sense, 6-inch or bigger, and there weren't any.

Now, we all know the resistance on the shoreline at Omaha Beach was very intense. At Omaha Beach the rough sea and the waves are pretty hard to get into when you're up to your waist in water and you're carrying a gun and ammunition and a gas mask and all the paraphernalia a poor soldier boy had to carry. They had a tough time. From 6:30 A.M. on June 6 until practically mid-afternoon, the successful attempt to get a foothold, let alone a beachhead, on Omaha had been—I won't say failed—but delayed.

In the early afternoon the V Corps commander had got ashore and telephoned back on the walkie-talkie: Couldn't the navy put some gunfire down on the German position? Well, when this appeal came to me that the general on shore wanted gunfire, I ordered the officer who had command of the distinctly supportive naval forces to send the destroyers in at once. They went so close that they darned near stranded themselves.

We were worried—I was worried, Bradley was worried—about Omaha Beach. We weren't too concerned about Utah Beach. The reports there were pretty good. But the delay in the movement at Omaha meant that all the follow-up forces coming in from across the Channel—the next division, the tanks, the merchant ships full of ammunition and stores—were piling up. Ramsay came down in a British destroyer. I went over to see him. He was perturbed about this and I said: "We'll straighten it out; don't worry!" He gave me a drink of whiskey, the only drink of whiskey I had from the fifth of June to the Fourth of July. I was disturbed too, frankly, but I assured him we'd get it straightened out, and by golly, on the seventh of June all those ships had been discharged. Their cargoes all had been landed. The reason—the beachhead had been enlarged from a toehold on the shoreline to a depth of several miles.

One day during the planning process before the invasion, General Bradley and I had gotten to talking about the supply of ammunition. He said he wasn't too sure that he'd get it from the normal supply ships. In other words, lifting the ammunition out of the holds of the ships with a derrick, lowering it over the sides of the ships into boats and taking it ashore, and then getting it to the front. He very wisely suggested that he might be in real trouble if we got in difficulties with the ship-to-shore movement of ammunition or if the weather got so bad that the little boats that were supposed to take it in couldn't carry it. He had said, "What do you think of the idea of getting some car ferries from the Eastern Seaboard—heavily loaded to the gunwales with ammunition—towed over and just landed up on the beach?"

I said I thought it was a fine idea, so we commandeered from the New York Harbor and Boston Harbor and Baltimore Harbor these car ferries. We loaded them with what the army called units of fire—so many rounds of small arms and so many rounds of machine-gun ammunition, ammunition for antitank guns and antiaircraft guns, and 105s, bazookas, 155s, and so on. Each barge was loaded with some of each kind of ammunition. The whole thing was what they called combat loaded for each type of gun. We towed those right over on D+1 and stranded them high up on the beaches, out of the way of the regular landing spots. So this reserve ammunition was available and, by God, when the great storm came in mid-June, it saved our bacon. A very well-conceived idea of Bradley's and very well executed.

Bradley came to see me on about the twenty-second or twenty-third of June, asking if it would be possible to use naval gunfire against the Cherbourg defenses, particularly those behind Cherbourg. The German artillery was placed behind the hills and firing over the hills. Our own artillery ashore at that time did not have enough of the howitzer type, the 105-millimeter and 155-millimeter howitzers. At this time most of the men-of-war had been withdrawn and sent over to Portland to replenish before going down to the Med for the operation against the south of France. I felt sure we could divide our men-of-war into two groups. We could use the shorter-range ones to subdue the fire of the batteries along the seacoast—the breakwater of Cherbourg Harbor and so on—while the longer-range ones could fire over into the backside of the hills where the German artillery was bothering Major General Joe Collins.

So I sent a signal to Portland to organize the expedition. Their immediate response was one of reluctance because of the time element. We had to get to Cherbourg awfully fast. We couldn't keep on tying down the VII Corps south of Cherbourg any longer. So I suggested that if it was not possible, I would go down there with the *Augusta* and a destroyer escort, and we would do our best with our 8-inch guns. That produced a result, and a proper attack was organized on the forts. We used the *Nevada* and several of the older battleships. One or two of the British cruisers also had long-range guns.

Well, here, I know, in fact, I actually stepped completely on the toes of the British Naval Commander in Chief and the Commander in Chief of the Portsmouth area because those sea areas did not belong to me. Ramsay, having been present in the disastrous Gallipoli affair in World War I, like many British men of that vintage, was nonplussed at the thought that we should now begin to take on shore batteries in this modern world with naval ships. Nevertheless, he did not interfere, did not intervene, did not veto it. My order had been so phrased that it was almost impossible, because I said, "In order to support the First Army at the request of General Bradley, we are going to do this."

Mind you, our ships didn't go in close to the shore. The long-range ships were seven or eight miles away from the shore so that their guns would shoot twenty-four thousand yards or so, and the shorter-range ships were about five or six miles off the shore. The German shore batteries returned the fire, but there were very few casualties. Then the Americans withdrew without any loss of ships. The bombardment probably wasn't very successful, but at least it gave the Germans something to think about, and it gave our navy a chance to participate in an action of a different type from what they had ever gone through before. Ramsay rushed down from Portland to see the ships as they returned, very nervous about what had happened, but he never made any comment to me, one way or the other, either approving or disapproving. Maybe I didn't do any good in terms of knocking out the enemy, but after all, Cherbourg was captured the next day by Joe Collins's army.

After this I sent the *Augusta* back to refuel and then head for operations in the Mediterranean. We sent the other men-of-war back and I transferred to a destroyer

Admiral Kirk climbs down a ladder on the side of the *Augusta* as he prepares to visit the invasion beach at Normandy on June 14. Note the hundreds of rivet heads in this ship that was built in the early 1930s. (*Navy photo in the National Archives: 80-G-253433*)

with some of my personal staff. It was time to turn over the beach to Rear Admiral John Wilkes, who was in charge of that under the basic plan, the combatant ships having left and the situation being as nearly stabilized as one could expect.

I returned to Portsmouth on the Fourth of July. One of my own staff group met me there, and I went at once and reported to Admiral Ramsay in his office. Pretty chilly interview—it was grim! It was too bad because he

was a decent guy, and we had been rather good friends up until the Normandy operation. I think he was among those British naval flag officers who had no real conception of the power the U.S. Navy had developed. And if they began dimly to perceive that, they were unconsciously or subconsciously rather resentful. Why not? After all, they'd had command of the sea for centuries. They were being displaced by a greater naval power, and they did not really quite like it.

ALAN GOODRICH KIRK (1888–1963) graduated from the Naval Academy in 1909 and spent his career largely in surface combatant ships, specializing in ordnance and gunnery. In the early 1920s he was a naval aide to presidents Warren Harding and Calvin Coolidge. In the 1930s he was operations officer on the staff of Admiral Claude Bloch, who served as Commander Battle Force and later as Commander in Chief U.S. Fleet. Kirk was commanding officer of the destroyer *Schenk*, executive officer of the battleship *West Virginia*, and commanding officer of the cruiser *Milwaukee*. He served as U.S. naval attaché in London from 1939 to 1941. He spent part of 1941 as Director of Naval Intelligence, then took command of Destroyer Squadron Seven. After brief duty as Admiral Harold Stark's chief of staff in London, Kirk became Commander Amphibious Force Atlantic Fleet in February 1943. He was involved in amphibious operations in the Mediterranean that year, later moving to England to command the Normandy task force, and still later commanding U.S. Naval Forces France. After duty on the Navy's General Board, he retired in 1946. He was U.S. ambassador at various times to Belgium and Luxembourg, the Soviet Union, and Nationalist China. The frigate *Kirk* (FF-1087) is named in his honor. (*Navy photo in the National Archives: 80-G-K-14112*)

ULTRA WARNINGS

By McGeorge Bundy

My assignment to the staff of Rear Admiral Alan Kirk was at his request. He and my father were friends, and our families had known each other. He knew that I was in the army, he asked for me, and the army gave me to him.

My army experience had been in signal intelligence: codebreaking and that kind of thing. I enlisted in the army in June 1942 and was assigned to the Signal Corps because of a high math aptitude. I was involved with Dr. William Friedman's organization, receiving training initially at Fort Monmouth, New Jersey. Later, I went to officer candidate school, was commissioned, and received still more training. I was studying the process of codebreaking and teaching it to others.

My service with Admiral Kirk began in early 1943, in time for me to be at Norfolk before his flagship *Ancon* sailed for the invasion of Sicily. He was Commander Task Force 85 for that operation and had on board Lieutenant General Omar Bradley, Commander of II Corps. Those two would be together again at Normandy.

After the landing in Sicily, I accompanied Kirk when he went to England to take part in the planning for Operation Overlord. We had a long London winter of staff work. I don't have any particular memories, because we were so busy not remembering things—everything was so classified. My job essentially was to keep track of the admiral's own paperwork, with the flag secretary, of course, doing the administrative work of the staff. I came to be the "guy at the door," as it turned out. Watching Admiral Kirk's copy of the Overlord plan, for example, was my problem. My own inputs to the plan didn't amount to anything. I was involved with him as his assistant in some of the drafting of messages and that kind of thing, but I had no substantive role.

I don't want to exaggerate my contribution, because I certainly didn't get between Admiral Kirk and his chief of staff, Rear Admiral Arthur Struble. Admiral Struble kept track of the staff and did an excellent job of monitoring what was getting done and not getting done. He kept the flow of business going. He referred to Admiral Kirk the issues that he knew Kirk wanted to

Landing craft stream past the flagship *Augusta* on their way to the beach. (*Navy photo in the National Archives: 80-G-45720*)

The eyes of the brass look shoreward from the bridge of the *Augusta* on D-Day. *Left to right are:* Rear Admiral Alan Kirk, Lieutenant General Omar Bradley, Rear Admiral Arthur Struble. (*Navy photo in the National Archives: 80-G-252940*)

decide, but didn't bother him with other things.

As a second lieutenant in the army, I wasn't really senior enough then to have an opinion on what kind of job Kirk was doing. Eventually, he became a great friend of mine. Much later, when I was in the Kennedy White House, I was involved in Admiral Kirk's assignment to be the U.S. ambassador to Taiwan. I had a high regard for him. He was just a very intelligent and imaginative commander.

He was very good at Alliance command, which was obviously an important factor in our dealings with the British and French. Admiral Kirk was under the British Admiral Bertram Ramsay. At the same time, Admiral Ramsay was under General Eisenhower. And both of them knew that the most important thing Kirk had to do was get Admiral King, the Chief of Naval Operations in Washington, to act as if Europe was part of the war. Admiral King regarded it as an army theater and was understandably concentrating his principal attention on the Pacific. We had to write the dispatches that helped get us some old battleships to cover the beaches with gunfire and things like that.

Shortly before the invasion force set out for France, Admiral Kirk and his staff embarked in the heavy cruiser *Augusta*, and General Bradley came aboard as commander of the First Army. Bradley was a wonderful man, and I observed that he and Admiral Kirk got along easily and well. There was no problem.

At the time that trouble developed on Omaha Beach on D-Day, a number of officers went in for a look from

a boat offshore. I was included—I suppose on the basis that I was an army officer, not that I was going to know anything more than the rest. Indeed, my ability to see was fairly limited because of my bad eyesight. I've never been able to spot things at distances.

Anyway, we did go in and look, and about all we could see was that we couldn't tell for sure what was happening. So we came back, and I reported that to Admiral Kirk. I thought the men from this party were giving him more information than they really had. We didn't really know yet what the score was. But that was only one small episode. The army, after all, was getting communication from the beach, and it was better than observation from fairly close offshore. We had a nervous twenty-four hours as the men on the beach battled the Germans.

My real role while the *Augusta* was off the beachhead was to serve as Admiral Kirk's Ultra officer. There had been no need for that earlier, because we didn't get any Ultra messages in London. Now we were receiving operational communications warning us that there was going to be an air attack at such-and-such a time from such-and-such a direction. These Ultra messages were sent to Kirk's flagship through a system known as the one-time pad. This is the most secure possible system, because it involves the sender and receiver each having a pad of individual sheets rather than a recurring system that involved mechanical means. These sheets involved random number-for-letter substitutions in order to encipher messages. Since each sheet on the pad was used only once, an intercepted message couldn't be combined with other messages to establish any sort of pattern that might facilitate codebreaking.

I don't know specifically who was sending the messages we were getting on board the *Augusta*. Presumably, someone ashore in England was intercepting and decoding the German messages. I got the resulting information on board ship in a form that my one-time pad would undo. We were not breaking the German messages directly, nor were we really supposed to know just how the information was obtained. We were told not to worry about that. My brother, incidentally, was at Bletchley Park in England at the time, working on the same stuff for the same reason. He also had enlisted in the army, and his aptitude had wound him up in signal intelligence.

When each message came in, I would decipher it by running it against the appropriate page on the one-time pad. I'd write out the plain-language version of the message and give it to the admiral. As far as I knew, he and I were the only people on board ship who knew the contents of these messages. Then he would translate the message into an alert that was sent out over the TBS voice radio. That is to say, suppose the message said that "Such-and-such is heading for the beachhead area from A to B. Will be approaching beachhead at about such-and-such a time." The admiral would find a way of saying, on the TBS, that if he were a German, he would be going to attack from approximately that direction at approximately that time, and he hoped everybody had his eyes out accordingly.

I can't remember the exact language he used to avoid letting the Germans know that we could read their messages. They might have been listening to the TBS and collating the information with their actual flight plans. I myself thought Admiral Kirk was up against the edge of what he was authorized to do in passing along such information. But as a practical matter, nobody was going to connect all that. Listening to the TBS was not what counterintelligence Germans were going to be busy doing.

Moreover, the Germans—like their Japanese allies— had a supreme sense of confidence that their codes couldn't be broken. So the Germans might simply infer that Kirk was getting advice from the aviation officer on his staff as to what the Luftwaffe's plans were. I don't know how many kills resulted from the information he provided, but there were some.

After the first few days of the operation, it came time for General Bradley to go ashore and take command of the landing force for its breakout from the beaches and on into France. With a smile, he turned to me— recently promoted to first lieutenant—and said, "You're now the senior army officer present afloat." But I never kidded myself that I made the landing a success. I was just lucky to be there.

McGEORGE BUNDY (1919–) graduated from Yale University in 1940 with a bachelor's degree. In 1942 he enlisted in the army as a private, underwent officer training, and then joined the staff of Rear Admiral Alan Kirk for most of the remainder of the war, including duty in the Mediterranean, in conjunction with D-Day, and later ashore in France. Following the war he was the research assistant for and coauthor of Henry L. Stimson's autobiography *On Active Service in Peace and War* (Harper, 1948). He subsequently served as a political analyst on the Council on Foreign Relations and taught at Harvard. In 1953, at the age of thirty-four, he became dean of Harvard's faculty of arts and sciences. He held that post until President John F. Kennedy made him special assistant for national security affairs in 1960. He remained in the White House under President Lyndon Johnson before leaving the government to serve as president of the Ford Foundation from 1966 to 1979. Mr. Bundy was a professor of history at New York University from 1979 to 1989 and is now chairman of a Carnegie Corporation committee on reducing the nuclear threat. He lives in New York City. (*Photo of Vice Admiral Kirk presenting a medal to Captain Bundy provided courtesy Mrs. Peter Solbert*)

As is the case with the Allied accounts that focus primarily on the land side of the Normandy invasion, so it is too when German forces are discussed. All too often, the view of German sea power concentrates on the surface raiders such as the *Bismarck* and on the ubiquitous U-boats that wreaked havoc on Allied merchant shipping until the tide turned in 1943. Vice Admiral Friedrich Ruge was a prime player on the German naval side, especially in developing beach defenses. Here he explains that aspect of the story, as well as describing the vessels of war the Germans were able to bring into play. Primarily, it is a story of frustration on the German side, traceable in large part to the flawed strategic vision of Adolf Hitler. Impatient, he took his nation to war before it was able to develop a balanced fleet, and then he interfered in the work of such capable commanders as Field Marshal Erwin Rommel. Ruge, who later became a distinguished author and a leader in the renascent postwar West German navy, tells us here what it was like to be on the other side as the Allies invaded France.

GERMAN NAVAL OPERATIONS ON D-DAY

By Vice Admiral Friedrich Ruge, Federal German Navy (Retired)

On June 7, 1919, I was a very young naval officer preparing to scuttle a German destroyer interned at Scapa Flow. Twenty-five years later, on the morning of D-Day+1, I realized that the Allies had established a permanent beachhead and that the war was definitely lost. I had been appointed naval adviser to Field Marshal Erwin Rommel in November 1943 when he received instructions to examine the defenses in northwestern Europe. He had orders (why, I don't know) to begin in Denmark. From there we moved over to France around December 20, 1943. From my previous appointments, I knew the coast very well, as I had swept and laid mines practically everywhere in those waters.

Rommel immediately made extensive tours of inspection to get a personal view of the situation. Soon it became evident that the defenses were weak in men and material. The only hope to beat off a large amphibious operation lay in integrating all available forces in one common plan, which held some prospect of success. When we arrived in France, there was no such plan for the defense. Rommel, however, soon developed one. The infantry were comparatively numerous, but only very lightly motorized. At first, there was only one combat-ready armored division in the west, but more were organized or sent to France, until there were ten in all. Our air force was extremely weak, only a few hundred bombers and fighters. Of course, they were unable to support mobile operations.

Rommel, realizing this at once from his experiences in North Africa, came to the conclusion that the best plan was to put the infantry and every single man, including the staffs, bakeries, supply trains, etc., into a belt of field fortifications. These strong points were to be protected by as many land mines, as much concrete, and as much barbed wire as possible. This "Rommel Belt" was to be about three miles deep all along the coast, with the armored divisions stationed behind it in such a way that the guns of their forward units could shell the beach. In addition, of course, as much artillery

Vice Admiral Ruge stands with Field Marshal Erwin Rommel, left, during an inspection of the "Atlantic Wall" defenses prior to the Allied invasion. (*Naval Institute Collection*)

as we could assemble was to be put into and behind that belt. In this way, when attacked, the infantry would quickly have armored and artillery support while the divisions on either flank of the attacked area would

Omaha Beach is at low tide on the afternoon of June 6, revealing the beach obstacles designed to rip out the bottoms of landing craft. On the beach itself are the corpses and vehicles hit by the withering German gunfire. (*Navy photo in the National Archives: 80-G-45714*)

form the reserves. With the good road-net in France, they would be available almost as rapidly as when stationed farther inland.

Rommel was a great believer in close cooperation between infantry and armor. He knew from Africa what it meant to fight without an adequate air force. He foresaw that the mobile operations would be slowed down so much that they could not be effective, particularly after the Allies had established a beachhead with landing strips for fighters. He realized and unmistakably stated that it would not be possible to eliminate such a beachhead once it had been formed. A third front in France, with our forces in Russia and Italy retreating, would mean disaster everywhere. In Rommel's opinion, the only hope for a tolerable end of the war was to beat off the attack either before or at the time it reached the beach.

In view of normal army experience, Rommel's defense system had the disadvantage of too little depth. This could be improved, however, by extending the defenses far into the sea—putting obstacles in shallow water, and placing various types of naval mines in deeper water. Because of the great differences between high and low tides (up to twenty feet in the Seine bight), putting obstacles all along the foreshore required an immense amount of work and material.

If we had known where the attack would come, work could have been concentrated there. After the raids on Saint-Nazaire and Dieppe, the ports themselves were fortified to such an extent that they could be ruled out. Rommel first expected the Allies to strike astride the Somme River, but later favored the Seine bight where they actually came. However, *Oberkommando der Wehrmacht* (OKW) and *Oberbefehlshaber West* (OB West), under Field Marshal Gerd von Rundstedt, did not agree with his reasoning. They were of the opinion that the invasion fleet would take—indeed had to take— the shortest way, and consequently expected the attack between the Somme River and the Schelde Estuary. Therefore, infantry divisions were stationed there in two rows—even in the Boulogne-Calais area, which was well defended by heavy batteries protected by concrete or armor. Farther west, infantry and artillery were spread out rather thinly.

In the western part of the Seine bight, between the Orne and Vire rivers, precisely where the attack came, there was only one weak division and no heavy battery. Along excellent landing beaches we found only observation posts, with nothing between them for three-quarters of a mile in places, and little behind them. This would not have mattered too much if we had had some naval strength, but for offensive purposes, the navy had become the weakest of the three services.

The Treaty of Versailles had restricted the German

navy to six armored ships of ten thousand tons, six light cruisers of six thousand tons, some minor craft, no submarines or airplanes, and only fifteen thousand officers and enlisted men. When Hitler started rearming in 1935, he did not expect a war against England, and he concluded the London Treaty, which fixed the German navy at 35 percent of the Royal Navy. In any case, the situation required that the army and air force be created first.

Grand Admiral Erich Raeder understood sea power and did not want a war against England. He was satisfied with a small, balanced fleet. Only in 1939, after Hitler had revoked the London Treaty, did Raeder examine the possibilities of a war with Great Britain as an opponent. Hitler assured him, even then, that there was no danger of war before the middle of the 1940s.

In 1939 Raeder embarked upon the Z-plan, which meant the creation of strong task forces of great endurance. These, together with submarines and raiders, were to attack British shipping in all oceans and thus compel the Royal Navy to disperse its strength. But not a single one of the large ships of that program was ever finished. When war broke out, the few surface ships that existed were used for commerce raiding until the submarines took over about a year and a half later. These operations were quite successful, but the surface ships were practically used up in the process. The last event was the *Bismarck* affair in May 1941.

The submarine war caused the Allies heavy losses, but in 1943 it broke down almost completely. The submarine staff had realized the implications of technical developments on the Allied side too late. Only a new type of submarine with a much greater underwater speed had any prospects of evading the antisubmarine warfare forces of the Allies. There were about a hundred submarines, mainly type VII, in the submarine bases on the Bay of Biscay. Some had been improved by snorkels and others were being converted, but it was an open secret that in case of an invasion, little could be expected from them. No submarines whatsoever were stationed in ports on the English Channel.

It should be mentioned that no naval aviation existed. When Hermann Göring began to build up the German air force, he claimed everything that flew. Only a few naval aviators were trained for the small planes carried by battleships and raiders. The two aircraft carriers under construction never reached the operational stage. Reconnaissance for submarines was flown by air force units when and if it was flown. Knowledge of the necessities of naval war was scanty in the air force commands. Consequently, the only naval forces available in France were destroyers, torpedo boats, and—for offensive operations—motor torpedo boats (MTBs). In addition, there were minesweepers, escort vessels, patrol boats, and subchasers. In June 1944 only four destroyers were operational in the Bay

Teller mines attached to posts offshore were among the devices waiting for American landing craft. (*U.S. Army*)

of Biscay, where they escorted submarines, raiders, and merchant ships.

In the case of torpedo boats, two types were stationed in the west. At the beginning of 1944, there were four so-called "fleet torpedo boats" of the "Elbing" class, so named because they were built in Elbing, West Prussia. They had a displacement of thirteen hundred tons. *T-21* was severely damaged by a fighter-bomber, went into dry dock in Le Havre, and had just been repaired when the invasion began. The other three were used for laying mines in the Channel. In March they were sent to the Bay of Biscay. On the way back, at the end of April, they were intercepted by superior British forces. *T-29* was sunk and the other two were slightly damaged. After repairs in Saint-Malo they had another fight with British destroyers. *T-21* was sunk along with the British *Ashanti*. *T-24* reached Le Havre, where it joined the Fifth Torpedo Boat Flotilla, consisting of five old torpedo boats of nine hundred tons. Ten days before the invasion, one torpedo boat was lost off Le Havre and two others damaged. Fifth Flotilla, therefore, consisted of two old and two new torpedo boats on June 6, 1944.

The MTBs—known as E-boats by the Allies—were better suited for operations in the Channel. They displaced about one hundred tons and were armed with two torpedo tubes and two light guns each. In theory, their speed was forty knots, but in practice, much less. Five squadrons of eight boats each were stationed in the west. Early in 1944 there were two squadrons in Ostend, one in Boulogne, and two in Cherbourg. Early in May one squadron was moved from Boulogne to Le Havre.

In January 1944 they carried out nine operations in the English Channel. On one they sank five ships (twelve hundred gross tons) off Land's End. In February they undertook thirteen operations, four of which were to lay mines. They sank or damaged a number of vessels with a loss of two boats. Thirteen operations in

March were unsuccessful because the MTBs were located too early by the British for an attack. In April they carried out fourteen operations with one loss. They sank two LSTs and damaged one in Lyme bight. On another occasion they claimed to have sunk a floating dock. In May there were twelve operations, mainly devoted to laying mines.

It became impossible to reach the English coast undetected. Over and over again they were attacked by planes and destroyers that chased them almost into Cherbourg. Two were lost, two others damaged. When the invasion started, only thirty-five motor torpedo boats were ready for action.

The defensive forces were far more numerous. Four hundred and fifty-eight small craft operated on D-Day. But their actual fighting value, of course, was low, in spite of the great experience and bravery of their crews. The types of vessels mainly used were minelayers, minesweepers, and larger minesweepers of five hundred to six hundred tons, with one or two 105-millimeter guns and some other light guns. There were six squadrons of eight ships normally. They were most frequently used in the Bay of Biscay and in the western Channel.

In the narrows, R-boats played the main part. They were motorboats of one hundred to two hundred tons, containing one or two light guns and possessing a speed of about twenty knots; very handy for sweeping and also for minelaying. They could each take eight of our large mines. We had five squadrons of twelve R-boats each. There were two hundred trawlers and drifters that had been converted into patrol vessels and auxiliary minesweepers; one squadron of subchasers

Among the remnants of "Fortress Europa" after the invasion was this gun emplacement blasted by naval guns from offshore. (*Navy photo in the National Archives: 80-G-253241*)

consisting mainly of small whaling vessels that my good friend Captain Ernst Felix Krüder had captured in the Southern Polar Sea and sent to France; and a number of large and small steamers that were equipped as big magnets for sweeping magnetic mines. For local sweeping purposes, we had commandeered fishing vessels, pilot steamers, tugs, and even lobster boats for use in the Bay of Biscay.

A new development was the so-called "gun-carriers," small landing craft with one or two 105-millimeter guns.

Altogether, they were a motley crowd, but they had one thing in common: all were armed to the teeth with small guns (in part taken from unprotected air force fields) and heavy machine guns, and their crews knew how to use them.

As to the coast defense proper, the navy's contribution in men and material was considerable. Coastal artillery was installed in several steps. The commando raids on Saint-Nazaire and Dieppe had shown that isolated batteries outside the port defenses could be eliminated from the rear. This led to the next step: moving batteries of that kind closer to the ports; integrating them in the system of defense there; and, at the same time, setting up more guns for the protection of those ports. Owing to lack of reserves, this took a long time. Therefore, two heavy batteries of three 380-millimeter guns, one west of Cherbourg and one at Le Havre, were not ready on D-Day. The final step, putting batteries behind the threatened parts of the coast between the ports, started late and the program was not very far advanced.

The army was for placing the guns behind the coast and camouflaging them. The navy, however, wanted them forward and under armor or concrete. This was better for firing at moving targets, but concrete was in short supply, and fixed concrete embrasures restricted the arc of fire to an angle of a little over 90 degrees. Too late, navy engineers hit upon the bright idea of revolving turrets made of concrete. Taking everything together, naval coast artillery greatly contributed to coastal defenses in general, but little toward defending the coast of Normandy against the invasion.

Another naval contribution to the defense was a chain of radar stations all along the coast. At that time German radar was not as good as the Allied radar, but it had discovered and reported the landing fleets about three hours before the first troops arrived on shore. Our radar stations were attacked many times in the last weeks before the invasion, but on D-Day almost all of them were in working order again.

A distinct asset was our monitoring service. Early in May it found out from an Allied landing exercise on the southern coast of England that the landings would begin about two hours after low water. In previous years it had monitored the British radar results so exactly and quickly that we were able to give our small convoys their correct positions from English radar and warn them of impending MTB attacks, which was of considerable help.

The net of naval communications was excellent. We had teletypes to all the main ports, whereas the army relied mostly on telephones. Nobody could listen in on teletype messages, and we always had in print what had been communicated. The only problem that arose was training our people to condense their reports, questions, and so on.

Finally, German naval contributions to the defense included providing motorized units for transporting ammunition, torpedoes, etc., and making available a number of naval training units that could serve as infantry battalions under certain conditions. They were transferred from Germany to places behind the coast, where they relieved army units for the defense proper.

The organization of the three armed services in France had simply happened after the campaign of 1940 and had never been streamlined for defense purposes. Basically, the navy was to fight the enemy on the sea, and the army was to defend the coast. But it was complicated by the fact that the enemy might arrive by sea and then fight ashore. After long discussions, orders were given that the "Sea Commandant," a naval captain or rear admiral responsible for one or two hundred miles of coast, would be in charge as long as the enemy was on the water. As soon as the landing began, control of the fire direction went over to the army division that held the sector under attack. All the batteries were under the orders of the senior coast artillery commander of that sector.

On the whole, this system worked quite well, although there were some further complications. Local commanders tended to switch fire too soon from the ships to the infantry units who had already disembarked and could attack them directly.

Under the name of "lightning fields" (*Blitzsperren*), Navy Group West prepared a system of minefields to be laid by all vessels as soon as the attack was imminent. Considering the lack of reliable reconnaissance and the short distance between the coasts, this was a plan of doubtful value. As things turned out, most of these fields were laid on D-Day, but not a single one off the landing beaches. The Allies were there before the minelayers, just as we had predicted. Shortly before the invasion, MTBs laid some mines near the Isle of Wight. But "oyster mines," the pressure mines, were not laid because their use was not allowed by OKW until after the invasion. On the whole, much more could have been done with naval mines.

So much for the naval preparations and situation. As to the actual events, the German navy did very little on D-Day. As far as I remember, the last air reconnaissance was on May 26. The large Allied minesweeping operation on June 5 was not recognized and evidently

not sighted, although at least two squadrons approached the French coast so closely that they could make out details ashore. In any case, no report reached the various headquarters.

The landing force was reported by radar between two and three o'clock on the morning of D-Day—at about the same time that the first alarm was given because paratroopers and dummies had landed in several places. Our meteorologists had predicted continuing bad weather. They had no news of the approaching area of high pressure that enabled General Dwight Eisenhower to come to his momentous decision. No German patrols were at sea, and the minelaying excursion had been canceled. Only the four torpedo boats at Le Havre and one MTB squadron at Cherbourg were ready at short notice.

The torpedo boats, under the command of Captain Heinrich Hoffman, left Le Havre and attacked the Allied forces screening the landing fleet to the east. They torpedoed the Norwegian destroyer *Svenner*, but they left the battleships HMS *Warspite* and HMS *Ramillies* unharmed, even though they were immediately behind the *Svenner*. Hoffman attacked again in the following nights, but without success. The first night, patrol vessels from Le Havre tried to clarify the situation and suffered some losses. Two squadrons of MTBs went to sea from Cherbourg but were unable to find any targets. They had been alerted rather late, and evidently the radar reports had not been evaluated when they were told where to search.

The following night one MTB was lost on a mine. The other MTBs had their first success on the night of June 7-8, sinking two LSTs in the Bay of the Seine and one LCI and one LCT to the west of Fécamp. During the following nights, the MTBs attacked repeatedly, had some successes, and suffered considerable losses. From June 9 on, the German air force also dropped mines in the Bay of the Seine. At least forty-three Allied vessels were sunk or damaged by mines.

On the night of June 8-9 the German destroyers stationed in the Bay of Biscay tried to penetrate into the western English Channel. They were intercepted, however, by Allied destroyers. Two German destroyers were lost, and one Allied destroyer was heavily damaged. The two remaining destroyers returned to Brest and did not make another attempt.

On the evening of June 14, 325 Lancaster bombers attacked Le Havre. The German antiaircraft batteries had orders not to fire because an attack with radio-controlled glider bombs was planned at the same time. Consequently, the British attack was a full success. Three torpedo boats, ten MTBs, and numerous minesweepers, patrol boats, and other vessels were sunk or damaged. There remained only one operative MTB in Le Havre. The following night a similar attack was directed against Boulogne, where a considerable num-

Captured German coastal battery at Normandy (*Coast Guard photo in the National Archives: 26-G-2513*)

ber of minesweepers and other craft were destroyed. By that time the Allies had a large bridgehead ashore, and there was no possibility of throwing them back into the sea. Still, the fight went on.

As for the naval batteries, the 210-millimeter battery at Fort St. Marcouf to the east of Cherbourg initially fired at targets at sea and sank one destroyer, the USS *Corry*—possibly in conjunction with a mine. When visibility permitted, the battery turned its fire toward Utah Beach. Several ships, among them two battleships, tried to silence it. One of the guns was put out of action by a direct hit, and the two others were damaged. But the crews succeeded in repairing the first one, and when it was damaged again, the other. In this way they continued to fire for two days, although the battery was already under infantry attack and cut off from the German main force. Nevertheless, it defended itself for three more days. By that time all the officers and petty officers had been wounded or killed. Those who could walk retreated through inundated country and reached the German line five miles back.

The other naval battery, four 150-millimeter guns at Longues, north of Bayeux, was not quite finished, but all four guns could fire. Its commanding officer and crew evidently were inferior to those of Fort St. Marcouf. Heavy air attacks before D-Day did not harm the guns but destroyed much of the fire-control equipment. On D-Day the battery took several ships under ineffective fire. It was bombarded by battleships and cruisers until three guns were knocked out. The fourth fired for the last time on the evening of D-Day. The next morning the crew surrendered to British troops after an infantry company, which was to defend it, had been ordered back to the defense of Bayeux.

The difficulties of cooperation between the army and the navy on the German side are illustrated by events at Sword Beach in the British sector. For the

British it was imperative to get supplies to their paratroops east of the Orne River, and they occupied the bridge across the river at Bénouville close to the sea before it could be blown up. At an inland shipyard between Bénouville and Caen, some patrol boats and minesweepers were under repair. They raised steam and went downstream, only to find the way out to sea blocked at the bridge. As the situation was not at all clear, they went back. When they were told about the importance of the bridge, they formed a party of volunteers and, together with army engineers, proceeded to blow it up. The sailors reached it, but the engineers who carried the explosives did not make it. Thus, the bridge remained unharmed and in British hands, although it could have been destroyed right at the beginning.

So far, I have not mentioned any submarine activity. Of course, the U-boats were alerted on D-Day, and thirty-six left their bases on the Bay of Biscay within twenty-four hours. It was soon realized that submarines without snorkel equipment could not operate in the Channel. Eighteen formed a group in the Bay of Biscay. They did not find any targets, and some of them were lost by attack from the air. The submarines with snorkels attacked the 12th Support Group with T-5 (wren) torpedoes, homing on the noise from the propellers.

It was June 14 before the submarines reached the Allied shipping lanes in the English Channel. The following day they sank an LST, a frigate, and a destroyer escort. Operating in the Channel was most difficult. Losses were high and results meager. Without intending to get there, one of the submarines found itself in Spithead Roads off Portsmouth. But there was no target in sight that would have merited a torpedo, and the submarine crept out again and reached one of the bases on the Bay of Biscay.

A group of submarines left their Baltic and Norwegian bases to take up a defensive position off the Norwegian coast. Five were sunk by planes, and five others were damaged. One was sunk by a submarine; four more were sunk in the Atlantic, and two were damaged. Submarines with snorkels laid mines off Plymouth and Land's End. One attacked a U.S. battleship off Cherbourg, but the torpedoes detonated too early. Altogether, the submarines arrived far too late to be of any influence, and their losses were so high that the operation was a complete failure. From D-Day to the second half of August, at least thirty-six submarines were sunk and fourteen damaged in the Channel, its western approaches, and in the Bay of Biscay on the way to and from the submarine bases.

A few days after the Allies had landed, Army Group B, commanded by Field Marshal Rommel, was informed that the navy intended to attack the invasion fleet with small assault craft. This new arm had been organized by my classmate Vice Admiral Hellmuth Heye. At that point, it consisted of one-man torpedoes and crash boats. The former was a torpedo used as a carrier and operated by a man inside with some sort of navigational aid. He carried another torpedo that he could maneuver and launch. The crash boats had explosive charges in their bows. They were meant to ram. The pilot, with a watertight suit, jumped overboard after putting the boat on a direct course toward the target. He was then picked up by a following boat. It worked better than one would expect. Two-man submarines were not yet ready to be placed into operation.

All this had been kept top secret. If we had known it earlier, I could have contacted Heye, and we might have moved some men and these new weapons to France in time. It took exactly one month until they began to operate in the Bay of the Seine. On the night of July 5-6, twenty-six one-man torpedoes proceeded against the ships off the mouth of the Orne River. They sank two minesweepers while losing nine of their own. Two nights later, a midshipman succeeded in damaging the old British light cruiser *Dragon* so heavily that she had to be beached, forming part of the artificial port at Arromanches-les-Bains.

Still later, one-man torpedoes sank a destroyer and a minesweeper, but their losses increased. When they attacked for the last time on August 16, they lost twenty-six out of forty-two, and they sank only one small steamer of seven hundred tons. At the same time, MTBs used long-range torpedoes for the first time with some success. There were also many bitterly fought engagements between Allied and German small craft, with losses on both sides. The German patrol and minesweeping forces suffered heavily.

On September 4 the last thirteen MTBs left their bases on the English Channel and went to ports in the Netherlands. The German armies were in full retreat. France was lost. Navy men took part in the defense of the few ports that were held until the end of the war. What remained of the navy was concentrated in the Baltic, where ships of all types did good service until the last days of the war ferrying back over two million people fleeing from the Russians.

In the attempt to counter the invasion, the German navy had lost heavily without corresponding results. This was due partly to material weakness, but also to a lack of insight into the problems involved. Before the war, nobody in the German armed forces had examined these problems. Consequently, they were not understood, and there was not enough cooperation between the services, which alone could have brought better results. But that is another story.

FRIEDRICH OSKAR RUGE (1894–1985) began his career as a cadet in the Imperial German Navy in 1914. During World War I he served in a destroyer in the North Sea. After war's end, his ship was interned, and he was a prisoner of war until 1920. His book *Scapa Flow 1919* (Naval Institute Press, 1973) dealt with the scuttling of the defeated German fleet. In the 1920s he began specializing in mine warfare. At the beginning of World War II, Ruge, then a captain, was in command of German minesweepers in the Baltic, where he participated in operations against Poland. In 1940 he was in charge of minesweeping along the Dutch, Belgian, and French coasts. He was involved later in escort and patrol. In 1943, following an assignment in Italy, he became naval adviser to Field Marshal Erwin Rommel. He was in that position until the invasion of Normandy, after which he headed the German navy's ship bureau in Berlin until the end of the war. He was a prisoner for a time after the war, then became an author and lecturer. He served as head of the new Federal German Navy from 1956 until his retirement in 1961. His book *Der Seekrieg: The German Navy's Story, 1939–1945* was published by the Naval Institute in 1957. (*Naval Institute Collection*)

For many years after 1944 the story of Exercise Tiger was known primarily in the form of rumors, and there were hints of a massive cover-up. Two American landing ships—the *LST-507* and *LST-531*— were sunk and the *LST-289* damaged off Slapton Sands in southern England. German torpedo boats attacked the LSTs during a rehearsal intended to prepare the invasion forces for the sort of environment they would face when they got across the English Channel to Utah Beach. All told, 750 perished during Exercise Tiger. Those who have investigated the matter suggest there was no deliberate cover-up; word of the disaster was closely held in 1944 for reasons of military security. By the time it could be publicly discussed, it was old news.

In the 1980s, ABC-TV brought out a good deal of new information on the subject, as did Dr. Ralph Greene, who had been an army physician in England in 1944. Englishman Nigel Lewis wrote a book called *Exercise Tiger* that presents an excellent account of the disaster and its aftermath, although he does go to some length in discussing any number of hypotheses and wild flights of imagination that sprang up in the wake of the exercise.

Several results emerged from the Exercise Tiger fiasco. One apparent consequence, discussed later in this book, was the suicide of Rear Admiral Don Moon, commander of the amphibious task force for Utah Beach. Another was the desire to get more small craft into the theater as potential rescue vessels in the event that people went into the water as they did that terrible night off Slapton Sands. Thus it was that the Coast Guard brought eighty-three-foot boats into the theater and the navy inserted several dozen motor torpedo boats.

Any number of men could tell of their experiences in Exercise Tiger. Among the foremost experts on the subject is Dr. Eugene Eckstam, who has made himself into a clearing-house and data bank on the subject of Tiger. But he is more than a collator of data. He was there, and his memories are filled with the horror of a night when German E-boats pounced upon LSTs as if they were wolves raiding a chicken coop.

EXERCISE TIGER—SCREAMS OF AGONY

By Eugene E. Eckstam, M.D.

Less than two months after I took the oath as a Naval Reserve medical officer—and became an instant lieutenant (junior grade)—I was on my way to war. I had started at the huge Great Lakes Naval Training Station, where I was part of a team that examined an average of sixteen hundred naked recruits a day. To add some variety to the procedure, we looked at a different part of the body each day. After a week of this, a lieutenant commander shouted across the drill hall, "Eckstam, we don't want you here anymore. We're sending you overseas."

The navy was gearing up for the invasion of Europe and for the requirement to provide hundreds of medical personnel to deal with expected casualties. I joined a large group of medical officers and pharmacist's mates at Lido Beach, Long Island. There we assembled in a huge gymnasium for assignments and for instruction in amphibious warfare. A gruff but efficient chief petty officer divided us into units of the overall activity, which was designated Foxy 29. In designating each unit, the chief barked out the names of two physicians, one chief pharmacist's mate, two first class, four second class, ten third class, and about twenty hospital apprentices.

Once the assignments were made, the units began shipping out—six to ten each week. Around the first week in March I reported to the landing ship *LST-507* in the port of New York, and we were soon under way for Europe. I spent my first wedding anniversary, March 14, at sea.

The LST crossed the Atlantic as part of an eighty-ship convoy, then picked up landing craft at Roseneath, Scotland. We discharged oil at Milford Haven and trucks at Port Talbot before arriving at Falmouth, England, in mid-April. As we were leaving one of the ports on our itinerary, an intoxicated British pilot guided our ship directly over a buoy and bent one of the *LST-507*'s propellers. The ship went into dry dock at Falmouth to get a new screw, and we of the medical staff trooped off to Fowey for instruction in treating the effects of chemical warfare.

The executive officer of the *LST-55* pointed his camera through the rigging of his own ship to photograph the *LST-507* in Plymouth, England, the day before she was sunk in Exercise Tiger. (*Walter Trombold photo courtesy Karla Powell*)

We had come to England so we could prepare to invade France. Part of that preparation was Exercise Tiger, in which ships of Force U, destined for Utah Beach on the Normandy coast, would hold a practice landing at Slapton Sands on the south coast of England. On April 25 the ship loaded army troops, trucks, Jeeps, and other equipment aboard at Brixham Harbor. All told, as we prepared for the exercise, we had on board the *LST-507* 125 navy men as ship's company, the 42-man medical detachment, and about 300 soldiers. We rode at anchor for about two days while other ships loaded for the practice landing. The ship's main deck and the enclosed tank deck below it were completely filled with vehicles and army personnel. The soldiers slept anywhere they could find a space and paraded around in a circle on the main deck in order to get the C rations that constituted their meals.

41

The motor torpedo boat was known to the Allies as E-boat (for enemy boat) and to the Germans as *Schnellboot* (for fast boat). The E-boats wreaked havoc on American LSTs engaged in Exercise Tiger and later posed the principal seaborne threat to the invasion fleet. This is the *S-142*, which was destroyed in a British air attack on Le Havre the night of June 14. (*Courtesy Bibliothek für Zeitgeschichte, Stuttgart, negative number 188136*)

At last the loading was complete, and during the day on April 27 the force got under way and prepared to make a looping approach to Slapton Sands, adding some extra distance to make the drill more realistic. After we cleared the harbor at Brixham and were a few miles out into the English Channel, I heard that a British frigate assigned to protect our convoy of landing ships had been damaged in a collision. Thus we would be proceeding with only a lightly armed trawler as an escort. But it was only an exercise, only a drill.

Night fell, and our group of three LSTs from Brixham and Torquay joined up with five that had loaded in the port of Plymouth. The convoy proceeded onward, and I turned in early to get some sleep in anticipation of the next morning's practice invasion. I was jarred awake around 1:30 in the morning by the sound of the ship's general alarm. German E-boats were approaching the force, although we got that information only gradually. I got fully dressed, outfitting myself, as always, with helmet, foul-weather gear, and gas mask, then reported to the wardroom, which was the ship's first-aid station.

Upon arriving in the wardroom a few minutes after hearing the general alarm, I heard reports of some shooting outside. I remember talking about the possibility that some gunner on one of the ships in company with the *LST-507* was shooting at shadows or something equally dubious. The report was that some of the bullets had come fairly close to us; the people firing those guns needed to be more careful!

After that, all was quiet for about twenty minutes, so I decided to go out on deck to see what was going on. The passageway to the hatch on the starboard side led past the captain's cabin. Just after two in the morning, as I was passing the captain's door, I heard the sound of a tremendous explosion. In quick sequence came the sound of crunching metal, a painful landing on the steel deck with both knees, falling dust and rust. In the ensuing darkness and silence, distracted by aching knees, I wondered, "My God, what happened?"

Later, I learned that a torpedo launched by one of the German E-boats had rammed into the starboard

The *LST-289*, torpedoed during Exercise Tiger but still afloat, enters Dartmouth Harbor for repairs. (*Navy photo in the National Archives: 80-G-257908*)

side of the ship, about thirty feet forward of where I was standing, and penetrated into the auxiliary engine room, where it exploded. Since the auxiliary equipment was knocked out, there was no electricity for light, none for water pumps to fight the fires soon raging on board the ship, and none for lowering the landing craft that might provide escape for those of us on board. Fortunately, I had done my homework and knew where all the battery-powered battle lanterns were stored. As I stood up, I found one by my right hand, just across the passageway from the captain's door. Aided by that first light, I located the rest of them.

When I got back to the wardroom, I discovered that the force of the explosion had popped the first-aid cabinet partly off the bulkhead, and supplies were all over the place. Slowly the injured men came in, some by themselves, some by litter, most half-carried by shipmates. But there were only a few, including one man with a broken thigh bone. As more reports of damage came in, we realized that the center part of the LST-507 was an inferno. Consequently, no one could pass from one end of the ship to the other, either topside or below decks.

Since I was stuck at the stern, I decided to search for wounded men and to ensure watertight integrity to whatever degree might be possible. That meant closing all open hatches to prevent water from flooding into dry compartments. I knew that the other officers were busy trying to maneuver the ship, fight fires, and so forth, so I set out to do what I could. The result was one of the most difficult decisions of my life.

As I moved about below decks, I approached a hatch leading into the tank deck, a large open area filled with vehicles and men. As I looked in, I saw only fire—a huge, roaring blast furnace. I tried to enter and to call out to the men inside, but it was futile. Trucks were burning; gasoline was burning; and small-arms ammunition was exploding. Worst of all were the agonizing screams for help from the men trapped inside that blazing inferno. But I knew there was no way I—or anyone else—could help them. I knew also that smoke inhalation would soon end their misery, so I closed the hatches into the tank deck and dogged them tightly shut.

There was nothing more I could do, so I checked still more compartments and returned to the wardroom. One or two more injured men had been cared for. By then, men were jumping overboard to escape the flames on board the ship. I didn't relish a sudden entry into water that had been reported earlier in the day as 42 degrees, so I checked out the landing craft. There were two on each side, but they had been jammed into place by the force of the explosion. Without electricity to raise the boats, they couldn't be launched.

A life raft seemed the next alternative, but the metal pins that released the rafts were rusted in place, and only a few rafts could be used. The cargo net was one thing that worked. I inflated my life belt. Rather than wear the bulky vests that would impede us in providing medical care, we wore a type of belt that resembled an inflated inner tube. It was made up of two tubes about two inches in diameter; the belt folded and snapped to take out the slack as necessary. I squeezed two handles together to puncture two CO_2 cartridges, and my life belt inflated. Once I had that nice inner tube around my middle, I proceeded down that cargo net on the side of the ship.

The water was chilly, so I entered slowly and gingerly. As I swam away from the LST-507, I settled through the life belt, and it pulled up my jacket, shirt, and underwear—exposing my bare abdomen to the cold water. I managed to pull the clothes down and felt a bit warmer, but only a bit. I swam quickly away from the ship to avoid being dragged down by her suction if she sank. I felt someone or something tugging on my neck, and I kept hitting something with my left arm. I thought someone was trying to hang on to me, and I hollered out for him to let go. Dr. Ed Panter, the ship's other physician, happened to be swimming twenty yards to my left, and he asked what was wrong. Finally, I figured out the problem—my gas mask was interfering with my swimming. He told me to toss it. Indicative of the degree to which our indoctrination had become part of me, I said, "But I have to check it in." Then common sense prevailed, and I tossed it away.

As I got away from the LST-507 I looked back and saw that the flames from the ship were shooting high in the sky and lighting up the whole area. I found a life raft about three hundred yards from the ship; on it was

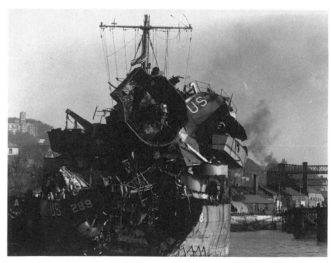

Closeup of the torpedo damage inflicted on the stern of the LST-289. (Navy photo in the National Archives: 80-G-283500)

Survivors of the LST sinkings in Exercise Tiger pose near a Nissen hut ashore in England. Dr. Eckstam is all the way to the right in the row of standing men. (*Courtesy Dr. Eugene E. Eckstam*)

one of our very responsible pharmacist's mates. He had rescued from the wardroom the man with the broken leg and lowered him into the water with a piece of line. Now he was protecting the man by keeping off the raft all those who were clamoring to get on. To allow too many on would capsize it.

At first I was hanging on to other men circling the raft; I was in about the fifth or sixth ring myself. As those in front of me lost consciousness, I had to leave them to drift off. There was nothing to hold them to the raft so we could stay together. As I got closer, I was eventually able to reach in between two men and twist my hand around a piece of line that circled the perimeter of the raft; that kept me from drifting away. But I could feel myself becoming very sleepy and no longer cold; I knew that I would be unconscious soon. Before, I had been concerned about being strafed by the Germans; that was no longer a worry. A couple of miles away, the *LST-507* was still burning brightly.

What happened after that I do not know, because the next thing I remember clearly was climbing up the side of a ship. It was daylight, and I was halfway up; I have no memory of beginning the climb. In recent years I have had the vague remembrance of hearing the engines of landing craft, of putting a knee on the lowered ramp of a landing craft, and sitting along the side once inside. None of these recollections is more than fuzzy; none presents a continuous picture.

The ship was torpedoed about 2:05; we were picked up by the *LST-515* at about six o'clock. Somewhere in between, I was hauled out of the water. I doubt if I was on board the landing craft for three hours, but it's difficult to say. My reading on the subject of hypothermia tells me that none of us should have survived in 42-degree water for more than an hour. The insulation of foul-weather gear probably helped keep our body temperatures from dropping rapidly, as did the struggling to get nearer the raft. But just when I came out of the water remains a mystery. My hero and the man responsible for rescuing so many of us was Lieutenant John Doyle, skipper of the *LST-515*, the only LST to rescue any of us.

After I had slept for a while on board the ship that provided a safe haven for us, I was awakened by Arlo Gregory, our pharmacist's mate first class. I was delighted to see him. He offered a shot of whiskey, which I took along with a cup of coffee. Then I started making rounds with Dr. Panter, who had already been hard at work tending to the survivors. I had been on active duty since January 10 and had an idea that some of the officers and men on board the LST carried bottles of booze, even though all the navy regulations I had studied said this was taboo. But the number of whiskey bottles suddenly available was astounding. It was a good thing too, because we found out it worked just as well—if not better—than a lot of hypodermic needles, and it was easier to give in a mass casualty situation.

We sailed for a long time, and it seemed about noon when we had some food and went ashore in a small port called Portland Bill. We filed into a two-story square red building. Personnel from the Red Cross, army, and navy registered us there. We soon received small duffel bags containing green fatigues and all the clothes needed for two changes. Included also was a kit containing a toothbrush and comb, the two most valuable possessions I owned at the time. After we showered to get the salt water off, we dressed and boarded trucks. After what seemed a long ride, we arrived in a survivor camp in Plymouth. There were large metal Quonset huts on a graveled area, and there were slit trenches everywhere. After a month at that camp I was reassigned to the *LST-391* for the invasion of Normandy.

Many years have passed since that terrible night in the English Channel in the spring of 1944, but there is some pain that the lengthening span of time has been unable to deaden. To this day I can still hear the screams of those burning men, my former shipmates in the tank deck of the *LST-507*. The agony of their final few minutes of life is embedded so deeply into my memory that I still have nightmares about them.

⚜   ⚜   ⚜

EUGENE EMANUEL ECKSTAM (1918–) received his bachelor's degree with high honors from the University of Wisconsin in 1940. After completing his medical training at the same university, he became a doctor of medicine on March 2, 1943. He did his internship later that year at St. Luke's Hospital in Duluth, Minnesota. He later received a master's degree from the Mayo Graduate School of Medicine, University of Minnesota. His active duty as a naval reservist included brief service in the *LST-507* until her sinking. He was in the *LST-391* for the invasion of Normandy in 1944 and in the invasion of Mindanao in the Philippines in 1945. He was released from active duty in 1946. Dr. Eckstam's postwar career included long service with the Monroe Clinic and the St. Clare Hospital, both in Monroe, Wisconsin. He was chief of surgery for the hospital and also a long-time preceptor for the University of Wisconsin Medical School, serving in that capacity as a mentor for young students. Dr. Eckstam, who is now retired from his medical career, lives in Monroe, Wisconsin. He has done considerable research on Exercise Tiger and maintains a large file of material on the subject. (*Courtesy Dr. Eugene E. Eckstam*)

STRIPE FIVE
AND YOU'RE OUT

By Admiral Alfred C. Richmond, U.S. Coast Guard (Retired)

Because of all the U.S. merchant ships heading for Great Britain in the summer of 1943, the Coast Guard decided to send me as a representative to the British Isles. The Coast Guard is the foremost regulatory body for the merchant marine, and I had had some experience in previous months in dealing with merchant complaints on a variety of topics. So I gathered up a number of officers, including Lieutenant Commander Quentin Walsh, and put together a team. Before my tour of duty was over, I'd dealt with many more items than originally contemplated. Included was the Allied invasion of Europe.

The job was considered sufficiently urgent that I was able to fly overseas on a flying boat. I remember that I was quite thrilled at flying across the ocean because this was long before the era of transatlantic air travel became commonplace. I got aboard and sat down next to a young man who was a State Department courier. He had a dispatch bag chained to his wrist so it couldn't be stolen. I asked him how many trips he'd made, and he said, "I think this is my thirtieth trip."

Of course, I was quite excited to be flying, so I said, "Gee, you must find it enjoyable."

He looked at me kind of sorrowfully and replied, "I'll tell you. I wouldn't take $2,500 for my first trip, and I wouldn't give you a nickel for any one since." As I flew more during the war, I began to appreciate his sentiments.

Once we got to England we set up our offices with the navy in London's Grosvenor Square. They provided us space, and we started operating. The additional personnel for the outer ports came over by ship. I distinctly remember that because they brought a lot of supplies, including toilet paper. Anybody who was in England during the war knows the hardships of British toilet paper, even in peacetime, much less in wartime. It was really rugged.

I had been appointed senior Coast Guard officer in the European theater. Gradually, we got our organization set up throughout the British Isles. One of the big problems we ran into very quickly wherever we went was that there is little distinctive about the navy uniform. For an officer, the only things that set it apart in those days from a Coast Guard or merchant marine uniform were the buttons and the cap devices. The uninitiated person was not likely to look for these small differences, so the result was that merchant marine officers were getting in trouble ashore, and reports would come back that they were naval officers.

One interesting case turned up in Glasgow, where there were some tugboats that were part of the U.S. Army Transportation Corps but were run by merchant seamen. These men went ashore in civilian clothes but weren't making much headway with the local populace, particularly the girls in the bars. So the captains of these tugs got blue coats and put four stripes on each sleeve; the engineers got coats with three stripes. I got a call from Glasgow because of a complaint about the tugboats' cooks and stewards, who saw that the captains and engineers were making more time than they were. They decided that if four stripes and three stripes could do the job, they would get blue coats and put five stripes on. It worked for a while, until we got the stewards to knock it off.

In addition to the merchant marine questions, I was part of Admiral Harold Stark's overall staff building up for the invasion of Europe. One of the concerns that came up had to do with men lost overboard from invasion ships and landing craft. Those at the top wanted Coast Guard patrol boats available to save lives. Actually, they wanted boats with diesel engines, but the Coast Guard's eighty-three-footers were powered with gasoline engines. There were a lot of conferences as to how this requirement could be met, and in the end it was decided that there was no answer but to accept the eighty-three-footers. A number of them were shipped over from the United States, and a base was established for them in the port of Poole.

When these patrol boats first came over, we had to take them out and run them at different speeds through the water while airplanes took aerial photos of them. I asked why this was so, because it didn't occur to me. The answer was that the British were using what they called HSLs, high-speed launches, against the German E-boats. When the British had planes over-

Commander Jack Dempsey of the Coast Guard Reserve, heavyweight boxing champion in the 1920s, holds a press conference in London with British reporters. At right is Captain Richmond. (*Navy photo in the National Archives: 80-G-281142*)

head, they couldn't differentiate the nationalities of the boats from silhouettes or side views. But they knew that the wakes had different appearances at different speeds, so the only hope for the British planes to be sure they were attacking enemies instead of friends was to recognize the wakes. By taking the photos and educating the pilots, our people wanted to forestall an attack on our own boats.

I was also involved in the Phoenix project for forming an artificial harbor off the beach at Normandy, and the Coast Guard manning of LCIs, LSTs, and some of the large troop transports that were going to be used in the invasion. The base for the landing craft was at Portsmouth. The government had taken over mystery writer Agatha Christie's house there, and some enterprising artist in the group painted a mural over the bar. Later, I often wondered if the mural remained there when the house was returned to Agatha Christie after the war.

There were also day-to-day situations to handle. One of the interesting things that happened, for example, was that we decided it would be good publicity to bring over the former heavyweight boxing champion Jack Dempsey, who was a commander in the Coast Guard Reserve. I had the pleasure of taking him around and was struck by how popular he still was in

the era of Joe Louis, considering that Dempsey's heyday had been in the 1920s. Jack was an excellent representative of the service, and I thoroughly enjoyed the three or four weeks that I had with him over there. He was a prince of a fellow—maybe not the best-educated person in the world, but a good diplomat and a very likable person.

During the invasion itself, of course, our ships participated, and the Coast Guard public relations people provided some excellent photography. We worked out systems to get the pictures back to the States after they had been cleared by the navy. I did have problems with one man in particular. I don't know whether all photographers are nuts, but this one certainly was, and I spent some time keeping him out of trouble. For some reason he had gotten separated from his unit after the landings at Omaha and Utah beaches. He went off on his own and had gotten up with the British on Juno Beach and gotten into Caen before anybody else. He meant well, but apparently he hadn't been trained in military procedures.

People of all sorts were continually coming over, drifting through for one reason or another. After our forces got onto the Continent and Supreme Headquarters Allied Expeditionary Force (SHAEF) moved to Paris, a Coast Guard Reserve officer showed up in

The crew of a transport hoists aboard a stretcher with a wounded man in it so he can receive treatment. To the right is a Coast Guard eighty-three-footer that served as a seagoing ambulance. (*U.S. Coast Guard*)

London, on his way to SHAEF. He had been a lawyer in the Treasury Department and was going to be on General Eisenhower's staff to deal with the finances of the occupied countries. I regret to say that he was a brassy fellow and a self-seeker. The first thing I noticed when he came into my office was that he had the SHAEF shoulder patch sewn on his uniform even before he reported to the SHAEF staff. As I questioned him as to why he was wearing it, he began explaining the patch, which showed a sword cutting chains asunder and so on. He was brokenhearted when I told him that there was no authorization for wearing patches on the Coast Guard uniform except for those designated by the service, so he had to get the thing off in a hurry. And he did.

Another example of his brassiness was a call that came in from Paris during the spring of 1945. He'd been recommended by SHAEF for promotion from lieutenant commander to commander. It was early one Sunday morning, and he called my apartment to ask if his promotion had come through yet. All the phones from France were scrambled at the time, and you always got a warning, "Remember, the enemy is listening." I told him, "Hell, no."

He made a few more comments and then said, "By the way, the general asked to be remembered to you."

I said, "General who?"

"Why General Eisenhower, of course." I won't repeat what I told him over the phone, but the substance was that I told him to get the hell off the line because there was a war going on. This was typical of this officer's approach, because General Eisenhower didn't even know I was alive.

The eighty-three-footers performed valuable patrol and rescue services while operating with the invasion fleet. (*Coast Guard photo in the National Archives: 26-G-2346*)

In the port of Poole, England, the Coast Guard used a marine railway to perform maintenance and repair work on the boats of its Rescue Flotilla One. (*Navy photo in the National Archives: 80-G-356344*)

I should conclude by mentioning the eighty-three-foot patrol boats that we had shipped over to Poole to rescue shipwreck survivors. My recollection is that they picked up more than one thousand people from the water, some alive and some dead. There was a story of one boat that picked up a couple of bodies—either directly out of the water or transferred from one of the larger transports. The crew stuck the bodies down in an aft storage area called a lazaret. When the boat got back to Poole, they took the cover off the lazaret and nearly fainted when they discovered one of the "corpses" wasn't dead. The ride in the lazaret had revived him.

On another occasion in the spring of 1945 I was visiting down at Poole. We were driving along a street in the port, and there were houses between us and the harbor. As we looked out over the houses, we could see a barrage balloon approaching. It would come down just about to the housetop, and then it would rise maybe thirty or forty feet, all the while progressing forward. We couldn't figure out what was making it move so strangely, so we raced down to the harbor, and there came one of our eighty-three-footers. This balloon had gotten loose and the crew decided it would be a nice prize to take home, so they lashed it to the stern of their boat. The balloon had just enough buoyancy that every so often it would lift the boat out of the water, then it would settle again as the weight of the boat took over. So the boat was bouncing happily along toward the port as the crew attempted to bring home its prize. It was one of the funniest sights I've ever seen.

ALFRED CARROLL RICHMOND (1902–1984) graduated from the Coast Guard Academy as the top-ranking member of the Class of 1924. In the 1920s he served for a time as aide to the Coast Guard Commandant, as aide to the commander of the Special Patrol Force operating against rumrunners, and at the Coast Guard Academy. He subsequently performed a variety of shipboard duties, including service as executive officer of the cutter *Haida* during patrol duty in Arctic waters. In 1938 he was awarded a law degree from the George Washington University in Washington, D.C., and later served as a delegate of the United States to the International Whaling Conference in London. Early in World War II Richmond commanded the Coast Guard training ship *American Sailor* and the cutter *Haida*. From 1943 to 1945 he was senior Coast Guard officer on the staff of Commander U.S. Naval Forces in Europe. In the latter part of the 1940s he served in Coast Guard headquarters in connection with budgeting and program planning. From 1950 to 1954 he was Assistant Commandant of the Coast Guard, with additional duties as chief of staff from 1951 onward. From 1954 to 1962 Admiral Richmond served as Commandant of the Coast Guard. (*Naval Historical Center: S-008-E[14]*)

IKE REMEMBERED ME

By Vice Admiral John D. Bulkeley, U.S. Navy (Retired)

When I left the Philippines in the spring of 1942 and came back to the United States to receive the Medal of Honor, General Douglas MacArthur sent a message along with me. MacArthur asked for two hundred PT boats to protect against the Japanese fleet in the vicinity of the Philippines. In my opinion, that wouldn't have been enough. He would have needed a lot more than that to be able to destroy the Japanese fleet. But I carried the message back, including talking with Admiral Ernest King, the Chief of Naval Operations. He was cordial—or at least as cordial as Admiral King could be.

During my trip to Washington, I also talked with Secretary of War Henry Stimson about MacArthur and the situation in the Philippines. Stimson was an elderly gentleman at the time, in his mid-seventies, but his mind was just as sharp as a tack. He questioned me for two hours. Nearby was an army officer in uniform; he sat there for the entire time and never said a word. I

President Franklin D. Roosevelt presents the Medal of Honor to Lieutenant Commander Bulkeley in 1942. In the center is Rear Admiral Randall Jacobs, Chief of Naval Personnel. (*Courtesy Vice Admiral John D. Bulkeley*)

didn't pay any attention to him during my briefing, but I later learned that it was Brigadier General Dwight Eisenhower. He and MacArthur disliked each other intensely. I think he was there to see if I would say nasty things about MacArthur, which I did not. But that meeting started a sequence of events.

The next development in the sequence took place over in England in April 1944. During Exercise Tiger off Slapton Sands, German E-boats torpedoed and sank two American LSTs and badly damaged another one. Hundreds of American soldiers and sailors were killed. I was told that General Eisenhower, who by now was in command of the forces for Operation Overlord, was absolutely furious about the whole thing because this exercise was a rehearsal for the invasion of Normandy. He wanted the bodies accounted for and divers sent down to make sure no papers could be recovered that would tip the Germans off on what was coming up. The other thing he was furious about was that the escort for these LSTs was a British corvette that didn't have the speed to keep up with the German E-boats, which could make pretty close to forty knots. So Eisenhower, remembering me from my meeting with Secretary Stimson, asked the navy to get Bulkeley.

Fortunately, the navy had me nearby. I was already in the area, running agents and spies into Brittany and Normandy on behalf of the Office of Strategic Services. I had three fast boats and was operating out of Dartmouth, England. Rear Admiral Arthur Struble, Rear Admiral Alan Kirk's chief of staff, sent for me and told me what Eisenhower had ordered. Struble asked me how many boats I needed. I said I'd like to have at least five squadrons—that was sixty boats—and anything else I could pick up. He had the power to make it happen, and I wound up with a total of sixty-seven. Seven of them were manned by the British, French, or Norwegians. Struble backed me up on whatever I needed. He was a great guy.

One of the big problems we had initially was finding a place in England to park our boats. My supply officer and I appealed to the Royal Navy, and one port captain after another said he didn't have room. Finally, we went to Portland Bill and saw Captain Farquharson. My

The American PT boats were crowded into close quarters once they reached England. In the foreground is the *PT-502*. (*Courtesy Vice Admiral John D. Bulkeley*)

mother was a Scottish gal and a Farquharson. The captain was also a Scot, so I told him of the connection of clan lineage. He immediately made room for us, including seventeen hundred men altogether. Many were sleeping in tents. As part of his command, Captain Farquharson had women from the Royal Navy, and they did a great job of providing service for us. Whenever we came in off a mission, they would clean up the boats, put chow aboard, belt the ammunition, and check the torpedoes. The sailors loved that, although they didn't get much chance to enjoy the situation. Since they'd been up all night on patrol, they got their sleep during the daytime.

When the invasion was only a week or so away, King George VI and Prime Minister Winston Churchill came down to visit. Admiral Kirk had alerted me that they wanted to see a PT boat. So we went through meticulous preparations to get the *PT-504* ready for them. It was polished to a fare-thee-well. When the king came aboard, there were a number of admirals there, both British and American. Kirk told me to entertain the king for about half an hour with some sea stories. With all that had happened up to that point in the war, I had plenty to talk about. We got along fine.

While all this was going on, one of my quartermasters was supposed to go around and record the names of all the visitors for the deck log. For example, he'd say: "What's your name, Admiral?"

"Kirk."

"What's your first name?"

"Alan."

Then the quartermaster would write down "Rear Admiral Alan Kirk, U.S. Navy," and so forth.

When the quartermaster got around to the king, he looked at his blue uniform and saw the big broad stripe and four smaller ones. He said, "What's your name, Admiral?"

The king smiled and said, "My name is Windsor." All the rest of the people, including Churchill, were so amused they could hardly contain themselves.

Then the quartermaster asked, "What's your first name, Admiral?"

"George."

So the quartermaster dutifully made his log entry: "Admiral of the Fleet George Windsor, Royal Navy." The king handled it beautifully, reminding those of us present that he really was a naval officer. He had been a midshipman in the Battle of Jutland in 1916.

Bulkeley gives a tour of his PT boat to Admiral of the Fleet "George Windsor" (aka King George VI) shortly before D-Day. (*Courtesy Vice Admiral John D. Bulkeley*)

Another crew member had some contact with "George Windsor" as well. The PT boat's cook, a petty officer third class from Rome, Georgia, brought up a cup of coffee for the king. He drank it, and thereafter the cook would brook no complaints at all about his coffee. He said that if it was good enough for the king of England, it ought to be good enough for American sailors.

The visit provided us with some amusing moments, but the part to be played by the PT boats in the upcoming operation was unquestionably serious. We had several missions to fulfill. One was to run the German E-boats out of Cherbourg, and we promptly went after them. Another was to serve as a screen, if you could call it that, to protect the minesweepers when they were going in to clear the channels on the way to the invasion beaches. The big concern of the Allies prior to the invasion was to prevent the Germans from knowing where we would hit.

In the planning phase for the assault, I had been called over by Rear Admiral John Hall, who was commander of the amphibious task force for Omaha Beach. He told me that my boats would be providing the screen and escort for the minesweepers that would be clearing the channel on the way to the beaches. He said, "You will take charge. Get those minesweepers in

and get those lanes swept, then get out by 5:15 in the morning." He underlined the importance of our mission by telling me, "You will proceed with the utmost determination, regardless of losses."

Beginning around midnight the minesweepers went back and forth for hours, detonating mines. The PT boats blew up some with their machine guns. We kept on the alert throughout the night for a possible challenge from the E-boats, but fortunately they remained in Cherbourg. After the minesweepers cleared the lanes that morning, they put down dan buoys to mark them. But it was awfully hard to keep those minesweepers going straight and in line. We did our best.

Dawn came and with it the invasion force. As I watched from the *PT-504*, large numbers of American bombers were clobbering the beaches, and we could see tremendous clouds of smoke, dust, and dirt being raised. But the bombing was too far inland, not on the crest of the bluffs where the damn Germans were. With our shallow-draft PT boats, we were able to go in close to the beach and use our .50-caliber machine guns against those Germans. We kept their heads down. It was a tremendous team effort that day on the part of many elements of both the navy and the army. The result was that more than 130,000 troops went over those beaches on D-Day.

In the ensuing days of the operation some of our ships set off mines, including the destroyer *Rich* and the minesweeper *Tide*. The bad thing about those mines is that the explosions would break the legs of the men on board ship or bounce their heads off the overhead. Fortunately, the draft of a PT boat was pretty shallow, so we were able to go alongside the *Rich* and the *Tide* and pick up these survivors. Some mines went off while we were alongside, but they didn't bother me. The captain of the *Rich*, Lieutenant Commander Ed Michel, was a good friend of mine because we'd served together in the cruiser *Indianapolis* in the 1930s. He said he wasn't going to abandon his ship. He was up on the bridge, so I sent two sailors up to grab him. He still wouldn't come, so I had to go up and grab him and take his pistol away. Then we carried him on down. He was in great pain; both of his legs were broken.

Still another task for our boats came along in the days after the invasion itself. German bombers came over at night to attack the Allied forces that were getting a bigger and bigger toehold on the beachhead. The lead bomber would drop bright magnesium flares in the water to serve as a point of aim for the rest of the bombers coming in. The PT boats just loved that job; we'd go in and sink the flares with machine guns. Of course, we had to do that quickly; otherwise, we'd still be there when the bombs started falling.

The E-boats weren't really a threat during the daytime; nighttime was when they were going to make their penetration, if they could. So we had the nightly job of maintaining a patrol line to protect the invasion forces from any more incursions out of Cherbourg. Those tangles with the E-boats were interesting. The threat they posed, remember, had been the impetus for the PT boats' presence off the French coast.

When the E-boats were out of their base and on the prowl, we would get a radio warning from Captain Harry Sanders in the *Frankford*, his flagship as commodore of Destroyer Squadron 18. Then we would start stalking the enemy with our radars. Once they knew they had been detected, the Germans would turn around and start running, so it became a stern chase. Our secret was that we had a 37-millimeter antitank gun mounted on the bow of each boat. We'd be speeding along at maybe forty-five knots and firing explosive shells at the fleeing E-boats. The 37-millimeter gun was belt fed and tracer aimed, and it worked a lot better for our purposes than it did against tanks.

Naturally, the E-boats put up a fight of their own and sent a hail of machine-gun bullets back in our direction. When we managed to hit one of the Germans, those explosive shells would set the E-boat on fire. Quite a spectacular sight at night. It's a matter of record that none of the E-boats got through my patrol line. We were such a deadly and effective strike force that after a while they decided not to challenge us anymore.

Before these operations, as I mentioned, we had such high-level visitors as the king and prime minister. I also had one while we were in the thick of things. That was a Naval Reserve captain named John Ford, much better known as a famous movie director from Hollywood. And he was a rascal. When he first arrived, he was a pain in the tail to have on board the *PT-504*. How the hell are you going to take care of the guy when you've got plenty of other worries just trying to do your job? He wasn't really there in a naval capacity; he had come to gather firsthand observations for a movie he was going to film about our PT boats in the Philippines. It was the movie version of the book *They Were Expendable*. In the interests of realism, he wanted to see men react under the intense stress of battle so he could depict that same atmosphere in his film. At one point he was on board when the German E-boats were firing machine guns at us, poking holes through our mahogany boat at the waterline. Ford thought that was just great.

Ford did his research and certainly got plenty of the authentic atmosphere he was looking for. He then put it to use in directing his picture. I thought he made a splendid film. It still shows up frequently on Ted Turner's network. I hadn't known John Ford at all before that encounter, but he turned out to be one of my closest friends. I saw him often in later years when I visited the West Coast.

We were on the line for more than a month altogether, because the work of the PT boats was an ongoing thing, even when the troops had moved

George Samson's painting "Clearing the Lanes" depicts Bulkeley's *PT-504* escorting minesweepers off the Normandy beach on the morning of June 6. (*Naval Institute print program*)

beyond the beachhead. Cherbourg was one of the key objectives, and it was the target of a big naval bombardment on June 25. Rear Admiral Morton Deyo had one of the task forces for that bombardment, and he had a role for us. Two boats went in to within a few miles of the three forts there to try to entice the Germans to open fire and disclose their positions. Deyo's battleships and cruisers were then in position to try to destroy the German batteries as soon as they opened up.

The Germans didn't bite, so with the *PT-510*, accompanied by the *PT-521*, I went in as close as I could—maybe five hundred yards from the forts—and opened up with machine guns. They opened fire on us all right. We got out of there quickly as the enemy projectiles were falling around us. I don't like being straddled like that. Of course, it is a whole lot better than being hit. And it was one more mission accomplished for the versatile PTs.

JOHN DUNCAN BULKELEY (1911–) graduated from the Naval Academy in 1933 and was delayed a year by the Great Depression before receiving his commission. In the Thirties he served in the cruiser *Indianapolis*, gunboat *Sacramento*, and aircraft carrier *Saratoga*. Shortly before the United States entered World War II, he took command of Motor Torpedo Squadron Three. In March 1942 his PT boat evacuated General Douglas MacArthur and his family from the Philippines. Bulkeley was awarded the Medal of Honor for his achievements in the Philippines. Subsequently, he was involved in the New Guinea campaign, then moved to the Atlantic for PT operations in the European theater. He later commanded the destroyers *Endicott* and *Stribling* and served on the staff of the Naval Academy. He was involved with the Atomic Energy Commission, then commanded a destroyer division in the Korean War. He commanded the fleet oiler *Tolovana*, Destroyer Squadron 12, and the naval weapons base at Clarksville, Tennessee. In the mid-1960s he commanded the U.S. naval base at Guantánamo Bay, Cuba, and had a notable confrontation with Fidel Castro over the supply of water to the base. He commanded Cruiser-Destroyer Flotilla Eight, then from 1967 to 1988 served as president of the Board of Inspection and Survey. His remarkable career of more than fifty years' commissioned service ended in 1988, and he was promoted to the rank of vice admiral in recognition of his manifold accomplishments. Admiral Bulkeley and his wife, Alice, live in Silver Spring, Maryland. (*Howard Chandler Christy painting, courtesy Naval Academy Museum*)

Altogether there were five landing beaches for the Allied forces that invaded Normandy on June 6, 1944: Omaha, Utah, Juno, Gold, and Sword. The first two were American and the latter three were British. The fiercest fighting was on Omaha, and indeed it is here that the stereotypical picture of D-Day has evolved in the minds of most Americans. The army-navy team worked together to get thousands of olive drab-clad soldiers from their billets in England aboard ships, across the English Channel, and into position to fight Germans at both Omaha and Utah beaches in northwest France.

The doctrine for such amphibious landings had been developed in the 1930s through the collaboration of the U.S. Navy and Marine Corps. As soldiers of the sea, the marines had sought a role by which they could be useful in the event of a second global conflict. Slowly, sometimes painfully, the techniques and the equipment had been worked out. Operations in the Mediterranean and in the Pacific had added still more to the doctrine and led to the development of increasing numbers of craft and methods to get the job done.

It is a measure of the industrial capacity of the United States in World War II that it was able to mount a vast armada of landing ships off Normandy just a week or so before another huge amphibious force was about to descend on the island of Saipan in the Marianas, on the other side of the globe. To be sure, the U.S. Fleet had not just been divided equally to get the job done, because the two major theaters of war were considerably different in their requirements.

In the Pacific the war was one of distance and mobility—and a major naval power in opposition. The bulk of the aircraft carriers, battleships, cruisers, and destroyers were there. In Europe the British Isles were able to serve as billeting and staging areas. Aircraft carriers were not needed because airplanes could easily fly across the Channel from Britain to attack targets in France. Moreover, the German naval forces could be countered mostly by destroyers and small craft such as PTs. Only a handful of battleships and cruisers were assigned to the Normandy operation, and the battleships that did go were the real antiques. The naval workhorses of the Normandy invasion were the landing craft and the ships just offshore that supported them.

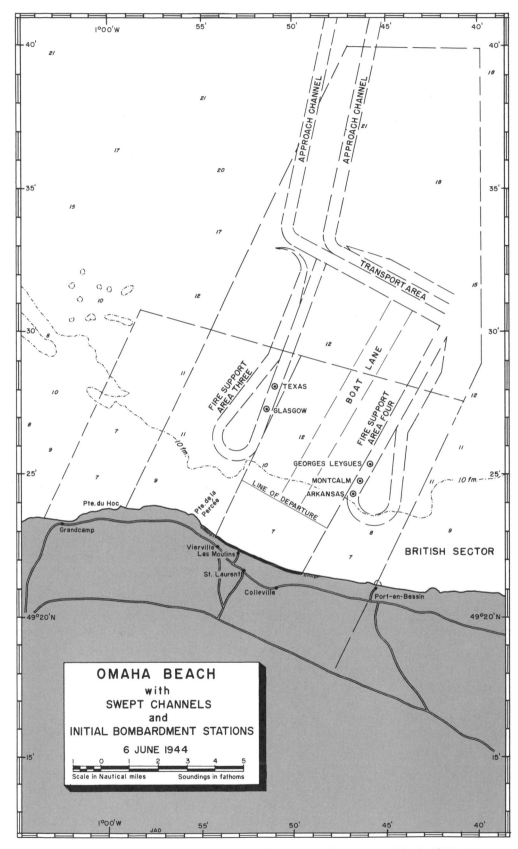

Drawn for Samuel Eliot Morison's *Invasion of France and Germany: 1944–1945*. (*Courtesy Naval Historical Center*)

CLOSE-IN SUPPORT AT OMAHA BEACH

By Vice Admiral Lorenzo S. Sabin, U.S. Navy (Retired)

There is a long morning twilight off the Normandy coast in early June, a phenomenon in that part of the world which worked well for the personnel of Force O, who were trying to clear away the confusion of the predawn hours. Under almost any conditions the dawn of a new day is refreshing, and it surely was in our case. The darkness had been dissipated and along with it our serious concerns of the previous few hours. The first bright streaks of light had given us a lift. We felt good

Rear Admiral John Hall was one of the navy's most experienced amphibious force commanders in World War II. He commanded Force O off Omaha Beach. (*Navy photo in the National Archives: 80-G-59419*)

just as one generally does when he is bathed in the fresh atmosphere of early dawn. The situation appeared to be shaping up well.

My primary duty during the assault was as commander of the close gunfire-support group for Omaha Beach. In addition, my collateral task was to serve as close inshore observer for the force commander, Rear Admiral John L. Hall. In accordance with the latter task, the LCI(L) in which I was embarked set out for the line of departure. It arrived at 5:40, exactly fifty minutes before H-hour.

All the way to the line of departure those of us on board had the feeling that either the enemy was being very generous not to interfere with our activities, or, unbelievably, he was not aware that we had gathered in his front yard for a bit of fireworks. He had given no indication that he had observed us, and up to then it had been just like one of our exercises. Actually, it was incredible. How could it be possible for a naval armada of the size and composition of Assault Force O to approach within a few miles of a fortified enemy coast without opposition or even detection?

But there we were, getting ready to blast the daylights out of the place, and the enemy hadn't even given one sign that he was concerned. There was not a sound from the beach nor from any place else except for the unmuffled engines of our landing craft and the salty comments of the wave-control officers as they herded their charges along the line of departure. It was so quiet that on our bridge we found ourselves talking in whispers as though the enemy might hear us and wake up.

With forty-five minutes still remaining until H-hour, we began moving in slowly toward the beach line to reconnoiter the inshore situation. Just east of Beach Dog Green we could see the concrete wall that had appeared on our overlays, and with binoculars we could see openings in the wall that we surmised were—and later proved to be—gun ports. The steeple of the Catholic church at Vierville-sur-Mer, also on our intelligence overlays, stretched upward like a finger

An LCI, similar to the one in which Captain Sabin was embarked, is trapped by the receding tide at Omaha Beach on June 6. This one was holed by German mortars and 88-millimeter shells. Prominent in the foreground are beach obstacles. (*Painting by navy combat artist Dwight C. Shepler*)

pointing to the sky. To the left on top of the hill overlooking the beach we saw a few houses, and about a third of the way down the slope of the hill we could make out pillboxes and what appeared to be concrete gun positions. Along most of the beach line were barbed-wire impediments that we assumed were booby-trapped. Every officer and man on our bridge was searching the area for some sign of life, but, except for a mongrel dog scampering along the top of the hill, there was none. Nor was there any sound except the beat of our diesel engines and the swish of our propeller wash.

We relayed the result of this first look-see by flashing light to Admiral Hall and to the wave-control officers. On our way back to the line of departure we received a prearranged flaghoist signal that the guns of the small gun ships were loaded and ready and that the rockets in the rocket craft were on their pads with switches on full salvo and ready to go. Zero hour was approaching for the Army Air Forces bombers and the opening salvos from the heavy bombardment group. As the minutes ticked off, the tension mounted. By now the enemy had to know we were out there and that we had

not just dropped in for a friendly call. Thousands of eyes searched the enemy's shores for some sign of reaction, but there was none. He just kept quiet and did nothing.

Shortly before six o'clock the eerie silence was shattered by a deafening roar. The big guns of the heavy bombardment group had opened up. We wondered how the Frenchmen in the light cruisers *Georges Leygues* and *Montcalm* felt as they hurled bullets on their homeland. For the rest of us it was an inspiring spectacle, and for this spectator, personally, it was a scene filled with emotion and pride. Among those great ships was the U.S. battleship *Nevada*, and as I watched her big 14-inch rifles belching forth fire and smoke, my mind went back two-and-a-half years to Pearl Harbor and another scene.

At that time we had watched in horror as the *Nevada* floundered helplessly in the channel while taking a terrible mauling from the bombs of Japanese aircraft. The Japanese had good reason to believe that they had scratched her from any further combat usefulness. But here she was, halfway around the world from Pearl Harbor, with her battle ensign again proudly flying and her guns again roaring in angry answer to another challenge to freedom.

In the midst of the bombardment, Lieutenant Robert Lee Smith, U.S. Naval Reserve, the operations officer for the close gunfire-support group, shouted, "Where are the airplanes?" It was a question no one could answer at the time. Not one bomb was dropped on Omaha Beach by our airplanes during the assault. Later, we heard that the bombers did come over but, due to faulty navigation, their bombs were dropped harmlessly on vacant land inland. Our troops would not have walked across the beach at their leisure—as an Army Air Forces general had promised at a pre-invasion briefing—even if the bombs had found their targets. It is probable, however, that the initial lodgment would not have entailed quite such a bitter struggle.

The initial assault waves had been dispatched from the line of departure and were on their way to their designated beaches during the bombardment. As the landing craft in the first wave reached a point about two hundred yards from touchdown, approximately six thousand rockets left their pads on the rocket ships. Firing these rockets at the proper time was a heavy responsibility for the young reserve officer, Lieutenant Ed Carr, in command of the rocket ship division. The launch time was a minute and a half before touchdown—provided a constant speed and course were maintained by the craft in the first wave. Carr had to ensure that the rockets were fired at the last possible safe time but not so late as to endanger our own troops. He did just that.

Due to excessive dispersion, however, the rockets inflicted very little damage on the enemy. They did pay some dividends; they acted as a temporary harassing agent to the enemy and, in the absence of the air attack, they were a morale booster for the troops who

Flame and gun smoke erupt from the 14-inch barrels of the battleship *Nevada* as she shoots over Captain Sabin's close-in craft to reach the Normandy shore. Two-and-a-half years earlier, Sabin was present at Pearl Harbor when the Japanese put the *Nevada* temporarily on the disabled list. (*Navy photo in the National Archives: 80-G-59420*)

were in the first waves. It was the last morale boost those troops, boat coxswains, and beach personnel were going to get for hours, for the enemy finally let us know that he knew we were there and that if we wanted Omaha Beach, we were going to have to pay for it.

Even without opposition, making a touchdown on Omaha Beach was not the easiest assignment. Irregular contours and currents between the line of departure and the beach line had caused numerous runnels and floor rises under the surface of the water. Many of the landing craft struck the rises and were grounded on them. Unable to retract, the troops were forced to

Among the close-in fire-support ships were LCT(R)s, tank lighters equipped with rocket launchers to provide a barrage of fire. (*Navy photo in the National Archives: 80-G-257288*)

In the center of the picture, army rangers use scaling ladders to get up the steep cliffs in back of Omaha Beach. (*Navy photo in the National Archives: 80-G-45718*)

disembark several hundred yards from the beach. Under the heavy load of their combat packs, some of the soldiers fell or stumbled into the deeper runnels, where they were drowned. Others struck booby-trapped obstacles and were blown to bits. Those who managed to discard their packs and swim or wade ashore were immediately pinned down by enemy gunfire. In dire need of tank support and artillery fire on the beach, the troops were unable to get it because the landing of tanks and artillery had been stopped.

The decision of the wave-control officers to stop the landing of tank- and artillery-loaded LCTs was due to unacceptable losses from enemy gunfire, especially mortar fire, and to the hazards of underwater obstacles in uncleared boat channels. As measured by military standards, the intensity of enemy gunfire would have been classified as moderate, but its accuracy was excellent. Enemy mortars were particularly effective and seemed to be zeroed in on their targets every time they let go. LCTs that escaped being hit by gunfire but which tangled with underwater obstacles had holes blown in their hulls and foundered. Under those conditions the wave-control officers notified the force commander, Admiral Hall, that they were stopping the advance of follow-up waves.

Failure to open all designated boat channels was costly, but it could not be blamed on the underwater demolition teams. This valiant corps of navy super-sailors simply did not have the time to complete their

job. They were delayed in starting because of the confusion when they arrived in the objective area, and when they were able to commence their dangerous task, they were slowed by the clever, intricate, and hazardous system of underwater obstacles the Germans had devised. Successive rows of high-explosive hedgerows were paralleled by lines of stick detonators, each interspersed at varying intervals with booby-trapped wire mesh and with shallow mines embedded in the sand. No one works in haste amid that sort of surroundings—not even experts—and navy frogmen *are* experts.

Even so, they performed a heroic task. By H-hour they had succeeded in opening five channels and partially clearing three others. Nevertheless, of the sixteen channels designated for clearance, half of them had not been cleared at all and a third of them only partially cleared. With landing craft halted between the line of departure and the seaward edge of the obstacles, the troops and beach personnel who had already landed were in a precarious position.

Contributing to the unhappy conditions was the disaster suffered by the so-called super-secret DD (duplex-drive) tanks, a British-conceived innovation to amphibious warfare which was a complete flop. The tanks were mounted in a canvas arrangement called "bloomers" as flotation gear. The idea was to launch these floating tanks from their parent craft, after which they would propel themselves in to the beach with guns blazing. Once ashore, the bloomers would be discarded and the land tractor system of propulsion would take over. Unfortunately, almost none of them ever reached the beach. They either capsized when launched, sprang leaks and sank, or were destroyed by enemy gunfire. It might be added that the carefully guarded secret of those washouts was no secret at all. Captured enemy documents revealed that they were known down to the last minute detail. Sketches had been made by the enemy showing their more vulnerable points.

While the underwater demolition teams were working feverishly to clear additional boat channels to allow more waves to move in, the shore party was urgently requesting fire support to knock out enemy batteries while at the same time sending warnings of probable heavy losses to follow-up waves. The wave-control officers were understandably cautious about releasing additional waves, not from what they were hearing from the beach alone, but from what they could see with their own eyes. What they could see was that anything that came inside the fifteen-hundred-yard beach markers was immediately subjected to punishing gunfire. This was a dilemma facing Admiral Hall. On the one hand, if the troops pinned down on the beach were going to be able to advance, they would need immediate tank and artillery support. On the other hand, if the tank- and artillery-loaded LCTs could not land without unacceptable losses, they could not be sent in.

About H+5 we received a message from Admiral Hall requesting a situation report. Turning inshore, we moved to about a thousand yards off the beach, where we were taken under immediate fire. At five hundred yards we paralleled the beach, zigzagging at maximum speed. We saw our troops on the beach, the dead lying still and the living digging into the sand. Machine-gun fire from the pillboxes was quite heavy, and it was accompanied by intermittent artillery fire coming from emplacements in openings in the hill. Mortar fire, still moderate but increasing in intensity, was deadly accurate, causing by far the greater part of our casualties.

It seemed apparent to us that if our troops were to advance at all, that mortar fire would have to be silenced—and soon. I thought there might be a possibility that our troops could advance under a rocket barrage, so, with two rocket ships still loaded, I sent a message to Admiral Hall requesting permission to lay down a barrage. It was promptly refused with an additional order to proceed to the force flagship immediately and make a personal report.

On the flag bridge with Admiral Hall when I arrived were Major General Leonard Gerow and Major General Clarence Huebner. After briefing the situation as I saw it, I repeated my request to lay down the rocket barrage. It was again refused. I did not think so then, but later I realized that Admiral Hall's decision was

correct. In those days the fire-control equipment for rocket fire, especially rockets mounted in landing craft, was crude at best. Accuracy of fire was far from pinpoint, as had been demonstrated a few hours earlier. Adding to the hazards to our own troops was the high incidence of premature explosions in the rockets. Undoubtedly, our people would have suffered casualties, and this was Admiral Hall's concern. He figured that they had had enough casualties from the enemy without suffering any more from us.

General Gerow wanted to know what the chances were of getting more tanks onto the beach. I said that if they were sent in, some of them, of course, would get through, but the casualties would be heavy. General Huebner asked why the small gunships could not get at the mortars. I replied that the mortar locations were not accurately known and, further, that their apparent locations were out of the gunships' range. I suggested calling in some bombers if the admiral had any on immediate call, but the press of time ruled this out, even if they were available.

Throughout the conversation everyone except Admiral Hall seemed to be tense, worried, and disturbed. Perhaps he was too, but if so, he never showed it. In this calm manner he kept insisting that the enemy was not going to stop the landings and that final victory would be only a matter of time. I recall his saying to no one in particular, "I did not come here to fail."

As the discussion was ending, a message came in

Soldiers pack the deck of a Coast Guard–manned LCI(L) while waiting their time to go ashore on D-Day. (*Coast Guard photo in the National Archives: 26-G-2315*)

from the shore party giving the coordinates of the mortar locations. Admiral Hall immediately passed this information to Rear Admiral Carleton Bryant, commanding the heavy bombardment group of Force O, with orders to destroy the mortars. Then, to fill the gap of tank and artillery support, he decided to turn Captain Harry Sanders, Commander Destroyer Squadron 18, loose with a division of destroyers. This turned out to be redundant, as Harry had already anticipated the order and had swung his destroyers inshore as close as possible at high speed where, under a protective cloak of heavy smoke, he opened up with a blaze of 5-inch gunfire.

Taking advantage of the smoke screen, the little gunships moved in to the beach to take targets of opportunity under fire—meaning to engage anything from which enemy gunfire seemed to be coming. One of them, unable to find a target he could reach, moved a few miles to the east, where, of all things, he found a small Nazi merchantman hiding in a cove. He promptly sank it. Although this action had absolutely nothing to do with enemy resistance, it must have made the crew feel good, as evidenced by the message the skipper sent us: "Have just removed one Nazi coaster from Hitler's merchant fleet. No survivors in the water. They all jumped over the side and made it to the beach."

Meanwhile, a company of army rangers, attempting to open exits behind the seawall, were getting a rough deal from German machine-gun nests in the steeple of the Catholic church. The rangers requested naval fire support, and Captain Sanders directed Commander George Palmer in the destroyer *Harding* to silence the enemy machine guns. Palmer complied by the simple expedient of knocking most of the steeple off the church. In fact, between the guns of the heavy bombardment group and Captain Sanders's destroyers, things were becoming so uncomfortable for the enemy that the troops were now advancing, and follow-up landings were resumed.

We noticed an LCT apparently in trouble about a half mile off the beach. He signaled us that he had a load of wounded rangers and was en route to a hospital ship when one of his engines broke down. Going alongside, we started transferring the wounded to our headquarters LCI(L). As the last soldier, mortally wounded in the throat, was being passed over to us, an enemy battery of two 88-millimeter guns opened up on us. The first two shots were just over and the next two just short. Since we were dead in the water, it was a lead-pipe cinch the next two would be right on top of us. So we ordered the LCT skipper to cast us off, and we moved out at full speed. Both shots from the next salvo landed in the slick we had just left, and the following two shots struck the stern of the LCT.

The situation was becoming more optimistic by the hour, just as Admiral Hall had predicted. Pressure on the enemy was steadily increasing as additional tanks and artillery were landed. Exits from the beach on the right flank had been opened by the rangers, and troops were pouring inland through them. By midnight of D-Day the army had landed a sufficient number of units ashore to form a line from the Vierville-sur-Mer/Saint-Laurent-sur-Mer sector to a point just south of Colleville-sur-Mer. Follow-up waves were landing forces over the beaches, and by noon of the next day Admiral Hall could safely report that Force O had established a firm lodgment on Omaha Beach. If the subsequent buildup of men and material came as planned, the Allies were on the Continent to stay. Admiral Hall's calm confidence in ultimate success had been justified.

After the D-Day operation, when I was writing the action report for the close gunfire-support group, I included a few observations to indicate that everything did not go as planned. In that document I classified them under the merciful term of "constructive criticisms." But I didn't get away with it. When I called on our inspirational boss to bid him good-bye after I had received a change of orders, I found that my timing was bad. I caught him reading my battle report. Fixing me with a stony stare, Admiral Hall said icily, "I have been reading your battle report, and I am getting sicker by the moment." Then, with just the right amount of salt in his voice, he added, "After all, we *won* the damn battle, didn't we?"

LORENZO SHERWOOD SABIN (1899–1988) graduated from the Naval Academy in 1921 and later received postgraduate education in ordnance engineering. Sea duty prior to World War II included the *Tennessee*, *Northampton*, *Augusta*, Base Force staff, *O'Bannon*, *West Virginia*, and Battleships Battle Force staff. During the war he commanded LCI(L) Flotilla One and Flotilla Two and Landing Craft and Bases Europe before reporting to the OpNav staff. Subsequently, he commanded Destroyer Flotilla One and was chief of staff to Commander Destroyers Pacific Fleet before being selected to flag rank in 1948. Sabin held eleven billets as a flag officer. Among them were command of the Amphibious Training Command Pacific Fleet, Amphibious Group One, Task Force One during Operation "Passage to Freedom" in Vietnam, Amphibious Task Force Seventh Fleet, Naval Gun Factory Washington, D.C., Potomac River Naval Command, and Amphibious Force Atlantic Fleet. Admiral Sabin retired from active duty in 1961. During and after his active naval career he was a prolific contributor to the U.S. Naval Institute's *Proceedings* magazine. His memoir of the battleship *Nevada* at Pearl Harbor is included in *Air Raid: Pearl Harbor! Recollections of a Day of Infamy* (Naval Institute Press, 1981). (*Photo of Secretary of the Navy Frank Knox awarding the Legion of Merit to Captain Sabin courtesy the National Archives: 80-G-43842*)

TRAFFIC COP

By Captain Richard H. Crook Jr., U.S. Naval Reserve (Retired)

As the hundreds and hundreds of landing craft headed toward the invasion beaches on June 6, they needed traffic cops to mark the route. That's where the eighteen patrol craft at Normandy came in. I was the executive officer of the *PC-553*. I think there were ten PCs at Omaha Beach and eight at Utah. These 173-foot-long, 400-ton ships could be described as miniature destroyer escorts—smaller and less well armed. Their primary mission for operations at sea was antisubmarine warfare, which is why they were armed with depth charges and Hedgehogs. Their 3-inch guns made them a good deal less potent than either destroyers or destroyer escorts.

The ship checked in with the transport *Samuel Chase* by blinker light about three o'clock in the morning, and she told us to proceed to our station. We took station around five or so. As the operation order directed, we were to be offshore about a mile and a half, serving as primary control vessel in the Easy Red sector of Omaha Beach. Our sister ship, the *PC-552*, was off to our left as the guide for Fox Green Beach.

The PCs' job called for us to be in precise positions to serve as reference points for the landing craft. We had British QH gear installed; it was the antecedent of the American Loran. The gear was able to pick up radio signals that gave us lines of position. When we plotted the intersection of those lines, we had a

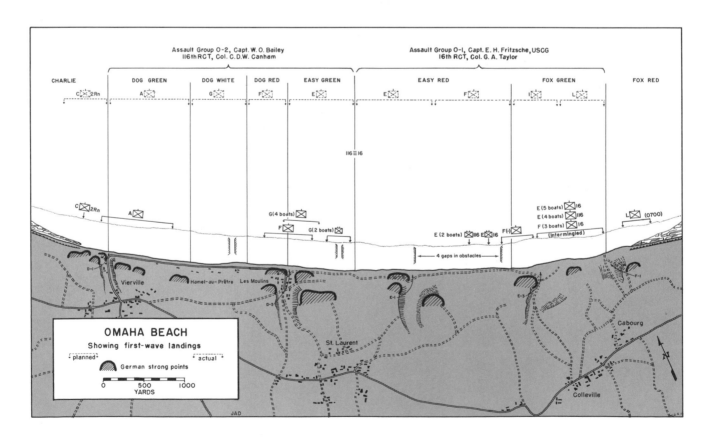

Drawn for Samuel Eliot Morison's *Invasion of France and Germany: 1944–1945*. (*Courtesy Naval Historical Center*)

navigational fix. So we knew within fifty to one hundred yards where we were at all times. That was important, because we were fighting a swift tidal current—ten–twelve knots—going from west to east off Omaha. If we didn't know where we were, we could be swept off station quickly. Eventually we anchored.

Shortly before 6:00 A.M., by the time the American presence had been revealed to the enemy, the German 88-millimeter guns did a pretty good job for a minute or two of bracketing the ship. We moved temporarily and avoided being hit, then we returned to our spot, because our role was to be there and be seen by the boat coxswains. To identify the ship for the benefit of those coxswains, we flew the signal flag for E and a red flag for the beach sector. ("Easy" was the word for the letter E in the phonetic alphabet then in use.) Because of the concern for being hit by expected major-caliber gunfire from the beach, the transports were anchored out of range, ten or eleven miles offshore. That meant the landing craft had a long run in before reaching the control vessels. By going past the PCs, the waves of LCVPs would be able to orient themselves and get into the right position for the final run-in to the beach.

Unfortunately, after the boat waves passed by us, they veered to the left in their journey toward Omaha; they didn't steer to starboard enough to counteract the current. For the most part, the landing craft wound up east of where they were supposed to be. We had no radio communication at all to tell the landing craft what was happening, and we really hadn't rehearsed with the LCVP coxswains beforehand. We were supposed to have a beachmaster on Easy Red, but we never did make contact by radio to find out what was going on. And we didn't really see the LCVPs for all that long either because they quickly disappeared into the smoke and haze after they went past us. From a mile and a half offshore I couldn't actually see them hit the beach, in part because I didn't have binoculars. The skipper,

The *PC-553* under way at some speed. Notice the cylindrical crow's nest on the mast. (*Courtesy Captain George Atterbury*)

who had glasses, did see some of them land on Easy Red.

For the most part, the early waves that went in to land on Omaha Beach were fairly well on schedule in our sector. We didn't really have a concern about being hit from that point on. Part of it was that the Germans didn't have the major-caliber guns that were anticipated and also because the German machine gunners were mostly zeroing in on the beach line rather than the ships offshore.

Since radio communication with the beach broke down completely, we had to get the word of require-

Two PCs, smaller than destroyer escorts, maneuver near the Omaha Beach flagship, USS *Ancon*, off the coast of France. This photo gives an idea of the relative sizes of the ships. (*Navy photo in the National Archives: 80-G-257287*)

Lieutenant (junior grade) Ben Fairchild, left, skipper of the *PC-553*, poses with Crook, the executive officer. (*Courtesy Captain Richard H. Crook Jr.*)

indication was that some of the boat waves were circling offshore rather than going in at the assigned times. As the coxswains saw the LCVPs ahead of them getting blasted and troops jammed up at the shoreline, they held back rather than adding still more to the jam. The whole thing was a very confused situation.

We really felt sorry for the poor soldiers in the duplex-drive tanks that were supposed to be kept afloat by canvas collars. They weren't seaworthy enough for the rough conditions that day; they just went down to the bottom like rocks. Some men were able to jump out in time, but not all. We picked up perhaps twenty-five to thirty men from those tanks, and more of them were corpses than survivors. They were all around us. The *PC-552* picked up even more than we did. After our crew pulled the bodies out of the water, they were laid out on deck. The live ones were given such medical attention as we could. Then we sent the soldiers—both living and dead—back out to the transports in landing craft. Our pharmacist's mate was a mortician in civilian life, and he supervised the disposition of the bodies that day. He'd had that same unhappy duty in April when he dealt with the bodies of men killed in Exercise Tiger back in England.

ments ashore from the landing craft as they came back out. As they passed, the crews would yell out to us the messages they wanted sent to the transports by radio. The call was for more of everything—more troops, more ammunition, more tanks, etc. That gave us a real sense of how desperate things were ashore. Another

The ships that really saved the day at Omaha Beach on June 6 were the U.S. destroyers. They operated

The destroyers *Emmons*, foreground, and *Doyle*, steam among splashes from German 88-millimeter guns as they operate close to Omaha Beach to provide fire support for the struggling soldiers ashore. (*Painting by navy combat artist Dwight C. Shepler*)

inshore of us and were pinpointing the German 88s, which had not been knocked out at all by the Army Air Forces planes. They dropped their bombs two miles inland—nothing on the shoreline. Destroyer Squadron 18, under its commodore, Captain Harry Sanders, really did a magnificent job. The *Frankford*, commanded by James Semmes, was the flagship, and she went into shallow water, less than a thousand yards off the beach, to engage the German batteries. The others that contributed were the *McCook*, *Carmick*, *Doyle*, *Emmons*, *Thompson*, *Satterlee*, and *Barton*. They all did a lot of firing—very close in.

The *PC-553* just wasn't up to that job because our guns didn't have either the range or fire-control capability of those on the destroyers. We shot about forty or forty-five rounds of our 3-inch/50-caliber at the beach. Our gunner's mates and the gunnery officer claimed they scored some hits on the pillboxes close to the waterline. I was too busy on the bridge, backing up the skipper, Lieutenant (j.g.) Ben Fairchild, to get a good look at our shooting.

We had a couple of high-level visitors to the ship on D-Day. Brigadier General Willard Wyman, assistant commander of the 1st Division, came aboard around seven in the morning. In late afternoon, Major General Clarence Huebner, the division commander, was on board briefly before heading ashore. Both had come in from the *Ancon*, flagship for the Omaha Beach task force commander, Rear Admiral John Hall. By the end

A group of LCVPs circles in the foreground, while others head toward the Normandy beach. (*Navy photo in the National Archives: 80-G-231234*)

of the day we had the sense that the landings had succeeded. General Huebner was eager to get ashore, but in the meantime, he had lost his pearl-handled pistol on board our ship. Maybe one of our boys took it; I don't know. There was a big furor about that. Fortunately, his mood had improved as the day had proceeded. He finally left in late afternoon—without the pistol—to take command of his men on the beach and begin the movement inland.

RICHARD HENRY CROOK JR. (1921–) graduated from Princeton University in 1942. He went to midshipman school at Notre Dame and Northwestern as part of the V-7 program and was commissioned in November 1942. Following duty at the Subchaser Training Center in Miami, he reported aboard the *PC-553* in early 1943 for Atlantic convoy duty and subsequently the invasion of France. He commanded the ship from September 1944 to January 1945. He spent the remainder of the war ashore, first as navigation instructor at the midshipman school at Columbia University, later running the laundry for the naval training center at Bainbridge, Maryland. He left the service in June 1946 and entered Harvard Law School, from which he graduated in 1948. After that he worked in the commercial world as assistant secretary and corporate secretary of two large corporations—Atlas Powder Company and Champion Spark Plug Company. Following the war Mr. Crook affiliated with the Naval Reserve and served as an administrative officer at the naval air station in Willow Grove, Pennsylvania. Captain Crook retired from the Naval Reserve in 1971 and from Champion Spark Plug in 1983. He lives in Toledo, Ohio, where he collects books about military and naval history. (*Courtesy Captain Richard H. Crook Jr.*)

DD SPELLED DISASTER

By Dean L. Rockwell

In early March 1944 I was detached from duty in a flotilla of large landing craft known as LCTs. I was ordered to report to Dartmouth College in England for an assignment that was completely new and strange to me. I became involved in a ten-week training program, working with three tank battalions: the 70th, which would go into Utah Beach; and the 741st and 743rd, which were destined for Omaha Beach. They were equipped with special DD tanks, duplex drive. The DDs were regular Sherman tanks that were designed to be launched from landing craft offshore and then swim in to the beach. They had two small propellers apiece to push them through the water and treads for operation on land. They had nine-foot-high waterproof canvas shrouds that were inflated by heavy rubber struts attached to bottles of compressed air. These collars were intended to keep the tanks afloat while in the water, but they had only about nine inches of freeboard, even in a calm sea. Unfortunately, the tanks were makeshift at best. At worst, the DDs were a disaster.

During our ten weeks of training we had practice launchings and landings with these amphibious tanks at Slapton Sands, on the south coast of England. In the course of this I worked with thirty-two different LCTs that were going to Normandy. I also drilled the LCTs in the standard navy procedures: man-overboard, fire, battle stations, first aid, and so forth. The crews were well prepared when it came time for the invasion, and they were well supplied. At a time when civilians had to endure meat rationing in both England and America, the LCTs got so much fresh meat aboard they could hardly close the refrigerator doors.

On May 25 we went to the harbor at Portland-Weymouth to make final preparations. I was on the receiving end of briefings for Operation Overlord. They were held in the garret of a little building along the waterfront. When we left after each day, we just walked away without locking doors or trying to hide anything. This was much in contrast to the situation I found in late 1944 when I arrived back in Washington, D.C. Security of classified information was so tight there that you would think Washington was about to be invaded. The lesson I drew from this was that the closer you got to the action, the less people cared about security and the more with getting the job done.

For the operation itself I was put in command of a group of eight LCTs ordered to land the DD tanks of the 743rd Tank Battalion at Omaha Beach. The normal operating speed of these craft was about four knots, so we left Portland-Weymouth on the night of June 3 for the originally scheduled invasion date of June 5. Early on the afternoon of the fourth we learned that the landings had been delayed because of weather, so we turned back. It was just as well because we had had a hell of a time getting out of that harbor and had some damage to LCTs that collided with other craft. We were hampered by orders to use no radio or visual communications and the fact that Force U for Utah was trying to get in while we were trying to get out. It was an unbelievable snafu—a World War II acronym that in its sanitized form meant "situation normal, all fouled up." We finally got things sorted out, mostly by cursing at the ships of Force U.

Early on June 5 we set out again, and I spent most of the morning gathering up the ships in my group. I looked all over the place trying to find the *LCT-713*. At last I found her, sailing blissfully along as part of the wrong convoy. She had a large O (for Omaha) on her conning tower, while all the LCTs around her had a U (for Utah). The skipper evidently hadn't looked around. I went alongside and asked the captain what force he was supposed to be in. He looked around, saw the U's on the other ships, and the light finally dawned.

Once I had everybody together, we followed the English coast to Southampton, then turned almost 90 degrees and headed southeasterly across the Channel toward France. June 5 was a dull, overcast day up to then, but about two o'clock in the afternoon, soon after we made the turn, the sun came out briefly. Looking back toward England, I saw the horizon completely filled with ships and realized the enormity of the operation. It was a fantastic display of naval might. The others weren't behind us for long. With our slow speed, practically all of the other ships of the invasion force passed by us during the voyage.

Barrage balloons float overhead as landing ships of the invasion fleet make their way across the English Channel toward France. (*Navy photo in the National Archives: 80-G-231247*)

We were really low in the water with our load. Those DDs were normally thirty-four-ton Sherman tanks, but they were so loaded up with ammunition, fuel, and provisions that I estimated they displaced close to thirty-nine tons apiece. The deck of our LCT was awash almost constantly during the Channel crossing because of the load on board and the rough seas. Each tank carried five or six men, and there was no room for them in the crew quarters of the ship. The soldiers were trying to bed down on top of those tanks with life belts for pillows. Others may have slept on the deck in the crew quarters. These men weren't used to rough seas. I suspect a number of them were seasick and miserable just from the weather, and they also had to think about going to face the Germans the next morning.

We arrived at the rendezvous area off Omaha Beach about four o'clock the next morning. Our responsibility with the LCTs was to go in to roughly five thousand yards off the beach and launch these tanks. This was supposed to happen about 5:30, and then they would have an hour to get ashore in time for H-hour, 6:30 A.M. One mishap occurred in the meantime when the swift current pushed one of the flat-bottomed LCTs

into the side of the battleship *Arkansas*. We went toward the beach in a column formation. I was in the lead ship, *LCT-535*, and when we got to the five-thousand-yard mark, I ordered a left turn so we would run parallel to the beach in preparation for launching. The next maneuver was to be a 90-degree flanking movement to starboard in order to turn the bows of all the LCTs toward Omaha Beach.

At that point it was apparent to me that the seas were too rough to launch the DD tanks, because they had so little freeboard above the water. I was in radio communication with army Captain Elder, who was on board one of the other craft in my group. He was the senior company commander of the tank companies of the 741st that we had on board our group of eight landing craft. There were eight tanks in a company, thirty-two altogether. The 743rd had another thirty-two tanks. Even though we weren't supposed to break radio silence, I figured the Germans knew by this time that we were there. More importantly, I knew that we had to change from our original plans in order to get these tanks ashore. Captain Elder reported to me that

The destroyer *Emmons* provides gunfire support in the battle for Fox Green Beach at Omaha on D-Day. In the foreground are dozens of Allied landing craft with enemy shells splashing among them. (*Painting by navy combat artist Dwight C. Shepler*)

an LCT in another group had launched some tanks, and they had sunk immediately.

At that point Elder and I made the decision jointly that we would go directly to the beach rather than force the tanks to try to swim for it. Officially, I was the one responsible for making the decision. Even though they were Elder's tanks, naval regulations dictated that the senior naval commander was responsible for them until they went either into the water or onto the shore. Fortunately, Elder agreed, because he could see the situation as well as I could. But if he had insisted on following the original orders to launch offshore, we would have gone to the beach anyway.

As we moved through those last five thousand yards to Omaha Beach, quite a bit of machine-gun fire was splashing around us. In my mind I can still hear those bullets rattling off the steel sides of those LCTs. We didn't have any casualties there because everybody was smart enough to get down and take cover. On the right flank of the beach was a German 88-millimeter gun that was in a heavily fortified pillbox. It was protected from both the sea and the air by thick layers of concrete. The gun could shoot only horizontally through a narrow slit in the pillbox, producing enfilading fire down the beach. As soon as we closed the beach, the gun began firing at the LCTs. Two of my LCTs were hit; in one of them three men were killed and three others wounded. Fortunately, my own ship was at the extreme left flank of the landing area, farthest away from the 88, so we were not hit.

We landed on that beach thirty seconds before the designated H-hour of 6:30. Because of the rough seas, our wave was the only one that got in on time. We lowered our bow ramp, and the four tanks rolled off directly onto France; they didn't have to swim at all. The other seven LCTs in my group off-loaded their tanks within thirty seconds. As soon as the tanks landed, they were in position to provide cover for the waves of infantry as they came in from LCVPs. As soon as we disgorged the tanks, the 88-millimeter gun lost interest in us and started concentrating on the tanks. They were now a prime threat to the Germans, which the LCTs weren't. I remember that one of the tanks was already on fire even before we got off Omaha Beach. At that stage of the game I thanked the good Lord that I had joined the navy and hadn't decided to be a tanker.

We saw the corpses of a number of the dead tankers in the water. I had put another naval officer in charge of the group of eight LCTs carrying the 741st Battalion's DD tanks to Omaha. Obviously, I chose the wrong man. Instead of going all the way to the beach, this officer launched his tanks offshore, according to the original plan. They were swamped by the rough seas and went right to the bottom. Perhaps he had been overruled by the army and wasn't strong enough to assert himself. Maybe he didn't want to go in close to the German guns. I don't know. I never did talk to him later to get the story of what happened. By that time, the tragedy was done, and nobody really wanted to talk about the damn thing.

We went out to an anchorage to await the time to land the rest of our rolling stock. We still had on board some Jeeps and trailers for medical detachments. The row of four tanks had been down the center of the landing craft, and these vehicles were parked outboard on each side of the tanks. About two o'clock in the afternoon we went in to off-load the rest of our cargo. By that time the tide was in, and we couldn't see the beach obstacles that had been out of the water and exposed when the tide was low in the morning. We tried to find an open path cleared among the obstacles by the combat demolition teams. Unfortunately, many of them never reached their assigned sectors. When we nosed in at one place, we hit a submerged obstacle, and it had a mine on it. It damaged the ramp gear on the bow, so we weren't able to open the ramp and get the Jeeps off.

We did put the medical personnel ashore, and I can tell you that they were most reluctant to leave the security of that ship. I don't blame them. By that time the beach was just clogged with men and the accoutrements of war. Most of the men were hunkered down on the sand as mortar rounds rained down on them from the bluffs beyond. A salvo of four mortar shells would land on the beach and men, material, and sand would fly up into the air. We were dodging around ourselves, trying to outguess the Germans who were firing the mortars. In my mind's eye I can still see a single file of soldiers finding a path up the bluff so they could take out the gunners who were devastating the beach.

With the ramp jammed, we went out to anchorage to spend the night of June 6 and await the events of the following day. By that time I was truly tired because I hadn't had any sleep for something like forty hours. At the end of a long, long day, I was ready for a rest.

DEAN LADRETH ROCKWELL (1912–) was born on a farm in Michigan. He graduated from Eastern Michigan University in Ypsilanti in 1935, then became a teacher and football, wrestling, and track coach at East Detroit High School. He was appointed a chief petty officer athletic specialist in the navy in February 1942, part of the Gene Tunney program for physical training. Seeking a more active role in the war, he sought reassignment and was sent to the amphibious force. He participated in D-Day in LCTs and was awarded the Navy Cross for his heroism in taking the DD tanks to Omaha Beach. Later in the war he took command of LCT Flotilla 42 and went to the Pacific. After leaving the navy in late 1945, he enrolled in the University of Michigan at Ann Arbor and earned a master's degree, which prepared him for teaching on the faculty of Albion College in Michigan. Since 1948 he has been in industry as a sales representative for companies involved in making metal die castings. Mr. Rockwell coached the U.S. Greco-Roman wrestling team in the 1964 Olympic Games. In 1968 he was chairman of the National Amateur Athletic Union wrestling committee and head of the U.S. wrestling delegation at that year's Olympics in Mexico City. He lives in Ypsilanti, Michigan, where he collects antique ceramics. (*Courtesy Dean L. Rockwell*)

LANDING THE BIG RED ONE

By Robert E. Adams

At the time of the Normandy invasion I was twenty-five years old, assigned to the Coast Guard, aboard the USS *Samuel Chase*, an attack transport. I was boat coxswain of an LCVP. Prior to Normandy, our boat division had participated in landings in Sicily, so we were a fairly experienced group. Our ship was destined for Omaha Beach, and we had men of the 1st Infantry Division—the Big Red One—on board. We had taken them ashore during several invasions in the previous year, so we had a lot of respect for them. That was particularly true for those of us in the boat crews who knew by experience what those soldiers were going to have to go through.

After a good breakfast on the morning of June 6, I went to my boat. The crew consisted of an officer and three enlisted men besides myself. As we were gathering, I heard the captain saying over the public address system, "Expedite the loading of LCM number three [or whatever] aft on number-four hold."

Hearing that, a gnarled old chief petty officer with years and years of service said, "Why doesn't the old man speak plain English? These [expletive deleted] don't know what expedite means."

We got the boat in the water and took aboard a load of troops, probably twenty-five or thirty of them. One memory that sticks with me is that the soldiers had condoms over the muzzles of their rifles to keep them dry.

Once the men were in the boat, which we loaded about twelve miles off the beach, I was struck by the roughness of the water. I was thinking to myself, "My God, these soldiers will all be seasick before we get them to the beach. Whose side is God on anyway?"

As we approached the beach sometime between eight and nine o'clock, I was standing to steer the boat, and the officer was standing as well to keep posted on where we were going. Everybody else was down. When we got in fairly close to the beach, I could see a haze and smell the cordite odor of gunpowder. It was like going into a new world. We could hear the chatter of machine-gun fire and then the sound of mortars. There is almost always a sandbar out from any beach, and my routine was to cut the engine for a second and let the backwash carry the boat over. I must have done so unconsciously, because I was able to get the boat right up to the edge of the beach.

Once we got near the beach, it seemed that all hell was breaking loose. I had decided not to get too close to the other landing craft, and that was wise because there were lots of obstacles put down by the Germans, including those made of telephone poles and some made of railroad rails. As I looked around me I could see the bodies of dead soldiers floating; they were probably from the army's amphibious DUKWs. The

Soldiers embark in a Coast Guard transport for the ride to Normandy, where they will again enter LCVPs for the last lap to the beach. *(Coast Guard photo in National Archives: 26-G-2238)*

men were floating with their rumps sticking out of the water. Their life belts were around their waists, not their chests. They couldn't keep their heads up when they hit the water, and they drowned. All the belts did were keep their asses up out of the water. I suspect that the waves had engulfed the DUKWs easily, because they did not appear to be very seaworthy.

When maneuvering an LCVP, I had found that I needed to keep the boat in forward gear at low speed. That provided enough steerageway so that the boat would remain perpendicular to the beach and not broach sideways. That was especially important at Normandy because of the high waves washing in astern of the landing craft. When our LCVP's ramp opened, our brave group from Big Red One bounded out onto Omaha Beach. I recall that I looked to my left and two soldiers were holding up another one in between them and yelling words of encouragement to him.

Fortunately for my crew and me, I was able to back off the beach without mishap. Even so, I have a memory that will stick with me the rest of my life. My boat grazed one of the Germans' telephone-pole beach obstacles. On top, so close I could almost touch it, was a teller mine. It could have blown us all to bits. So our first landing was successful—but just barely.

Our orders then called for us to seek out any support boat and take whatever orders we were given. So I approached one of the boats and picked up a one-star general and about four or five people from his staff. The general said to me, "Son, how is it on the beach?"

At this time we were a couple of hundred yards off the beach, and I responded, "Pretty hot, sir."

Then he said, "Well, take us in as close as you can." During my time as a kid I had read cowboy and Indian stories as to how men on whatever side would try to knock off the enemy's leader. They could spot the

Here are two views of the Coast Guard–manned attack transport *Samuel Chase*. The attack transport concept was developed by the navy as a means of dealing with the challenge of amphibious warfare. Commercial cargo ships were converted to carry bunks and also outfitted with davits and landing craft such as the LCMs shown here. Soldiers went over the side on debarkation nets and into the craft below. *(Both photos from the U.S. Coast Guard)*

leader because he always wore some distinctive insignia. Here was this general in my boat, and he had a distinctive insignia all right—a star painted on the front of his helmet. It was extremely visible. I just kept thinking, "Why don't I have the guts to ask him to turn

Soldiers look anxiously toward the shoreline as their LCVP approaches the beach. (*U.S. Army*)

it around? I'm going to get killed just because he's a general and they'll try to blow this boat out of the water."

Well, neither thing happened. I didn't ask, and we didn't get hit. I put those soldiers so close that the general and his group hardly got their ankles wet.

While we were at the beach we were summoned by an army provost marshal to take three men in stretchers back to our ship, along with a few who were standing. The latter were evidently shell-shocked, because they were like mummies. They were like dead

One of Adams's shipmates, Coxswain Delba Nivens, is at the helm of this burning LCVP from the *Samuel Chase*. The boat was set afire by German machine-gun bullets. Nivens unloaded the troops on the Normandy beach, helped his crew put out the fire, and then returned to the transport. (*Coast Guard photo in the National Archives: 26-G-2342*)

guys—walking but not saying anything. Later in the day, after another run in to the beach and safe return to the ship, we all felt a sense of relief, although it was interrupted by the process of trying to get back aboard in the heaving seas of the English Channel.

Wire cables from the four corners of the LCVP converged in a large metal ring in the center of the boat. In order to get aboard, one of the boat crew members had to grab a lanyard attached to a hook lowered by the ship, pull the lanyard through the metal circle, and then give a hefty pull to get the ring onto the hook. The problem with these waves was that at a given moment, the hook was slack and down in the bottom of the boat; then it was ten feet above and out of reach. At some moments it was swinging back and forth like a vicious pendulum. I recall ducking and thinking, "Wouldn't it be tough to survive all that we saw on the beach, only to get killed by this damn hook?" Obviously, it didn't happen. My crew made the connection, and we were lifted back aboard safely.

Getting on deck I saw dead soldiers stacked like cordwood on the port side aft. Many still had their boots on. Helmets were in a big pile on the deck. I just had to turn away from that sight.

In thirty minutes we were under way, headed back to England with our cargo of corpses and wounded soldiers. We were safe on board and had a hot meal that night. To most of the crew of the *Samuel Chase*—those who had not been in the boats as we were—it was almost a normal routine. It was the easiest invasion they'd ever been through because they hadn't had to fight off the sort of Luftwaffe air attacks that we remembered from Sicily.

But for me it was not so easy. A number of questions went through my mind on that evening of D-Day: How were the guys of the Big Red One doing now? How many of the guys who went ashore in my boat were still alive? Where in the hell would they sleep the night? Would their K rations be all wet? How many would make it through the night? Most all of us on board the *Samuel Chase*, particularly those of us in the boat, thought about it and prayed for our soldier comrades every night. We saw only a small piece of what they went through daily.

Many of our LCVPs didn't make it back, particularly those whose crews had been recently assigned to our ship and lacked the landing experience most of us had had at Sicily and Salerno, Italy. It's pretty obvious that any sailor or soldier who survived that day—D-Day at Normandy—should be thankful every day of his life. I had a chance to reflect on that idea when I was lucky enough to tour the area during the fortieth-anniversary year. I saw it all once again, and what we had achieved became more unbelievable.

ROBERT E. ADAMS (1919–) enlisted in the U.S. Coast Guard in January 1943. He reported to the crew of the USS *Samuel Chase* in May 1943. As a member of the ship's boat division he participated in the invasions of Gela, Sicily; Salerno, Italy; Normandy, France; and Saint-Tropez, in southern France. After that he trained for the quartermaster rating. He left his ship in the waters of Japan and was discharged in November 1945 as a quartermaster second class. In January 1946 he enrolled in the U.S. Maritime School at Fort Trumbull, New London, Connecticut, and four months later received his third mate's license from the Coast Guard. For a few years he sailed on board tankers and freighters, ending his sea career as third officer of the Grace Line's SS *Santa Luisa*, sailing the west coast of South America. As a civilian Mr. Adams worked thirty-four years for the Pillsbury Company, retiring in 1983 as a regional manager. He now lives in Minneapolis, Minnesota. (*Courtesy Robert E. Adams*)

MY ONLY JOB WAS TO STAY ALIVE

By Lieutenant Commander Paul S. Fauks, U.S. Navy (Retired)

After I graduated from high school, I went to work with my cousins on their ranch near Sturgis, South Dakota. I was there when my draft notice came in March 1943. I think just about everybody that got drafted went into the army. They actually gave us a choice. You could go through this door, and you were in the navy; if you went through the other door, you were in the army. I thought at the time maybe those ships would be better than the trenches, and I think I liked the uniform better.

I was inducted into the navy at Camp Crook in Omaha, Nebraska, and left the next morning for Farragut Naval Training Center, way up in northern Idaho. It's long since been torn down, but it was a big base at the time, constructed to deal with the wartime manpower requirements. I went through my boot training there, and then immediately after that they sent me to signalman-quartermaster school. I was rated as a signalman third class when I got out of there.

Then they sent a group of us over to Treasure Island, San Francisco, for training in merchant marine signaling. The idea was that we would go aboard merchant ships as part of the armed guard. I think they had gunner's mates, perhaps a boatswain's mate or two, a signalman, and a radioman. After we had been in this school for some time, the navy evidently concluded that the threat from Japanese submarines wasn't as great as it had been, so we were rerouted to amphibious force training at Camp Bradford, Little Creek, Virginia. From then on to the end of the war, my wartime experiences in the navy were in the amphibious forces.

Our next stop was another temporary wartime base, at Lido Beach on Long Island. We were pretty well restricted to the barracks, but naturally we all wanted to see New York. This is where the ingenuity of the American sailor comes into play. The barracks had green blinds on some of the windows, and that was the same color as the liberty cards men were being issued. So we just took some scissors and created imitation liberty cards. We flashed them at the gate guards, and we got to see some of New York.

We spent part of the time chasing the girls, of course. Some of my friends liked to party, and they got over to Jack Dempsey's bar and restaurant. I was too young to drink, and the shore patrol seemed to show up fairly often, so I played tourist instead. For instance, I went to the top of the Empire State Building, which had been a goal of mine if I ever got to New York.

During the first week of January 1944 we were ordered to prepare to head overseas. We had a long walk—carrying our hammocks and seabags—from Lido Beach to Long Island City and caught a train to Pier 90, New York City. There we boarded the British troop transport *Mauretania*. She was big and she was also fast. She and some of the other liners went across the Atlantic unaccompanied because they could outrun the U-boats. We had to start the voyage twice. The first time, we got about thirty miles from New York and collided with a merchant tanker called the *Hat Creek*. So we had to go back to Pier 90 for repairs, then started out again the next day.

The ship didn't have bunks for the passengers, so we had to hang our hammocks from vertical stanchions. During the entire twelve-day voyage there was always the fear that the *Mauretania* was going to be hit by a torpedo. We played a lot of cards, but there were no required activities, no mess-cooking duties, no watches to stand or anything. The odor of vomit was constantly with us. I recall that I just got dirtier and dirtier as each day passed. I finally took a salt-water shower about the last day we were aboard. It wasn't worth it. They had special soap for use with the salt water, and I felt dirtier when I got out of the shower than when I started. It wasn't a pleasant experience.

Back in Norfolk the navy had given us all kinds of issues—winter clothing, carbines, canteens, backpacks, blankets, and at least four or five different types of gas masks. They were always issuing something, but these items didn't give us a clue where we were going. In fact, we didn't know our destination until we got there. It

War is indeed hell. Here navy enlisted man Albert Gesswein says goodbye to his pinup collection in England before heading for France. (*Navy photo in the National Archives: 80-G-46900*)

Fauks signals by semaphore flags from the Normandy beachhead. (*Courtesy Lieutenant Commander Paul S. Fauks*)

turned out to be Liverpool, which we reached on January 18, 1944. For the next several months we were in training in various bases in southern England. For a while we lived in Quonset huts—the rounded metal buildings shipped over from the States. More than just in training, we were in the vicinity when the time came for the invasion. The United States couldn't send everyone over at once, so we went in stages and stood by for the order to go into action against the enemy.

Our regimen during that waiting period wasn't too demanding, and the people in charge weren't keeping good track of our liberty time. So, we just kind of came and went as we pleased. On February 18 I caught a train and went up to London. That's when I met my future wife, during an air raid by German bombers. All over London the British had their ack-ack guns, so we heard an awful lot of gunfire. At one point a group of us got really frightened, so we went into a pub. That was the only place we could really get into. While we were in there, we heard knocking sounds, so we got under tables. And we thought, "Well, they'll let these people in. There's somebody knocking to get in here."

Some guy said, "No, that's not it. That's shrapnel hitting up against the building." When we left there we got down into the subway system, which was the most

secure bomb shelter. That's where everybody went if he could. The British even took their beds down there because it was safe.

While I was passing the time down there, I struck up a conversation with a British girl named Barbara Clare, who was then sixteen years old. We talked that night, and I said, "Well, I'd like to come out to your home and visit you and your family tomorrow." So she gave me directions on how to get there on the subways. Actually, I couldn't find her house right away and was about ready to give up. Then I asked a youngster from the neighborhood where the Clare girls lived, and he told me. It was another several weeks between then and when we went over to France, so I saw her one more time. We went out to lunch, probably went to a dance that night.

During this waiting period when we were in England, I did make some progress in getting advanced to signalman second class, but there wasn't a lot of training. The officers seemed to go their way, and we'd go our way. There was no great cohesion, and that even applies to the invasion itself. There just was not that closeness like when you're aboard ship.

When we had left Little Creek, we went over as part of the 294th Joint Assault Signal Company. But that JASCO concept apparently faded away. On the tenth of April I was attached to Company B, 4th Platoon, of the 7th Beach Battalion—strictly a navy outfit. These were the people who would run the beachhead once the invasion was made and American forces were set up ashore in France. Included were some pharmacist's mates and some boatswain's mates along with the radiomen and signalmen. We did do some training at Slapton Sands, including the period when two LSTs were sunk by German E-boats during Exercise Tiger.

Members of a navy beach battalion lunge for cover as a German plane strafes their position. (*Navy photo in the National Archives: 80-G-252841*)

We would go ashore and pitch a tent and dig a hole and send messages, just as we would be doing when we got to France. We signalmen used our semaphore flags and flashing lights. After five days of that, it became very repetitive and boring.

We were not told a great deal about the specifics of the mission for which we were training. Time after time they would load us in trucks with our carbines but not give us any ammunition. We'd put everything we owned in these trucks, and they'd take off. The people in charge were timing all this to see how long it would take to reach the embarkation ports. We did that a number of times, and we had the idea each time that it might be the real thing. Then they did finally issue us live ammunition and started sending us to the marshaling areas. This had to be the invasion.

On May 25 we started receiving briefings on the invasion of Europe. And there was another interesting tipoff. Up to then each man cleaned his own mess kit after he'd finished eating. In the marshaling area were fifty-five-gallon drums filled with boiling water. Everybody had to dip his mess kit down in to clean it off and kill germs. Some guy was standing over the drum to make sure you actually did it. They didn't want any outbreaks of illness just before the invasion.

On June 1 we went to the debarkation port of Weymouth. I boarded the *LST-372* that day; most of the rest of the passengers were army engineers. Security was really tight by that time, so we didn't go ashore at all for the next few days. On the evening of June 5 the ship got under way for Omaha Beach. On the way across the English Channel I remember seeing every type of ship that you could imagine—ranging from a World War I battleship to tiny craft the size of fishing boats. Some German bombers dropped bombs near our ship during the trip. The vibration we felt down below decks was enough to rattle our teeth. We had the sensation of being in a metal coffin. There was a lot of praying going on then. That's probably the most scared I've ever been in my life. Being with a bunch of seventeen- and eighteen-year-old kids didn't do a lot to provide reassurance. Our fears were feeding everybody else's.

When we got within two or three miles of the beach, I saw dead bodies floating by on the water—the first encounter with death I'd ever had. We arrived at the assault area and debarked from the LST about one o'clock in the afternoon. I climbed down a rope ladder to board an LCVP for the trip ashore. I was wearing long gloves and smelly clothing impregnated to protect against gas attack. I had rifle, canteen, backpack, and an 8-inch signal light with tripods to set it on and a

Members of a navy beach party are shown after setting up their headquarters ashore on Normandy. A portion of the invasion fleet can be seen in the background. (*Navy photo in the National Archives: 80-G-252733*)

Paul Fauks and his beach battalion "shipmates" visit Utah Beach shortly after D-Day and get a look at the Germans' remotely controlled miniature tanks. They were intended to function as movable land mines, but they served only as a curiosity after the fact. (*Navy photo in the National Archives: 80-G-252746*)

gasoline-powered generator to provide electricity for it. When we got in to Omaha Beach, the coxswain of the landing craft opened his ramp too soon. I can't say that I really blame him, because he was eager to unload and get away from the beach as quickly as he could. I stepped out into water up to my neck, and it didn't help that I was wearing all that heavy clothing and had things to carry. We had a good fifty to a hundred yards before we reached the sand.

I thought I had a pretty good idea what I was supposed to do on the beach, but once I got there, it was turmoil. I saw smoke, fires set by the shelling from offshore, and more dead bodies. My only job at that point was trying to stay alive myself. With all the heavy fighting in progress, I was still terribly frightened. I joined the men with me in digging a hole in the sand, and that was it. There was pretty heavy fighting in progress. For the remainder of June 6 and probably a good part of the next day as well, I don't remember getting out of that hole. We were pinned down. There was no sense trying to signal for LSTs to come in and

beach, because Omaha wasn't anywhere near being secure enough yet. I figured the only thing I'd get for my trouble would be a bullet in the back. A fellow in a nearby foxhole had a .50-caliber machine gun, and he was popping away at the German reconnaissance planes that came over during the night.

After a couple of days we were able to come out of our holes, and we met up with some soldiers who brought supplies ashore in one of those amphibious trucks called a DUKW. I remember the first food I received that way was a package of candy Lifesavers, which was highly appropriate under the circumstances. As soon as we could, we moved from the beach itself to an abandoned German pillbox that had housed an 88-millimeter gun. It was close to the cliff attacked by the rangers at Pointe du Hoc—within a couple of good long baseball throws of it. When we got to the pillbox, it had some parts of bodies in it and one thing and another. After the body parts were removed, someone took some gasoline, sprayed it around in there, then set it afire. It wasn't the greatest place to live but still much better than the foxholes on the beach. We stayed in the pillbox for a week or two and had our communication station up above it.

Then we went perhaps a mile inland, toward the town of Sainte-Mère-Église, and set up pup tents for our shelter. We stood watches to coordinate ship-to-shore communications and kept pretty busy as the flow of men and supplies being landed grew progressively larger. For example, a blinker-light message might say, "This is LST so-and-so. I'm supposed to land. Would you give me directions which beach to come in to?" And we'd get an answer from the beach people and send it out to the ship. We stayed pretty busy with that, getting a little sleep whenever we could. Cherbourg was not really in a position to handle much cargo, so the beaches at Normandy were still vital for getting the goods ashore and to the troops as they battled their way eastward across France. I have to say that we were good signalmen but not much use as combat people. After all the time I spent carrying that carbine around, I doubt if I shot it in France more than a time or two.

There were a few opportunities for "liberty" during our time on the beach. One day some men from the beach battalion on Utah Beach came over for a visit, and then we went to their beach the following day. On Utah we saw an interesting curiosity, some remotely controlled weapons called "doodlebugs." They looked like miniature tanks and were fitted with explosives. The idea was that they could be sent in among the invasion troops and detonated. They were not at all successful. Another trip we made was a one-day visit to the city of Cherbourg. We were there long enough to find a small bar, and that was my introduction to cognac. I thought it was great, especially after the Spartan life we'd been leading in our tent city.

We carried on our communication activity until mid-August, when we boarded another LST and left Normandy to return to England. We were put up at the naval college at Sandhurst, and one evening I resumed my interest in Barbara Clare. I really kind of went AWOL and headed off for London to be with her. I got caught, but a couple of my good buddies swore that I'd been to the movie with them.

We made the voyage back to the United States in the transport USS *Wakefield*, which had previously been the passenger liner *America*. During that trip I was one of several men up at captain's mast for disciplinary action. There were a few threats, such as loss of leave or demotion in rate, but no actual punishment. Perhaps the record of what we'd been through at Normandy was put on the scales of justice.

When I got back to New York, I bought an engagement ring and sent it to Barbara. After that I went to serve in the Pacific, and Barbara and I wrote to each other as often as we could under those wartime circumstances. Memory's starting to get away from me, but I know that I had to visit the British consulates in San Francisco and various other places to get the paperwork going to bring her to the United States. It wasn't an unusual thing for those officials who had to do that, because they were getting an awful lot of applications from guys who had met English girls over there and wanted to bring them to this country. It was new to me, though, and thus quite a hassle.

I often felt lonely during the latter part of the war and the period when I was trying to deal with all that red tape. And I'm sure the two-year separation from 1944 to 1946 was a trial for Barbara also, but eventually things worked out. There was no sense to our relationship at all, because we were both just kids, but we were married in July of 1946 in Oklahoma. All the odds were that this marriage would never take, but we're going on fifty years together, and it's been a great life for both of us.

PAUL SAMUEL FAUKS (1924–) entered the navy in 1943, served in the European theater, and then was in the USS *Arenac*, an attack transport that was among the first Pacific Fleet ships to take occupation troops to defeated Japan. He was discharged from active duty in late 1945 as a signalman first class. As a civilian he attended Oklahoma City University, graduating with a degree in journalism in 1950. He had been commissioned as an ensign in the Naval Reserve in 1949, and the following year was recalled to active duty for the Korean War, serving in the destroyer *Blue*. He augmented into the regular navy in 1953. Training courses at the Naval Postgraduate School included communications, general line school, and navy management. His various assignments as an officer included Naval Air Station San Diego; communications adviser for the Nationalist Chinese Navy; USS *Virgo*; USS *Mount Katmai*; commanding officer of the Macon, Georgia, navy recruiting district; executive officer of the stores ship *Pictor*; and executive officer of the St. Louis, Missouri, navy recruiting district. Fauks retired from active duty in September 1967, then worked in the front office of the St. Louis Cardinals baseball club, mostly in the areas of player procurement and development. He retired from the Cardinals after the 1987 season and now lives in Glendale, Missouri. (*Courtesy Lieutenant Commander Paul S. Fauks*)

SURVIVING THE LONDON BLITZ—AND MEETING A HUSBAND

By Barbara Clare Fauks

Before the war we lived in East Acton, which is a suburb about thirteen miles from London in the county of Middlesex. I think we moved there when I was about nine years old, and I thought it was really a pretty area. It was a nice middle-class neighborhood with single-family homes rather than rowhouses. I well remember all the trees and the beautiful flowers. The rain and fog there are conducive to the growth of plants. A lot of our family lived nearby—my grandparents and aunts and uncles and cousins—so that made it even nicer.

In 1939 we went down to visit my uncle in the country. We could see men practicing with guns, so we knew that the war was coming. When we got back to London, we didn't stay long, because most of the schoolchildren were shipped out of the city for their own protection. There was a concern about the threat of air raids against the city. It was terrible to be separated from our parents. In fact, Mum and Dad didn't even know where we were going. The authorities took us first to our school and then marched us to the train station. I was crying, Mum was crying, and my sister Evelyn was crying. My cousin, who was a little older and later served in the war, went to the movie house not long after our evacuation. He saw me in the newsreel because there had been a cameraman present as our group of children was going away from home. I never saw the film myself, because I was in the country by the time it was shown.

I was sent first to Abbotsbury, Dorset, for a while. Then they moved me to be near my sister in Banminister, Dorset. But that didn't last, because Dad decided, "If we're going to go, we'll all go together." So he came down and brought us back home to the London area. We were gone only a few months. One of the things that struck me about that period was the contrast in attitude from peacetime. Normally, the English are very reserved and hardly know their neighbors. But when war broke out, we all helped each other. Facing an enemy such as Germany really pulled the country together.

Food became scarce during that period, but we did better than most because my grandfather was in the grocery business. My mother had chickens, so she would help out our neighbors with eggs. On Saturdays I would go to the butcher shop. The butcher liked to flirt a little bit with the girls. I flirted back, so we frequently got a nice beef roast. When Mum heard that some oranges had come in at the green grocer's, she would go down and join the queue. We didn't have a refrigerator, so we had to shop practically every day. There were some black-market operations for items such as sugar and tea. The English do like their tea.

My father was born in 1902, and so he was too young for World War I and too old for World War II. He was involved in building Rolls Royce cars before the war. Then the factory where he worked was turned into an aircraft plant to build Spitfire fighters. He was also a home guard, dressed up as a soldier for civil defense. He took great pride in that. These home guards were older men, and we referred to them as "England's last hope." He got so mad at us for that.

In our home in East Acton we had an Anderson shelter out in the backyard. It was made of heavy steel. You dug a big hole and put the shelter into it. It wouldn't have helped us against a direct bomb hit, but it was supposed to protect us from flying debris if the bomb struck some distance away. We used to go down there every night, because Dad made bunks in it for us. We even took our little dog in with us. As soon as we heard the air-raid siren, we grabbed our gas masks and headed for the shelter. But after a while it started filling up with water, and that was not good. So then the government provided something called a Morrison shelter, which was a huge iron table that was assembled from the pieces supplied to us. We put the table in our dining room and tried to sleep under it when the

A once-placid residential neighborhood in London lies in ruins after an attack by German buzz bombs. (*National Archives: 306-NT-901A-9*)

German planes came over. The table wasn't really big enough to protect all of us.

We lived on kind of a hill so that we overlooked London. I remember how unpleasant it was when London was under air attack night after night, particularly when the bombers were concentrating on the docks in the east end of the city. We could see the fires burning, and it was just awful. The Germans dropped incendiary bombs around us, and some of my friends from school were killed. They were in a shelter where many families would go, and they had a direct hit one night. Oh, it was so terrible. The area where my grandmother lived was hit, and the people who lived near her were killed. Her home was destroyed, but Dad went down and managed to rescue her. Then she came to live with us, and that meant one more person trying to take cover under the iron table.

When I was a little older, I got a job selling cosmetics in a department store in London. When I'd go to work in the morning, I never knew if my parents would still be there when I got home. That was frightening, especially when the buzz bombs started in the spring of 1944. When the buzzing stopped, you knew they were about to land and explode. It was quite an exciting time for a teenage girl. I suppose maybe the fact that I was young kept me from taking it so seriously as older people did. Still, life was different than it had been in peacetime. We didn't get to enjoy proms and wear pretty dresses because the war limited people to the necessities. There was more of a social life before the war.

I remember when the American servicemen showed up. Some of the English—particularly the servicemen—didn't like the Americans because we British girls were so interested in being with them. You know, you'd walk down the street, and the Americans would say, "Hi, Honey." They were really friendly, really nice guys, and the Englishmen were much more reserved. And, the Americans certainly had more money to spend than the British soldiers. There were also a lot of servicemen from the Allies: Canadians, Australians, New Zealanders, Free French, Polish, Norwegians. It was interesting to get to meet some of them. In fact, there were so many that it's a wonder England didn't sink from the added people. The Americans used to joke that it was all the barrage balloons that were holding up the island.

When I went to the underground at night to go home, all sorts of people would be sleeping down there. That's where I met Paul, one night during an air raid. He had on his little sailor hat and his peacoat. He was with a friend, and I was with a girlfriend. The four of us started talking. I remember that Paul was really awfully nice—he still is, of course. We went to Covent Gardens together that night, and then he came out to our house to see me the next day. Then he had to go back to his camp at Salcombe, and I didn't see him for a while. After all the worries about our family members being hit by bombs, now I was concerned about his safety as well when he went off for the invasion of France. I kept a close watch on the news reports during that period. As it happened, Paul and I were together only three times that year before he went back to the United States.

He wrote me some wonderful letters while we were apart. Then he sent me a ring, and little by little he sent over money so I could pay for a plane ticket to get to America. I couldn't come over as a war bride like my sister Evelyn, because I wasn't married yet. Paul's dad had to write a letter saying that I would not be a burden once I got to the United States. I had to go to the embassy in London and apply for a passport. The whole process took a long time. Then I had trouble getting a flight out because they were scarce right after the war. Finally, I made it, and we were married.

Two American servicemen pose with their future wives in England in the spring of 1944. *Left to right are:* Melvin Schaffer, Evelyn Clare, Paul Fauks, Barbara Clare. (*Courtesy Barbara Clare Fauks*)

Coming to this country meant quite a change for me. In England we hadn't had a refrigerator or a washing machine. When I got to America and saw all the appliances, I thought I was in heaven. We didn't have much when we first got married, but it was still more prosperous than England. This is really a beautiful country.

We've been together now since 1946—in the navy and afterward. We have three children and five grandchildren. We've been very lucky.

BARBARA CLARE FAUKS (1927–) was born in Notting Hill, London, England, and was educated at John Perryn School, East Acton, Middlesex. She was an employee at Peter Robinson's Department Store, Oxford Circus, London, from 1943 until 1946. She and her husband Paul were married in Oklahoma City in July 1946; the union has endured for more than forty-seven years. Barbara has been a housewife, mother, and grandmother during that time. Because of her husband's frequent, and sometimes long, absences from home because of military service and professional baseball commitments, she was instrumental in the rearing of the couple's three children: Paula, Pamela, and William. The family has lived in a variety of locations in the United States and other countries. For the past thirty years the St. Louis suburb of Glendale has been their home. For the most part, Mrs. Fauks has lost contact with relatives and old friends in England. Her only return to her native country came in 1988. (*Courtesy Barbara Clare Fauks*)

NOIC UTAH

By Commodore James E. Arnold, U.S. Naval Reserve

Upon detachment early in April 1944 from command of the U.S. Naval Advanced Amphibious Base at Falmouth, Cornwall, I reported to Rear Admiral John Wilkes at Plymouth, Devon, for a very hush-hush assignment. This new assignment was NOIC Utah. NOIC stood for naval officer in charge. That was comparatively simple to interpret.

In trying to make plans, I decided to talk with officers of the Royal Navy. "I'm Captain Arnold, U.S. Navy, gentlemen, and I'm looking for NOIC, British Forces," I began. "I wanted to discuss . . ."

"Aye, sit down and have a spot of tea. I'm the ruddy NOIC Gold himself [Gold being one of the British beaches at Normandy]. I've been wanting to talk with you American blokes. Y'see, we don't know a damned thing about this NOIC setup. New and all that sort of thing. A bit of a beastly puzzle, what? I've made no plans, myself. Seems to me it will be an on-the-spot-decision sort of mess. Any plan you make can't work anyhow. The ruddy army won't know what they want, and if they did, it wouldn't be there, and if it was, they would decide they didn't need it by the time you got it ashore. So, y'see, plans wouldn't be any use. And don't forget Jerry will jolly well see that any carefully formulated plan will be knocked into the king's whiskers. It's going to be a sticky mess at best. But it's surprising how well all our blokes will get in and solve their problems when the bombs and shells are batting about. Don't you think so, Captain?"

Exercise Tiger, held in late April, was the last full-dress rehearsal for Force U. It confirmed the prophecy that NOIC's plans were bad, almost unworkable. Communications proved to be the most critical stumbling block. Also, many officers whom I had chosen for key jobs had to be shifted to less responsible assignments. Discouraged, I called on the force commander, Rear Admiral Don Moon, letting my hair down. He listened patiently to my tale of woe. I was thoroughly discouraged. I was afraid that I had made a complete flop of the whole deal.

Admiral Moon stared thoughtfully at me a moment when I had finished. "Yeah," he said, rising to shake my hand. "If you didn't feel like that, I'd be worried. I picked you to do a job on Utah Beach. Don't let me down, Arnold."

That was that.

As the invasion neared, all England and Wales—from the Bristol shore to the Channel ports—swarmed and seethed with men in khaki. Thousands upon thousands of alert, serious soldiers moved through the silent, blacked-out countryside. Stealthily, at night, endless convoys of men and vehicles embarked with their impedimenta onto thousands of naval vessels concealed in rivers and bayous. The embarkation of these legions was accomplished with quiet orderliness. Packed into their allotted vessels, they were sealed aboard for the greatest military operation the world has ever known. For too many of these heroes it was to be their greatest and last adventure.

I embarked at Dartmouth on the *LCI(L)-530*. It was the evening of June 4, 1944, and it was one of the most beautiful, peaceful nights I ever remember in England. Just as we were about to cast off our lines, a messenger from the decoding room thrust a flimsy copy of a dispatch into my not-too-steady hands: "D-Day postponed twenty-four hours." We doubled up all lines again. Each sixty minutes of those delayed hours was an eternity for me. There was no use to turn in; I couldn't sleep anyhow.

Boatswain's Mate Kare, who had served with me for months in a variety of capacities, brought me a steaming cup of coffee. I sat on the little folding chair on the starboard wing of the bridge. The LCI skipper took my advice and turned in while I sat and gazed at the silent, eerie waters of the Dart River, watching the incoming tide slack the mooring lines. Silent, ghostly sailors took in the slack of the lines, stepping carefully around dark, khaki-clad soldiers—two hundred infantry for the sixteenth wave of the assault.

Just before dawn, the LSTs, which had sailed out to the rendezvous for the original planned D-Day, crept silently back into their berths, only to turn about and sail down the river again without dropping anchor. It was now June 5. They deployed to their same rendezvous again, sailing on the delayed schedule. Twenty-

Army troops in England practice landing and breaching the beach defenses they expect to encounter at Normandy. (*Navy photo in the National Archives: 80-G-231231*)

four hours more life for some of the youngsters; thank God they didn't know it.

Dusk again found our crew singling lines and casting off for the new D-Day schedule. Clearing the lighthouse at the mouth of the Dart, which was lighted for a few hours for the first time in many war-weary months, we took position in column with hundreds of other vessels. It looked like a veritable "bridge of ships to France." It occurred to me that Hitler's Luftwaffe could certainly have had a field day if they decided to attack this column, and I wasn't too sure they would not.

The speed of the convoy was limited to the top speed of the slowest component—in this case, the wallowing little LCTs laden with their precious burden of modern fighting equipment and carefully trained men. Many of the soldiers manning this gear had been sealed aboard the little craft for more than a week, living in unbelievably cramped and uncomfortable quarters.

Through the silent night, the LCI skipper and I studied charts, following the plan. The ripple of the bow wave sounded like Niagara Falls in the tense silence. Though we were still so far from the French shore that Hitler's reception committee couldn't possi-

bly have heard the report of a 40-millimeter, everybody on board spoke in whispers. It's funny about that too. It is the same on submarines when diving off soundings.

Three hours before H-hour my gaze-weary watch read 3:30. My knees were shaking so much that I'm sure they were causing the ship to vibrate. My skipper glanced at me. In the dim glow of the shaded binnacle light his face looked ghoulish. My return grin must have looked as forced and silly as his did.

I reflected on the plan. We were due to reach the convoy area off Utah Beach by four o'clock, when it would be light enough to make a landfall on the Normandy coast. I knew that the airborne troops of the 82nd and 101st divisions were just about due to land in their gliders around Sainte-Mère-Église behind Utah Beach. A rugged job was that one. Thinking of their hazardous mission, my knees steadied down a bit.

My eyes have been a source of pride to me for over a quarter of a century in and out of the navy. But I wasn't the first to pick up the coastline of France, slinking out of the fog and mist of the English Channel at four o'clock on that memorable morning. It was Kare, I think, who standing by my side with more hot coffee, whispered, "Land ho, sir." I swear he didn't speak above a whisper, yet every shadowy form hunkered down on that gently heaving deck sprang erect to man the rails.

Then we all spied it. A red glow lighted the western horizon. Silhouetted by this light was the unmistakable outline of low-lying land. It flashed through my mind that this indelible picture was identical with the silhouettes pasted on the walls of the super-secret room ashore, where we studied the intelligence reports describing Utah Beach. What caused that red flash which gave us our first landfall remains a mystery to me. It wasn't a bomb, because there was no concussion or sound. It might have been a flare from the defenses ashore expecting a continuation of the daily bombings from the Allied air forces, which had pounded this area relentlessly for weeks.

"How's your courage, Skipper?" asked the LCI captain, munching a three-inch ham sandwich.

"Well, Bill, if it wasn't for this glorious opportunity to die for democracy so this world could exist in everlasting peace and tranquility, I fear my courage might be a little on the brittle side."

"Yeah," said Bill, taking a huge bite out of the sandwich.

It might have been my imagination, but I'll swear he glanced at my knees.

It was 4:15 now. Land was plainly visible. The rapidly approaching dawn revealed the thousands of ships and craft. As far as the eye could see, they stretched away toward the English coast.

The transport *Bayfield*, flying Admiral Moon's two-star flag, had anchored and swung to the gentle breeze. Already her LCAs were lowered away, loaded to wallowing gunwales with helmeted men in khaki. The *Bayfield* marked the transport area: it was thirteen miles from the beach and in mineswept waters leading to the boat lanes. At the head of the boat lanes and about four miles seaward from the beach were the control vessels that would start the assault waves on the scheduled race for glory and victory—or defeat and indescribable slaughter.

Wriggling uneasily on my hard chair, I glanced anxiously at the sky. Then I peered again at my watch. It was 5:15, and I wondered where the hell the air fleet was. Then they came, thousands of them crowding the meager dawn light, like wild geese on a hunter's morning. That mighty armada roaring over the assault fleet off Utah Beach on that fateful June morning was the most welcome sight I have ever witnessed.

For the next half hour the low-lying coast of France seemed to leap into the air in a sheet of jagged flame and thunder, nor did it settle back until the last bomb

The attack transport *Bayfield* served as Rear Admiral Don Moon's flagship for Force U during the invasion of Normandy. She is shown here with four LCVPs moored at the stern. (*U.S. Coast Guard*)

bays were emptied by those welcome harbingers of courage to sailor men.

Meanwhile, we headed for the starting line to check the position of the control ships. Just before we jockeyed into position, a terrific explosion to starboard a few hundred yards rocked our LCI. It was the *LCT-707*. She had hit a mine, turning her completely over. Then all hell seemed to cut loose. German shore batteries recovering from the shock of surprise were returning the slugging salvos of the naval fire-support ships, raising great gouts of water as they plumbed for the correct range. They got it on the little *PC-1261*, the control vessel of Green Beach. She was standing broad on our starboard bow about three cable lengths when she took it. The little 173-foot hull seemed to disintegrate in a belch of flame and noise. I doubt if a man aboard survived.

The first two waves had left the line of departure on schedule. The third wave was joining, while the components of the fourth and fifth were circling slowly, ready to take position on signal from control. The noise was deafening: returning planes roaring back to Britain to reload; fire-support ships belting away at unseen targets inland, making an almost continuous wall of sound; Jerry batteries banging and barking, indicating definitely that the element of surprise attack had passed.

Another large transport hit a mine. She seemed to rise from the water on an even keel. It was a gentle heave rather than a savage jerk, which might have been expected from the power of the mine. Then she seemed to hang a moment just clear of the water. Breaking gently in two, she slid back. The two great masses which were once a ship upended crazily and disappeared to add to the graveyard of that glutton, the English Channel.

The white crescent of sand that was Utah Beach was now visible through the glasses. Tiny columns of men wading ashore from beached ferry craft, dodging and running between shell bursts, disappeared suddenly into the white sand. Black columns of smoke arose from some of the convoys creeping along the dunes.

Then two LCMs came close aboard. The young officer in one cupped his hands, trying to make himself heard in the uproar. I beckoned him alongside, racing down the ladder to the rail.

"Blankets and blood plasma are needed desperately ashore, sir."

My skipper nodded that we had both, so I ordered the two LCMs alongside. To the wide-eyed young army captain in command of the two hundred infantrymen aboard, I issued an order, trying to keep my voice steady. "Get your men over the side, Captain. Have each of them carry two extra blankets. You carry this blood plasma. On the double now! This craft makes a good target for Jerry at this range."

An alert photographer on board the cruiser *Quincy* took this picture of YMS-type minesweepers exploding a mine off Utah Beach on D-Day. (*Navy photo in the National Archives: 80-G-231649*)

Before I could check my own equipment—carbine, canteen, gas mask, rations, papers, etc.—the soldiers were swarming into the landing craft. Kare helped me over the side and leaped down after me. Skipper Bill made a motion with his hands like a prize-fighter greeting his audience. I tried to return a halfhearted grin. Then to the coxswain of the LCM, a pasty-faced kid who was a hero without a decoration, I gave the order: "Cast off. Hit the beach where you were told to bring the blankets."

In reality, it must have been twenty minutes, but it seemed like less than three when we grated to a shuddering stop in three feet of muddy water off that inferno which was Utah Beach. As the ramp lowered, I was shoved forward, up to my knapsack in cold, oily water.

German 88s were pounding the beachhead. Two U.S. tanks were drawn up at the high-water line, pumping them back into the Jerries. I tried to run to get into the lee of these tanks. I realize now why the infantry tries to have tanks along in a skirmish. They offer a world of security to a man in open terrain who may have a terribly empty sensation in his guts. But my attempt to run was only momentary. Three feet of water is a real deterrent to rapid locomotion of the legs. As I stumbled into a runnel, Kare picked me up. A little soldier following grabbed my other arm. Just for a moment he hung on. Then he dropped, blood spurting from a jagged hole torn by a sniper's bullet.

The rows of wounded lying on the narrow strip of sand between the high-water line and the concrete seawall supplied the answer for the need of blankets and plasma.

Never before or since have I seen Kare or any other enlisted man work so hard, or his commanding officer help him so vigorously. Kare dug a foxhole in the sand.

Brigadier General Theodore Roosevelt Jr., assistant commander of the 4th Division, landed on Utah Beach on D-Day. He died of a heart attack the day this picture was taken in France in July 1944. (*Army photo in the National Archives: SC-191911*)

This would be Headquarters NOIC until some of the savage German fire could be silenced. It was near noon when an army officer wearing the single star of a brigadier general jumped into my "headquarters" to duck the blast of an 88.

"Sonsabuzzards," he muttered as we untangled sufficiently to look at each other. "I'm Teddy Roosevelt. You're Arnold of the navy. I remember you at the briefing at Plymouth. If you have any authority here, I wish you would stop bringing in my troops down on Red Beach. They're being slaughtered. The navy ought to know better than send them into that sector where the darn Krauts have them bracketed."

I had in mind to explain to him that NOIC Utah was not supposed to function until the assault phase was over. Looking at his grim eyes, however, I decided against this procedure. "Seems to me, General, there was something in the plan about you soldiers neutralizing this Kraut artillery. But wait a moment . . ." I could almost feel the blast he was about to erupt. "I'll shift the unloading from the Red sector over to the Green Beach area."

"How?" he demanded.

"By the simple expedient of alerting the navy beach battalion on Red Beach to send the incoming craft over to the Green Beach area. I'll station a ship off a couple hundred yards and divert them. Somebody's going to raise hell because it isn't according to the book, but I have to agree there's no use landing dead men down in that suicide area. Meantime, General, suppose you alert your outfit to change the staging area, or post guides to direct the incoming troops to wherever you want them staged after they land."

Before he could argue, Kare and I were on our way to execute the idea. It was remarkably successful too, until German spotters finally notified their batteries to shift their fire over to Green Beach. That was some three hours later. Shifting his barrage, Jerry gave us an opportunity to clear up the wreckage and carnage on Red Beach.

Early in the afternoon I contacted the army general and his executive officer in that area. They were commanding the 1st Special Engineering Brigade, which would work with me in consolidating all beach operations. Together we decided on sites for operations installations. Two stout German concrete pillboxes right on the seawall would serve as the general's command post and my headquarters. At nightfall the beach was swarming with men and vehicles huddled on the thin strip of sand dunes between the seawall and the inundated field shoreward. Jerry's fire became more desultory and less accurate as the reluctant darkness hovered. Led by Seabee officers, men were frantically working, forgetting the danger of enemy fire.

Other elements of our command landed. Deputy NOIC Utah arrived with the nucleus of operations control, a few communicators, and part of the ferry-control group. Plans were discussed in the candle-lighted dugout where mooring charts and landing diagrams with their overlays were placed upon the bulkheads of the concrete stronghold, evacuated less than sixteen hours before by Rommel's defending supermen. At least two of the "master race" still lay sprawled on the steps leading down into the shelter. Kare said these were probably two of the best Germans in Europe. They were awfully dead.

Once I was satisfied that our setup ashore could be expanded for proper function of NOIC's operation, I stumbled aboard an LCVP and headed out to the *Bayfield* so I could report our readiness to take over the mission. The captain of the transport, a doughty Coast Guard officer, met me at the gangway. Dirty, wet, and resembling a ghoul seeking a contract to haunt a house, I was ushered into the wardroom. Admiral Moon said, "Sit down, Arnold. We are advised that the show on Omaha didn't go quite according to plan.

Looks like your beach may have to take a little extra burden."

"Well, sir, we are set up to take over on a scale commensurate with the plan. But if you expect to land stuff quickly, we'll have to move the LSTs in closer to the beach. You can see by glancing over the rail that we can't unload them out here. Seas are too rugged."

"Can't bring them in closer to the beach until the German shore batteries are silenced," somebody ventured.

"Can't silence the shore batteries until we have the heavy stuff ashore to silence 'em," somebody else suggested.

Then a quiet army general with a quiet manner said, "Sort of a vicious circle, isn't it, gentlemen? Perhaps Captain Arnold, whose responsibility it is to get these vital troops and supplies ashore, will give us his opinion on the problem."

Admiral Moon then directed that the LSTs close the beach to anchorage "Fox," four miles from the mean low-water line. He also directed me to assume the duties of NOIC Utah at once.

I left the *Bayfield* in a PT boat at three o'clock in the morning of D+1. Hitler's Luftwaffe was over us again in some strength. Flares lighted the transport and beach areas. It was a spectacle indescribable and fearful. It was weird and awesome to see planes burst into flame at night and plunge into dark water, with a momentary flash and then complete blackness. Repetition of this spectacle almost nightly in the ensuing chaotic two weeks renders it now, in retrospect, almost unworthy of mention, but in that dawn of D-Day+1, it left a lasting impression on my mind.

It was nearly daylight when the German planes left the area, defeated and blasted. NOIC Utah slopped ashore on the teeming sands of Utah Beach. My staff officers were in the busy operation dugout, surrounded by milling army officers, many of whom wore the insignia of brigadier and major generals on their netted helmets. These warriors immediately encircled me. Their attitudes were varied. Some were anxious and nervous; some were belligerent and bellicose. All were deadly earnest. My deputy sneaked a gleeful wink in my direction. He had apparently spent the entire night with these restless heroes.

I had to tell them something. Yet just what could I tell them that wouldn't be too far wrong? I certainly did not know how many of their units would not be disembarked for another twenty-four hours.

"Sure, General, what is the number of your outfit? The 62nd?" I glanced through a sheaf of papers which in reality had no bearing on the unloading plan at Utah. "Yes, General, your outfit is to be unloaded very shortly." The general hustled off to pass the word to his staff, who passed the word to the non-coms, who passed the words to Joe Blow, who ended up sitting on

Soldiers transfer from a Coast Guard–manned LCI to an LCVP for the last lap to the beach. In the distance, more landing craft dot the horizon. (*Coast Guard photo in the National Archives: 26-G-2408*)

the sand on his ditty box—waiting along with his restless superiors.

And so it went. Through the long twilight they milled around the operations dugout, until Jerry put on his evening show with his overrated Luftwaffe. Junior staff officers and non-coms sought shelter in foxholes. The generals eased into the stout pillbox which couldn't house the entire army. I myself decided to inspect the beach. Jerry's bombs were less punishment than the scowls and caustic remarks of impatient soldiers wearing helmets with stars.

"By the way, gentlemen, General Eisenhower should be here shortly. He will no doubt straighten everything out," I remarked as I left the smoky, stinking pillbox to the surprised flock.

Somehow, the troops were landed. Somehow the generals dissipated as their commands were landed to take their belated places in the slugging, fluid front. Meeting these same people later in the war, when many of them were real heroes, they laughed about the panic and snafu times on Utah Beach, when I had set them out on the wet sand to await an imaginary visit from General Eisenhower.

JAMES EARL ARNOLD (1895–1971) graduated from Worcester Polytechnic Institute, Worcester, Massachusetts, in 1917 with a degree in mechanical engineering. He received an appointment as ensign in the Naval Reserve Force in May 1918 and subsequently transferred to the regular navy in September. He served at the Naval Academy, in the submarine service, and finally as executive officer of the destroyer *Edsall* before resigning his regular commission in 1926. In civilian life Arnold worked as a sales engineer for the Leland-Gifford Company of Worcester, and in 1933–34 was also a member of the Massachusetts state House of Representatives. He volunteered for return to active duty in 1940 and became administrative officer for the supervisor of shipbuilding at the Bethlehem Steel Company, Quincy, Massachusetts. In 1943–44 Arnold was commanding officer of the Advanced Amphibious Base, Falmouth, Cornwall, England, then moved to Utah Beach and later to Le Havre, where he set up an operating port. He described the latter experience in an article in the U.S. Naval Institute *Proceedings*. Following the war he served as a commodore in the First Naval District, OpNav in Washington, and the Ninth Naval District. He retired in 1951 and was promoted to rear admiral on the basis of his combat awards. From 1951 to 1971 he worked as the Washington, D.C., representative of the Inland Construction Company of Omaha. (*Navy photo in the National Archives: 80-G-356263*)

COMBAT DEMOLITION UNIT

By Orval W. Wakefield

After getting to a construction battalion (Seabee) training camp at Williamsburg, Virginia, in December 1943, I spent the next month and a half sawing firewood to keep our Quonset hut warm. So I was ready for a change when a recruiter came around and asked for volunteers for a navy combat demolition unit (NCDU)—as the underwater demolition teams were then known.

About forty of us showed up to hear his pitch as to why demolition men were needed. It seemed that at Tarawa, one of the recent landings in the Pacific, marines had been hung up on a coral reef offshore from the island. Some of them then stepped off into deep water and drowned. So the navy needed men who could blow up reefs, beach obstacles, or whatever else might be in the way to prevent soldiers from getting ashore safely. The recruiter warned us that the duty would be extremely hazardous, and that those who volunteered would be considered expendable. He said that the applicants must be good swimmers, and they would receive special physical and mental training for the work they would be doing. The good news—if you could call it that—was that the demolition teams would be excused from mess-cooking duty immediately and would be able to get out of the navy as soon as the war was over. *If* they lived, that is.

Of the forty interested sailors who showed up to hear about combat demolition training, all but two quickly disappeared. The other man and I began to take the training, and everything the recruiter had promised turned out to be true. We were trained by men who were explosives experts in civilian life—quarrymen and coal miners—and then sent to Fort Pierce, Florida, for additional navy training as part of NCDU 132. The unit was made up of one officer, one chief petty officer, and four junior petty officers. The training at Fort Pierce included more work on explosives, as well as hard physical conditioning. This was before the days of scuba gear, so we had to be able to make long, difficult swims with only our own lungs to supply the air.

In mid-April of 1944 our unit flew from New York to England. Maybe eight other demolition teams were there ahead of us, preparing to go into action. Wher-

ever we went, it was in secrecy. We said as little as possible when asked who we were and what our jobs were.

Our team went aboard an amphibious transport to prepare for going ashore on June 5. We were so excited that we couldn't sleep. The invasion was called off for that day, so we waited still longer. By the morning of June 6 we had been standing around for hours, wondering what it would be like on the beach. Then it seemed that everything lit up. Bombers went in, and so many shells exploded from ships' gunfire that it looked like the biggest Fourth of July anyone could make. I told the chief petty officer in our unit that no one could survive a bombardment like that. He said, "You can bet there will be someone waiting when we get there." He was right.

The combat demolition teams went ashore in small landing craft known as LCPs. We had eight men in the team by then because we picked up two seamen who had been sent to England by mistake, then volunteered to join us. The LCPs approached Utah Beach together as part of the first wave. It was a hectic experience because the big guns of the battleships were booming behind us. They were so loud that they seemed to shake the boat. The surf was so rough that I was feeling seasick. By the time we hit the shore and put our feet on solid ground, we were just glad to be there. That sense of relief was especially true in my case. I am only five feet, six inches tall, so when I got off the landing craft, I was in water up to my chin.

The popular notion of frogmen is of rubber wet suits, but we weren't so glamorous. We were outfitted with marine-green coveralls, boots, helmets, and the type of sacks that newspaper boys wear while hawking their wares. The sacks were strapped on in front and in back and were full of plastic explosives wrapped in good old black navy socks. When I got out of the landing craft and found that my legs would hardly hold me up, I thought maybe I was a coward. Then I realized that the problem came from those two heavy seabags; the load of water and explosives in them probably came to more than one hundred pounds. I used my knife to cut the bags and let the water drain out, then

Orval W. Wakefield

Two LCPRs are shown alongside a transport. A man is climbing down over the side on a debarkation net of the type that was used in great numbers at Normandy to transfer soldiers from ships to landing craft. (*Navy photo in the National Archives: 80-G-44523*)

moved up onto Utah Beach, about 250 yards from the seawall.

All the obstacles on our part of the beach were like children's jacks—made for the children of giants. The obstacles were made by twisting sections of six-inch I-beams together, so that each one was about five feet tall. The idea was that they could rip the bottoms out of landing craft at high tide. Our job—as explained to us before we went ashore—was to get rid of those giant obstacles before the fourth wave of soldiers came in. We set to work, tying prima cord to the obstacles. Prima cord is not a fuze; it is an explosive itself, so if it got hit by a tracer bullet, it would blow up, and so would we. Fortunately, we were too busy to stop and think about that aspect of it.

Soldiers of the first wave were already coming in as well, dodging around us, and sometimes taking cover behind those giant metal pretzels because machine-gun bullets and mortar rounds were arriving on the beach in large numbers. We had to keep chasing the GIs away because they didn't realize how hazardous those obstacles had become.

We finally got all the explosives hooked up and took cover ourselves in a slit trench by the seawall, alongside the enclosure for a German 88-millimeter gun. Someone shouted the usual warning, "Fire in the hole," and soon pieces of steel were flying into the air and then raining down. We had been successful. I don't think anything could have gotten by those obstacles because they were too solidly made. Of course, there was much more ahead for the soldiers who had to fight their way

"Belgian gates" were among the various types of beach obstacles deployed by the Germans at Normandy in their efforts to rip open the hulls of Allied landing craft. (*Walter Trombold photo courtesy Karla Powell*)

inland. The GIs gathered at the seawall, sort of working up their courage to charge ahead. The officers would say, "Go," and finally one brave man went up and over, then a second, and finally the rest. They looked like ants when they all went over that wall.

For those of us who had come ashore first, we had done our job with the explosives. Now there was another one. An officer came by and said that he needed volunteers to carry wounded men down to the shore, where a landing craft would take them aboard

Soldiers huddle behind beach obstacles on D-Day for protection against German gunfire. (*Naval Institute Collection*)

and carry them to a hospital ship. He said, "Are you guys going to just sit here, or are you going to volunteer?" We didn't think much of that idea, because we had just come off the hot end of the wire, but we finally did volunteer to do it for him.

When we came back and sat on the line again, I found myself next to our warrant officer, a man named Carl R. Noyes. Soon I heard a clang alongside my head, and when I looked down beside me, there was a jagged piece of iron. I touched it and found that it was red hot. So I turned to Mr. Noyes, who was sitting on my right, to say, "We better duck a little lower; there's lots of stuff flying around in the air here." Then I saw that he had been hit on the side of the head by the shrapnel. He was taken away for hospitalization.

There were other wounded as well. Some of our paratroopers who had been wounded inland were brought out to the beach for evacuation to hospital ships. They were more or less lying there in a group. Down a ways on the beach was another group of soldiers; these were the German prisoners. Those wounded paratroopers were trying to do everything they could to get at the prisoners. Bloody or not, they were ready to do more fighting on the spot if they had been permitted.

By the middle of the afternoon on D-Day, Utah Beach looked like a small city. When we first got ashore, there had been nothing but obstacles—then men running, turning, and dodging. With the obstacles blown apart, the beach was transformed into a beehive. Even though the tide was rising higher and higher on the beach, both landing craft and amphibian vehicles were now able to move ashore safely. By evening there was a rush of vehicles. It was as busy as you could possibly believe. It was apparent that all the other combat demolition units had done their work well, because as far as I could see, the beach had been opened.

We were able to relax by then, but when things calm down is when you have a chance to think. I wondered just who would have been crazy enough to do what we did. June 6 turned out to be a pretty good day for the men of NCDU 132. Overall, I understand that our units at Utah Beach had 30 percent casualties that day, while it was 70 percent on Omaha Beach. I guess we were lucky that we lost only two of our eight men. In any combat situation, people wonder if they can handle it. I remember that moment when I was in the water, struggling with those heavy bags, and wondering if I was a coward. When I found out that I wasn't, it was a great feeling. I believe my most important thought that day was this: Yes, I could do the job I had volunteered to do.

ORVAL WOODROW WAKEFIELD (1913–) worked during the early part of World War II as a steampipe welder at the Kaiser shipyard in Richmond, California. He enlisted in the navy's Seabees in November 1943 after deciding that he wanted to make a more direct contribution to the nation's war effort. After his experiences in Europe, he went to the Pacific, where he was part of the initial contingent to go ashore during the occupation of the Japanese home islands in August 1945. He was discharged from the service that November. As a result of his wartime experience in combat demolition, Mr. Wakefield had lost the hearing in his left ear and part of his sense of balance. In December 1945 he began work at Coast Records in Vernon, California, a company that made phonograph records; he became plant manager in 1948. In 1955 he moved to the Murcon Manufacturing Company in Vernon, California, as a supervisor and developer of machinery. In July 1973 he retired as the result of physical disability. Since March 3, 1946, Mr. Wakefield has been married to the former Phyllis Shiffermiller, whom he describes as "the absolute best woman." Mr. and Mrs. Wakefield live in Oceanside, California. (*Courtesy Orval W. Wakefield*)

THE BEST SEAT FOR A REALLY BIG SHOW

By Captain John R. Blackburn, U.S. Navy (Retired)

At about ten o'clock on the evening of June 5 the signal went to ships of the formation to go to general quarters at eleven. On board the heavy cruiser *Quincy*, I went below for my last cup of wardroom coffee and a nervous half-smoked cigarette. Everyone was talking in excited low voices. Conversation was difficult because no one was listening to the talker's words. It was as if we all had our ears cocked awaiting the alarm of battle stations, which—if sounded before eleven—would indicate that we were under attack.

Surely, if the vaunted Luftwaffe had any striking power left, then would have been the time to strike our force and cause at least partial disruption of our plans. But they didn't. So we went to our stations on schedule; mine was in sky control, well above the bridge. It afforded me the best seat in the house—an ideal vantage point for the many events that followed. At midnight I could still see a faint glow in the western skies. To the southward we could make out flashes of light where our air force was beginning its mammoth task of dropping fifteen thousand tons of bombs in a six- or seven-hour period.

The ships ahead of us were warily feeling their way along the channel that had been swept of mines. Every fifteen or twenty minutes we passed a small green lighted marker buoy close aboard to starboard. (The buoy system in Europe is the opposite of the one we're used to: red, right, returning.) The red ones on the port side of the channel were given a much wider berth.

Although this "dazzle" pattern of camouflage was normally a Pacific Fleet measure, this is how the heavy cruiser *Quincy* looked when she bombarded Normandy on D-Day. (*Navy photo in the National Archives: 80-G-281858*)

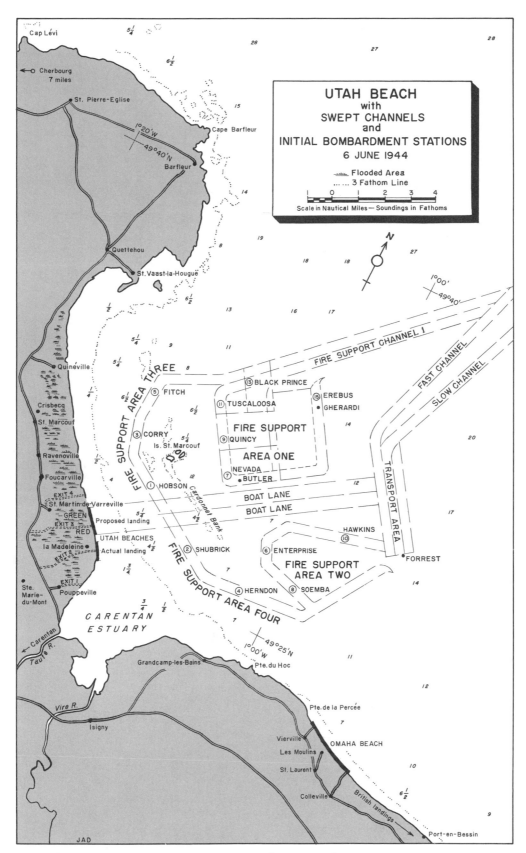

Drawn for Samuel Eliot Morison's *Invasion of France and Germany: 1944–1945.* (*Courtesy Naval Historical Center*)

An American soldier stands atop a German emplacement that was blasted by naval gunfire during the invasion. (*Navy photo in the National Archives: 80-G-253242*)

Our swept channel was supposed to be eight hundred yards wide. The Germans were known to have sown extensive minefields in the area we were traversing. By a combination of luck and excellent minesweeping we avoided any mines in crossing.

A destroyer or an escort vessel was pathfinding our column of ships through the channel. I could hear the "feeler" talking to the leading ship in our column. On several turns we were to make, the conversation would wax excited until the "feeler" found the turn buoy. Several times the engines were stopped while the lead ships sought the elusive bobbing lights. We had been on radar silence since the morning of the fifth. With the SG surface-search radar cut off, the navigators must have had a feeling of a missing right arm. From our intelligence we knew that the enemy was prepared to jam our radar or use it for direction finding. The best indication was that we were not fired upon by the long-range coastal guns during the hours of darkness. We fully expected this to happen when we came within range and had a plan (of questionable value) to provide

counter-battery fire in the event that the coastal batteries cut loose at us with their 6- to 11-inch guns.

As we headed toward France we watched for a flight of some five hundred C-47 Skytrain transport planes scheduled to wing over the convoy. These planes were to fly south of Cherbourg, cross the Cotentin Peninsula, drop a division of paratroopers, and return northward over our force. After midnight we observed heavy sporadic antiaircraft fire ahead of us and on the starboard bow. Most of it appeared to be machine-gun fire. Often, a yellow ball would start glowing out in the middle of a field of red tracers. This yellow ball would slowly start to fall, forming a tail. Eventually, it would smash into the black loom of land, causing a great sheet of light to flare up against the low clouds.

During the night I must have seen this reenacted a dozen times, with minor variations. Sometimes the yellow ball would explode in midair, sending out streamers of burning gasoline. This tableau always brought the same reaction from those of us observing from sky control—a sharp sucking in of breath and a muttered, "Poor goddamn bastards." The only planes we could see were the ones that were put on fire. How many were disabled and forced down I have no idea, but it must have been a considerable number.

Shortly after 1:00 A.M. we heard the drone of motors ahead and the first Skytrains appeared, silhouetted against the light clouds like groups of scudding bats. By this time the full moon had risen, and although the overcast was still fairly solid, it lighted the clouds with a peculiar degree of luminosity. This caused the transport planes to be outlined at a fairly good range, as the German machine gunners well knew. A few of the planes—especially the singles—were flying very low, at a height of twenty-five to fifty feet above the waves. I fully expected several to crash into the water, but they always seemed to recover sufficient control to plunge on through the darkness. I wonder what the results would have been had the Germans given us an air attack a half hour or ten minutes before, or if they had slipped a few Ju-290s in with the returning transports. I suspect that the effort would have paid rich dividends to the enemy and given us a taste of chaos. The transports came trickling back for almost two hours.

We anchored about three o'clock on the outskirts of our bombardment anchorage and waited for the attack transports and landing craft to get into position for the beach assault. During this period we saw the really heavy bombing taking place. The pathfinder planes flew in over the coast and dropped brilliant red and green flares on our assault beach, Utah. These flares fell on the ground and provided markers for the heavy bombers that followed. The throb of their engines was so heavy that it seemed to press in on our eardrums. The explosives that tumbled from the bellies of the four-engined bombers ripped across the land in strings of blinding yellow flashes. In a short while the dust clouds were so thick it was impossible to see any more explosions, but the noise continued.

After the landing area had been thoroughly worked over, a group of dazzling million-candlepower parachute flares were dropped to the north of our beach, in the area where the heavy gun emplacements were supposed to be. The flares drifted down slowly in a long, unbroken line. When the landscape of Cap de la Hague and Barfleur had been lighted like day, the big boys opened up their bomb bays, and again the sear of yellow flashes tripped across the black beach lands. It was one of the most awful and shocking things I had ever seen. I tried to imagine what those pleasant, quiet French natives were doing and feeling as they trembled in their cheese cellars.

Soon the dust filled the skies and reached out to us at anchor. The dust had the smell of fresh-cut grass. For a moment I had a twinge of homesickness for the fertile valley of my home in West Virginia—rich, green,

fragrant fields of alfalfa awaiting the mower. But the mood was as short-lived as it was out of place.

The first hint of dawn began to fill the sky about 4:00 A.M. The heavy bombers shifted their effort to the southeast, toward Omaha Beach. They dropped a considerable load around what appeared to be the Cherbourg area. About 4:30 we got under way and started moving toward our bombardment anchorage, three miles north of the St. Marcouf Islands.

Low water was due at about 5:40, sunrise at 6:00, and H-hour scheduled for 6:30. That gave the boat waves almost two hours of light to get organized and run in to the beach. Everything was worked from an amazing timetable that took—so it seemed—everything into consideration. The *Quincy*'s secondary battery of 5-inch guns was supposed to open fire on a machine-gun emplacement in the middle of the northern beach—Green Beach. The ship was supposed to fire for about forty minutes—sixteen rounds of 5-inch a minute, plus a number of 8-inch rounds from the turrets. We would stop if a black smoke rocket was shot up, indicating that we were to check fire because of the first wave's contact with the beach.

As we rounded the bend about 5:15, heading down toward our anchorage, we heard a sharp "splat" off our starboard bow and looked over to see three shells fall and explode about a thousand yards away. We were the target of one of the shore batteries. Everyone looked at the other men with a mingled feeling of fear and excitement. I put on my helmet, and the rest of the lads followed suit. The next salvo of enemy projectiles landed even closer—only about five hundred yards short this time. Instinctively, we all placed ourselves

The *Quincy* used her 8-inch rifles at Normandy, Cherbourg, and southern France (shown here) in support of the campaign to liberate France. (*Navy photo in the National Archives: 80-G-367853*)

Lieutenant Commander William Denton Jr., commanding officer of squadron VCS-7, normally flew a U.S. Navy
floatplane from the *Quincy* for spotting. Here he poses
with the British Spitfire he used during the Normandy
operation because it was more of a match for the German
planes than were the floatplanes. (*Navy photo in the
National Archives: 80-G-302107, via Peter Mersky*)

This German pillbox, armed with an 88-millimeter gun,
was put out of action by a direct hit from U.S. naval
bombardment. (*Navy photo in the National Archives: 80-G-
252574*)

behind the three-quarter-inch armor shield around sky
control, feeling a little sheepish as we did so. All of us
were doing some rapid mental calculations along the
same lines: "Will the next one be a hit for the German
gunners and, if so, what is the chance of it getting me?"

Our three 8-inch turrets were trained toward the
beach targets with their guns somewhat elevated to
provide the necessary range. The crews of the 20- and
40-millimeter gun mounts in the vicinity of the muzzle
blast were directed to move to a more sheltered
position, subject to telephone recall. The visibility in
morning twilight had improved to the point at which
targets could be located on the beach.

Lieutenant Commander Bill Denton, our ship's
senior aviator, had been checked out by the Royal Air
Force and was flying a Spitfire fighter over the target to
provide spotting for our main battery. He was given
our selected target coordinates for softening up the
Green Beach landing area. Well before sunrise, the first
of many 8-inch salvos erupted from our turrets and sped
toward the offending German battery. The belch of nitrous
brown smoke and yellow flames from the *Quincy*'s two
forward turrets gave us the reassuring feeling that at last we
were in the fray and doing something about those pesky
gun emplacements that were firing at us.

The explosions from the turret firing were less
bothersome to my gun crews in sky control and gun
mounts than was the sharp crack of the twin 5-inch/38-
caliber guns. For one thing, those thirty-eight-foot-

long barrels of the 8-inch naval rifles were pointing
away and, in most cases, over the side of the ship. In
addition, when they were about to shoot, those of us in
air defense were alerted so we could protect ourselves
from the blast. During D-Day the ship expended
almost half of her supply of 8-inch ammunition. The
Quincy was shooting 225-pound high-capacity projectiles with point-detonating fuzes for instant explosion
when they hit their targets ashore.

The ship's crew members who were most nervous—
and saw the least—were the engineers in their relatively
protected stations below the main deck. They could hear
and feel the enemy salvos landing near the ship. So the
engineers demanded over the sound-powered telephones
to know what was happening "up there" and what we were
doing about the situation. We finally worked out a system
for keeping them advised of our gunnery progress and
general activities on board ship and ashore.

Planes roared overhead. I glanced up in time to see
a P-38 firing into a Junkers 88. Fascinated, I watched
the German plane burst into black, oily flames and
come tumbling down. And we all wondered about the
next enemy salvo. The *Nevada* and *Tuscaloosa* cut loose
with their main batteries at the troublesome shore
emplacements. The next incoming salvo landed short
and farther to the right of us. Apparently, the point of
aim was being shifted to the *Tuscaloosa*. We must have
been about at the extreme range limit for the shore
batteries. A few more salvos of 8-inch and 14-inch
high-explosive American ammunition seemed to dis-
courage the German artillery. They closed up shop
when the big stuff started going off around them.

At last it was time for us to open fire on the
machine-gun emplacement in the middle of Green

Beach. The destroyer *Benson* had already been shelling the beach for some time. Bomb clouds of dust and rubble obscured the beach, but I could see where the salvos from the tin can were landing. Since she was much closer and better able to see what she was shooting at, we would just plunk ours in nearby—one four-gun salvo every fifteen seconds. I watched them landing and called in the spots to our plotting room people. They applied the spots so that the shells would cover a maximum area.

It was nearly H-hour—the moment long awaited by both the Allies and the Germans. The first waves of tank and infantry lighters approached the beach under heavy fire. One of the lighters stubbed her toe on a mine and was lifted almost bodily out of the water amid a column of spume some one hundred feet tall. She settled back down and began sinking stern first. I

anxiously watched for the black rockets that would give us the signal to stop shooting. But at 6:30, with still no sign of the rockets, the *Benson* was blanked out by the smoke. I gave the order to cease fire.

Our next target was another strong point in the coastal network, a small white blockhouse. The *Quincy* opened fire with 5-inch, but had trouble bringing the shots on target. I discovered that air plot was trying to combine and evaluate spotting corrections from both Lieutenant Charlie Biltmier in spot two and me. We were apparently looking at different targets without realizing it. We tried to order the corrections in opposite directions to get on target. Lieutenant Paul Anderson in the plotting room was in a dilemma. He tried using my spots on one salvo and Charlie's on the next. The result was that the 5-inch battery got nowhere. Our bullets were falling into a swamp on the

An Army Air Forces B-26 bomber flies over the beach line at Normandy. The three stripes on each wing are special markings for the invasion, designed to protect Allied planes against attack by friendly fighters and antiaircraft gunners. (*U.S. Air Force: 51988 AC*)

other side of a neck of land and throwing up columns of spray. Eventually, we realized the problem and got things worked out. Just in time too, because the shells were walking toward a French farmhouse.

While all this was going on, I was watching the *Corry*, another of the close-in fire-support destroyers. She was having a duel with a shore battery to the northwest of our target. I saw the splashes falling around the little destroyer and saw her blazing back with grim determination. Suddenly, her stern hit a moored enemy mine, opening up her smoke-making tanks. Her steering gear was disabled by the mine. The shore battery seemed to sense a victory and kept pouring out more shells at the disabled victim.

As we were watching this drama unfold, the *Quincy* was ordered to use 5-inch projectiles to lay a smoke-screen on the landward side of the *Corry* because she was sinking by the stern. All the while, I wondered why the destroyer didn't get the hell out of the way and clear of that German battery. It took us a while to start blasting out the 5-inch white phosphorous shells that might provide something of a curtain for the stricken destroyer. We had to empty the antiaircraft shells from our ammo hoists and bring up the white phosphorus from the magazine and lower handling room. Finally, after the seeming passage of hours, our smoke began drifting between the *Corry* and the shore battery. But it was too late, because the plucky little tin can was mortally wounded by the mine blast and sinking rapidly. A white mist of steam spouted up from her smokestacks.

We watched as boats and life rafts pulled away from her sides. Several landing craft came alongside to assist in the evacuation. By this time the big guns of the *Quincy* and the other heavy support ships were blazing—aimed at the batteries on the hillside and using

spotting corrections called down from a pair of our pilots circling overhead in Spitfires. The shore guns fell quiet at last, and rescue operations proceeded. The *Hobson* steamed up alongside the *Corry* and put her two bits' worth of shooting into the cloud of dust arising from the offending guns. The destroyer *Fitch* also aided in picking up survivors.

Great flights of American fighters still whirred overhead, almost always traveling in multiples of two. One of our P-51 Mustangs came drifting down, a mile off our beam. The engine was smoking a little, and the pilot was bringing his plane in for a water landing. But he came in too fast. We held our breaths and crossed our fingers for the poor lad, but that wasn't enough. He smacked in hard, the wings tore off, the nose went down, and the plane disintegrated on the water before us. We knew that the pilot could not have survived. Only a wing and an oil slick marked the remains of an American airman—someone's son, one of the many missing in action. He was smiling and confident one minute, dead the next.

Finally, hunger prevailed over the excitement that was coming at us in waves, and we sent down for breakfast about ten o'clock. We had hot beans and hot coffee, and they tasted wonderful. By then the gun crews and I were feeling a bit cocky. Our landing craft seemed to be getting ashore, and the fighter blanket overhead was warding off the Luftwaffe. And then, with our stomachs refilled after the long night and morning of waiting, we felt a sense of drowsiness in the morning sun.

We could not afford to be complacent for long, however, because in the early afternoon we had a series of "duels" with a persistent and elusive shore battery designated Seven Able. The northern ship in the bombardment area was lying to, waiting for her spotting plane to pick up an active target or a target designation from the shoreline fire-control party.

Then, in a repeat of the early morning activity, a cluster of enemy shells landed nearby. We peered in the direction from which the offending shots came, saw the smoke of gunfire, and checked our target reference maps. By then, a second salvo had landed, probably half as far away as the earlier one. By the time a spotting plane was put over the target and the 8-inch guns trained toward it, a third salvo landed—this one on the seaward side of us. This was too close for comfort, and everyone proceeded to get a little jumpy about the prospect of a fourth salvo. We had had a lot of fun laughing at the *Tuscaloosa* as she squirmed around in a similar plight, but it wasn't so comical when the same thing happened to us. The closest landed about fifty yards astern of us—where we had just been a few seconds before—wetting down the men on the 40-millimeter quad mount on the fantail.

As midday approached and the sun warmed our topside gun crews into a less-than-alert state, we asked

The invasion fleet lies in the background, beyond a French building shattered by gunfire. (*Navy photo in the National Archives: 80-G-59421*)

to stand down from general quarters to Condition II, a watch-and-watch situation that would allow some eating and sleeping for part of the crew after fifteen hours on full alert. This kept half of our antiaircraft batteries on station to respond to threats. The main battery could handle call-fire requests with one turret fully manned and the control stations with half the GQ personnel. Our hope was to avoid wearing the crew so thin that they wouldn't be able to perform in case of emergency.

I tried to grab a sandwich and some shut-eye after Condition II went into effect. I was so sleepy after eighteen hours of fresh air and adrenaline that I don't have a memory of going to my bunk. We probably talked with each other a bit, but I suspect that the conversation among the living zombies was at a low threshold. I do recall that when I got to my stateroom in mid-afternoon, my roommate, Lieutenant Lyle Keator, the main battery assistant, was already trained fore and aft in the upper bunk, conked out but preparing for whatever lay ahead.

An hour before sunset we went to evening general quarters in case the Luftwaffe attempted to pull any twilight surprises. An evening overcast had crept into our landing area. In mid-twilight some antiaircraft firing started to the north of us. We finally spotted the low-flying aircraft, which shouldn't have been where it was. Other ships were shooting at it even before it approached the *Quincy*. I identified the plane as British

and called out to the director for sky one, "Spitfire!" The director officer, Lieutenant Bill Ball, thought he heard, "Open fire!" so he obliged by shooting at the plane, which splashed a short time later. Our task force commander, Rear Admiral Don Moon, was more than upset, and the downstream flow of unpleasantness started.

The flow reached me when our good skipper, Captain Elliott M. Senn, asked me for an explanation. I didn't dare try the "Spitfire—Commence Fire!" story. I said that the plane was headed for us on a hostile attack course, and under the circumstances we were required to shoot. That didn't do much to soothe the captain. He directed me to keep "your damned gunners" under tighter control.

The following day, D+1, we heard that one of our PT boats had pulled the pilot out of a downed Spitfire. This could have been the one we hit with our 5-inch proximity shells; we shot about four rounds before the order to check fire. The Spitfire pilot, who had apparently been killed on impact, was dressed in a Luftwaffe uniform. The Spitfire had on it the three white wing markings used by all our Allied assault aircraft. We surmised that the Germans might have assembled this plane from pieces of Spitfires that had been shot down previously. They may have painted it with the invasion markings and then sent it out on a photoreconnaissance mission, believing that it would be perceived as friendly and thus immune to our shooting. If so, they guessed wrong.

JOHN RICHARD BLACKBURN (1917–) graduated from the Naval Academy in the Class of 1939. He served in two battleships and two four-stack destroyers before his assignment to the heavy cruiser *Quincy*, in which he served for the duration of the war. He was air defense officer, later gunnery officer, and finally the last commanding officer at the time of the ship's decommissioning in 1946. He had a destroyer tour, served in the Naval Academy's executive department, and then was commanding officer of the USS *Samuel N. Moore*, named for the skipper of a previous cruiser *Quincy*. Blackburn participated in the final phase of the Korean War in 1953, then was assigned to the staff of Commander Cruiser-Destroyer Force Pacific Fleet. He commanded Escort Squadron Three, then served on the staff of Training Command Pacific. He commanded the repair ship *Ajax* in Sasebo, Japan, and finally was chief of the navy section of the Military Assistance Advisory Group in the Philippines. He retired from active duty in 1963 and afterward worked for GTE Sylvania and General Electric in the nuclear energy field. After retirement in 1982 he moved to Rohnert Park, California, where he deals with the "unrelenting task" of daily golf. (*Courtesy Captain John R. Blackburn*)

MAKE LOVE AND WAR

By Rear Admiral F. Julian Becton, U.S. Navy (Retired)

Even before the destroyer *Laffey* arrived at Plymouth in late May of 1944, Allied counterintelligence had begun its work of hermetically sealing off millions of men who were to take part in Operation Overlord. On May 29, a total security blackout was dropped over every ship, unit, and man involved in Overlord. All of the ships of Destroyer Division 119—the *Laffey*, *Barton*, *O'Brien*, *Walke*, and *Meredith*—moved out of Plymouth Harbor on May 30 for some exercises off a place called Slapton Sands. After firing a total of thirty-eight rounds of 5-inch ammunition at targets, we made an uneventful return to Plymouth. It was a rather limited preparation for the kind of shooting that would soon be expected of us. Most of our gunnery training had been for engaging ships or enemy aircraft. We had not received a lot of training in acting as a floating battery of artillery supporting troops advancing ashore.

By the time we returned to Plymouth Harbor, the final, most stringent security measures were in force. No one aboard the ship was allowed to go ashore. We were in quarantine, restricted to the ship just as if we carried some dread, contagious illness—and in a sense, we did. The "illness" was our knowledge about the upcoming invasion. Had it accidentally spread to the wrong ears ashore, it would have killed hundreds, perhaps thousands, just as surely as any plague.

The time we spent at Plymouth before we finally sailed for France did have its lighter moments, and a sequence of these had begun not long after we arrived. Ashore, some distance from our mooring, there was a high hill with a number of bombed-out buildings on top of it. In front of these there was a level, grassy area. Farther down the slope facing us, the ground was steeper; and near the bottom there was another level area close to the water which was shielded from above by some bushes.

The level, grassy area at the top of the hill seemed to be a favorite gathering place for couples who would sit on the grass, enjoy the view, talk, and occasionally embrace, though in a very proper manner. But late one afternoon a young man and woman left their spot at the top of the hill and made their way down the slope.

When they reached the bottom, those above could not see them because they were behind the bushes.

Apparently, the young couple wanted to enjoy the view from a lower vantage point, because as soon as they were behind the bushes, they lay down on the grass near the shore and were soon enjoying each other thoroughly. But unknown to them, so too was someone aboard the *Laffey*. Though the ship was moored a considerable distance away, and the couple was well beyond the range of unassisted vision, neither of the pair apparently realized that warships carry optical instruments. They did not realize it the next day either, because they showed up at the same time, same place, and went through a repeat performance.

The following day when the couple again reappeared, they played to a much bigger audience. Since security regulations had been tightened and liberty could no longer be granted, the *Laffey* had her full complement aboard, and word had begun to spread. Matt Darnell, our doctor, told me later he was almost knocked down and trampled by the rush of sailors to the bridge at the 5:30 P.M. "curtain time," and quickly every pair of binoculars and every telescope on the ship was focused on the shore. Not just on the shore, of course, but on that couple who were again making love.

The next day we had to go to sea for that shore bombardment exercise at Slapton Sands, and we returned too late to catch that afternoon's performance. But on Wednesday and Thursday the performers ashore played to a packed bridge. And on Friday the audience was the largest ever. Not only were chief petty officers borrowing long glasses or a pair of binoculars, but at exactly 5:30 P.M. there were sounds of whirring motors as the *Laffey*'s three 5-inch gun mounts swung around toward the Plymouth hillside. Even the gun director atop the pilothouse was pressed into service just as the performance began. All, of course, had excellent optical devices which gave their users a front-row seat.

There were only two flaws in this otherwise enjoyable situation. Where the men were concerned, probably the most important was that this daily performance provided no means for audience participation "on

106

stage"; but for a few like Signalman Bill Kelly, it was something else. That Friday he was lying on his bunk fully clothed when he heard two shipmates talking about the crowd of chiefs on the bridge.

The bridge? That was his territory. What the hell were chiefs doing on his bridge? Kelly certainly knew what they were doing, because they had been doing it for some days, but Bill Kelly was fed up. He dropped to the deck, his legs moving before his feet touched the ground, and he raced up the ladders two steps at a time. When Kelly reached the crowded bridge he took one look and burst out with a disgusted, "What the hell is this?"

Chief Quartermaster William Ryder, who was Kelly's immediate boss, turned around, lowered his glass, and said, "RHIP, Bill."

RHIP is an old service acronym for "Rank has its privileges," but it didn't satisfy Kelly. This sort of thing had gone on too long as far as he was concerned, and he looked around trying to think of some way he could end it. Then, spotting an ally, duty Signalman Ted Purrick, Kelly motioned him over. Purrick, Kelly knew, wasn't any happier about the situation than he was. The way I got the story was that Kelly suggested they

"clear these [expletive] chiefs outta here," and Purrick agreed with the plan. They flipped a coin. Kelly lost the toss and he headed for the pilothouse.

Kelly went in through the door on the port side, tripped and fell. Then he got up and came hobbling out onto the bridge, bent over, holding his knee, and using some rather expressive words. Meanwhile, as the "Clang! Clang! Clang!" of the general alarm shattered the quiet, Purrick collected the glasses and binoculars from the departing chiefs, who were anxiously hurrying to their battle stations.

As I rushed to the bridge, I couldn't imagine what the emergency might be, and all sorts of things ran through my mind. On reaching the bridge, I quickly found out otherwise. Signalman Kelly came to me at once. He told me what had happened, then said he was sorry, and I immediately had word passed over the public-address system that the alarm had been sounded accidentally.

I wasn't very happy, but I didn't chew Kelly out. After all, he could not help it that his knee, "injured playing high-school football," had buckled under him. It was just an "accident" that his hand had grabbed the general alarm switch when he fell. And to prove it, he

The quarantine finally nears its end when troops load LCVPs in Plymouth Harbor so they can transfer to LCIs for the trip across the English Channel. Anchored in the background is the task force flagship *Augusta*. (*Navy photo in the National Archives: 80-G-252141*)

The newly commissioned *Laffey* on her shakedown cruise to Bermuda in March 1944, shortly before heading for England and the invasion of Europe. (*Navy photo in the National Archives: 80-G-237952*)

certainly was limping badly. As he said, "It could have happened to anyone." I agreed with that; but as Kelly talked on, I had a chance to think about it a little. The pilothouse was full of buttons and switches and certainly an "anyone" might grab one by accident—but not a man who knew the place by heart. A light began to dawn, and I had a great deal of difficulty to keep from chuckling.

As the skipper, I was not completely unaware of what had been taking place on my ship the last few days. Since no regulations were being broken or orders disobeyed, and it had not endangered the ship or interfered with duties, I had let it pass. We were moored in a safe harbor, restricted to the ship, and waiting to be sent into battle. Watching the shore and whatever could be seen there helped take the men's minds off their worries. But now I could see it had also created some problems, and I really didn't want to punish Kelly for trying to solve his, even if I didn't like his methods of solution. Any sailor resourceful enough to clear a bunch of chiefs off his turf was a sailor worth having in the *Laffey*. The bridge was Kelly's domain. The chiefs didn't belong there.

"Kelly," I said, trying to sound as stern as possible and glad that the light was too dim for him to make out the look on my face, "next time that trick knee of yours gives away, fall clear of that switch!"

And Signalman Bill Kelly, whose face I couldn't see too well either, replied, "Aye, aye, Captain," like the good sailor he was—and continued to be in the future. The invasion of France actually began around 1:30 in the morning of June 6, 1944, when about thirteen thousand paratroopers were dropped at selected points inland from the invasion beaches. Their objectives were causeways connecting the beaches to the mainland, bridges, crossroads, and other key positions. And they were to hold them until our troops stormed ashore, pressed inland, and could link up with them.

As the *Laffey* approached the coast of France some time later, C-47 transport planes could still be heard flying overhead. They were towing gliders filled with troops of the 82nd and 101st Airborne Divisions who had with them equipment that could not be dropped by parachute. They would land at dawn to support the paratroopers already on the ground, and there seemed to be hundreds of them.

By then I assumed that the Germans had been alerted and were taking every measure to counter our assault. Shortly, however, it became evident that some at least were not. The tall lighthouse at Point Barfleur was still brightly lit, just as it had been fourteen years earlier. Then, I had been at Cherbourg on a midshipmen's cruise. And long ago as that was, when I saw that lighthouse I remembered the taste of those strawberries dipped in sugar that I had eaten at a fine Barfleur restaurant.

The Germans, apparently lulled into a false sense of security by the recent bad weather, were stunned and confused by the air drops. Not only that, but they were not expecting the Allies to make a major landing effort in the Normandy area. As it began to grow lighter, the Germans manning gun positions ashore suddenly began to wake up to what was happening. By then it was too late. Our main bombardment groups were in position and at anchor. They had missed their chance to hit us during that critical period when mines were being swept and our heavier ships were still maneuvering to get into their correct positions.

H-hour at Utah Beach was to be 6:30 A.M. The naval bombardment of designated targets began on schedule at 5:50 A.M. and lasted forty minutes. Then, as soon as our warships stopped shooting, about three hundred B-26 Martin Marauder two-engined medium bombers swept in to attack. More than four thousand bombs smothered the German positions; though the bombs did not destroy many of these, they did explode many enemy land mines. So too did the rockets from seventeen LCTs that were specially equipped for this bombardment role.

The first wave of twenty LCVPs moved in at H-hour and unloaded troops on the beaches. Following came eight LCTs, which put ashore four tanks each, then two battalions of infantry in thirty-two LCVPs which also carried eight navy demolition teams. These last were to destroy the wood and metal beach obstacles, and they were followed in the third wave by combat engineers who would complete the job.

We stayed with her LCTs until they were very close to the beach, and then she moved out to a station in the defensive screen around the bombardment ships. Since the ships in the screen—like those they were guarding—had limited room for maneuver in the mineswept area, they had to anchor, and this meant that we had to remain especially alert.

The *Laffey* did not remain at anchor throughout D-Day, nor in the days after. Our squadron commander, Captain Bill Freseman, had ordered all his ships to stay at anchor each day only until minesweepers had swept the surrounding areas; on D-Day, once this was done, the *Laffey* was able to move, continuing her screening operations. Every gun, every position, was manned and ready for action. By dusk, the situation on all the beaches was fairly well in hand. At Utah, Sword, Juno, and Gold, troops and naval gunfire had overcome German resistance. Troops had pushed well inland to link up with our paratroopers. And even on Omaha, where just about everything that could have gone wrong did, the enemy's back had been broken.

On June 7, D+1, the *Laffey* continued her patrolling and screening around the bombardment ships. Again, all stations were manned. But being too far offshore for our 5-inchers to take part in a bombardment, we spent most of the day in a frustrating holding pattern watching the larger ships support the army ashore.

Then it came. At 4:30 A.M. on the morning of June 8, we were on station a couple of miles off the beaches, ready to shoot. The heavier ships with their longer-range guns were now firing at targets well inland in support of VII Corps army troops under Major General J. Lawton Collins. These were advancing up the Cotentin Peninsula toward Cherbourg. But our assignment involved a little more direct shooting. There were still a number of coastal guns and groups of enemy troops closer to the shore and a number inland that we could reach. And all of them were giving considerable trouble to the soldiers.

We got our first target at 7:57 A.M. The whole ship shook as we opened fire. From then on, for the rest of the day, the sounds reverberated through compartments with very little letup. A lot of the enemy were out there with howitzers, field guns, machine guns, mortars—just about every weapon you could imagine—and they were playing hell with the troops of the 4th Division.

Sometimes even the shore-fire control party couldn't help us. Once, instead of range and deflection corrections, all we got back over the radio was, "We're lying on our stomachs in a ditch. Can't see! They've got us pinned down." But by then we had enough information. We gave the Germans a ten-minute barrage, and it ended with, "Right on target! You did it! Whoever was shooting at us has stopped," over the radio.

Altogether, the *Laffey* got eleven calls for support on June 8; each shoot helped the 4th Division move closer to Cherbourg. June 9 brought more of the same. At 6:30 in the morning we started off on some cement pillboxes and fortifications; and, for the next hour and twenty minutes, we fired more than 275 rounds of 5-inch ammunition into various enemy positions.

There was a lot of shooting, and it meant an awful lot of work for the men crowded into the mounts and those below in the ammunition handling rooms. Both locations, even in the relatively cool weather, were soon hot and stuffy; the men manning them were dripping with sweat and exhaustion. There was a certain amount of power-assisted automation like powder-and-projectile hoists in the handling rooms. But the process wasn't really automated. It operated mostly on muscle and sweat and depended on just plain stick-to-it guts to keep going. Because it was a carefully organized team operation, if one man fell out or collapsed, the rate of fire might slacken.

In that hour and twenty minutes of steady, high-speed shooting, not one mount faltered—not even mount 52. This was our second forward 5-inch twin mount, located just forward of the bridge and pilothouse. At some point, not long after the shoot began, there was a problem in the handling room of mount 52. The regular hoist operator stationed there suddenly doubled up with what, in polite company, is known as an urgent call of nature. There was no question about the urgency of the situation, nor what might have happened had the man not gone to the head. The last thing you need in a place full of gunpowder and explosives is a human being stumbling around in agony. One little slip and you have real trouble.

With the hoist operator out of action for a while, mount 52's rate of fire should have slackened. But it didn't. Down in that handling room was a steward named Henry Teague, and Teague took up the slack. He handled over half the shells fired by the mount before the regular man was able to get back to his station, and he did it without anybody in the rest of the ship even being aware that anything was wrong.

On the face of it, the situation may not seem all that unusual. Teague was a husky fellow. He was agile and he was intelligent. He was also a hard worker. But Teague, a black man from Mississippi, could neither read nor write. He had never been trained to handle both hoists at the same time, much less trained to handle them at high speed. It was an amazing performance, one that a lot of other men couldn't have managed. But Henry Teague did it; and when I heard about it later, I made darn sure he knew I appreciated it. Henry Teague may have held the rating of steward, but as far as I was concerned, he was something else too. He was a gunner, and off the Cotentin Peninsula on June 9, 1944, he proved it.

Exactly one month to the day after that bombardment, when we were back in Boston, I found out just how much that opportunity had meant to Henry Teague. I was told by Lieutenant (j.g.) Harvey Shaw that Teague always carried the letter of commendation I'd given him in his pocket. Teague knew what was in it because I had told him. But, not being able to read it himself, he had asked Shaw to read it to him again later on. And when Shaw had finished, Teague had thanked him, carefully put the letter away, and said something to Shaw which almost brought tears to my eyes when Shaw repeated it to me.

Teague said, "In the years to come, when I'm back down in Mississippi, and someone tells me I'm no damn good—as a lot of 'em do—I'll tell 'em maybe not, but one time I was. Then I'll pull out this letter and prove it." I always hoped he did. Henry Teague was not "no damn good"; he was damn good, and he had proved it. Some men with a lot more chances in life than he had ever had never do.

It was not until June 12 that the *Laffey*'s gunners had a chance to engage the German E-boats. When they arrived in the area about 1:00 A.M., the *Laffey* was in position on the Dixie screening line and right across their path. To the west-northwest of us, some seventeen hundred yards away across the calm water, was the destroyer *Nelson*, and to the east was the USS *Somers*. We could just barely make out both of them. It was very dark, with thick clouds overhead. And there was no horizon at all. Nothing was in the immediate vicinity except the three of us and blackness.

We knew these were perfect conditions for a torpedo-boat attack. We'd been on alert for hours, but at 1:00 A.M. we didn't have to wait much longer. Our radar had picked up a very faint, fuzzy contact about eight to nine thousand yards away. The *Somers* picked up the same contact very shortly thereafter. And, as the *Nelson*'s radar recorded this contact as solid blips on her screen, she challenged by signal light and opened fire. As I maneuvered the *Laffey*'s bow on toward the targets, and our 5-inchers opened up, the blips suddenly slowed. Then, quickly, there followed a muffled explosion from the direction of the *Nelson*. The blips reversed course and fled, and the *Nelson* reported she had been hit with a torpedo.

The *Somers*'s radar lost contact with the E-boats about fifteen minutes after they had been spotted. That left the job to us. It was a job I wanted to do, especially after hearing that the *Nelson* had been hit; and everyone aboard my ship felt the same. When I called for more boilers to be put on line, Lieutenant Al Henke, the chief engineer, had us working up to top speed in jig time. But as fast as the *Laffey* was, she was chasing a very fast and elusive foe. We used our two forward 5-inch twin mounts, 51 and 52. Mount 51 fired star shells to illuminate the targets; mount 52 fired high-explosive rounds to destroy them. Our gunners kept up a fast rate of fire, and some of our rounds seemed to come fairly close, but spotting them was very difficult. The powder we had ready at the guns and in our magazines was for day bombardment. Every time a pair of guns went off, we were blinded by the flashes.

As time passed, the range increased, and slowly it became apparent that we had a long stern chase ahead of us. But we kept at it. The *Laffey* roared through the water like an express train, her guns blasting, our eyes blinking, trying to regain their night vision. Then our own ships did us in.

The E-boats were racing northwest, trying to reach their rat holes at Cherbourg, when suddenly our radar screen was full of blips. These weren't more E-boats; they were Allied ships moving across our bow on their way from England to the beachheads in France. The skippers of those E-boats had spotted them too, and before we knew it, they split into two groups. These dove in among those ships like rabbits diving into a briar patch to escape a dog. And the minute this happened, we had to cease fire; we were unable to tell friend from foe. The E-boats had finally escaped. It was a disappointing end to what had had a painful beginning.

Generally, I avoid using bad language, but there are times when it does serve a purpose. Later, in the privacy of my cabin, a few well-chosen words helped— not much, but some; though frankly not enough to overcome my disappointment. I had wanted very much to get those E-boats.

FREDERICK JULIAN BECTON (1908–) graduated from the Naval Academy in 1931 and served in a variety of ships in the 1930s: the *Texas, Arkansas, William B. Preston, Breckinridge, Guam,* and *Pope.* He also had a tour of duty at the Naval Academy. At the outbreak of war he was executive officer of the destroyer *Aaron Ward,* then was skipper at the time of her sinking. After duty on the staff of Commander Destroyer Squadron 21, he commanded the destroyer *Laffey* in both the Atlantic and Pacific, earning the Navy Cross for his role during a devastating kamikaze attack off Okinawa in 1945. Becton told the story of his experiences in the *Laffey* in the book *The Ship That Would Not Die,* published in 1980 by Prentice-Hall. After the war he served in the Bureau of Personnel and did postgraduate work in personnel administration. He was executive officer of the cruiser *Manchester,* Commander DesDiv 202, skipper of the transport *Glynn* and battleship *Iowa,* and served in OpNav. As a flag officer Becton was on the Joint Staff in Washington, Commander Cruiser Division Five, Commander Mine Force Pacific Fleet, Commander Naval Base Los Angeles, Commander Naval Reserve Training Command, and Naval Inspector General for the Navy Department. He retired in 1966. Admiral Becton and his wife, Betty, live in Wynnewood, Pennsylvania. (*Courtesy Rear Admiral F. Julian Becton*)

DREAD OF THE UNKNOWN

By Lieutenant Davis C. Howes, U.S. Naval Reserve (Retired)

The story of the invasion of Europe is going to be told by many, many who know the story better than I can ever hope to tell it. All I want to tell is my own reactions, troubles, and problems felt, met, and defeated during the operation. I know this will never be published while I am in the navy, but sometime it may be. The story is about the part one ship [the destroyer *Baldwin*] took in the venture, and a rather insignificant part it was, but to those aboard it was important. Perhaps somebody will care to read it. At least maybe my children will be interested, but then I forget, as did my father, they also will probably be fighting—fighting for something they can't quite express, but are fighting for anyway.

The story begins in Portland, England, May 26, 1944. We arrived there early in the morning, and when dawn broke I saw assembling a sea of ships. I knew then the invasion wasn't far away. Days, perhaps weeks, but not months. No longer were the rehearsals going on. This was in deadly earnest. The transports and smaller landing craft were all assembled, getting ready, and although nobody said so, everybody knew this was it.

That same night we had the first taste of war. Ju-88s roared overhead and bombs fell, mixed with mines. Nothing very dangerous, but nevertheless, we knew at long last we—who had never seen war before—had arrived. Hitler was playing for deadly stakes now and his chances were running out. We all returned to our bunks a little uneasy, but I soon fell asleep. The next morning sweepers rapidly cleared the mines, but everybody wondered whether or not they had done a complete job. We soon found out. Our motor whaleboat, returning from the shore, passed over a spot, and not five seconds later, the water rose fifty feet in the air.

The days dragged on; aboard ships a selected few began reading secret publications which told the story—a story people had been wondering the answer to for some years: where and how the landings would be made. Days dragged past, and finally May 30 the ship was sealed. Now a few more officers had access to the secret operational orders. I was among the lucky few, and I began reading pages of information with an enthusiasm I had never shown for any college work, or even a Nero Wolfe mystery. What planning—pages of plans worked out right down to the last detail. Corrections were still arriving daily by dispatch, but in general, the plan was complete.

Three groups were to hit the French coast: two American groups and one large English outfit. We made up the middle group, and were called by the unromantic title Assault Force "O," or Oboe. [This group's landing area was Omaha Beach.] Assault Force O was made up of all types of ships, from lowly landing craft to mighty battleships and transports. Battleships, cruisers, and destroyers made up the screening and bombardment group. It was in the latter that we took our place. Plans called for us to close the beaches forty minutes before H-hour, and to fire at previously designated targets before the troops landed. We were to close within one or two miles of the beaches, well within the range of the coastal guns lining the entire area.

Very interesting, I thought, my heart pounding with increasing speed. And what, may I ask, are the Germans doing while we are slowly pounding their beaches into dirt? I decided somebody must have figured that out also, so read further. "Probably enemy opposition." "The enemy has several fortified strong points along the beaches which will make some trouble."

"Yes, yes, Howes, read on," I told myself. "You're in this now." This description of the enemy defenses was complete. Casement guns, 75-millimeter and bigger—in fact, much bigger. Very interesting, and yours truly was going to be within two miles of said guns even before the troops arrived. There was some brief mention of air bombardment, but I didn't have much faith in that.

Cold sweat began to break out on my faithful brow, but I read on. "Mines! Mines will without doubt be encountered but must be passed on the down wind side." All well and good if you can see the damn things. "The enemy probably will use submarines, E-boats, and all air strength to defeat the landings." Without doubt, I reasoned; after all, he must have a few planes left.

By now I figured I would be swimming shortly after dawn on D-Day, but then I would be lucky to be able to

112

Aerial view of the destroyer *Baldwin*, taken in March 1944. (*Navy photo in the National Archives: 80-G-426227*)

swim. Then I came to the sentence which ended all sentences: "The assault must be pressed without retreat, regardless of the cost or consequences." So we were expendable!

I continued reading the more technical details of the operation, the vast plans for communication and radar operations. Gunfire support organization, and shore-fire control party dope, but behind it all remained the sentence, which I recorded to read, "The assault must be pressed without retreat, regardless of what happens to anybody." How could I possibly get out of this mess alive? Of course, the planes would soften up those casement guns, but the chances of staying afloat seemed remote.

The following day I was less worried and began to stop worrying about being sunk, and studied the plans with vigor.

Finally, June 4 arrived. We expected to sail that afternoon, with D-Day to be the next morning. We wrote last letters, and everybody began wondering just what would happen to us. The crew heard the captain [Lieutenant Commander Edgar S. Powell] read an order of the day from several Allied chiefs, and were told where they were going. Suddenly, postponement was announced. For one day.

The next afternoon we finally got under way. Every-

body not on watch was topside, taking what might be a last look at the hills of England. People were exchanging addresses with each other on the chance one might live to tell the other's family what happened. I gave my address to Jack Page, the communication officer, who lives in Massachusetts, and also to Tom Atwood, a machinist's mate, who lives in Barnstable. One of them, I hoped, would be able to tell my family how it happened, if it did. But naturally, it couldn't, I kept telling myself. Not to me, Old Doc Howes, that happy-go-lucky yachtsman who could hold his own with any racing man, the little boy who had gone to Avon for four years and emerged a grown-up lad of eighteen, only to go through three years of further education before entering the navy.

During that late afternoon, as I watched the shore of England disappear, I thought of the things I had gotten from life, and the things I knew were to come. True, I had had a lot of fun. College and school had been fun, and since I had gotten out of college—at least up until this afternoon—life had been rosy. I was proud, in a way, that I was going to be part of this great adventure, but nevertheless, I knew I had a lot to discover in life. I had been in love, but never married. There was something I had to live for. Maybe I should have gotten married; well, it was too late to worry now.

General Dwight Eisenhower speaks to the crew of the *Baldwin* during a visit at Belfast Lough, Northern Ireland, in May 1944. At left is Commander William J. Marshall, Commander, Destroyer Division 36; the *Baldwin* was his flagship. In the center is Rear Admiral Morton Deyo, commander of the heavy bombardment force for Utah Beach. (*Courtesy Lieutenant Davis C. Howes*)

The ship went to general quarters at sunset, and the long night was on. We were on the way to France. The same France from which the English had retreated four years ago. The same France from which Napoleon and Hitler had tried to invade England. History was being made over again this night, and I was part of it. Exciting thought, but one which failed to keep me from feeling nervous. The hours crept slowly by as we crossed the Channel. One o'clock, two o'clock, and finally three o'clock, and still no news that the Germans knew we were en route. Five o'clock, and we were starting in toward the beach through the mine fields. Mine fields which were supposed to be swept, but were they? I rather doubted it.

Ahead of us the sky glowed as the planes bombed the beaches again and again. Keep it up, boys, I thought to myself. Nearer and nearer the beach we crept, the speed of our advance even too slow to record on the pit log. Yet we were moving nearer and nearer, for on the radar scope, which all of us in CIC [combat

information center] watched anxiously, the land grew plainer, until it finally looked entirely too close. We had nearly arrived. It was now about one hour before H-hour. At H-40 we were due to open fire. The next twenty minutes were terrible as we edged a few yards closer before opening fire.

Then at H-50 somebody fired. Then we began, and soon everybody was firing. We had been one of the first ships to fire on French soil in our area! Now if we only lived to tell about it. Minutes passed, shells were bursting somewhere, and we in CIC couldn't tell how close they were. All seemed to be too close for comfort. Suddenly the true state of affairs came to us. The firing was our own ships firing around us. Actually, the bridge finally reported, very few shells were being fired from the beach, and most of those at the larger ships. We continued firing, and still no opposition. Where was the mighty German air force, the shore batteries whose positions we had plotted on the chart in front of us? Surely there must be some opposition!

Then it happened. Number one gun was set afire by a small hit. Our motor whaleboat was smashed by another shell. Bang, bang, we fired a couple of rapid salvos. The battery that had fired on us was out of action and we soon had the fire out, and were okay, except for the loss of the boat.

By then it was H-hour, and the troops began to hit the beaches. It was astonishing. Almost no opposition. Apparently, the shore batteries were put out of action by the heavy bombardment. Anyway, in our area it looked quite easy. Offshore of us, ships of all types filled the area. From where we were, nothing could be seen of the horizon but ships. In close to the beaches, out five miles, the area was filled with landing craft of every type. Every time we moved ahead or astern, we ran into some type of craft. Overhead, not a single enemy plane was in sight, while fighters flew in constant vigilance. We were completely protected overhead. The much-talked-of German air force didn't get anywhere near us on D-Day.

As the morning dragged on, we sat almost motionless, firing only when a shore battery opened fire on our ships or the beaches. This was D-Day—the Day that was to have been living hell. The troops weren't having it too easy on the beaches, but as far as the navy was concerned, it was a picnic so far. Everybody kept wondering how long it would be before the Germans started a counterattack. Surely the air force must be on the way, but it never appeared. During the afternoon the sun came out, and we relaxed a little, but gun crews kept right at their stations, for we were entirely too near the enemy to take any vacation.

Just before sunset we established radio communication with our shore-fire control party, and the second phase of our work began. They reported no targets, and we stood by for them to call us. As dusk settled over the area, one shore battery up on a high cliff began firing at three destroyers near us. Everybody started firing at the enemy, and soon even the battleships offshore had joined in. For a few minutes shells were going toward the beach at a rapid pace, then a shower of sparks filled the air, and black smoke bellowed up. We must have hit an ammunition dump, for the batteries stopped firing. Shortly afterwards the entire area burst into flame, and we believe the battery was destroyed.

So ended D-Day, a day I will never forget. Successful—at least I thought so, and further developments sustained my guess.

With the end of D-Day came the Germans. It wasn't a very heavy raid, but it was our first raid, and we wondered how much it would develop. All the ships in the assault area began firing, and the barrage was overwhelming. Two German planes were shot down that we could see, and I heard later more were destroyed down the beach. One plane passed very low over the ship, but the captain withheld the order to fire, feeling a shooting ship made a better target. The plane passed over so low we could nearly touch it, and the machine-gun crews were screaming for permission to commence firing, but the captain kept his decision.

Throughout the early morning of June 7, I kept on calling our fire-control party. Finally, shortly after the raid was over—0330—they started calling us. I was half asleep on the deck behind the plotting table, but woke instantly and switched on the transmitter. "Mike-Charlie-Mike! This is Dog-Love-Baker! Go ahead, over," I whispered into the transmitter. Instantly, the receiver began designating a target for us to fire artillery support at. In a few seconds, the ship was alerted, and the guns began swinging toward the target. We fired two ranging salvos, then fired rapid fire as designated by the shore-fire control party. "Target destroyed, mission completed," came back from the tired men on the beach. We relaxed again until they might need the support of our guns again.

With dawn, all the shore-fire control parties for all the support ships began calling for fire, and all along the line ships began firing. [Rear] Admiral [Carleton] Bryant [commander of the bombardment group for Omaha] started urging the ships to fire only at targets of designation rather than targets of opportunity, because yesterday we had been firing too much on our own troops. Throughout the day we kept calling our fire-control party by radio in hopes of getting more targets, but despite the fact we had two parties, we fired only a few times during the day.

Finally, late in the afternoon, I switched over on the common fire-support frequency. I heard a party calling for someone to support them. We promptly offered

our guns and within a few minutes were firing shells into German positions. They also gave us a "mission completed," and we relaxed again. It was a very easy day, for we only fired a few times, but the ship remained at general quarters because we never knew when we would have to fire.

The second night was about like the first where we were, but out in the screen it was hot. Shortly after midnight we received the red air-raid signal, and soon a few German bombers were overhead. Out in the screen they hit one of our newest-type destroyers [the USS *Meredith*, hit by a radio-controlled glide bomb], and she sunk the next morning. We started making smoke to protect the transports near us, but the raid was over before it ever developed into anything worth worrying about.

With the dawn, peace and quiet settled over the area. We could see the unloading going on steadily on the beaches, but hardly a gun was being fired except when a fire-control party requested support. We fired a few times during the day, and toward the end of the afternoon were ordered to report out to the screen for

General Eisenhower and Lieutenant Commander Edgar Powell, the *Baldwin*'s commanding officer, pass between two rows of crew members during a ceremonial inspection on the ship's port side. (*Courtesy Lieutenant Davis C. Howes*)

the night. Our magazines were two-thirds empty, and fresh ships moved in to give fire support.

The screen was where the hottest action had taken place to date, and we wondered whether or not tonight would be as hot as usual. We took our station on the Dixie Line just before dusk and waited for action. I stood in CIC with the same old gang of people, everyone very tired from having lived there for three days. What would tonight bring? I rather expected something, and it wasn't long in coming. The radar operator reported several small targets coming around the point from Cherbourg. We knew our forces weren't operating in that area, so we tracked the targets in deadly earnest, watching them grow nearer by the minute. I reported the targets to the screen commander by radio, and he shouted, "Open up, Baldy, let them have it."

We illuminated with star shells, then shifted into rapid fire. The 5-inch guns began firing like 40-millimeter machine guns, for the crew knew they were firing to save their own necks. Five-inch shells were flying toward the target like rain. We watched the scope with anxious expectation. Would the little E-boats press the attack? Generally, when fired on, they ran, but now Germany was being pressed to the wall. Would they sacrifice all in a last gallant attempt to hold the Atlantic Wall? Once through the screen, they could do a lot of damage, but would they get through? There was a blinding flash, and then the targets began to turn and retreated at rapid speed.

The squadron commander credited us and another destroyer with sinking one E-boat. Whether we did or not makes little difference. The main thing was that the German navy had turned around and headed home. Still afraid to fight, once discovered—unlike the American PT navy which had fought against battleships and destroyers throughout the Pacific. I lost all my respect for the German navy right then and there. Any navy that wouldn't fight, even against odds, would never drive us away from France.

"Only one hundred rounds of flashless powder left," the gunnery officer reported from control. That wasn't good. If we had to fire flash powder, we wouldn't be able to see very well, besides making a better target for the enemy. I wondered how many more German E-boat attacks we would have that night.

"Enemy destroyers!" The rusty voice of Captain [Harry] Sanders [Commander Destroyer Squadron Eighteen, the screen commander] spoke without emotion over the radio. Never did he sound excited. Enemy planes dropping bombs, enemy E-boats, enemy destroyers—they never bothered him. I didn't feel so calm. Here we were, low on ammunition and nearly out of flashless powder, faced with a possible destroyer attack. Shortly afterwards, we picked up the same targets the squadron commander had been watching and began tracking them. Three of them, all big targets, coming in from the north, headed straight for the screen. Everybody was talking into the radio, reporting courses and speeds, ranges and bearings. I stood where I could handle both radio transmitters, and watch the plot and scope, all at once. I was our mouthpiece and had to assume an outward calm, which I certainly lacked within. The three targets drew closer until finally Captain Sanders designated which target should be engaged by whom.

We waited with mixed emotions. It would be exciting to fight a duel with a German destroyer, but we were rather low on ammunition, so it didn't seem very healthy. The squad dog [Captain Sanders] must have been aware of that, for he assigned three other destroyers to engage: "Sidney, that one looks about right for you on the left." Sidney promptly rogered, probably not too happy about it. "Charlie, you take the one in the middle, and Fred, you tackle the boy on the right." We relaxed a bit, for at least we wouldn't be in the initial action. All this time Captain Sanders was keeping the cruisers behind us informed of conditions on the screen. I rather imagine them moving out in hopes of getting a few shots in also.

For about five minutes we waited for the word that would start the three destroyers out to engage, and then the letdown: "Those three targets are three friends, three LSTs." Captain Sanders still spoke without emotion, although he had just discovered in time what otherwise would have been a fatal accident. I leaned weakly against the bulkhead for a second, then hurriedly rogered the message. It was nearly dawn now and everybody suddenly seemed tired; at least I know all of us in CIC were dead.

Shortly after morning twilight we headed for England. The ship secured from general quarters, and I crawled into my bunk for a few minutes' sleep before we reached what now seemed almost like home. We reached Plymouth the next morning, and for the first time I felt like relaxing. Once inside the nets guarding the harbor, I felt as secure as in Portland, Maine. The fact that German planes might raid the town never worried me. At least we were away from the war for a few happy hours.

English sailors climbed aboard to help us load fresh ammunition, much to the astonishment of our crew, who never had much respect for the English. I headed toward our navy base in Plymouth and found out what it was like to be a minor hero. We were one of the first ships back from "over there," and the few people I talked to wanted to know all about the invasion. "Was it a success?" "How many ships had been sunk?" They flooded me with questions, most of which I didn't know the answers to.

At dawn the following morning we sailed again for France. We all felt rested now, and almost anxious to return, for fear we might miss something. We had proved we could slug it out with the best of them, and loaded with fresh ammunition, we wanted to go E-boat hunting. Would we get a chance? Tonight should tell, for we were returning to the now-famous Dixie Line. Vacation was over, but somehow it had been long enough. Everybody was again keyed for action.

EDITOR'S NOTE: *Howes wrote this account soon after experiencing the events described. It is presented virtually as he inscribed it.*

DAVIS CROWELL HOWES (1922–) graduated from Brown University, Providence, Rhode Island, and was commissioned an ensign in October 1943 after completing the Naval ROTC program there. He spent approximately two years in the destroyer *Baldwin*, primarily as a CIC officer. The ship provided shore-bombardment support to the forces landing at Omaha Beach and later took part in the invasion of southern France. Following the surrender of Germany, the *Baldwin* was en route to participate in the invasion of Japan when the war ended. Mr. Howes received his LL.B. degree from Boston University in 1950. He was recalled to active duty during the Korean War, during which time he was assigned to the Office of Naval Intelligence in Washington, D.C. When the war ended, he returned to civilian life and rejoined the firm of Prescott, Bullard & McLeod in New Bedford, Massachusetts, for which he continues to practice law to this day. In 1964 Mr. Howes officially retired from the Naval Reserve with the rank of lieutenant. In 1993 he completed his fiftieth year of Naval Institute membership and became a Golden Life Member. Mr. Howes lives in South Dartmouth, Massachusetts. (*Courtesy Lieutenant Davis C. Howes*)

In the wake of the first day's landings, American forces settled into a pattern of providing massive reinforcements to sustain and enlarge the toehold accomplished on June 6. That meant fighting off air attacks and bringing more and more men, equipment, and supplies to the beachhead. It was not an easy chore, even in the absence of significant German naval opposition. What the Germans had done was sow mines, and those mines wreaked havoc. Here are two dramatic stories of ships sunk by mines. In one case the narrator merely abandoned ship and went about his business. In the other, the victim suffered such massive injuries that his life was forever changed by the instant when a mine's explosion hurled his ship into the air.

SHIPWRECKED IN THE CHANNEL

By Lieutenant General Orwin C. Talbott, U.S. Army (Retired)

As the invasion of France approached in the spring of 1944, I was a captain serving as a rifle company commander in the 90th Infantry Division. Until about May 20 we were training in the Midlands area of England, on the extreme western edge, right up against the Welsh border. Some friends in a nearby town invited me for breakfast one Sunday morning, and I was due to have a rare treat—three real eggs. We had been used to eating canned powdered eggs. At ten o'clock Saturday night the camp was closed, and before dawn Sunday morning we were gone. No eggs.

We moved down to southern Wales, to the little town of Abergavenny, and stayed there until it was time to board the ship for France. While we were there—perhaps about May 25—I was briefed on the invasion by the captain serving as battalion intelligence officer. His setup was in a large squad tent, surrounded by three bands of barbed wire, with a guard at the entrance to the outer band and a guard outside the inner band.

When I went in for my explanation of the plans, the intelligence briefer had a large map of Europe posted inside his heavily protected tent. He asked me to show him where I thought the invasion would be. I put my finger on the exact spot on the Normandy coast. Of course, he was stunned. How had I learned that? He was almost ready to throw me into chains. As a matter of fact, it was pretty easy. And if it was that easy for me, it should have been for the Germans also. Why they didn't figure it out, I don't know to this day. We had the last large dress rehearsal at Slapton Sands, on the south coast of England, near Torquay. If you look at the beaches there, right behind them is a marshy area. So we just looked from Cherbourg all the way around to Pas-de-Calais, and the only place we could find that was similar was what became Utah Beach. And that's exactly where we went.

After dark one evening we went by train down to Cardiff. The 4th Infantry Division was slated to invade Utah Beach, but the division commander wanted an extra regiment in reserve so he could commit all three of the regular regiments in his division to offensive missions. So my regiment, the 359th Combat Team, was attached to the 4th Division. The 1st and 3rd battalions landed about 10:30 on the morning of D-Day. It was basically an unopposed landing—certainly in comparison with Omaha Beach, which was a bloody mess. The fighting at Omaha was done by the 1st Infantry Division, which I commanded years later in Vietnam.

The 2d Battalion, which I was in, was the reserve battalion of the regiment. As such, we were loaded aboard the navy transport *Susan B. Anthony* on June 3 and moved to an anchorage in the Bristol Channel, which divides Wales from southwest England. In the terminology of those days, it was a "pre-loaded buildup." In other words, we got on board before D-Day, but we were to land after the assault. During the waiting period on board I befriended the ship's communication officer and got my first acquaintance with radar, something I hadn't even heard about previously. It was interesting to be able to see blips on the screen and realize that they were airplanes flying in the vicinity of London.

The ship got under way shortly before midnight on the fifth, then headed west, went around Land's End, and then east into the English Channel. As the *Susan B. Anthony* steamed slowly along, we briefed the troops of our battalion on what the mission would be. We had a foam rubber mock-up of Utah Beach, made from a series of reconnaissance photos taken just above water level. This rubber map was perhaps six feet by four feet, and it depicted the beach at low tide. When the briefing was over, this map was just an impediment, so the battalion executive officer and I rolled it up and wrapped it in brown paper and mailed it in the ship's post office. We wanted it to go back to Texas to be saved along with the memorabilia of the 90th Division that had been preserved from World War I.

I have a clear memory of the morning of the following day, June 6. We were sailing eastward along

For most of her life she was a civilian passenger liner, launched in 1930 as the SS *Santa Clara* of the Grace Steamship Company. She was commissioned as the navy transport *Susan B. Anthony* in September 1942 and soon took part in the invasion of North Africa. (*Navy photo in the National Archives: 80-G-176124*)

the south coast of England, in sight of land off in the distance. Three army transports were steaming in company with the *Susan B. Anthony*, and we had seven Royal Navy ships as escorts. As we got opposite Normandy, but still along the south coast of England, I was struck by the amount of air traffic. There was one path going to France, and one path coming back, and each was a steady stream. I made the comment at the time, "There are so many planes up there, you could walk from England to the Continent." It was so crowded at any one moment that it was almost dangerous. This thing was being refed all the time, sort of like a bicycle chain going around endlessly.

For a day, the ship had been dawdling around off the beach until it came our time to go ashore. On the morning of June 7, we got up and looked over at the coast of France. My company of soldiers was berthed in the assault quarters, on the bridge deck level. We were the only army unit that high up in the ship. Everybody else was below, and most of them were down in the hold. Since we were on the highest deck, we had an excellent vantage point. We were off Omaha Beach, where we could see shells from naval guns hitting against the cliffs in back of the beach. The ships offshore were firing against German fortifications.

Because we were about to go ashore, our troops were all fully clothed, wearing backpacks, and carrying their arms. A few minutes before eight o'clock I was in our company's quarters, leaning against a bunk, when the *Susan B. Anthony* hit a mine. My impression was that there were two separate explosions, very close together. I also have the most distinct memory of being thrown straight up in the air, coming down and landing on my knees, being thrown up in the air again, then coming down again on my face. After that, everybody piled on top of me with guns and everything else.

After a moment of shocked silence, the air was filled with the sound of loud chatter. While still down on the deck, I hollered, "At ease." Everybody quieted down and became calm. We didn't know yet what had caused the explosion, but everybody knew immediately that we were in trouble. Even so, the discipline took over totally. I was very proud of how well they responded. As soon as I could make my way through the mess of soldiers around me, I went over to the starboard side of the ship and opened a door out onto the deck. I looked out and saw that there was a huge solid mass of dirty water coming down. It had been thrown up by the explosion. I had the impression at the time that it had gone over the ship and was coming down on the other side. It was very black, very dirty.

About six weeks after D-Day a service magazine called *Yank* came out with the news that the *Susan B.*

Anthony had been sunk. It quoted a Canadian officer who had been in a nearby ship as saying that the blast had been so great that he'd been able to see other ships underneath the keel of our transport. I'm skeptical, because it looked to me as if there would have been too much water in the way for him to see what he reported.

We had a few bruises, but the only man seriously hurt was an individual with a broken leg. He had been coming back from the head and had the misfortune to be stepping through a watertight door just as the explosion rocked the ship. Down in the hold areas many soldiers had been badly injured when heavy timbers forming the hatch covers had been dislodged by the blast and thrown down onto the men. Miraculously, not one of the more than twenty-three hundred troops on board was killed.

Because our quarters were in the superstructure, it was obvious that we were in the best position of any unit in terms of evacuation from the ship, so I just held them right there. Of course, we hardly had any problem with being rescued because there were some six thousand ships and craft of all kinds in sight. I remember going out on the starboard side and aft down to the well-deck area to make a check on the troops there. By that time the stern had settled so far down that I had to grab the lines rigged around as handholds in heavy weather. I used those to help me get back to the ladder that took me to the superstructure deck where my men were waiting. We were directed to go to abandon-ship stations.

Around nine o'clock the British frigate *Narbrough* came alongside to starboard to begin evacuating passengers. She was soon joined by an American LCI and the frigate HMS *Rupert*. I told my men to leave behind all the crew-served weapons—machine guns and mortars—but take all the rifles, pistols, and personal arms with them, as well as their backpacks and so on. Debarkation nets made of pieces of line woven into a grid pattern were suspended over the side of the ship. These were designed for soldiers to climb down and into the landing craft that would take them ashore in an amphibious operation. Now we were using them to go down the side of the ship, but not into landing craft. I joined the rest of my men in climbing down and onto the deck of the *Narbrough*. Even though I was leaving a sinking ship, I managed to be rescued without even getting my feet wet.

Remember, there had been a heavy storm shortly before that delayed the invasion. As a result, we encountered heavy wave action when we were going down the side of the transport. The frigate was bouncing up and down while we were making the transfer over from that debark net. Sailors on the frigate were holding the net to make it easier for men to climb down, but one time the wave action was so great that the sailors lost hold of the net and it slapped back against the side of the frigate. As our battalion chaplain was coming down the net, the frigate bounced back up and went past him, so he was now below where he wanted to be instead of above. Fortunately, he didn't bang against the side of the ship. Otherwise, he would have been mincemeat. When he came back up, about a dozen of us reached out to grab him and practically threw him on the deck because we didn't want it to happen to him again.

As we pulled away about 9:40, we looked back at the *Susan B. Anthony* and saw about two hundred men still on board, mostly sailors. They were gathered around the hatch area forward of the bridge, and the bow was beginning to come out of the water. It occurred to me that the only way those men would get off the ship would be to jump. They did just that, according to the action report written later by the captain of the *Susan B. Anthony*. He reported that everyone was rescued. The captain went into the water about ten o'clock, and the ship disappeared from view completely at 10:10. By that time, I was headed away and didn't see her go under. Among the things that went to the bottom with the *Susan B. Anthony* was that rubber relief map of Utah Beach that we had tried to mail to Texas.

The *Narbrough* was nearly identical to a U.S. *Buckley*-class destroyer escort, lacking only torpedo tubes. We were interested to note from a plaque on the bulkhead that she had been built in the United States the year before and was transferred to Britain as part of the Lend-Lease program. So a U.S. Navy transport got me halfway across the English Channel, and it took the Royal Navy to get me the rest of the way. The hospitality was great. The British crew began serving our troops tea and hot chocolate right off the bat. I went up to the open bridge and met the captain, who was a lieutenant commander in the Royal Navy Reserve. Also on the bridge were Brigadier General Sam Williams, assistant commander of the 90th Division, and his aide. The captain of the ship invited us to go down to the wardroom to eat. When I got there, someone set an open bottle of Johnnie Walker whiskey in front of me, but at that hour of the morning I wasn't inclined at all.

Back on the bridge after that we said we wanted to go to Utah Beach, and the ship's skipper said he didn't know where it was. Over our regular uniforms, everybody in our division wore a two-piece fatigue-type uniform that had been impregnated to make it relatively gas proof. The uniform had big side pockets in it, and I had in one of those pockets our invasion maps, which I had wrapped in plastic and brought along. So I hauled out my map and showed this British captain where Utah Beach was. Since he didn't have any charts, he used the army maps to take us where we wanted to go.

When we got near the beach, he communicated with the *Ancon*, the command ship for Rear Admiral John

C-47s fly low over the invasion force while returning from a raid against France. (*Coast Guard photo in National Archives: 26-G-2406*)

Hall. The staff on board arranged for three LCVPs to be sent over to take us ashore from the frigate. None of the sailors manning these LCVPs had been ashore yet during the course of the operation. They weren't going

to the right opening in the beach obstacles, so I pointed this out to the coxswain. We got to the beach and went ashore with no opposition whatsoever. That's when I finally got my feet wet.

On Utah Beach I saw no resupply or anything else going on at that point. I was stunned, because I thought it would be as busy as a beehive, trying to get some buildup before anything bad happened. My initial task was to make a count of the individuals in the company who had come ashore. I had been quite proud of myself, because I thought I had brought my entire company with me on to the *Narbrough*. When I got ashore, however, I found that I had about eighty people—only half the company. Without my realizing it, the other half had gone on to the *Rupert*, which was outboard of us during the rescue from the *Susan B. Anthony*, and the *Rupert* had gone back to England instead of taking those soldiers on to France. So it was two weeks before I got all of my company back together. I wasn't nearly as smart as I thought I was.

As we started out from the shore, I went into a German pillbox that General Williams was using as a temporary command post. He told me to report in to the headquarters of the 4th Division since we had lost equipment and our men were widely scattered. So we marched in about three-quarters of a mile to the road that paralleled the beaches, inland from the marshes. In a little apple orchard there, I found the headquarters with about five people in it. It was close to noon

View of the *Susan B. Anthony* shortly before she sank off Utah Beach on June 7. (*Courtesy Lieutenant General Orwin C. Talbott*)

Gliders from the Ninth Air Force clutter fields in France after landing as part of the support force for the invasion. C-47 tow planes fly overhead. (*U.S. Air Force: 51618 AC*)

when I was directed to the château that served as headquarters for Major General J. Lawton Collins, Commander of VII Corps. He wasn't there, but when I went in I saw Rear Admiral Don Moon, who had commanded the task force for Utah Beach. He was in a chair, leaning back against the wall, sound asleep. It was unfair of me to think this, but I concluded, "No wonder there's nothing happening on the beaches; the commander's asleep."

After that I went back to my company, and we joined up with the 359th Regiment. I had gotten the location from headquarters of the 4th Division; we were about where our outfit was supposed to operate, but not quite. I had a chance to look around and saw some of the effects of the airborne part of the D-Day operation. I saw a fair number of soldiers whose parachutes hadn't opened after they had jumped out of the transport planes. Of course, that was the end of it for them. Their

bodies were still lying on the ground more than a day after the drop that took place in the early hours of June 6.

A lot of gliders were sitting around in those fields. The second field in which our company was placed—this was probably on the eighth—was a large one, and it must have looked attractive to the pilots trying to find a safe place to set their gliders down at night. Unfortunately, running diagonally across the field was a telephone line held up by reinforced concrete poles. I remember seeing a plywood glider that had hit one of those poles and shattered; you can imagine what happened to the people inside. Later, I saw an American glider that had brought in a small bulldozer. It was so heavy that no troops had been on board—only the dozer, pilot, and copilot. The glider landed right into the corner of a hedgerow. Then the dozer broke loose and went forward, crushing the pilot and copilot. It was pretty messy.

On June 10 we began to marshal, getting together more people and more equipment. I was about to embark on the first combat experience of my life. I remember being in a large field surrounded by hedgerows. When the German machine guns started shooting at us, the lead seemed to be coming at us from all directions, although I'm sure it wasn't. I had a wonderful weapons platoon sergeant with me, Abe Jamail. He had a rifle that could shoot hand grenades—the advantage being that it could shoot them a lot farther than they could be thrown by hand. He was able to silence both machine-gun positions. The sergeant wound up losing a leg about July 7. By that time, he had won two Distinguished Service Crosses, which, of course, is phenomenal.

A day after that machine-gun action, we got into a couple of skirmishes, and another day later we got into a real mess. Having a company that was understrength and short of weapons was not helpful. The field was kind of level, and then there was a line of trees, beyond which there was a vertical drop of four or five feet down to a stream. The Germans were down by the stream, and my men were by the trees. I was just walking back and forth; I was actually in full view but didn't think too much about it. A German bullet hit one of our soldiers, killing him instantly, then it went on through the helmet, out the back side, and hit me in the leg. It wasn't all that serious, because I can't even find the scar now, nearly fifty years later. But that one bullet gave me a quick education in combat survival; it taught me to be more careful about where I was walking when in close proximity to the enemy.

ORWIN CLARK TALBOTT (1918–) was in the ROTC program at the University of California at Berkeley while majoring in political science and history. He was commissioned a second lieutenant in the California National Guard in March 1941 and commissioned in the regular army in February 1942. He served for the remainder of the war as a member of the 90th Infantry Division, rising from platoon leader to battalion commander. In the 1950s he went to Washington to attend the National War College and later served as senior aide and executive officer to the Chief of Staff of the army; executive officer to the Chairman of the Joint Chiefs of Staff; and as executive officer to NATO's Supreme Allied Commander Europe. After a series of assignments in the United States, General Talbott reported to Vietnam in 1968, first as Assistant Division Commander and later as Division Commander of the First Infantry Division. Later assignments included service as Commander of the U.S. Army Infantry School and as Deputy Commanding General of the U.S. Army Training and Doctrine Command. He retired from the army in 1975 to become full-time director of the Maryland Historical Trust. He lives in Annapolis, Maryland. (*Courtesy Lieutenant General Orwin C. Talbott*)

BROKEN SHIP, BROKEN BODY

By William D. Branstrator

When the minesweeper *Tide* went to Normandy, I was a motor machinist's mate second class, and that included a good deal of practical experience. For instance, I had worked on race-car engines and later had been a coal-shoveling fireman on a steam locomotive for the Pennsylvania Railroad at the beginning of the war. After I joined the navy and completed boot camp, that railroad experience probably was a factor in my being assigned to the ship. I was part of the crew when she went into commission in May 1943. I was, naturally enough, assigned to the engine room. After a while I got so I could tell by the sound whether an engine was running right. When a bolt needed to be tightened, I knew which wrench to reach for without looking to read the numbers on it.

As for the mission of the ship as a whole, all I knew was what I heard. One of the things I was told was that Montgomery and Eisenhower got into quite an argu-ment over our size. Montgomery thought we were too big to do the job. He wanted the little British wooden minesweepers to go in and clear the channels. Eisen-hower told him that our ship and her sisters—all with steel hulls—were built for this purpose. They were the latest ships available for sweeping mines. They had more electronic gear than anything in other navies built for minesweeping. Our sonar and radar were the latest that the navy could put on a ship. We had a lot of electrical generating capacity to supply the power for all of our equipment. We had diesel engines and diesel generators.

Even before we went to France, we had a lot of convoy duty in the Atlantic and Mediterranean. We had an experienced crew, and we knew what we were doing. During the time before the invasion, we spent time in England, exercising with the British and sweep-ing the English Channel to get rid of as many mines as we could. We tore up quite a bit of minesweeping gear

The *Tide* is shown at the time of her commissioning in May 1943. Her antiaircraft gunnery was beefed up before she went to Normandy a year later. (*Courtesy Ted Dietz*)

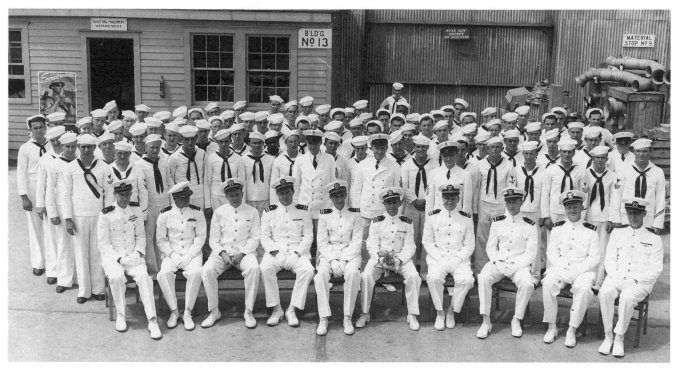

The first crew of the *Tide* poses at the time the ship was commissioned. Many of these men were killed when the ship set off a German mine at Normandy. One who escaped that unhappy fate was Electrician's Mate Ted Dietz, third from right in the third row. Chronic seasickness got him transferred off the ship before D-Day. (*Courtesy Ted Dietz*)

when it got tangled with ships that had been sunk and were resting on the bottom.

On the morning of June 7, D+1, the *Tide* was doing some sweeping off the beach at Normandy. She finished that job, and the crew brought the sweep gear back aboard. A breeze from offshore was blowing the ship toward the beach. There was a motor machinist's mate named David Spencer who worked with me; he was the ship's oil king, which meant he kept track of how much fuel we had and in which tanks. A little before 9:30 he called me up from the engine room. I was down there logging the engine hours, the amount of diesel fuel we had used during the past few days, and the amount of fresh water available. I was putting this together so I could report to the engineering officer.

Spencer came over to the trunk leading to the engine room and hollered down for me to come up and see the planes that were taking a load of paratroopers into Normandy. When I came up to the engine room trunk door, my life jacket was lying there, so I just grabbed it and stuck it on, and went on up the ladder. In one direction we saw the C-47s heading toward France, and coming back the other way were empty ones with only a tether trailing behind to show where the troops had jumped out.

After I got up on deck, I sat down on a seat that folded down from the bulkhead on the port side. It was right by the door to the trunk to go back down to the

engine room. I was in the middle of the seat, with a fellow sitting on each side of me. Another man was sitting on the rail. The chief engineer was standing underneath a gun tub, which was right above us. There was another gun tub forward, and in between them was a ladder that was just wide enough so that a man could get up to the guns. I happened to be sitting right where this ladder was.

Spencer had gone to the mess deck and picked up a box of K rations. He came back out and was standing near me opening up that box. I said to him, "I've wasted enough time looking at this. I've got to go down and top off the freshwater tanks so I can get this report in to the engineering officer."

He said, "Branny, you've been down below decks long enough. I've been able to come and go." He handed me the K ration box and said, "Take this and open it and give the guys the cigarettes and cheese out of it. Whoever wants the candy bar can have it. I'll go down and top off your water tanks."

So I said, "Okay." I tore the box of rations open, and I handed the can of cheese in there to a chief motor machinist's mate named John Quigley. He opened the can and cut off a piece for the fellow sitting on my left side. Then I leaned forward with my elbows on my knees to reach the piece of cheese that he was cutting off for me. Just at that moment, the *Tide* detonated a German mine.

According to a report from men on board nearby ships, the *Tide* lifted completely out of the water—rising up maybe five feet in the air—from the force of the explosion. This was not just a boat; the *Tide* was 220 feet long and displaced more than a thousand tons. A chief petty officer who was near me came up underneath that gun tub and smashed his head on the bottom of it. The fellow by the rail was blown clear out into the water. The men on either side of me went up into the underside of the gun tubs. All of these men were killed except the one blown over the side. None of us had helmets.

I went up into the air like a rocket, over the gun tub, and lit back on the depth-charge rack on the fantail. When I hit, I did the splits. My right leg bent back under me. I broke my back over the edge of a K-gun used for launching the small depth charges. There was a big gear around a winch that pulled our minesweeping equipment in. I guess when I fell backward, the big teeth on that gear mashed my skull in. That's where it would have helped to have a helmet on when the mine exploded. I think the life jacket is what kept me from breaking my neck.

From where I had been sitting to where I was when I regained consciousness on the fantail was about thirty feet. I cleared the 20-millimeter gun tub that was just aft of me, a 40-millimeter mount, and this winch. I probably went about twenty feet up into the air, though it's hard to say. I was conscious when I went by the gun tubs because they appeared to me at the time just like a sheet of gray. I must have passed out when I hit the depth-charge rack.

When I came to again, the ship's carpenter, a shipfitter first class named Elmer Schmidt, looked down at me and said, "Are you all right, Bill?"

I said, "Well, yeah, I am, but my leg hurts me so. Just straighten my leg out."

He looked, and he said, "Hell, you don't have any leg from the knee down, Bill."

I said, "Yeah, I do, because it's up under me here by my hand." My left arm was broken, but I could feel my foot with my hand. Smitty straightened my leg out, and that caused me to pass out again. When I recovered the next time, I was coughing because the explosion had set off the smoke pots on the railing on each side of the fantail. These were the things we used for making smoke screens. We were all gasping for air and choking.

People were hollering, "Abandon ship! Abandon ship!"

I felt someone holding onto the collar of my life jacket, and it was Motor Machinist's Mate Second Class Harry Turner, a kid that worked for me in the engine room. He was pleading with anyone who would listen, "Take Branny. Take Branny." He and some helpers dragged me over to the port side of the ship where a PT boat had pulled up alongside. I don't think I would have made it off the ship if it hadn't been for that kid.

The boat alongside was the *PT-504*, commanded by John Bulkeley; he was the guy who saved my bacon at Normandy. Some men dragged me across from the *Tide* over onto the PT boat. The minesweeper was sinking fast; by then she was far enough down in the water so that they didn't have to lower me to get me over to the PT. They practically slid me across. In one place, where the force of the explosion had been the worst, the deck was rolled back like you'd stick a key into a sardine can to wind the lid off.

Bulkeley was standing on the starboard side of the PT, right by the cockpit where the controls were. He

With the *Tide* mortally wounded, a PT boat stands by at left and the minesweeper *Pheasant* at right. (*Navy photo in the National Archives: 80-G-651677*)

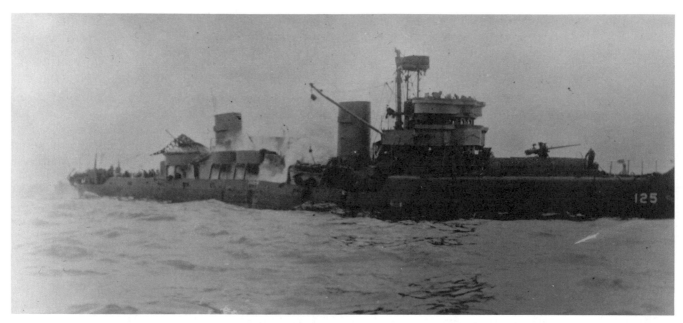

A close-up of the shattered *Tide*, smoking amidships shortly before sinking off Utah Beach. (*Navy photo in the National Archives: 80-G-651676*)

had a megaphone, the type that cheerleaders use. He was hollering orders, telling people to move the injured fellows who showed some signs of life. I was put in a position so that my feet were pointing toward the bow and my head aft. In fact, my head was lying right near Bulkeley's feet. He was standing half a deck down in the cockpit. When the PT boat was just getting ready to pull away from the minesweeper, he looked down at me and said, "Are you going to make it, son?"

I said, "Yeah, if I just had a cigarette." At that time, of course, I was still smoking. Nearly everybody did then.

He had just lit a cigarette himself. He took the cigarette out of his mouth and put it down in mine. I took a couple of drags off that cigarette. Then the PT pulled away, raising up the bow and my feet. I passed out again when that happened.

The boat took us to the *LST-282*, which had been converted to a small hospital ship. Inside the tank deck there were bunks mounted on the bulkheads. When the PT came alongside, I was in a sort of metal basket, a Stokes stretcher made of a frame with a wire mesh on it. The LST's boat davit picked up the stretcher and lifted me up toward the deck. Two guys with lines were supposed to keep them taut so the stretcher wouldn't sway around while the ship was rolling. Unfortunately, they didn't do their jobs too well, because I swung out and banged into the side of the ship a couple of times. That woke me up again.

I wound up down in the tank deck, and one of my shipmates came up to me. It was a black man from the *Tide*, a hell of a nice fellow. He said, "Mr. Bill, are you going to make it?"

I said, "I hope so."

He said, "Here, I've got some pears for you." He had a tablespoon, and he spooned half of a pear into my mouth. I asked him about some of my other shipmates. Some of them were in the LST with us. I remembered the man who was cutting off the piece of cheese when we blew, and asked, "What about Quigley?"

"Nobody's seen Quigley." I asked about a couple of others, and he hadn't seen them either. (One of them I didn't see again until a few years ago when I ran into him at a ship's reunion in New York. He was Boatswain's Mate Second Class Walter Smith, the man who had been sitting on the rail of the *Tide* and was blown into the water by the explosion.)

The LST took us over to England, and when we got there, some corpsmen picked up my stretcher in the tank deck and carried it over to the big bow doors at the front of the ship. I had been passing in and out of consciousness during this whole period, and I must have been out when I was carried. Hearing the LST's anchor chain go rumbling out and the engines backing revived me again. I probably wasn't completely awake, because I got the idea that the LST was sinking too, and I had to drag myself off. With my one good arm, I was trying to drag my body. They corralled me back onto the stretcher and said, "Where are you going, and what are you doing?" I told them I thought the LST had just been hit too. That's when they explained to me that we were safe in England.

About this time I realized that I didn't have stitch one of clothes on. So I asked one of the pharmacist's mates about it, and he said, "Oh, we cut your clothes off of you. You're torn up from one end to the other."

I said, "I know, but I had something in my shirt pocket. That's the only thing I've got in this world besides these dog tags."

He said, "What did you have in your shirt pocket that's that important?"

I said, "Well, I think there's two twenty-dollar bills and a picture of my wife."

He said, "Well, they'd be all water-soaked and everything."

I said, "Oh, no. I had two rubbers—one one way and one the other way—and had them tied. It was waterproofed."

He said, "There's a ton of clothes back there, stacked from the deck clear to the overhead. They just took them off and threw them in a pile." I asked him to go look anyway. I don't know how long he was gone, but when he came back, he said, "Here, slide this under your arm." And he gave me my picture and my money. So I came off the LST with only that and my dog tags.

When I got into a hospital and the doctors had a chance to look me over and X-ray me and so forth, they found out just what kind of shape I was in. My skull was fractured above where the collar on the life jacket had been. My back was broken in two places lower down. My left arm was broken. Both knees were dislocated. Both legs were broken—nine places altogether. Both heel bones were jammed up into the ankle joints. I had a hole in my side and a hole in my head.

The mine exploded on the port side of the ship, right at the break of the deck between the forecastle and the main deck. Down below the crew's quarters was a magazine for 3-inch ammunition. Those projectiles blew up, and so did the Hedgehog antisubmarine rockets on the bow. The forward ammunition magazine blew also. Some of the depth charges may have gone up too, but I'm sure we didn't explode every depth charge we had on board. If we had, I don't think they would have left any pieces big enough to recognize as parts of a ship.

I think being called up that trunk to look at the C-47s carrying the paratroopers probably saved my life, because most of the men down in that engine room were killed. You just never know when sitting or standing in one place instead of another is going to make such a difference.

WILLIAM DAYTON BRANSTRATOR (1921–) enlisted in the navy in November 1942 and underwent recruit training at Great Lakes, Illinois. He was in the commissioning crew of the USS *Tide* and served on board until the ship was sunk at Normandy in June 1944. He was evacuated to England, where he received army medical treatment for his multiple injuries. In October of that year he was sent to the United States for continuing hospitalization, then was discharged from the navy in February 1946. After that, he returned to his home state of Indiana for treatment by the Veterans Administration. One leg did not respond to treatment and was amputated in 1947. In subsequent years he has received continuing care for the disabling injuries that resulted from the mining of the *Tide*. In all, he has been hospitalized for a total of more than thirteen years and has undergone fifty-four operations. He has been unable to work since his return to civilian life. Mr. Branstrator's wife, Maxine, died in 1983. Their only child, a son named William, was born in late June 1944. Mr. Branstrator now divides his time between Fort Wayne, Indiana, and St. Petersburg, Florida, accessible to Veterans Administration hospitals in both places. (*Courtesy William D. Branstrator*)

A truly little-known aspect of Normandy is the role of merchant shipping. The soldiers and cargo moved across the Atlantic in dozens and dozens of troopships and merchant vessels. Then it was a matter of getting those men and materials to the beachhead and moving them ashore. In the case of the Liberty ships, smaller craft did the unloading and moved the cargo to the beach. In other cases, ships such as LSTs and LCTs loaded the cargo in England and moved it across to land directly on the French beaches. Such was the range of the tides that these amphibious craft deliberately beached at high tide, then waited for the water to recede so they could off-load directly onto the shore.

GETTING THE TROOPS 'OVER THERE'

By John L. Horton

A heavy shroud of fog enveloped our convoy as we headed toward Europe with a load of more than two thousand soldiers destined to take part in the invasion. The curtain of mist was so thick that at times we could not see the ships ahead, astern, or to either side. On board a ship not equipped with radar, we were dependent for station-keeping in convoy on a fifteen-foot-long piece of wood towed by the ship ahead. It had a plow-like device at the front end to kick up a plume of water that we could see from our bridge. We tried to keep it right alongside; if we lost it, we were in trouble.

Our ship was the U.S. Army transport *Excelsior*, headed from Boston to the British Isles, and we in the crew were part of the civil service. We were civilian mariners, licensed by the Coast Guard and employed by the Army Transportation Corps; we were not union men. In fact, that was part of the appeal of working for the army; the civil service people were highly disciplined types. Passenger ship duty was the top of the pecking order in merchant ships, compared with break-bulk cargo ships, tankers, and so forth.

I had received my officer training in 1942 in the fifth class at the U.S. Maritime Training School, located at the Coast Guard Academy in New London, Connecticut. I had the required sea duty on the Great Lakes to qualify for entrance. The coming of war—and the heavy losses of ships—created such a great need for merchant officers that many able-bodied seamen from the lakes were recruited for third mate ocean licenses. We prospective officers were treated with some respect because the construction of new tonnage and the heavy losses in the Battle of the Atlantic—on the merchant run to Russia, as well as off our East Coast—demanded trained replacements. Later, after getting my third mate's license, I was assigned to the U.S. Army port of embarkation at New York for a berth on board a troopship.

While in New York I had seen a high degree of patriotism on the part of the citizens. I remember in particular a period of several weeks when the "Star-Spangled Banner" was periodically played on the music systems in restaurants, and everyone would dutifully stand up. It became so bad, they finally had to stop playing it because people couldn't carry on business.

The troopship *Excelsior*. (*Courtesy Mel Lizotte*)

On May 11, 1944, while I was on standby duty at the Brooklyn Army Base, I received hurry-up orders to take a train from Grand Central Station in New York to Boston so I could sign on the *Excelsior* as second mate. I had a high priority for transportation because the ship was set to sail. Though I didn't know it at the time, the invasion of France was less than a month away, and the *Excelsior* was to play an important part.

Sharing a first-class room with me on the train was a navy commander returning from leave; he was the captain of the *Susan B. Anthony*. She was a former commercial passenger ship that had been converted to a navy transport and radar command ship and would also be carrying troops in the coming invasion. The captain had been in the crew of the ship when she was the SS *Santa Clara* of the Grace Steamship Company. He was also a Naval Reserve officer, so when the navy took the ship, it took him too by calling him to active naval duty. He and the ship were part of the nation's vast mobilization for war. He was the only person I could talk to during the train trip because we had been warned to be extremely security conscious as we were on a special mission. We took to heart the motto, "Loose lips sink ships."

The departure from Boston was at six o'clock on the morning of May 13. We left in fog, a precursor of the conditions we would encounter during the upcoming voyage. Since the *Excelsior* didn't have radar, the *Susan B. Anthony* kept us in position on the way to rendezvous with the New York main body of the convoy. We had eight ships coming out of Boston and joined up with about forty out of New York. We were a fast troop convoy, traveling at fifteen knots. The normal steaming formation had a thousand yards between columns of ships and seven hundred yards or less between ships in each column.

On the occasions when the fog cleared enough to let us see the scope of the convoy, it was impressive: twelve columns wide with four ships per column. (Most columns had four ships; a few had five.) Troopships were up front, followed by tankers. The escort commander was in the old cruiser *Marblehead*, which had been mauled by the Japanese early in the war. One small aircraft carrier was along, but only to transport planes, not to provide protection.

The *Excelsior* carried a navy gun crew to help defend the ship in case we encountered enemy submarines or aircraft during the course of the operation. Altogether, the ship had eight 20-millimeters, four 3-inch guns, and one 5-inch. Actually, we had little contact with the navy contingent because they had their jobs to do and we had ours. An exception was that merchant crew members were assigned to assist the navy gun crews during alerts.

With so many men on board the ship, water was a scarce commodity, available during three half-hour periods per day. Two of those three came during my daily bridge watches. But my life was actually quite comfortable compared with those of the soldiers down below. I had a nice stateroom, outfitted with woodwork, a closet, a desk, and stainless steel light fixtures. Down below, the troops were crowded into berthing spaces made in what had been the ship's cargo holds. Bunks were stacked four high. In some places they went higher than that, but the army finally halted the high stacking because men were injured falling out of bunks.

It was crowded down there, and the air was so-so. The lavatory facilities were tight, particularly when men had diarrhea. The army medical people made frequent patrols to clean off handrails with antiseptic solutions as one means of preventing soldiers from passing along germs to their shipmates.

The army contingent ran the ship's hospital and coordinated troop activities. They also controlled the cleanup of troop quarters. The merchant marine crew operated the ship—bridge watches, lookouts, engineering watches, and so forth. There was no way we could supply services to two thousand men. The army also ran its own galley to bake bread and feed the troops. At night, for example, ten or twelve GIs would cook bacon, throw it in tubs, then heat it up early the next morning and serve it. There were so many men on board that the army provided only two meals a day. The chow lines seemed almost continuous.

The trip across the Atlantic, being in late spring, was calm compared with winter North Atlantic weather. But the troops were still seasick. I think some of them became seasick right at the dock, as soon as they came aboard. A lot of the men tried to stay up on deck because they felt better up there. No wonder, because when you were down in those crowded compartments, the collection of human smells—including sweat, diarrhea, and vomit—made the situation much worse.

Army MPs had to keep men from congregating on the stairways leading to troop quarters. Some of the soldiers were uneasy staying below. They wanted to play cards and sleep on the stairways so they could get out if something happened to the ship. I don't know what difference it would have made, because if the ship was hit, your chances were slim. The water on the North Atlantic run is so cold that thirty minutes is about as long as one can live—unless by chance the ship is south in the Gulf Stream flow to England.

Without question, the soldiers on board experienced a lot of stress. In the America of that day, some of them had never been on a train before joining the army. Now they were put in a claustrophobic situation in the totally unfamiliar environment of a ship, which was like a small floating city. While at sea they faced the possibility every minute of being torpedoed by a U-boat. When they reached the end of their journey,

These soldiers are on board a troop transport bound for the invasion of Sicily in 1943, but the crowded conditions were doubtless the same as on the ships headed for England and Normandy a year later. (*Navy photo in the National Archives: 80-G-86312*)

they were expected to step ashore and confront German soldiers.

Because of the submarine threat, everyone had to be up before dawn, no matter when his watch was. That was a crucial time, because the submarine skipper could get on the dark side of the formation, with the convoy ships silhouetted against the light in the east. The reverse was true in the evening, as dusk fell. We had army men stationed topside as extra lookouts trying to spot submarines.

As we neared the eastern end of our transit, we went around the northern end of Ireland to try to minimize the likelihood of submarine contacts. On May 22 the convoy broke up into two long columns that stretched from horizon to horizon. We had been running blacked out across the Atlantic. In the heavily congested Irish Sea we showed running lights to avoid collisions while unescorted. We reached the port of Liverpool, England, on May 23 and began the period of waiting for the invasion itself. One of our merchant mariners was a British man who had come from Liverpool and was especially eager to get ashore to be with his wife and the four-year-old son he had never seen. He had shipped out early in the war and was only now getting home.

I found Liverpool to be a grim, dirty place because of all the beating it had taken from German bombing in the preceding years. I walked down the middle of one street that was lined with burned-out buildings.

Alcoholic beverages were in short supply in England. About the only thing I found in my wanderings was Scotch, because the English people couldn't afford it. Beer was available only from 6:00 to 9:30 P.M. There was little to do because the movies closed early, and at night the blackouts turned Liverpool into a ghost town. A few times I went into hotel lobbies but discovered that I was not welcome to sit and relax because I wasn't registered.

As May ended we went to Milford Haven in Wales, then to Bristol at the eastern end of the Bristol Channel. We had beautiful weather, and I was able to look down from the bridge on the soldiers on deck below as we steamed. The chaplain was holding a different service every twenty or thirty minutes at any location where soldiers assembled. He had a full schedule, he told me, when we had a chance to talk. He'd have a Jewish service when a group of Jewish soldiers gathered. Another time it was a group of Catholics. At other times it would be different types of Protestants. He did it all day long, and there were so many requests that he had to assign some services to his assistants. He had a portable organ that either he or a GI played for services. The troops were getting their religion, and we could see it all from the bridge. I suppose I spent a bit of time contemplating my own

mortality as well, but fortunately, I was too busy most of the time to dwell on it.

On the last day of May we prepared the *Excelsior* for the invasion. Two of the 20-millimeter guns were moved to a better firing position. We ran a hawser the length of the ship so that landing craft could tie up to it. Debarkation nets were rigged on the sides to facilitate unloading. Ship identification numbers were secured under the flying bridge so the ship could be located by the landing craft due to take our load of soldiers ashore. On June 1 our sight-seeing trips ended. We were restricted to the ship until it was time for the invasion.

On June 5 the soldiers practiced climbing down landing nets rigged for them between decks. This was preparation for leaving the ship once we arrived off France. That evening we shifted to an anchorage at Swansea Bay. As we arrived, four transports, including the *Susan B. Anthony*, left with an escort of destroyers. On the morning of June 6 we heard the initial reports that the invasion had begun in the Bay of the Seine River, off Normandy. We had some tense moments as we listened to the accounts coming in over the radio. The radio was hooked into the loudspeaker system so that the reports went throughout the ship. But at least the uncertainty was over. Everyone on board the *Excelsior* seemed glad the operation had finally started.

At eight o'clock on the evening of the sixth we left Swansea in company with four other transports and headed for the English Channel. Down below, the troop officers opened their sealed orders and briefed the men on the job they were to do. I had noticed a change in mood among the soldiers. Their leaders were more abrupt and snappish than they had been earlier. In fact, apprehension had mounted at various stages in our journey: when we left Boston initially; when the escorts left us upon our arrival in Ireland; and now as we reached the English Channel and joined up with the massive traffic of the invasion force.

Everybody was getting jittery, including the escorts. One destroyer dropped three depth charges about a mile from the *Excelsior* and, because of the shoal water, set up a concussion that blew out the fires in our boilers. We had to drop back for a while as the engineers relighted them. The entire time we were in English waters the ship was cold, because the steam lines for heating had been turned off to minimize the danger of escaping steam and confusion if the ship was hit. One time I walked into the boiler room alleyway just to warm up. That was the only place we had heat.

Flares illuminated us overhead on the night of the seventh, and then we anchored off Utah Beach at Normandy early on the morning of June 8. We saw hundreds of landing craft on the water, as well as the bow of a destroyer that had been damaged by a mine. On the beach I could see a steel landing craft broken in two and turned over on its deck. Dozens of planes were overhead providing cover, and a couple of battleships were pouring shells inland at the supposedly impregnable German defenses. As we watched the shells land, we could see eruptions of dirt falling from the cliffs near the town of Sainte-Mère-Église. Late in the morning, we were placed in tandem between the battleship *Nevada* and the cruiser *Quincy* as we sailed along Utah Beach. Their guns silenced the German armament in the cliffs. We were in such close formation, I could look down on their decks. I wondered that the water depth could accommodate such large ships.

The *Excelsior* anchored and began unloading troops at noon. We had two debarkation stations on the port side of the transport, and in less than two hours the navy's landing craft had completed the entire process of unloading more than two thousand soldiers and landing them ashore. It was practically a parade. As soon as one landing craft was filled, another would move in and take its place. At any time, two were alongside and two more were waiting.

In the afternoon, after the battleships left for another mission, the Germans took aim at us. Shells from shore batteries straddled us at times, and that was rather uncomfortable. Any time you take a straddle,

you know the next one might be it, but they never hit us. The destroyers with us had a lot of nerve; they kept peppering away at the beach. At times the German shells fell right off their bows.

At one point I watched a plane head for us, but luckily it crashed about eight hundred feet from our ship and only about seventy-five feet from another ship at anchor. Our skipper wanted to move out, but he had to wait for orders from the navy, which wanted all the outgoing ships to depart together. We finally got under way about 4:30 in the afternoon, joined the escort, and began steaming toward the Bristol Channel and to safety from beach attacks, but not German E-boats. As we worked our way out through the swept channel, our skipper went below to eat. He had been up all night and all day, but he didn't get much chance to rest, because I soon had to call him back to help out. The traffic was congested and out of control because of a strong cross current, and we also faced the hazard of mines. Eventually, we got clear.

Our initial mission, begun weeks before in Boston, was at last over. We had landed our first contingent of army men "over there" in France. Now we had another mission as we headed for Belfast to load General George Patton's soldiers and return to the beachhead.

JOHN LOUIS HORTON (1914–) is a career merchant mariner who has sailed and managed a fleet of Great Lakes vessels. He holds an unlimited ocean master's license with first class pilot endorsement for the Great Lakes. He was awarded the Admiral Hallert Shepheard Award by the American Bureau of Shipping; received a public service commendation from the U.S. Coast Guard; and won the Cameron Award from the National Safety Council for his innovations and promotion of ship safety in the merchant marine. He is a past vice president of the Society of Naval Architects and Marine Engineers. Mr. Horton served in World War II as a deck officer in the U.S. Army Transportation Corps hospital ships *Acadia*, *Seminole*, and *Larkspur*, and the troopships *Excelsior*, *Henry T. Gibbons*, and *General R. E. Callan*. Mr. Horton retired from Great Lakes shipping in 1981. He now researches French/American and Great Lakes history at Cleveland State University. His French/American Endowed Library Fund supports the history department's annual Great Lakes Prize for scholarly essays concerning the French and the Great Lakes. Mr. Horton lives in Rocky River, Ohio. (*Courtesy John L. Horton*)

SUB-ORDINARY SEAMAN

By Richard A. Freed

In 1942 I was called up for the draft, but I was rejected as a 4-F because of a childhood injury in which I was badly burned and suffered a deformed foot. I went to work as a shipyard inspector for the War Shipping Administration. In the fall of 1943 I was trying to get into the Canadian air force when I got a call from my brother Frank, who was stationed at Quonset Point, Rhode Island. He told me of the demand for crews for merchant ships. Because of the heavy casualties in the early years of the war, the merchant marine was undermanned. To alleviate the shortage of experienced men, the merchant marine had established stations that provided a two-month training program before sending men to sea. I applied for the training.

In March 1944, while I was waiting for a response to my application, Frank called again and said he knew of a Liberty ship, the SS *Oliver Wolcott*, that was short-handed. I told him I was willing, so I went down to a Coast Guard office the next day to be sworn in. The lieutenant in charge said he'd never heard of anybody going right to sea without any training. Fortunately, a chief yeoman was there, and he explained to the lieutenant that if the master of the ship was willing to take me under his wing as a sort of protégé, then it

would be legal. The lieutenant agreed, and off I went. My official rating was ordinary seaman, but I was so inexperienced that I would have been classified as a "sub-ordinary seaman" if there had been such a category. In such a situation, however, one learns quickly.

The ship sailed from the navy construction battalion (Seabee) base at Davisville, Rhode Island. We loaded up with supplies and went to New York City. There we took aboard four of the Coast Guard's eighty-three-foot search-and-rescue boats. They were lashed down to the deck so they wouldn't be carried away in heavy seas. The carpenters built walkways between them so we could get forward and aft on the ship. The boats hampered us in several ways, including making the ship a bit top-heavy and interfering with forward visibility from the bridge. But this was wartime, and there was a mission to be accomplished.

The *Oliver Wolcott* left for England in the middle of the night. That was the safest time, because the German U-boats used to lie outside Sandy Hook, waiting for convoys so they could pick off the tail-end ships. By leaving at night and running at darkened ship, we hoped to get past the danger area without being spotted. As we made our way to sea, the night was cold and windy, and snow was falling. At the time, I

The Liberty ship *Oliver Wolcott* rides high in the water in March 1944, soon after completion. (*Courtesy William Hultgren*)

Seamen work on the deck of a Liberty ship carrying a load of Sherman tanks to England. In the ship's hold is still more cargo for the British Isles. Topside members of the navy armed guard man 20-millimeter antiaircraft guns. (*Painting by navy combat artist Dwight C. Shepler*)

concluded that I must have been crazy to leave a nice warm home and shoreside job for this. My sense of discomfort was reinforced when the first job I was assigned that night was to go up to the bow and be a lookout.

Soon we settled into a routine of watches for crossing the Atlantic. The engineers, of course, stood their watches down below in the engine room and boiler room. The on-deck portion of a watch included an officer, two able seamen, and one ordinary seaman from the ship's crew. We also had members of the navy armed guard manning the guns, doing signaling, and serving as lookouts. A watch lasted for four hours, and I was on a routine that had me on duty from four o'clock to eight o'clock, morning and evening. I liked that watch, because you got to see the sun rise and the sun set. I normally spent about a third of each watch steering the ship. I didn't have any experience, but I picked it up quickly.

The Liberty ship was constructed for wartime conditions: designed to be built quickly, in large numbers, and to provide basic transportation. The wheelhouse on the bridge was an example of the fairly primitive setup on board. It was a rectangular room with three windows straight ahead of the helmsman. Under convoy conditions, this didn't provide enough visibility, because you couldn't see the ships around you. So we were always in danger of running into some of the other ships we were steaming with.

Since it was such a bad design, there was a flying bridge above the wheelhouse, but the disadvantage was that the officer and helmsman on watch were right out in the weather. Thankfully, the carpenters in the *Oliver Wolcott* built a protective house on the flying bridge. It wasn't heated, but at least it kept the officer and helmsman dry. During a North Atlantic run, the weather could be brutal. The crossing through the northern iceberg lanes was cold, and the seas were heavy. In a way the heavy weather provided some protection against submarines because it was difficult for them to operate.

Time went by quickly during that voyage. When we weren't on watch, we were sleeping, eating, playing cards, or chatting with our shipmates. The only time we took our clothes off was to take a shower, and then we put them back on right away. The Atlantic had been really perilous because of U-boats, although by March of 1944 the tide had begun to turn in our favor. Even so, I kept my life jacket close at hand almost all the time. The crossing took something like seventeen days. We made it safely to Milford Haven, Wales. It was beautiful to see land after all that time at sea—especially for someone making his first trip. The ship's cargo was quickly unloaded.

Security was a big concern during this period, because it was apparent that the invasion would take place shortly. What we didn't know was the location—possibly France, Norway, or even Russia. We were cautioned against sending home letters that told where we were. All the letters were opened, read, and marked "passed by censor." Or they might be sent to naval intelligence if anyone wrote something suspicious. We were also warned that we would be punished for keeping diaries. We swabbies didn't know that much about what was going on anyway. Only the higher-ups kept the diaries and wrote books about them afterward.

Shortly after the ship arrived in England, we left and formed into another convoy. We started heading up the Irish Sea, and I thought we were going home. Instead, we went to Glasgow, Scotland. The *Oliver Wolcott* went into a dry dock there so she could be converted from a straight cargo ship into a troopship. The shipyard workers cleaned out number four and five holds and put in bunks for 450 men. They installed portable toilets out on deck and a mess in which the soldiers could eat. Then they sent all of us, particularly the merchant seamen who had no experience in gunnery, to training schools for the 5-inch, 3-inch, and 20-millimeter guns. I can't say that we were very good at it, but we did the best we could.

After that we spent most of the month of May in the Orkney Islands, north of Scotland. We were so far north that we had only about two hours of night time out of twenty-four. We spent the time at anchor, presumably to keep us out of the way and keep a lid on security. We weren't allowed to go ashore. We weren't allowed to leave the ship, except for some rowing practice. There was even some question whether to take one kid ashore when he developed appendicitis. He was taken away, and that was the last we ever saw of him.

In late May we went to Cardiff, Wales, and loaded an artillery regiment of the 29th Infantry Division. We took on artillery shells, ammunition wagons, Jeeps, and howitzers. Then came the 450 men the ship had the capacity for. You talk about being crowded; they were everywhere—elbow to elbow. On June 4 we got

A Liberty ship uses one of her booms to off-load an army truck onto a rhino barge alongside. (*Navy photo in the National Archives: 80-G-252696*)

The Liberty ship *Charles Morgan* was near Freed's ship when she caught a German bomb aft and settled to the bottom of the English Channel. (*Navy photo in the National Archives: 80-G-252655*)

under way as part of a convoy of perhaps sixty or seventy ships, with a naval escort of maybe ten or twelve. We were held up a day because of bad weather and then arrived off Omaha Beach on the morning of June 6. The *Oliver Wolcott* was about six thousand yards offshore. The men and equipment on board the ship were supposed to be ashore an hour and a half after the initial landing, but the opposition was so strong that it was about forty-eight hours before we could get everyone ashore and the ship unloaded.

When we did do our unloading, the ship was so close to the shore that we had a clear view of what was happening on Omaha Beach. It was absolutely devastating—something I'll never forget. There were at least three thousand dead and wounded on that beach—all young men. There were bodies floating in and out. The noise was frightful—I can't really describe it—between the ships firing on shore and the planes bombing just inland. There were also special landing craft equipped with rockets, and they made a terrible noise.

The Liberty ship *Charles Morgan* was off to our starboard, and the Germans dropped a bomb into her number-five hold. Like us, she had about 450 troops on board. Thank God, about half of them had already left the ship, but she still had a tremendous number of casualties. She sank in about thirty feet of water. Coast Guard search-and-rescue boats of the type we had carried across the Atlantic went over to the *Charles Morgan* and helped take off a number of the troops.

Because of the need for our cargo of artillery equipment, the unloading continued day and night. It was difficult at night with only some dim blue lights to see by. We had nine seamen in the deck crew, and we had to do most of the unloading ourselves, with the ship's booms handling cargo nets that were lowered to landing craft alongside. We did receive a lot of help from troops on board. I was lucky enough to work on the winches, which I knew something about from my experience in shipyard construction before joining the merchant marine.

In the middle of the unloading one night, a raid of four or five German planes came down. We were told not to leave our posts—just keep unloading. We did so in the near-darkness. We could see firing in the distance: tracer bullets going up. In the midst of the raid, one of the German planes evidently strafed us. I didn't realize it until I heard the shells pinging around me. Even though we weren't supposed to leave our places, I went and hid under one of the winches until the planes went by. I figured I was no good to the ship if I was dead.

Richard A. Freed

In the foreground a Liberty ship lies partially sunk as the ships around it put up a crisscross pattern of tracer fire in their attempts to shoot down attacking German planes. (*Coast Guard photo in National Archives: 26-G-2565*)

RICHARD ANTHONY FREED (1924–) is one of five brothers, all of whom were in the U.S. armed services during World War II. During the war Mr. Freed was on overseas duty with the merchant marine for twenty-three months, serving in the North Atlantic, Europe, the Mediterranean, and the Pacific. After his service in the *Oliver Wolcott*, he was on board the Liberty ship *Abbot L. Mills* when she hit a mine in the Adriatic and had to be abandoned. He was repatriated from Dubrovnik, Yugoslavia, in January 1946 and discharged. Mr. Freed was awarded two British Stars, the Defense Medal and War Medal, the French *Médaille de la France Libéré*, and the Philippine Liberation Medal and Unit Citation. He also holds three U.S. War Shipping Administration combat ribbons and three theater of operation ribbons. After the war Mr. Freed earned a B.S. degree in business administration from Bryant College, Providence, Rhode Island, and worked for Texaco, Inc., until 1959. He recently retired from Johnson's Fuel Service as founder and chairman of the board. He has been married since 1948 to the former Alice Livesey. They have eight children and nineteen grandchildren. Mr. and Mrs. Freed spend most of their time at their home in Naples, Florida. (*Courtesy Richard A. Freed*)

LIBERTY SHIP SIGNALMAN

By Cornelius A. "Pete" Burke

Before reporting to the navy armed guard on board the Liberty ship *William Tyler Page*, I had been assigned as a signalman on the communication staffs of convoy commodores. The navy needed so many officers for wartime operations that it had recalled a lot of retired old-timers, and many of them were in charge of these convoys. The first one I sailed with was Captain Selah Montrose La Bounty, who had graduated from the Naval Academy in 1908. The second one was Commander Walter S. Carrington, Annapolis, 1916. So these were no young fellows. La Bounty was nearly sixty at the time. The first convoys I rode went between Key West, Florida, and Norfolk, Virginia. Later runs went to New York, Trinidad, Galveston, North Africa, and Sicily. Altogether, I was in twenty-one ships with the two commodores.

In March of 1944 I went aboard the *William Tyler Page* in New York as she prepared to go across to

Members of the navy armed guard man a 20-millimeter antiaircraft gun as a North Atlantic convoy plods toward Great Britain. Burke, a signalman, was part of the armed guard contingent on board the *William Tyler Page*. (*Painting by navy combat artist Dwight C. Shepler*)

England. The officer in charge of our naval armed guard for the ship was a reserve officer, Lieutenant Gordon Webber. When I first met him, we were riding in a cab to join the ship, and I gave him the same story I told everybody else. It was a little snow job on my convoy service. I was proud of all that I had been through, and I probably exaggerated a little bit in the process. I told him about sailing with Captain La Bounty and Commander Carrington and said these guys I was sailing with now were ninety-day wonders. I could tell by Webber's reaction that he wasn't buying any of this. Later I figured out why: in civilian life he had been a scriptwriter for NBC radio. I said to myself, "Christ, he's been bullshitted by experts!"

On April 15 we shipped out of New York and began our voyage across the Atlantic in a convoy of perhaps forty-five ships. That crossing was no big deal; when you've seen one sea, you've seen them all. My job involved the visual signaling. When the commodore wanted to maneuver the ships, he would send signals out by flaghoist. Typically, he would be in the center ship in the front row. His signalman ran up a flaghoist command, and then it was relayed to the rest of the convoy. The signal went sideways to the other ships in the front row and then aft down all the columns. When the flaghoist was hauled down on the commodore's ship, that was the moment of execution for the order. Any other individual message within the convoy would be sent by flashing light.

In our armed guard setup on board the Liberty ship, the gun crews slept in a berthing compartment at the after end of the superstructure. The signalmen slept amidships in quarters on the main deck. All of us ate together, so we had a lot of contact with our shipmates. The merchant marine crew members had their own mess. But when you weren't on watch, what the hell, there was no place else to go, so you got friendly with everybody—both navy and merchant seamen. It was like living in a rooming house.

Sometimes the navy men in the armed guard would ask me if it bothered me that the merchant seamen were making a lot more money than we were for serving in the same ship on the same trip. I was a

This line of Liberty ships was sunk off Omaha Beach to create the Gooseberry breakwater to shelter the landing area. (*Navy photo in the National Archives: 80-G-46818*)

signalman second class, and I said, "Look, pal, I get paid for the stripes that I've got on my sleeve. Regardless of where I go, that's the story. So what the hell's the difference?" I'm sure that there was some friction in other ships, but that sort of thing didn't bother me. Who the hell ever heard of a rich sailor?

At the end of the crossing the *William Tyler Page* pulled in at Liverpool, where she discharged her cargo. One night when we were there, Lieutenant Webber came back to the ship and called in the signalmen and two or three gunner's mates. We didn't normally drink on board ship, but he broke out a bottle and said, "Here, fellows, let's all have a drink." That was a surprise. He was a nice guy, but not what you'd call a friend. Then he told us that this was a going-away party. He said, "I've been reassigned."

I'll never forget that I said to him, "Do you need a good signalman? How about letting me come along?"

He replied, "I wouldn't wish this assignment on my worst enemy." That was all there was to it. We had a couple of drinks, and he left. I didn't find out what the hell had happened to him until later. He had taken a skeleton crew on one of those old rust-bucket ships that was deliberately scuttled off one of the beaches at Normandy to form the artificial harbor to aid unloading. As soon as the ship was scuttled, a small craft went out and picked up the merchant marine crew of the ship. They said they were going to come back later to pick up the armed guard sailors, and it was later all right. They didn't come back for a week. These poor bastards were stuck out there with Germans shooting at them from one direction and Americans shooting over them from the other.

In 1957, when I was working at a fire station in Philadelphia, I picked up a paperback book called *The Far Shore*. I was looking to pass some time between fires, and I spotted this novel on the watch desk. Most of the books there were mystery stories or horror stories or whatever. When I glanced through this particular one, I saw a mention of the armed guard. I turned a few more pages and saw something about scuttling a ship. I wondered who wrote it, so I turned to the front, and there was Gordon Webber's name. I wrote to him in care of the publisher and had a letter back from him within a week. By then he was with an advertising firm in New York. He told me in a subsequent letter that he had based most of the story on his experiences after leaving the *William Tyler Page*, but one of his characters was drawn from a boatswain's mate in our ship.

During our time in England I spent a lot of my time drinking and with the local women. The English girls were a lot friendlier than the English men. Those of us in the navy weren't making as much as the merchant

Overview of the breakwater created by sinking Liberty ships offshore. (*U.S. Air Force*)

sailors, but we were still doing a lot better than the British servicemen. They didn't have any money to throw around. What money I had, I believed in putting into the British economy right away. Going back to my first runs in convoys, I never went to sea with more than two dollars. When we were traveling with one of the commodores, we had a young radio operator who didn't drink, didn't smoke, didn't do anything. We used to kid him, "Christ, Jamie, you're going to be the richest man in the life boat!" because the Germans were blowing up tankers galore at that stage of the war. I figured I didn't want to have any money in my pockets when I went over the side.

After Liverpool they sent us down to Avonmouth, where we took on the load of cargo that we carried across the English Channel to support the follow-up elements in the invasion. We had small-arms ammunition, mail, all different sizes of tires, engineers' gear, barbed wire, pieces for the Bailey bridges, chloride of lime for sanitation, and more. After leaving England

we went to the Isle of Wight, picked up some escorts, and proceeded on to Utah Beach. We arrived there in mid-June, just in time for that big storm that damn near wiped out the whole operation. That was a rip-roaring one. We had anchors out to both starboard and port, but we were still dragging.

One time we were trying to tie up an LST alongside our ship. We tried to use heavy mooring hawsers, and they snapped like string. We never did get her tied up; she wound up on the beach. While this was going on, I was hanging on the after end of our ship with one leg over the rail and a pair of semaphore flags in my hands. I was trying to exchange signals with a signalman on the bow of the LST. You talk about being on a yo-yo. I didn't think anything of it at the time. When you're in the midst of all this stuff, you're concentrating on what you're doing yourself. You don't have time to pick your nose and think about your surroundings, so you're practically oblivious to what the hell else is going on around you. Later on, when you have time to think about what you've been through, then it hits you.

My nephew asked me once if I was scared. I told him, "When your knees are knocking and your ass is sucking wind, buddy, you're scared." I remember one time when I really was frightened at the time things were going on. We received a message saying that a floating object, believed to be a mine, was headed toward the *William Tyler Page*. I put a pair of binoculars on it and saw that it was a big black thing with prongs sticking out all over it. It was evidently a moored mine that had broken loose in the storm. We were fortunate that it didn't hit us.

Around June 19, when it was still pretty rough because of the storm, some LSTs went past us on the way to the beach. Our ship was about half a mile or so off the shore. One of those ships, the *LST-523*, hit a mine and went up. Those poor bastards never had a chance. I was on the bridge with a lieutenant, and we watched one man hanging on the jagged end of the stern of the LST after she hit the mine. A wave would come over and toss the ship up. We were praying for the man to be able to hang on. Another wave came over, and he was still there. Finally, another wave came over, and he was gone. Our ship put a lifeboat over the side and picked up six or seven of those survivors.

Because of all the storm damage in the vicinity of the beachhead, there weren't many boats available to take our cargo ashore. The people running the beach were in bad shape also. The army sent a liaison officer out to the ship, and he was a nervous wreck. We had stuff on the ship that he needed on the beach, and he was eager to get it off. The problem was, how to do it? He had me send visual signals to the port director three or four times a day. The answer was always the same, "As soon as we have anything to put this stuff on, we'll send it out." Eventually, the merchant crew and the armed guard from the *William Tyler Page* unloaded the ship. They used the ship's booms to move things over the side and into lighters alongside.

Later, the army sent some DUKWs out, the amphibious trucks. You could put two sling loads into one of those, and that was all they could carry. I remember being on board a DUKW when the crew on deck was loading it with tires. I was in the DUKW helping to stow the cargo. When it was loaded, I climbed out and up a Jacob's ladder to get back aboard the ship. They went only about two hundred yards, and then the DUKW sank. The two soldiers were treading water, and tires were floating all over the place. The army had to send a small boat out to rescue the two crewmen from the DUKW. Some of the tires sank, and the rest floated around among all the rest of the stuff off the beach: dead bodies and everything else.

One night, about two or three weeks after we got to Normandy, the ship was still anchored off Utah Beach.

Captain Andy Lund, master of the Liberty ship, was an American citizen during World War II but Danish by birth. Here he uses a sextant on the bridge of the *William Tyler Page*. (*Courtesy Pete Burke*)

I was down in the mess hall playing cards. One of the sailors came down from topside and said to me, "Hey, Flags, they want you up on the bridge. There's signal rockets going off." I got up on the bridge, and, sure enough, I could see them. I hadn't seen this type of flare before, but I knew that they were used in convoys. A sort of mortar would fire them up into the air, and then they would float down on parachutes. A specific sequence of rockets would have some meaning that you could interpret by looking in the signal book. For example, the rockets might be used to signal an emergency change of course if the convoy was in danger. This time I saw red ones, green ones, and white ones, but there was no sequence to them; they were completely haphazard. All of a sudden I found out the answer. Somebody was celebrating the Fourth of July.

All these ships at anchor had barrage balloons attached to them by wires as protection against low-flying aircraft. One of the flares came down and landed on top of the balloon hooked to the *Thomas B. Robertson*, another Liberty ship. That was the flagship for the port director at Utah Beach, Commander Isaac

Boothby. I saw that barrage balloon burn up and thought, "It couldn't happen to a luckier guy, because he's the boss of the whole lashup." And I had another thought that showed what kind of progress we had made: "They were shooting real ammunition a few days ago; now they're playing with fireworks."

After we left Normandy we headed back to England and pulled into the port of Falmouth. For weeks we had avoided the hazards of the invasion beachhead, but then we had a problem with one of our own ships. This was after midnight, and I was in the sack. All of a sudden there was a big crash. I grabbed a life jacket and went out the hatchway. All I could see in the night was a shower of sparks. I knew we were in port, and I thought to myself, "Christ, we hit a mine."

The truth was that a British ship had crashed into us. The British ship was anchored with her starboard anchor. The port anchor was hanging out of the hawsepipe and just about touching the water. When we came along, we evidently just sort of brushed the other ship. That loose anchor bounced up on our deck amidships. It pulled back the bulwark of the *William Tyler Page* like it was opening up a can of sardines—all the way back to the gunners' headquarters.

The two ships were locked together, because the anchor from the British ship was embedded in our deck. Our skipper was an American citizen, but he was actually a Dane, another old-timer who had been brought back on duty. The Limey skipper was on his ship, and our skipper, Captain Andy Lund, was on the stern of ours. With their two accents—British and Danish—they were screaming at each other across the water like two motorists that had been in a fender bender. You're likely to see anything in wartime.

CORNELIUS ALOYSIUS BURKE (1917–) entered the navy in September 1941. After boot camp in Newport, Rhode Island, and communication school in San Diego, California, he served as a signalman on the communication staffs of convoy commodores La Bounty and Carrington in 1942–43. He was later assigned as a signalman to the Liberty ships *John B. Hood*, *William Tyler Page*, *George Popham*, and the Victory ship *Winchester*. He sailed to Sicily, North Africa, West Africa, England, Utah Beach, and North Russia. Burke was in southern France when Germany surrendered and in Samar, Philippine Islands, when Japan surrendered. He was discharged from the navy at Bainbridge, Maryland, in November 1945 and then was a member of the Naval Reserve from 1947 to 1955. After leaving the navy he was employed as a firefighter in the Philadelphia Fire Department for thirteen-and-a-half years. Later, he worked for the F. W. Woolworth Company as a department manager, retiring from that company in July 1979. Mr. Burke is active in veterans' events and maintains a voluminous correspondence with other armed guard members. He has lived since 1945 at 3456 Tilden Street in the East Falls section of Philadelphia. (*Courtesy Pete Burke*)

The LCVPs, as we have seen already, were the small workhorses at Normandy, moving thousands and thousands of soldiers from the large oceangoing transports to the invasion beaches. In between the LCVPs and the large transports in both size and function were the medium-size workhorses: LSTs, LCTs, and LCIs. Here are several stories on the exploits of such craft, along with the recollections of John Niedermair, the naval architect who devised the tank landing ship.

In today's world, helicopters and air-cushion vehicles have added great sophistication to the ship-to-shore movement, enabling troops to vault over the shoreline or perhaps to hover over it while moving inland. No such luxuries were available in 1944. Landing craft had to put their bows onto the beaches, drop ramps, and let men and vehicles go ashore. LSTs were essential to the success of one landing after another in World War II. Here are several stories of their contribution to the success at Normandy, including a description of the way in which shipboard crews were drawn from the populace of America and turned into fighting men. The author of the latter article, Walter Trombold, also provides vivid testimony on the rough ride offered by the flat-bottomed LSTs. It's tough enough going to war without being tossed around in a seagoing mixmaster on the way.

WHEN SEVENS WEREN'T LUCKY

By Father Patrick W. Kemp

My navy assignments were the navy's choice, not mine. When I was undergoing training at New Orleans in 1943, I made the only duty-related request of my service time, and it was made in prayer. A number of submarines came in to put provisions aboard before leaving for the war zone. I thought to myself, "Oh, dear God, I don't want to go in one of those things."

That prayer was answered when somebody told me, "Don't worry. If you don't volunteer, you don't go."

I said, "Thank God for that." Little did I realize what lay ahead above the surface.

Soon I was sent to Little Creek, Virginia, for amphibious warfare training. After that, at New York, I joined the crew of *LCT-528*, a brand-new tank lighter. At two hundred tons and only 187 feet long, the landing craft was not designed to cross the ocean on its own. So it was hoisted onto the deck of an LST for the trip. The LST had some mechanical problem and thus missed two convoys before finally joining a group of ships at Halifax, Nova Scotia, for the trip across the Atlantic.

The LCT had a dozen men in the crew; we rode as passengers in the ship while our landing craft was up on deck. Our skipper was Lieutenant (j.g.) Allen Crowther, a very lovely man who had graduated from the University of Pennsylvania. He and his brother came from a family of means in West Virginia; I'll tell you more about his brother later.

We got to Britain in late November or early December to begin training for the cross-Channel invasion. At the end of the Atlantic crossing, we came around the north of Ireland and then down the Irish Sea to Milford Haven in Wales. From there we went around to Falmouth, which is in Cornwall, near the southwest tip of England. To get the LCT into the water, the LST was ballasted down on one side, and the landing craft slid off sideways.

While we were at Falmouth, our skipper allowed another boy and me to begin studying from a handbook so we could become petty officers. Tom Lafferty wanted to be a gunner's mate, and I was striking for quartermaster. Both of us had done well in high school, so the captain thought we could do that work and wanted us to get a rating if we could. I became a petty officer during the ensuing months.

The *LCT-528* was one of the newer-type tank lighters. In the older type, everything was in the stern. These new ones had the crew compartment on one side and the quarters for the two officers on the other. There was also a galley, which meant the crew could be self-sufficient once we left the LST. It was not bad, really, considering the size of the landing craft. We had an "older" fellow of about thirty-five, a chief motor machinist's mate named Pete Keller, and he was the one who kept the crew together. Lieutenant Crowther really relied on Keller because he was older than the skipper and had a lot more time in the service. He was the "sea daddy" for the younger men.

Being in the navy opened my eyes about people from different backgrounds. I had come from a homogeneous group of people. When I got in the crew with these other men, I was just shocked by some of the things they did, because I'd had a pretty strict Catholic upbringing. But it was a good experience to learn to get along with them, because in life that's the way it is. Among other things, I was surprised that they didn't go to church. I had grown up in a family where going to Mass was like breathing; you just did it.

Then I was a little shocked too at the sexual behavior of some of the married men. I wasn't accustomed to seeing married men be unfaithful to their wives. One fellow was a hotshot who used to read out loud to us the sweet things that he was writing in letters to his wife. But at the same time he was bragging to us about this woman and that woman he'd been with in England. I thought, "Oh, you jerk." But then I matured a little myself and gave it some more thought. I realized that as a single man, I was not accustomed to having a sexual relationship. These married men had gotten used to sex, and all of a sudden they didn't have that sexual relationship anymore when they were away from their wives. Even though I didn't excuse what they did,

The crew of the *LCT-528* poses on deck. To the left of center is the skipper, Lieutenant (junior grade) Allen Crowther. For some reason, Quartermaster Kemp was absent the day this picture was taken. (*Courtesy Father Patrick W. Kemp*)

it became more comprehensible to me.

I loved England, which surprised me at first. I had developed some built-in prejudice against the English, because I grew up in this country in an Irish Catholic environment. We were used to thinking of the English as snooty and uppity and all this other stuff. I found the English to be just lovely people. I enjoyed the country so much, and the people were so friendly. In Falmouth, you'd go in a pub at night, and the people were just delightful. They took us into their homes and shared what little they had. I couldn't say enough nice things about the British myself, even though my favorite joke is the one about the Englishman who said during the war that Americans were "overpaid, overfed, over-sexed, and—worst of all—over here." That was before I decided to become a priest, and I had a number of dates with English girls. In particular, I remember a pretty blonde who was part of an antiaircraft gun crew.

On the edge of Falmouth was a hard surface where the landing craft moored when they came in between exercises. A little fellow of about ten used to hang around there all the time. His name was George Bolitho, and he was a darling little kid with wavy blond hair. Of course, we all got to know him. One day he invited me to come home with him and meet his family. It was interesting to learn that his mother and father, though originally English, had met each other in Ohio. They had gone to America separately, she from Lon-

don and he from Cornwall. They married in America, but neither of them had become a U.S. citizen. When the Great Depression came, they decided to go back to Britain, and they settled in Falmouth. Mrs. Bolitho said to me, "Pat, that's like taking a girl from New York City to live in the hills of Kentucky."

We used to tie up sometimes in Dartmouth, which is where the Royal Navy College is—beautiful place. One time about three or four of us sailors went out walking from there. We went along a little country lane, over to Torbay and Paignton, which were British seaside resorts on the Channel coast. An Englishman and his wife were walking up the road as well. All of a sudden, we could hear some American trucks coming, and we all dove out of the way as they sped past. This Englishman shook his walking stick at us and said, "You bloody Yanks. The way you drive your lorries, it's a wonder that any of us are still alive."

One of the thrills of my life was the first time I rode an English steam train from Plymouth to London. It was a famous train, the Cornish Riviera Express, which runs from Paddington to Penzance. If you know anything about railroads and you're a railroad buff, that's one of the big express trains of the world. Of course, it was jammed with people, as our trains were during the war. You had a tough time even getting on, so there was something truly exciting about riding on that big-name train and arriving in London in the blackout.

Before departing for France, U.S. servicemen say farewell toasts over pints of bitters. Notice the seltzer bottle and the old-fashioned cash register. (*Navy photo in the National Archives: 80-G-46906*)

Much less enjoyable was the first Christmas away from the United States. I remember sitting in church and weeping all during the Mass.

We spent nearly six months in training, continually making practice landings with troops. During those exercises we practiced drying out, which is exactly what our landing craft did later, on D-Day at Normandy. The idea was to head in, drop the anchor astern, and go as far as we could on the beach. When the tide went out, we dropped our forward ramp on the beach, and the cargo could be unloaded. When the tide came in again, we used the anchor to pull the LCT back off the beach. We did that quite often, sometimes with troops and sometimes with vehicles. It was the same principle an LST used, but the LCT was a smaller version. I recall a number of the places where we tried this technique: North Devon, Bideford, Barnstable, and South Wales.

We loaded in Plymouth for the invasion. We'd been through so many drills that I didn't realize this was the real thing. My birthday is May 20, and we were loaded

by that time. Some of my shipmates took me out, and we got crocked that night to celebrate my twenty-first birthday. One of my shipmates said, "Well, Kemp, at least you'll die a man."

We went from Millbay docks at Plymouth up to Portsmouth to join the group that we went to France with. We left England the evening of June 5. I remember that the weather was not too good as we went across the English Channel. The LCT bounced around, but we had been on board so long by then that we were used to it. I didn't sleep that night because I was helmsman, steering the ship. In the bow we had a truck that belonged to the army amphibious engineers. Behind that were Bailey bridge forms, and behind them, blitz cans of gasoline. It's just a miracle that we survived the trip because there was shrapnel flying around. I wondered how we could have missed getting blown up, but we didn't. We saw a tank lighter like ours, and it was the *LCT-777*. Dick Simpson, a boatswain's mate, looked at those lucky numbers and said to me, "That would be a good one to be on." He had no sooner got the words out of his mouth than the thing blew right up.

There was a huge armada of vessels on the Channel that night; I was overwhelmed by the size of it. All I had to do was steer. I'm sure there were some real headaches for the guys who were in charge of the traffic patterns. We were doing perhaps eight knots, so I had a long, long night on the helm. But I didn't really feel tired. There was so much nervous anticipation that I stayed alert. That was really an exciting night, I'm telling you. When it got light, I never saw so many ships as there were in the English Channel that day. Fortunately, we went to Utah Beach and dried out at about ten o'clock in the morning. Then army people used their equipment to carry off what we had aboard. The bridge forms were needed to cross the marshland that was back from the shoreline.

During the day on June 6, a number of fellows who

were in the parachutes and the gliders got to the beach. Some of them were kind of banged up. I remember taking them aboard to give them whatever we had in the way of food or drink. Some of them were wounded or had been injured when they landed.

We stayed that night on the beach. We were anxious about the unknown, so fear crept in as darkness moved over us. For the second night in a row, I didn't dare close my eyes—this time because I was terrified that I would never wake up again. I had watch duty on a 20-millimeter gun. It seemed to me that only one German reconnaissance plane came over that night and dropped flares. We were petrified, but nothing else came over. The guys who were not on watch were allowed to go to bed, but I don't think too many of them were able to sleep. Maybe a couple of days after that everybody was sleeping more or less normally because things began to fall into a routine.

An LCT had the capacity to carry many more soldiers to the Normandy shore than did the LCVPs. (*Navy photo in the National Archives: 80-G-59422*)

The bow doors of an LST frame this photo of captured German soldiers marching toward the landing craft that will take them across the Channel to England. (*Navy photo in the National Archives: 80-G-252780*)

Kemp's *LCT-528* dried out on the beach at Normandy during low tide. (*Navy photo in the National Archives: 80-G-253009*)

The beach was still not ours up above us. The Germans were firing down on us, but they didn't hit us—thank God. In maybe a day or two that whole beach was secured. At the same time, a whole line of ships was sunk behind us to create a breakwater harbor. That gave us a new job as a ferry to transport cargo to the beach from ships anchored inside this breakwater. Landing craft were really a key to that operation, because we were the final step in getting supplies ashore after they had made the long trip across the ocean in cargo ships.

Then came the storm that just about wrecked us. I remember that I was the one who parted the anchor cable to our stern anchor. When the sea got under the stern, I reeled in cable and put too much stress on it. I had misjudged the amount of strain on the cable; it broke, and the *LCT-528* was washed up onto the beach. I thought the skipper was going to hang me, because it was embarrassing for him to be among those whose ships were stranded ashore. But he got over it.

A week or two later he became angry at me again. He was one of two children. He had a brother who was in the army, and the brother was killed by the Germans soon after he landed. By this time, we were taking German prisoners out from the beach to the other ships so they could be evacuated to England. There was one poor German guy who was horribly wounded and obviously near death. He looked like he had his genitals blown off. He kept pleading, *"Wasser. Wasser. Wasser."* So I went to give him a drink of water, and my skipper said that if I gave that guy a drink, he would blow me away. The captain had just gotten word that his brother had been killed, so he was taking revenge—in his way—on the nearest available German. That was out of character for Lieutenant Crowther, because I had known him to be a nice man in every way. Under the circumstances, his anger and harshness were understandable.

PATRICK WILLIAM KEMP (1923–) was born in Washington, D.C., enlisted in the navy in December 1942, and received recruit training at Bainbridge, Maryland. After his service in the *LCT-528*, he was transferred in 1945 to the attack cargo ship *Roxane* for the ship's Pacific duty at the end of the war and in the immediate aftermath. Discharged in February 1946, Kemp attended the George Washington University School of Foreign Service on the GI Bill, graduating with a bachelor's degree in 1949. In 1950 he began preparation for the priesthood and attended seminary at Mount St. Mary's in Emmitsburg, Maryland. After completing his studies, he was ordained in 1955. For nearly forty years thereafter he was a parish priest in the Archdiocese of Washington, serving both in the capital city itself and in parishes in the state of Maryland. Father Kemp retired from the active priesthood in the spring of 1993 and now lives just outside Annapolis, Maryland. (*Courtesy Father Patrick W. Kemp*)

DESIGNING THE LST

By John C. Niedermair

In late 1941 Captain Edward L. Cochrane was the assistant head of the design division of the Bureau of Ships in Washington. On November 4 of that year, he came in with a dispatch from the British. They had previously designed some landing craft, nicknamed "Winnies" after Churchill, that we were building in this country. But the drafts were too light on these, so the new message outlined in very brief manner the need for larger landing craft that could be seagoing.

The total weight of the military load called for in this new British requirement was five hundred tons, and the craft would have to carry the biggest tanks. Some of the tanks that were getting into the picture at that time weighed thirty or more tons, so you couldn't carry them on these little landing craft. In our LST that we were going to get into now, five hundred tons allowed for at least ten of these big tanks and the other equipment that had to be put in ahead of the tanks in order to get onto the beach and prepare a roadway.

As Captain Cochrane recited the need, the British specified a design to go on a beach whose slope was one foot in a hundred. I listened to that, and then I started thinking. I got busy and made a few sketches. The craft had to meet two conditions. One, it had to be able to cross the ocean and have enough draft to get there. Then, when it got to the landing area, the crew needed to pump the ballast tanks dry and go onto the beach. Instead of taking the one-in-one hundred slope, I decided that to be successful, it would have to be one in fifty, and that's the way we designed it.

Cochrane was satisfied that I had a solution. It seemed odd that I would be able to do it so quickly, because the British hadn't been able to hit on this scheme. I drew the original sketch in a couple of hours that afternoon on a scale of fifty feet to the inch. Then I went home that night and worked on it in my study, which had a drafting board in it. I made a larger drawing, one-sixteenth of an inch to the foot, and brought that in. The Bureau of Ships made copies of that, and a short time afterwards the officer courier flew off to England with the plan. That was the way of getting secret material over in a hurry, because they didn't want to talk about it over the air.

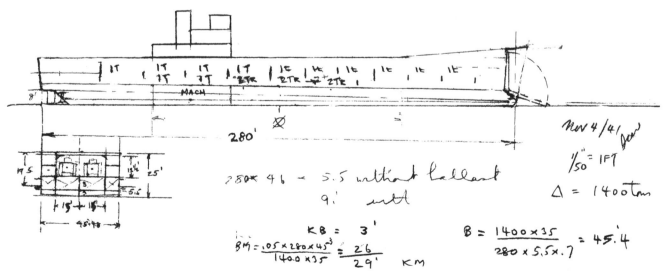

John Niedermair made this original sketch of the LST concept on November 4, 1941. The date and his initials are at right, just forward of the ship's bow. (*Naval Institute Collection*)

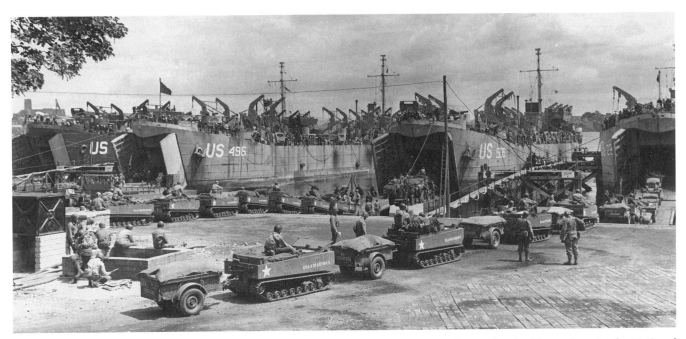

Army vehicles move toward the jaws of waiting LSTs at an embarkation port in England. (*Navy photo in the National Archives: 80-G-252143*)

The initial scheme was never changed, except that we increased the size of the ship. We were a little afraid of using quarter-inch plating on the sides and on the deck. We increased that to three-eighths of an inch, and to take the weight, we added a little to the beam and increased the length from 280 feet to around 300. The machinery would be located aft, and the bow would have a ramp inside the bow doors.

Rear Admiral J. W. S. Dorling and a team from Britain worked with the bureau in the design study and development of the detailed plans. We finished our study sometime in January. Mind you, all of this was started on November 4, 1941. Sometime after January 1, we had a preliminary design finished. Instead of taking those preliminary plans and turning them over to our contract design section in BuShips, we passed them to the firm of Gibbs and Cox to be developed into contract plans. They developed the details and the ventilation system that had to be put in there because the tank engines would be running inside the ship. The ramp that was on the forward end also had to be worked out. They made contract plans and the detailed plans simultaneously so the shipyards that got the job would receive detailed plans without delay.

The Dravo Corporation, Pittsburgh, Pennsylvania, was chosen as the prime yard to build this type. By October of 1942—a little less than a year after we began—an LST was finished. Then it wasn't very long after that when there was an LST available down at the Norfolk Naval Operating Base. It was cold winter weather, so I suppose it was either in December 1942 or January 1943. I went down there and joined Lieutenant Commander Ernest Holtzworth, who was a construction officer who worked in the preliminary design section in the Bureau of Ships. There was also a line officer, Captain Forrest Royal.

We started loading the LST. We put a big crane in it, and it seemed almost like magic that we had picked the size of hatch that would allow the crane to be lowered down in it without taking it apart. That was a very good thing, because it could go ashore without having to be assembled. We ran some loading tests there with sandbags and so on and tried to work out a method to get ashore. We weren't really practicing a landing operation, but we were practicing using the ramp location at the naval base there and then trying to drop sandbags over the end so that bulldozer operators would have half a chance of getting their machines ashore.

We came back to Washington, and it wasn't very long before I went up to Quonset, Rhode Island, during the early months of 1943 to run a landing test. As we were getting ready, everybody wanted to know how fast to go to hit the beach. They came to me, and I said full speed. So they hit the beach at about ten knots. That's pretty high for a landing craft, and most captains don't like to hit the beach like that. I wasn't worried about it. I was standing up on deck, at the side, and someone had strung a piece of line between the stanchions in place of lifelines so that no one would fall overboard. As we were approaching the beach, that speed of ten knots seemed to get faster and faster. I began to look around

Vehicles roll out of the *LST-21* on to a rhino barge on June 6. In the foreground, not yet experienced in battle, is a Sherman tank bearing the legend "virgin." (*U.S. Coast Guard photo in the National Archives: 26-G-2370*)

Evidence of Niedermair's handiwork is this panoramic view of Omaha Beach with LSTs lined up side by side to discharge their cargo. (*Navy photo in the National Archives: 80-G-46817*)

to see what I would hang onto. Well, we hit the beach, and it was just a gradual stop. It wasn't any problem. So it was quite successful.

I had made the plating under the bow one inch thick, compared with three-eighths in the rest of the ship. I was always very glad I had made it that heavy in the bow after I saw pictures of what happened to some of these LSTs landing on the Normandy beach, on top of rocks and all that sort of thing.

The LST certainly proved itself to be a great thing, and it was all done in that short time. It was so successful that a lot of other people try to take credit for inventing it. In fact, *Jane's Fighting Ships* called it a British design. When I was in Washington in 1974 I got a telephone call from someone in the Maritime Administration who said that the Maritime Administration designed and built the LST. But it didn't. The U.S. Navy did the whole job.

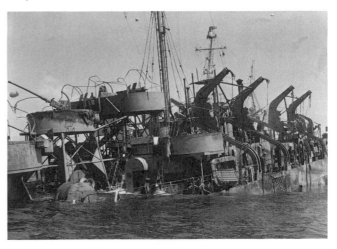

Some LSTs became casualties of war, as was the case with this one down by the stern at Normandy. The dogleg-shaped devices sticking up from the deck are davits used for lowering and raising the ship's LCVPs. (*Navy photo in the National Archives: 80-G-253021*)

An LST with a hefty load of trucks on the main deck heads toward the Normandy beach. The cylinders sticking up from the deck are ventilators to permit the removal of engine exhausts from vehicles in the tank deck below. (*Naval Institute Collection*)

JOHN CHARLES NIEDERMAIR (1893–1982) graduated from
the Webb Institute of Naval Architecture and Marine
Engineering in 1918. In December of that year he became
a ship draftsman at the New York Navy Yard. He soon
gained attention for his engineering skill and in 1924 was
chosen to correct faults in the operation of the passenger
liner SS *Leviathan*. Later in the 1920s he assisted in the
salvage operations of two U.S. submarines—the *S-51* and
the *S-4*—sunk off the East Coast. In 1929 Niedermair
participated in the International Conference for the
Safety of Life at Sea. His work on watertight integrity and
ship stability had an effect on practically every merchant
ship constructed after 1929. Afterward, he was transferred
to the preliminary design branch of the navy's Bureau of
Construction and Repair, which in 1940 was one of the
components when the Bureau of Ships was established.
He was the senior civilian in the branch and eventually
became the technical director, the position he held at the
time of his retirement in 1958. At that time he was the
highest-ranking professional naval architect in the U.S.
Navy. During his tenure he guided the basic design of
all types of naval ships and craft. (*Courtesy John C. Niedermair Jr.*)

CIVILIANS IN UNIFORM

By Walter Trombold

W hen the United States set out to engage in a global conflict in World War II, the navy had to expand greatly from its prewar base of personnel and equipment. It used types of weapons and equipment that weren't even in existence when the war began. To operate them, the navy essentially took hundreds of thousands of civilians, put us into uniform, trained us, and sent us off to face the enemy.

My own particular ship, the USS *LST-55*—she didn't even have a name—can serve as an example of how the navy geared up to fight that war. She was built inland—in Pittsburgh, Pennsylvania, of all places. Her crewmen, few of whom had been in the service before the war started, came from the cities, towns, and farms of America. They went back to those places when their service was done. The entire commissioned life of the

ship encompassed less than two years. During that brief period, she and hundreds of her sisters helped demonstrate the wisdom of the idea that LSTs were absolutely essential for carrying out an amphibious assault in the era before the use of helicopters became commonplace.

My transformation from insurance salesman to navy man began in my hometown of Wichita, Kansas, when I applied for an officer's commission. The nearest major naval activity with cognizance in such matters was the Ninth Naval District headquarters at Great Lakes, Illinois. At the same time, the draft board was coming at me from the other direction. It turned out that the draft board was working with a little more enthusiasm than the naval recruiting office.

When I reminded the people with the draft board that I was waiting for a response to my request for a

The officers and enlisted men of the *LST-55* gather on the main deck of their ship for a commissioning-day group portrait on January 6, 1944, at Pittsburgh, Pennsylvania. Executive Officer Trombold is third from the left in the front row. (*Courtesy Karla Powell*)

Naval Reserve commission, they gave me an ultimatum. "You've been telling us that. By Monday morning a week, put up or shut up." When that Monday came, I still hadn't heard about the officer commission, so I went to the courthouse in Kansas City and enlisted. When my commission arrived on Tuesday morning it was one day too late. I had orders to report as a seaman to the new naval air station at Olathe, Kansas, where I became a storekeeper. After serving in that for six months—to the day—I was able to activate my commission and be sworn in as a lieutenant.

My orders then sent me to officer training at Dartmouth College and later Fort Schuyler, New York. The navy by then had a well-developed training system and an established curriculum. It took people with the appropriate aptitudes and background, including college education, and then gave us the basics that would be enhanced by on-the-job training once we reported to our ships. That initial training included an introduction to such subjects as navy law, communications, signaling, navigation, naval history, engineering, gunnery, boat handling, and so forth.

Then came my orders to the *LST-55* as executive officer. I was designated as senior officer of the nucleus crew, which included one other officer and a half-dozen petty officers. The other officer was Ensign Arthur Kruggel, another recent civilian put into uniform. He had been a real estate man in Chicago. Our small group was directed to report to Pittsburgh, where we went aboard the *LST-271*, which had just been commissioned on September 1, 1943. (LSTs were obviously not all commissioned in numerical sequence. Our ship was part of a block of hull numbers assigned to the Dravo Corporation; the *LST-271* was built by the American Bridge Company.)

The idea was that we'd receive considerable practical experience before we had to begin operating our own ship. Each of us was matched up with his counterpart in the other ship. (My instructor was an officer who had been a pawnbroker in Kansas before entering the navy.) We got under way from Pittsburgh, then watched, listened, and asked questions as the *LST-271* made her way down the Ohio and Mississippi rivers, just as we would do later in the *LST-55*.

After we reached New Orleans, our small contingent took a train to the navy's amphibious training school at Solomons Island, Maryland. There we met up with our skipper, Lieutenant Alfred E. Mills, and the rest of the crew. Mills had been an executive with the Bank of Savings in New York City. He commuted there each day from Morristown, New Jersey, where he also served as a city alderman. Mills was a terrific person, with a great deal of native ability, but if he had any nautical background, it probably wasn't in much more than a rowboat.

We met the other officers as well. For instance, the

In civilian life Alfred Mills was a New Jersey alderman. In uniform he was the skipper of an LST and a leader who excelled as "a man among men." Here he is on one of the ship's signal lights. (*Walter Trombold photo courtesy Karla Powell*)

engineer officer, Joel Tom Ferris, was from Oklahoma, where he was a farmer. He wanted to get experience on diesel engines because he knew that when the war was over, he would want some diesel equipment on his farm. The communication officer, John Zimmer, was a beautifully trained musician. Harry Wright II, who later was an outstanding LCVP boat officer at Normandy, was the son of U.S. citizens who lived in Mexico. After completing college at the University of Colorado, he volunteered for service in the navy. He returned to Mexico City after the war was over.

We had a full range of people among the enlisted crew. Some of them had good IQs, and I'd say that some of them were what we now refer to as disadvantaged. The yeoman, Mike Leschak, was a top-notch man. Boatswain's Mate William Roth was older than many in the crew; he had previous navy experience that was a valuable asset for Art Kruggel. Those who were running the diesel engines were capable men who had received navy diesel training before they got to the ship. The communication people were sharp.

On the other hand, we had some who had never graduated from the eighth grade. Some were totally unskilled youngsters who just hadn't had a chance to apply themselves in school or anywhere else. In general, the people in the deck force were good workers who didn't have the abilities needed for the more demanding jobs. That was where we had the greatest lack of experience. Some of them turned out very well once we provided the opportunity.

At Solomons Island, and later at Little Creek, Virginia, the navy used ships already in commission to provide us with specific training in how to deal with the characteristics of this ungainly creature known as an LST. We found out how to operate the bow doors, since most ships don't open up at the forward end. We learned how to launch and recover the LCVP landing craft, how to ballast for beaching, and other specific LST skills.

Then it was off to Pittsburgh to pick up our own ship. She was commissioned at Pittsburgh on January 6, 1944, and then we began our own cruise down the Ohio and Mississippi. The river pilot assigned to the ship became persona non grata on board the *LST-55*. He was a retired officer who was really over the hill. He had serious problems with the LST's officers, and he was really no help to us in handling the ship. Mills was an intelligent, responsible person, and he was able to deal with situations as they came up, even if they were new to him. He was quick to pick up the business of running a ship and commanding personnel effectively. Mills was a man among men; I had the highest respect for him.

After the ship reached New Orleans and prepared for overseas duty, she proceeded to Panama City, Florida, to load ammunition. In the meantime, Mills was kind enough to let me catch a train to Wichita for the birth of our second child. Unfortunately, little Lynn Louise Trombold hadn't yet made her appearance when it was time for me to leave to meet the ship in New York City, so I had to shove off. She was born February 24, 1944, while I was en route to New York.

My brother was in New York at the time as an officer in the chemical division of the army. He deflated my spirits a bit one day when he said, "Walt, I saw an LST today. I was down on the 42nd Street dock, and it was right alongside the *Queen Elizabeth*. You know, I wasn't a bit impressed." We had a good time the few days that we were there. After that we went by convoy to Boston and Halifax. Our cargo for the Atlantic crossing consisted of half-tracks (which had wheels on the front and treads on the back), Jeeps, armored equipment, and other vehicles. A crane loaded an LCT onto the main deck, and its officers and crew lived on board the *LST-55* as we headed to Europe.

It was a fairly routine journey, but we got a real education in the kind of jolting an LST did. To facilitate beaching on the shore, her bottom was absolutely flat. The keel was on the inside of the ship and called a keelson. Thus, she didn't have the kind of tapered bow that cuts through the waves; instead, she would smack down hard on top of the water. In fact, we had a saying to describe the ride: "Some ships go over the waves; some of them go through the waves; some go under the waves; but an LST just clubs them to death." When that happened, you could feel the

The New York skyline is in the background as the *LST-55* (with an LCT mounted on her main deck) takes a brief respite in the spring of 1944 before heading for Europe. At left is a Hudson River excursion steamer with much more peaceful voyages in prospect. (*Walter Trombold photo courtesy Karla Powell*)

vibration through the whole ship. When you were down below decks, you could see the ship flexing at the compartments, sort of like a telescope opening and closing. That was the nature of it, because it was built to absorb the shocks of slapping at the waves.

Once we got to England, we ballasted down the *LST-55* on one side so the LCT could slide off and begin an independent existence of its own. We had beaching experience in Exercise Tiger in late April at Slapton Sands on the southern coast of England. That, of course, was the unhappy exercise in which two of our LSTs were sunk by German E-boats and a third damaged in the stern. Along with being the executive officer, I was the ship's official photographer, and on the morning of April 27 I happened to take a photo of the *LST-507*. She was sunk early the next morning, so that was probably the last picture of her.

Then it came time for the invasion of France. We had a medical team on board. On D-Day itself we sent our landing craft in to the shore to bring back casualties. The doctors were operating all night on June 6–7. Within a couple of days, about D+2, we were able to get ashore on Omaha Beach to off-load our cargo of soldiers and their equipment. One of the members of the army contingent was a U.S. Congressman, Representative Wint Smith from my home state of Kansas. But this was no junket for him; Smith was a major in the National Guard. It was apparent to me that he was well trained in warfare and knew his business.

After that initial landing, we developed a routine of cross-Channel trips between England and France to bring still more men, weapons, and equipment. By this time Captain Mills had really developed the crew into an effective team. The crew performed well and respected him. In particular, I was struck by his sense of integrity. One time when we unloaded our cargo on the beach in France, the army men went off and left a Jeep on deck. If we had kept it, the ship's crew could have a means of transportation any time we wanted. But Mills quickly agreed when I told him we should get rid of it; the only thing worse than getting a vehicle illegally would be to have women on board. So we just drove the Jeep off and left it on the shore. We didn't want the appearance that we were stealing the Jeep, because it was our responsibility to get all the cargo off the ship.

The months passed, and at various times we covered all the beaches at Normandy, including the British ones, and we even went around to Brittany. We had German prisoners on board many times, carrying them from France to England. They'd be herded into the tank deck, which was rigged as a hospital. There were stretchers lining the bulkheads. At a given time, there would be maybe a couple hundred in there. We herded them off again when we got to England.

Altogether, we made fifty-one trips, as I recall, between England and France. The fifty-second trip was a peaceful invasion of Norway. That was in June 1945, after the German surrender. We brought in troops to

LCVP crew members have a considerable audience of shipmates as they work on their landing craft. In the foreground is the davit used to launch LCVPs over the side of the *LST-55*. (*Walter Trombold photo courtesy Karla Powell*)

serve as an Allied garrison there. Our troops relieved the Germans who were still on guard there a month after the capitulation.

Another event that spring was sending one of the ship's officers to Paris. Our flotilla commander offered a few passes for crew members to make a trip to Paris, and the ship was allowed to select one person. Our navigator, Jim Donnelly, was chosen by lottery from among the ten line officers (we didn't even include the doctors). The enlisted men weren't allowed in that lottery either. The perk for the crew was that they got first shot at some rib steaks prepared by the ship's cook. The Paris trip was something we all envied Jim for doing. Our joy was in being represented; his joy was doing it personally.

In the summer of 1945, the LSTs came back to the United States by flotilla, although this time they traveled together for mutual support—a far different reason for sailing together than the trip going over as part of an antisubmarine convoy. We brought some released American prisoners of war back from Europe on that trip. They said their favorite pastime while in captivity was fantasizing about exquisite menus for meals that they would like to eat once they were released.

The men of the *LST-55* also used their imagination. One pastime was to talk about what we would do if we could convert her to use as a civilian cruise ship. We talked about how we would reduce the size of the crew, what bulkheads to cut out to make things accessible so only one man would be needed for both the main engines and the auxiliaries. We discussed where we would put in staterooms for tourists. We even thought about setting up gambling on the tank deck. One thing nobody ever mentioned, though, was where to put a pool table in a ship that sometimes rocked and sometimes rolled when she was at the mercy of the sea.

In addition, men were already talking about what pursuits they would get into in civilian life. The best entertainer in the crew was an enlisted man named Mike Cascio, who worked in the deck force. When we asked him what he was going to do when the war was over, he would say, "I'm going to open a bar." Just by the nature of his personality, we knew that he would be successful at it. No matter what he said, you grabbed every syllable of it and held on, waiting for the next one. He was a hale fellow, well met, and I'm confident he did well in later life.

The ship landed in Norfolk when she got back to the States, and all of us enjoyed being home again. Then we went to Staten Island and holed up there for a while. The war still remained to be won in the Pacific. The plan called for two thirty-day leave periods. Half the crew would go, then the other half would be on leave after the first contingent returned. After everyone had a chance for a vacation, I was due to take command.

With their flat bottoms, LSTs could go directly onto beaches to off-load their cargoes. Here is the *LST-55* "dried out" during low tide at Normandy while a truck proceeds down her bow ramp. To either side of the ramp are the large bow doors that close and seal shut to make the ship seaworthy. (*Walter Trombold photo courtesy Karla Powell*)

Boatswain's Mate William Roth was one of the few regular navy crew members in the crew of the *LST-55*, which was manned largely by sailors new to the navy and shipboard life. (*Walter Trombold photo courtesy Karla Powell*)

Then we would go down through the Panama Canal and use our trained, experienced crew during the planned invasion of Japan.

I went back home to Kansas on leave. By the time I returned to the ship, the atomic bombs had been dropped. The *LST-55* wasn't going to go to the Pacific after all. I relieved Mills as skipper and he became a civilian soon afterward. We spent the time that fall at Staten Island. I joined the Roseneath Tennis Club and lived the life of Riley. I made so many friends there on Staten Island that I think I could have run for mayor. It was not unpleasant duty at all.

The decommissioning of the *LST-55* was on December 19, 1945. We took the event in our stride—no real pangs of emotion. We had other ideas in our minds at that point. Even though this was the departure at the end of an adventure, everybody was more intent on where he was going than where he had been.

WALTER STEVENSON TROMBOLD (1910–) had an early interest in religion, serving as a volunteer personnel worker for evangelist Billy Sunday in 1928. He earned an associate's degree from Iola Junior College in 1930 and a B.S. in business from the University of Kansas in 1932. During much of the 1930s he was an assistant manager for an S. H. Kress retail store. From 1938 to 1941 he worked in the insurance field. The Wichita Junior Chamber of Commerce voted him outstanding young man of the year in 1940. He was commissioned in 1941 and served as a Naval Reserve Officer until released from the service as a lieutenant commander in 1945. Returning to the civilian work force after the war, he joined the Reid Supply Company, eventually becoming president and chairman of the board. From 1986 until the present he has operated the Trombold Consultation Service. He has been involved in a great many civic projects, including service on behalf of the Boy Scouts, Camp Fire Girls, YMCA, Salvation Army, and the Presbyterian Church. In 1990 he became charter president of the Kansas LST Association, helping to commemorate the role of LSTs and their crews during World War II. Mr. Trombold lives in Wichita, Kansas. (*Courtesy Walter Trombold*)

THE HAZARDS OF LONDON (AND NORMANDY)

By Commander Allen Pace, U.S. Naval Reserve (Retired)

By the spring of 1944, after I had commanded the *LST-386* for many difficult months in the Mediterranean, both the ship and her crew had accumulated battle experience and the type of war knowledge that doesn't come out of textbooks. At Bizerte, Tunisia, while the ship was loading for the invasion of Sicily, two members of a 20-millimeter gun crew were killed by a strafing German plane. At Licata, Sicily, we had been the direct target of a shore battery as we got under way to launch a spotting plane from a temporary flight deck constructed over our main deck. At Salerno, Italy, the ship struck a mine as she neared the beach while towing a pontoon causeway alongside. We were under continuous fire from 88-millimeter tank guns until we were able to retract from the beach with only one screw and one rudder in operating condition. During the course of our supply runs to Anzio, Italy, we were usually under air attack and also under fire from a huge railway gun.

Later, when most or all of the other LSTs in Sicily were sent to England while we were on a supply run, I wondered if the *LST-386* and her crew were going to miss "The Big One"—the invasion of the European mainland. I had somewhat mixed feelings about the possibility. I fully expected that it would be even deadlier than anything we had yet experienced and that we might therefore be lucky to be elsewhere. On the other hand, I realized—correctly, as it turned out—that all of our previous invasions would become mere footnotes to The Big One in future history books. I was not eager for the ship and crew to be relegated to that status. The issue was soon resolved when we were ordered to Britain. We arrived at Swansea, Wales, around the first of May and there drank our first fresh milk since leaving the States in February 1943.

Soon we proceeded to London and a memorable trip up the Thames River. We recognized such historic sights as Parliament and the Tower Bridge, but the most interesting things we saw were huge box-like concrete structures that lined the river on both sides.

We surmised that they must have something to do with the coming invasion, but had no idea of their function. We later learned that they were the Phoenixes, designed to be towed to Normandy and sunk in place to form an artificial harbor to facilitate the unloading of ships. For an LST, such measures were unnecessary because of the ship's ability to put her bow on the beach and unload cargo directly ashore.

For some two-and-a-half weeks the *LST-386* trained in the English Channel and lower Thames, becoming used to tidal currents and tidal ranges considerably greater than those we had known in the Mediterranean. In the Med we had seen a change in tide of only about six inches, and there were no tidal currents to contend with. Soon we were told what would happen to LSTs when they beached at Normandy before low tide. As the tide went out, they would be left on the shore with no water within several hundred feet until the next tide came in and refloated them. Every instinct and bit of experience we had acquired to that point told us that ships are not supposed to be left high and dry.

Probably because the *LST-386* did not arrive in England until about a month before the invasion date, she was assigned to a reserve unit. We embarked as part of a convoy headed for France on the morning of June 6. As we passed through the Strait of Dover, we saw several splashes as shells fired from the French coast landed in the water. Our convoy started out on a diversionary course in the direction of Calais. This was intended, as I later understood, to make the German high command believe that we would be landing in that area also and thus, perhaps, divert some forces from the main landing areas at Normandy.

Because of our little foray, we did not reach our assigned British beach, Juno, until D+1. We off-loaded our cargo of British troops and equipment, then had ample time to observe conditions on the beach as we waited for the next high tide to refloat us. I was so sure of success on the part of the British officer responsible for clearing the beach of mines that a couple of us walked to a nearby village, where we found a small shop open and ready to sell souvenirs.

So much for the uneventful portion of my invasion experiences. Soon all the LSTs in condition to do so became part of a continuous ferry program to carry supplies and equipment to the Normandy beaches from various ports in England. On one such trip the *LST-386* narrowly averted a tragedy that might have sent her to the bottom of the Thames. Not all the hazards were over in France, as I discovered one night when we were selected to make an emergency trip to transport thirty gasoline tank trucks to Normandy.

A Thames River pilot was supposed to conn the ship safely down to the English Channel. The pilot ordered full speed down the river, in keeping with the urgency of our mission (or perhaps his desire to get back to bed). We had a strong tidal current as well, so we were moving quite fast for an LST. The Thames was a crowded river, with ships anchored or moored all along the way. About halfway down the river, I was suddenly alarmed to see a large merchant ship looming dead ahead of us in the darkness. Realizing that the pilot was not aware of the hazard, I immediately ordered, "Full right rudder."

Before I could give the order to bring the rudder back amidships to get our stern clear, it grazed the side of the freighter and slightly damaged our stern boat davit. The freighter was completely at fault for not showing the required anchor light—or any other lights, for that matter. I'm sure that a head-on collision with the merchant ship would have torn the tank trucks loose from their tie-downs. The possibility of a great explosion in the Thames River still gives me shivers. I'm glad that didn't have to be written in the history books.

On a later supply trip to Normandy, the *LST-386* had the misfortune to arrive off her assigned beach during what was reported to be the most violent storm ever to hit the English Channel at that time of year. In the midst of gale-force winds and an already crowded anchorage, I had trouble finding a place to drop anchor. (I should digress here to explain why LSTs were unusually hard to handle when winds and seas were high. Because of the height of the two bow doors, the ship had a bow that rose above the main deck level. Also, to facilitate beaching, the LST had a very shallow draft forward. This combination of design factors meant that a strong wind against either side of the ship caused the high freeboard to act as a sail. The ship thus had a decided tendency to turn in the direction the wind was blowing.) Because of the violence of the storm we were in, this characteristic made for a frightening struggle, particularly because one of the anchored ships had a huge sign along her sides: "EXPLOSIVES."

Once I ordered the anchor dropped, I thought my troubles were over. No such luck. The navigator soon reported from his bearings that the anchor was drag-

Remains of the *LST-384* and *LST-312* after they were shattered by a German buzz bomb while sitting in a London dry dock in the spring of 1944. (*Courtesy Commander Allen Pace*)

ging, so we had to find another anchorage, and now it was dark. Again we anchored. Thinking I had found a good spot, I retired for the night. I was rudely awakened about dawn, however, by the feeling of the ship being bounced along her flat bottom. It was only a short time until we were broached sideways on the beach, where we were left stranded when the tide went out. This was one of those good news–bad news predicaments.

The good side was that while other ships continued to be buffeted about by the storm, the *LST-386* was sitting on the beach and able to off-load her cargo. The bad side was that we would stay on the beach until the next "spring tide," an event that occurred only once every two weeks and was still several days away. In addition to other concerns, we were "under fire" during our entire stay. The battleship *Texas* and various cruisers were firing directly over our heads at German forces that were holding up the Allied advance toward the town of Caen, about twenty miles inland from the Juno beachhead. I sometimes wondered what chance there was that one of those shells might be a dud that had just enough power to get to us.

When the spring tide did come, we were refloated, but disabled. The pounding on the beach had damaged one screw and one rudder. Moreover, the bottom of the ship was badly bent. Viewed from outside, at a point about halfway between bow and stern, the hull had been forced upward at least three feet. Viewed from inside the tank deck, we could see a large upward bulge close to the middle of the ship. After this particular crossing, we had been scheduled to have rails laid in the tank deck so that we could haul fully loaded freight cars from England to France. It was clear that we needed extensive repairs to be able to operate at all, so the ship was towed back to London, where we ended up in dry dock for repairs.

While we were being towed, we witnessed one of the earliest appearances of a new and deadly German weapon. It was a flying object with a fiery exhaust. We speculated that it might be a jet fighter plane, which the Germans were rumored to have started using. Soon after reaching England we learned that these were V-1 flying bombs—commonly called buzz bombs. They were capable of flying day or night, fair weather or foul, which is probably why many Londoners considered them to be worse than the bomber blitz of earlier days.

One night while the *LST-386* was in the London area we stood on deck and counted seven bombs in the air at the same time. No doubt there were others that weren't visible from our location. Shortly thereafter, we came in much closer contact with two of these awesome objects while docked at the Deptford base. I remember that four LSTs were tied up, two abreast. The *LST-384* and *LST-312* were directly ahead of our ship and another one. In the middle of the night a buzz bomb hit almost directly between the two forward ships. The explosion nearly demolished the officers' quarters in the two LSTs, and caused extensive damage in the stern areas, including the crews' quarters, which were directly above the ammunition storage space.

During the afternoon before this happened, the skipper of one of the ships had come aboard the *LST-386* for a visit with me. When I went aboard his ship after the bomb hit, I looked down into his cabin and saw what appeared to be a pile of hamburger meat—not even recognizable as a human body. Someone told me later that he had been blown through a bulkhead, although it seemed more likely that he had been blown *into* one.

We had another near miss—this one during daylight—when a bomb landed about five hundred feet away from the ship. We knew that one sailor had been killed when the heavy crane under which he had sought shelter was knocked over by the blast and fell on him. We later learned that two other sailors were killed in the attack.

In addition to the threat posed by these buzz-bomb attacks, there was an indirect effect as well. If a bomb had happened to hit close enough to the huge gates that were keeping the Thames River out of the dry dock, the result would have been catastrophic. So it was understandable that every time the air-raid sirens sounded, every worker scrambled as fast as he could up the ladders that would take him out of the dock. Needless to say, the men didn't return to work until the all-clear had sounded. The result of this stop-and-start routine was that the ship's stay in the dock was undoubtedly lengthened.

While the *LST-386* was immobilized, I took advantage of the opportunity to grant seventy-two-hour liberties to half the crew at a time. This gave them some much-needed rest and recreation and also removed them from the danger of the bombs, because most of the men got out of London. With only one exception, every member of the crew returned from liberty on time and in good condition. One mess attendant was so enamored of a woman he met that he came to me and asked if I could arrange permission for him to get married; I couldn't. As for the man who overstayed his liberty, I took no pleasure in sentencing him at captain's mast. He was one of the most capable members of the crew, and I am sure that he had been largely responsible for using ship's store items to bribe army bulldozer operators to help us out when we were stranded on the beach at Normandy.

As for my own use of the vacation time, I made friends with an English family. It all started when I

Bulldozers work around the hull of the *LST-386* after she has been broached sideways on the Normandy beach as a result of the ferocious storm in mid-June 1944. (*Courtesy Commander Allen Pace*)

Clem Leslie, public relations officer for the British Home Office, befriended Pace at church in England. Here he visits the skipper on board his LST while she was berthed in London. (*Courtesy Commander Allen Pace*)

attended a Wednesday night church service in London. After the service a lady near where I had been sitting introduced herself. She was Doris Leslie, and her husband Clem was Public Information Officer for the Home Office. As a result of our newfound association, Clem Leslie arranged for me to attend a session of the House of Commons. At the time, meetings were being held in an underground area of Westminster Abbey as a security measure. I was one of only a small number of observers and had the feeling that I was seeing a piece of history as I watched Prime Minister Winston Churchill in action. He fielded questions from members of the House with lengthy replies; as far as I could tell, he seldom, if ever, gave a simple, direct answer. It occurred to me that the ability to do this may be essential for anyone in high political office.

I also enjoyed the opportunity to get away from the ship for a Sunday dinner at the Leslies' home. The highlight of the meal was a beef roast, which I am sure used up a substantial portion of the family's ration coupons for the month. Teenage son David was given the honor of bringing the main course from the kitchen to the dining room. On the way, however, he let it slide off the platter onto the dining room carpet—to the consternation of everyone. With typical British aplomb, Doris quickly scooped it up and took it back to the kitchen for refurbishing. After that it was safely placed on the table and enjoyed by all.

Fifty years later, I still remember both the good times and the bad associated with those events of so long ago. Above all, I treasure the satisfaction of contributing to the war effort and the memories of friendships that were forged during the process of winning that war.

DAVID ALLEN PACE (1916–) graduated from the George Washington University in Washington, D.C., with a combined arts and law degree in 1941. He was commissioned an ensign in the Naval Reserve in 1942 and ordered to Cornell University for a sixty-day naval orientation course, after which he was sent to the amphibious force. He was the communications officer of the *LST-386* in the landings at Sicily and Salerno and the commanding officer in the Anzio operation and the Normandy landings. Later, he was operations and gunnery officer for LSM Flotilla One in the Pacific. After World War II he served for one year of active duty in the office of the Navy General Counsel and remained in that office as a civilian lawyer. Pace became counsel for the Office of Naval Research and served in that capacity until retiring in 1972. He retired from the Naval Reserve in 1976. An article titled "LST—Large, Slow Target," written by Mr. Pace and his *LST-386* shipmate Marx Leva, was published in the Spring 1990 issue of *Naval History* magazine. Mr. Pace now lives in Fort Worth, Texas. (*Courtesy Commander Allen Pace*)

Among the indicators of America's prodigious industrial capacity by 1944 was its willingness to sink a number of merchant ships deliberately to create an artificial harbor off the beaches at Normandy. Earlier in the war German U-boats had devastated Allied shipping in the Atlantic, sending one cargo ship after another to the bottom. The United States turned things around in two ways: by improving its antisubmarine warfare efforts and by building ships in such large numbers that it could overwhelm the enemy. Dozens of Liberty ships carried cargo and troops to Normandy, and then a number of them were sent to the bottom to fend off the waves rolling in from the English Channel. The effort was supported by the British in constructing concrete Phoenixes to add to the breakwater and a series of floating piers onto which cargo could be landed before a trip ashore on a pontoon bridge. It was quite an engineering feat.

Rear Admiral Edward Ellsberg was in Normandy in connection with the breakwater project, and later he contributed in a literary way. During his long and fruitful career, he added substantially to the body of naval literature with his tales of marine salvage. He had such a gift for imagery that his characters came alive. The reader could easily imagine being in one dire situation after another, working right along with Ellsberg to raise a sunken ship from the bottom. His book on Normandy, *The Far Shore*, is highly readable, focusing in particular on the artificial harbors but also including a stirring account of the battle ashore. The entire book deserves reading by those who want to know of the naval side of D-Day.

MULBERRIES AND GOOSEBERRIES

By Rear Admiral Edward Ellsberg, U.S. Naval Reserve (Retired)

Captain Dayton Clark set up a special group to handle and sink the vessels to form auxiliary breakwaters on Omaha and Utah beaches. They were known as Gooseberries. Twenty-three merchant ships were ballasted, fitted and wired with explosive charges, and gathered in the northern Scotch port of Oban, ready to sail so as to be off the Far Shore immediately behind the assault forces on D-Day. Since their depth of hull was substantially less than the sixty-foot-high concrete Phoenixes that were to comprise much of the Mulberry, these Goose-

berries would have to be sunk in shallower water. Still, their breakwaters would form adequate harbor space for coasting steamers and landing craft of all kinds, though not for oceangoing ships.

One day as I came into the office of Commander Albert Stanford, Clark's deputy, Stanford introduced me to a commander in the Royal Navy. I looked at him inquiringly. Had we met before, I asked. It seemed we had, in the Mediterranean. Did I remember the *Centurion*?

The *Centurion*? I remembered her all right. Immediately, my memory went back to Port Said, in the

Captain Dayton Clark briefs a group of Seabees on their assignments in connection with setting up the artificial harbors at Normandy. (*Navy photo in the National Archives: 80-G-46802*)

summer of 1942. There Captain Damant, Royal Navy, principal salvage officer for the Suez Canal, had just finished telling me the straits the Royal Navy was in, in the Eastern Mediterranean. It seemed they were trying there to hold off the entire Italian navy, dreadnoughts and all, with only four light cruisers; they hadn't a single battleship of their own left in the Mediterranean. Of the three they'd had, the *U-335* had sunk the *Barham* at sea, and some Italian frogmen, getting through the net defenses of Alexandria Harbor, had put the other two—the *Queen Elizabeth* and the *Valiant*—out of action for a year at least. Using limpet mines, the frogmen had blasted vast holes in those battleship bottoms.

Hardly had Captain Damant finished telling me that than I happened to look seaward. There, not a quarter of a mile off the quay, was moored a British dreadnought, bristling with 13.5-inch guns—as formidable a battleship as one might ever see. "What's that then?" I queried. "I thought you just said, Captain, that you hadn't a battleship in the Med."

Damant didn't even look to seaward to check what I was indicating. "That?" he answered. "Oh, that's not a battleship; that's a dummy. That's the *Centurion*."

I looked again. Before me was a full-sized battleship without a doubt—tripod masts, heavy guns, armored turrets. I recognized her; she *was* the *Centurion*, of the *Iron Duke* class; she'd fought at Jutland in World War I. "Quit trying to fool me, Captain," I objected. "I know a battleship when I see one."

"That's what our Italian friends think too," replied Damant. "We're pulling their leg, just the way we're pulling yours. Good job, isn't she?" Damant went on to explain that the *Centurion* years ago had had all her real guns and turrets taken off and had been reduced to service as a target ship. But when in World War II every battleship in the Med had been sunk or put out of action, the Admiralty had hastily fitted out the old *Centurion* with wooden guns and wooden turrets, mounted some real antiaircraft guns on her topsides, and sent her to the Med to fool the Italians. Cruising in the Med she'd kept four Italian dreadnoughts holed up, afraid to go to sea lest they should meet her.

Yes, I remembered the *Centurion*, all right. But all that was in 1942. What had that to do with me in 1944?

I soon learned. Before me was her new skipper. As he understood it, the *Centurion*, no longer needed anywhere as a dummy now that we had knocked Italy out of the war and controlled the Mediterranean completely, had been ordered home and the Admiralty had concluded she and her wooden guns could best serve the Allies, from here on out, as a Gooseberry. She was at the last minute being turned over to Operation Mulberry to be scuttled by her own crew as the key vessel in our line of old hulks to be sent to Omaha Beach. He, formerly her executive officer, had taken

HMS *Centurion*, disguised as the battleship she used to be, prepared for her final duty—being sunk as part of the artificial harbor at Normandy. (*Navy photo in the National Archives: 80-G-285146*)

over the command from the Royal Navy captain under whom she had masqueraded in the Med as a battleship in full commission.

So he was to scuttle the *Centurion*, eh? Queer end for a battleship. But it wasn't a bad idea—in death she would still keep on helping win the war. So huge a vessel, three times the size of any other ship we had, would make a wonderful anchor for the western end of our Gooseberry breakwater. And her antiaircraft battery, even after she was scuttled, would be a powerful addition to the air defenses of Omaha Beach.

The payoff came one day after D-Day. A huge battleship, three times the size of any troopship thereabouts, steamed from the transport area, headed inshore, far closer than any big ship ever before had gone. To the astonished Nazi artillery observers on the bluffs and to the unstrung GIs watching her from offshore, the black muzzles of her menacing 13.5-inch turret guns trained ahead as she steered in meant only one thing—she was going in with her main battery ready to blast those obnoxious inland guns off the face of the earth. On came that dreadnought, disregarding the shells bursting all about, evidently holding her own fire till she had a position that suited her.

When close in to the three hulks already protruding from the sea only a half-mile offshore, she swung slowly to starboard, obviously to present her whole port broadside to the shore, ready to let go a crashing salvo from all the guns she had.

She presented an even better target for them now, and the Nazi batteries inland, firing furiously, bracketed her from bow to stern as she swung parallel to the beach. And then to the horror of the GIs watching and to the delirious joy of the Nazi observers, before she could fire a single broadside, a series of internal

Storm waves wash over what is left of the *Centurion* as she sits in her watery grave off the Normandy beach. (*U.S. Coast Guard*)

explosions sank the ship and down went the *Centurion*.

I listened that night to the German radio program "Invasion Calling." Joseph Goebbels, the Nazi propaganda minister, had been in a tough spot on D-Day evening. Now, aside from gory prophecies of what should happen to us as soon as Rommel and his Panzers hit our forces behind the beachhead, "Invasion Calling" had hot news of amazing Nazi successes in the battle still going on for the beaches. To top off all, a British dreadnought, steaming in to strafe the beaches, had been sunk by the devastating fire of Nazi gunners. And more. The loss of life on that battleship had been terrific. So swiftly had she gone down, that out of more than a thousand men and officers comprising her crew, not more than seventy had been observed able to get on deck to abandon ship. The Allies had suffered a major disaster that ensured their swift defeat.

So, Dr. Goebbels? I couldn't keep from smiling as I listened. That harmless old dummy, the *Centurion*, to the very last still pulling the enemy's leg as she had in the Mediterranean, had now done her final bit for her country. She had gone down in a blaze of enemy publicity such as even the actual performance of her real 13.5-inch guns against the German High Seas Fleet at Jutland twenty-eight years before had never centered on her. Quite a finish for an innocuous old hulk.

Tremendous loss of life, eh? My thoughts ran back to the interview I'd had just the week before in Portsmouth with the *Centurion*'s new skipper. Hadn't

he told me then that his entire crew to steam the *Centurion* across the Channel on her last voyage had been reduced to seventy? He had. I chuckled. That Royal Navy three-striper had done an excellent job. In spite of all the fire Nazi artillery had laid on his ship while he was sinking her for our Gooseberry breakwater, he'd got his whole crew safely off and away from there. A good show.

On June 17, D+11, Lieutenant General Omar Bradley's troops succeeded in reaching the sea on the western shore of the Cotentin Peninsula at Barneville, slicing the peninsula completely across, cutting it off from the German army to the south, and neatly laying it out on the operating table, ready for the amputation of Cherbourg. Leaving three divisions to hold off the enemy on this southern flank, Bradley turned Major General J. Lawton Collins and his VII Corps northward toward his first main objective, Cherbourg, twenty miles away.

To shut Collins and his American troops off from any such access to the north, Lieutenant General Karl von Schlieben confidently expected to make a firm stand, hinged first on the city of Montebourg, and second and finally on Valognes. Both were heavily built Norman towns astride the road coming north to Cherbourg, both ideally suited for stout and long-dragged-out resistance from their thick-walled stone buildings and from the massive concrete pillboxes erected outside them long before to prohibit their being outflanked. The major delay Collins's VII Corps encountered at both Montebourg and Valognes came from waiting for his bulldozers to clear the blocked streets of shattered masonry so his armor could proceed northward through them.

On June 21 the siege of Cherbourg began. Bradley was ready for it. He had the men, he had the air support, he had the siege guns. He opened fire. But meanwhile, in Bradley's rear, real tragedy was brewing, which for the first time since the close of D-Day threatened to smash the invasion. On the afternoon of June 18 the seas in the Channel had started to roughen up perceptibly and the skies took on a peculiar appearance. A storm must be coming, the first since D-Day.

The regular weather report from the Allied Naval Commander Expeditionary Forces, posted on the bulletin boards for all to read, was for fair weather for the rest of the week, just gentle breezes. By nightfall of June 18 there was grave doubt all along the Omaha beachhead that the weather forecasters knew what they were talking about. Already the wind was above twenty knots—by no stretch of anyone's imagination any longer a gentle breeze. All work of unloading vessels from offshore by ferrying craft, whether DUKWs or LCTs, was suspended.

By morning it was blowing thirty knots. A storm was already kicking up a bad sea outside the harbor and was rapidly growing stronger. And now an even worse factor than the wind entered the picture. It was around the period of the new moon, when maximum spring tides were due. Between the high tides due anyway at that time, the falling barometer which of itself lifted the sea level, and those strong onshore winds piling the Channel waters high up on that lee shore, the sea level rose a full ten feet above any normal maximum and started to wash clear over the tops of the Phoenix breakwaters, as well as to sweep straight across the decks of the sunken Gooseberry ships.

It was evident the antiaircraft gun crews on board the Phoenixes were in danger; soon the seas would begin to wash them overboard. So they were hurriedly evacuated, no easy task with waves breaking over the Phoenix tops now. But it was done. Next, all traffic ashore over the floating roadways, undulating violently now on their heavy pontoons like writhing pythons, was suspended altogether. On the Lobnitz pierheads, everything portable was lashed down and extra hawsers run to secure more safely the vessels moored alongside.

The wind continued to increase as darkness fell on June 19. No doubt about it now; a real storm was already blowing; worse was likely to come. The weather reporting system had failed miserably; there had been no warning, giving reasonable time to get the hundreds and hundreds of small craft safely sheltered against a full-scale gale. All they could do now was to anchor inside the breakwaters, wherever they happened to be.

As a result, now came real trouble. The smaller landing craft—the LCTs and the LCMs, mainly, all ramp-type vessels—had no bow anchors. Their normal method of anchoring was by a wire line off a reel on their sterns, so that after touching down to unload over their ramps (having already dropped their stern anchors before beaching), they could then haul themselves astern and off the beach. But that method of anchoring had serious drawbacks in a storm. Stern to, a vessel—especially flat-sterned craft as these all were—does not ride storm waves so well as bows on to them.

Secondly, and worse, those wire lines, all that they had for moorings, had a woeful shortcoming as anchor cables in a storm. There was no spring whatever to them, as there is in a chain-link cable hanging in a long bight due to its weight, which under extra strain lengthens slowly into a flatter curve and eases the shock. But those wire anchor lines, already stretched as taut as bow strings by the tension on them, had no

Tugs maneuver concrete Phoenixes of the Mulberry harbor in preparation for sinking them to form a breakwater off the coast of Normandy. (*Navy photo in the National Archives: 80-G-46833*)

Army vehicles proceed toward the beach on a pontoon causeway connected to the floating Lobnitz pier in the foreground. (*Navy photo in the National Archives: 80-G-46827*)

possibility of any further give at all under any added strain. So when a heavy sea smacked the flat stern of one of those anchored craft, the inevitable happened— the already taut wire snapped under the blow, and that landing craft found itself instantly adrift in the storm, driving to leeward at the mercy of the seas.

The landing craft, caught without warning, anchored themselves by their sterns as usual and then did what they could to ease the strain on their anchor wires. They started up their diesels and kept them going full astern to mitigate the danger by easing the strain on their anchor wires. But it didn't always work. Some, half-waterlogged by seas breaking over them, couldn't get their soaked engines going; others, after long hours of such unexpected fuel consumption, ran out of fuel; still others, going full astern for such unusually long periods, suffered machinery breakdowns.

Regardless of the cause, the results in all cases, once engine power failed, were identical. Almost instantly after the next heavy sea smacked their flat sterns came a parted anchor line and then a landing craft with no motive power drifting helplessly before the storm.

Many drove up on the beach, which in itself was bad enough, but nothing compared to what followed when other helpless craft piled up on the same stretch of sand and then still others, with all of them churning against each other in the heavy surf and making hopeless masses of scrap iron of the lot, not to mention what happened to their crews caught between grinding steel and pounding surf.

Even worse occurred. Five LCTs, broken adrift, drove down before the storm in the night and crashed into the eastern roadway to the Lobnitz pierheads. Instantly, there was trouble. The battering LCTs smashed the concrete pontoons; banged holes in the steel ones; sank some pontoons completely; sank others on one end only, so that some of the bridge trusses submerged; and twisted other trusses sideways on upended pontoons. The Whale roadway was soon a terrible wreck.

The night dragged on, dawn came on June 20, the storm blew on. The tide during the morning was low. The Mulberry Seabees and their officers worked their hearts out, dragging those LCTs clear of their precious roadway and its pontoons, leaving the trusses free for resetting when the storm subsided. But the storm didn't subside. With afternoon came high water again and an increase in the storm.

Through all this Captain Clark had been shrieking orders—through loudspeaker and megaphone, into

The Lobnitz piers floated up and down with the tide, kept in place by vertical posts. (*British official photo*)

the teeth of the gale—for all adrift landing craft to keep clear of his Whales. When that failed to produce results, he reinforced his orders by frenzied threats of gunfire on any vessel disregarding them. But in the storm, orders and threats alike fell on deaf ears. The man who for a year had lived for nothing save to make a working reality of Mulberry had to stand impotently by and watch more and more of those fouled-up landing craft batter his priceless roadways to destruction. No longer did he have a tug left to drag them clear.

Night came, the storm increased—to what, nobody knew, but enough. And in those pounding seas now came still worse disaster. The Bombardons, a floating breakwater of dubious value, ironically turned now into an engine of further destruction for Mulberry. That twenty-four-hundred-foot-long floating steel barrier, set well offshore to form an outer harbor, tore from its moorings and broke up into its units. Those steel units, gigantic floating battering rams now, drifted to leeway before the storm waves to find a line of concrete Phoenixes directly in their path. There in the surging seas those ponderous two-hundred-foot-long sections of steel Bombardons started hammering away on the concrete Phoenix walls, battered many of them in, and as the tide fell, carried that destruction down to the low-tide line. Then, as the tide rose again, the unobstructed seas poured now through the gaps in the breakwaters to set up even worse waves in the inner harbor than before.

Another day, June 21, went by with the storm still continuing, the Bombardons making greater breaches in the Phoenix wall, the desolation over the harbor beyond description. And once again the waters off Omaha Beach were dotted with the bodies of the dead, mostly seamen from foundered landing craft this time, still clad in life preservers; a ghastly sight as they drifted amongst the spume and the spray of the breaking waves.

The storm waves began now to exert a powerful influence inland. What was beyond Rommel's power was well within theirs. Bradley, pounding away at the defenses of Cherbourg with every gun, large and small, found himself suddenly nearly out of ammunition. The steady flow from the beachhead which had heretofore at least kept up with the voracious demands of his guns, though allowing little leeway for building up a reserve, now stopped abruptly. Angrily, Bradley sent word back to the beachhead, demanding more ammunition.

When informed in reply that a storm at sea had shut down the port, he refused to believe it necessary, and sent some of his aides to order more landed regardless. The obedient aides, at the risk of their lives, made their way out over the twisted and tossing wreckage of the Whale roadways to learn what chance there was of somehow getting in some ammunition through the storm.

The only possible way was pointed out to them. Some small coasting steamers loaded with ammunition, riding out the storm at anchor well offshore, might be brought inside the Gooseberry breakwaters as near high tide as possible and stranded there. When the tide went out and left them completely high and dry, it might be possible to run trucks directly alongside the coasters on the wet sands and unload from their cargo hatches into the trucks, which, with luck, might then get all the way inshore without bogging down—some might, anyway.

The whole thing was dubious, but it might work. The only thing about it that didn't seem dubious was that the coasting steamers would most likely all leak like sieves thereafter from the pounding against the sands they'd get till the receding tide fell enough to leave them solidly on the bottom; they'd all probably be wrecks after that single unloading. It didn't seem worth it to sacrifice valuable ships for such a one-time operation in discharge; ships weren't that expendable; they could tell Bradley that.

The aides crawled back ashore to relay that message to Bradley on the battle front. The answer from Bradley was short and unequivocal—to hell with what happened to the ships—he had to have ammunition! If he didn't have some soon, the enemy could turn on his helpless troops and butcher them. More ammunition immediately, no matter what the cost to the ships.

So, storm or no storm, the coasters were run in,

Waves smash over a line of Phoenixes during the mid-June storm. Silhouetted at left is the antiaircraft cupola atop the concrete structure. In the distance is a Liberty ship on the horizon. (*U.S. Coast Guard*)

beached, and when the tide went out, unloaded directly into trucks—one thousand tons of ammunition on June 21, five hundred tons on June 22. Apparently, it sufficed as a stopgap.

Bradley, fuming and incredulous at what he'd been told, in view of the importance of the situation, came down on June 22 to see for himself, and then to speed up matters. But looking at a beach which to him seemed more littered with destruction than even on D-Day, he stood appalled, and made no further criticism of those running the harbor. Now he understood. For by night, when the gale finally subsided and a count could be made, it appeared that some eight hundred landing craft had been stranded on both British and American beaches, vast numbers of them beyond any hope of possible salvage and repair, three hundred of those hopelessly battered wrecks on our waterfront alone.

At Omaha Beach the wrecks were literally piled six deep against the shore end of our twisted Whale roadway. Other wrecks encumbered the waterfront from one end of the beach to the other. And one LCI(L), caught at sea outside the area of the harbor and there exposed to the full blast of the gale, had been flung bodily up on the rocks at the base of the cliffs near Pointe de la Percée, so high above any sign of high water in that vicinity that except by building launching ways under her and sending her down that incline, it was hopeless to expect ever again to get her back into the water.

It looked to every person gazing then on the remains as if the artificial harbors were through—and so also was our invasion. All the Nazis had to do now to toss our armies back into the sea was to stage their dreaded counterattack immediately. And surely now the Nazis knew it. The first night of the full storm—the night of June 19—when we no longer had any manned antiaircraft guns on the Phoenix line to keep them off, we'd seen more Nazi planes over Omaha dropping mines in our offshore shipping areas than on any night since we had first landed there. Undoubtedly, then, the Luftwatte had also scouted the harbors to see what the storm was doing to them; now they must know.

While the storm was still raging in the Channel, Commodore Howard Flanigan sent for me. He was deputy chief of staff to Admiral Harold Stark at U.S. naval headquarters in London. There had come in an urgent radio message from the Far Shore, asking my immediate return to Omaha Beach. I was to proceed instantly to Portsmouth and there catch the first dispatch boat able to get to sea again. I was to do what I could to get Mulberry back in service.

Early on June 23, on board one of the Coast Guard's eighty-three-foot picket boats, I was on my way out of Portsmouth. From the young ensign who was its skipper, I got an impression of what the storm, now

The storm sends its fury over the line of Liberty ships sunk to form the Gooseberry artificial harbor at Normandy. (*Painting by navy combat artist Dwight C. Shepler*)

subsiding, had been as seen by those at sea. He himself was much shaken. He (an experienced yachtsman before the Coast Guard grabbed him) had somehow managed to get his boat back into port the first day of the storm. That was more luck than some of his fellow Coast Guard skippers had had. Two of them at least, boats and crews together, had gone down in the gale—no survivors. And so had some of the Phoenix tows and much else that had been caught at sea on June 19.

Of course, after that, nothing had gone to sea again until this morning. All shipping in the Channel had been halted, all planes had been grounded. The weathermen in the U.K. were now announcing it had been the worst June storm to hit the Channel in eighty years. And we had caught it on the chin, wholly unwarned of its coming. As a matter of fact, we'd even been promised good weather instead! Our lack of warning had cost us plenty.

What it had actually cost us I never even vaguely appreciated till later that day as I stood again on Omaha Beach, gazing on wrecked landing craft in every direction and on such destruction as I could not have imagined possible from any cause—either from the fury of man at his worst or from nature at her most violent. Inshore lay a beach strewn with wrecks. Offshore lay the sunken ships of the Gooseberry breakwater, most of them now (including even the monster *Centurion*) with broken backs from the pounding they

After the big storm, landing craft lie tossed about as if they were toy boats. (*Navy photo in the National Archives: 80-G-46822*)

had received. And to their left, the concrete line of Phoenixes, with here and there huge chunks chewed out of that wall where the Bombardons had hammered them. And finally, two long Whale roadways, now two twisted and pathetic strings of wreckage running out to the heavily battered and partly foundered pierheads. It seemed wholly unbelievable. But it was so, and something had to be done about it.

Already the bulldozers were pushing or pulling aside enough wrecks here and there once more to allow workable though narrow passages for DUKWs up the sands and on to the beach road leading to the draws. And the DUKWs then saved the day, and no doubt the invasion also. For while the little landing craft—the LCMs and the LCTs—were being pounded by the hundreds to junk on the beaches or against the Whale roadways, the DUKWs (except for three or four lost the first afternoon)—all safely nestled well inshore on the plateau near their various dumps—rode out the storm on land, no more bothered by it than their half-brothers, the trucks, also parked on the bluffs above the beach.

The DUKWs now waddled down from the plateau and swam nobly into action alongside coasters and freighters brought into the inner harbor, and even out to those in the rougher water outside. Aided by the LCTs and LCMs, which had survived (about half the total), a veritable miracle in cargo handling was achieved. Ten thousand tons of cargo (most of it ammunition) were brought ashore on June 23, the first day after the gale, topping by a thousand tons the best record the port had ever made even before the storm. And next day, on the 24th, even that record went by the board—11,500 tons came in, to be topped again within two days, on June 26, when, working frenziedly to make good the deficit in ammunition before the enemy should strike at us, the men on Omaha Beach landed through the Mulberry Harbor 14,500 tons of supplies—not too far from double the 8,000 tons it had hoped for in preinvasion days.

Rommel had lost his golden opportunity. Heaps of artillery ammunition adequate to counter any attack now rested safely ashore in the dumps. With Cherbourg likely now soon to be in our hands, and the guns which were so voraciously chewing up ammunition in its reduction silent after that for a few weeks—till they should open again for a breakthrough at Saint Lo on the southern flank—those heaps could grow substantially. We were safe.

Meanwhile, a battle of a different nature was in the making on Omaha Beach. To back up the DUKW flotillas in unloading, the second order of business had been to clear away the wrecks from in front of the Colleville-sur-Mer and Saint-Laurent-sur-Mer draws where the LSTs had earlier grounded out to unload. That also was swiftly done since the wrecks there were all small. And soon, directly over the beaches, once again LSTs (none of which had been lost in the storm) were discharging their loads of warlike materials, from tanks rumbling ashore on their tractor treads to GIs stumbling ashore on their own two feet under inhuman packs.

The haggard Captain Clark, who literally had put his body and soul into the project, pressed eagerly for rehabilitation of the pierheads once enough clearance work had been done to get the DUKWs going again and the LSTs unloading on the sands. Would I next check the condition of the Lobnitz pierheads and their now-no-longer-floating roadways and advise whether it might not be possible to get at least part of them working again? It would practically double the usefulness of the LSTs, the most valuable vessels we had in

supporting the invasion, if only their turnaround time on Omaha could once again be reduced to the forty-minute period he had averaged in getting ashore the heavy artillery and the tanks in the three days before the storm.

Having put together in Massawa a whole naval base—from shops and piers to dry docks—from cannibalized pieces of smashed machinery, sabotaged by the Italians, I had no doubt a similar result could quickly be obtained from cannibalizing the wreckage of the floating piers in Omaha. I would guarantee it.

Eagerly, Clark rushed to the higher naval command afloat for authority to start. But all he got for his enthusiasm for rehabilitation was ice-cold water thrown in his face. The naval command afloat had never taken much interest in Operation Mulberry. It didn't then, when part of it was smashed by what some claimed wasn't even a storm really—just "a strong breeze."

And besides, Cherbourg was about to fall within a day or two; that was certain, and then we should have a real port. So Captain Clark was flatly refused permission to attempt any restoration of the damaged pierheads. The British could have what might appear salvable to them for repairs and extensions of their Mulberry B installation on their beaches to the eastward. That British artificial harbor, remarkably enough (due to its location—naturally less exposed to the fury of a storm from the northeast—and due partly also to

Mangled pontoon bridge sections lead to the Normandy beach; notice the jets of spray shooting up in the foreground through holes in the roadway. (*Naval Institute Collection*)

its still uncompleted state), had emerged with far less damage.

The most that would be done at Omaha would be to bring additional Phoenixes from England to patch the holes in the breakwater punched by the Bombardons, which, of course, would never be replaced. With only those minor repairs, our Mulberry Harbor might make out as best it could for the remainder of its existence, which would now not be long under any conditions. From the rosy estimates passed along to the higher command by the waiting salvage parties, Cherbourg should be operating within the week.

Captain Dayton Clark, utterly worn down anyway by

his hectic drive to get his harbor swiftly into operation after D-Day, then broken in body by his four-day battle with the elements to save it from destruction, now broken in spirit by this last rebuff, could take no more. The day after the capture of Cherbourg, June 26, he was on his way back across the Channel, bound for the Near Shore and hospitalization—as much and as badly wounded an invasion casualty as if, on D+1, one of those Nazi shells bracketing the first vessels he was sinking on the Gooseberry breakwater had burst in his face.

He had had it.

EDWARD ELLSBERG (1891–1983) stood number one of the 154 graduates in the Naval Academy's Class of 1914. After postgraduate training he was involved during World War I in the refitting of a number of captured German ships for U.S. service. In 1925, after the sinking of the U.S. submarine *S-51*, he dived on the wreck and eventually salvaged it. He established a reputation as one of the world's foremost experts on marine salvage and was later involved in submarine rescue work with the sinkings of the *S-4* in 1927 and the *Squalus* in 1939. In the late 1920s Ellsberg had resigned his regular navy commission to become chief engineer of the Tidewater Oil Company. With the coming of World War II, he was recalled to active duty and assigned to salvage work in the Middle East, Mediterranean, and later at Normandy. He was transferred to the Naval Reserve retired list in 1951 and worked thereafter as a consulting engineer. Admiral Ellsberg was a prolific author, writing seventeen books on such topics as his experiences in marine salvage and other naval subjects. His book *Pigboats* (Dodd, Mead, and Company, 1931) was made into the movie *Hell Below*. This chapter on Normandy is an excerpt from Admiral Ellsberg's last book, *The Far Shore*, published in 1960 by Dodd, Mead, and Company. (*Courtesy Edward E. Pollard*)

One lesson from any number of amphibious operations in World War II was that naval gunfire was an essential asset. Earlier accounts in this volume have addressed the fire support from armed landing craft, destroyers, and cruisers. Aircraft contributed as well, but the heaviest shelling was from the aged American battleships used in the operation. Most of the navy's battleship strength was in the Pacific, but the *Texas*, *Nevada*, and *Arkansas*—built a generation earlier—could still deliver the heavy ordnance. And because large navy ships carry marine detachments, the battleships provided several dozen marines an opportunity to participate in an operation thousands of miles away from where most of their counterparts were about to make an assault in the Pacific.

A particularly compelling facet of Rear Admiral Carleton Bryant's memoir is the description of German projectiles hitting his flagship *Texas* during the bombardment of Cherbourg. In one case, he got the happy news that a projectile was a dud. Similar news came to Commander Julian Becton of the destroyer *Laffey* during that same operation. Unfortunately, space limitations prevented inclusion in this book of Becton's account of his ship's role in the Cherbourg bombardment. In his *The Ship That Would Not Die*, Becton told of finding Czech markings on the unexploded projectile that landed in his destroyer. As he explained:

> When the Germans marched into Czechoslovakia in 1938, one of the prizes they took over was the giant Skoda munitions works. Skoda was recognized as one of the leading munitions makers of the time, and the Germans put Czech productive capacity to good use. But the Germans made one mistake. The Czechs didn't make very good slave laborers. They hated the Germans, and every chance they got, they did what they could to cause them trouble. That Czech shell that came to rest in the *Laffey*'s boatswain's locker—and many others the Germans fired at us at Cherbourg—must have been sabotaged.

BATTLESHIP COMMANDER

By Vice Admiral Carleton F. Bryant, U.S. Navy (Retired)

When I was promoted to captain, I began to hound the detail office in the Bureau of Navigation about getting a command. I said I would take anything, even a tugboat, to get me out of Washington. In April 1941 a classmate of mine in the detail office said the USS *Arkansas* needed a captain, then added, "But you wouldn't want *that*, would you?"

"Most assuredly," I replied. She was at the time more than thirty years old, the navy's oldest active battleship. But I was delighted to be afloat and have a command, no matter what. I took command of her at the Norfolk Navy Yard in April 1941 and turned her over to my good friend Dick Richards in 1943 after two of the most interesting and exciting years of my naval career. The ship spent much of that time escorting transatlantic convoys. After I was relieved and promoted to rear admiral, I became a battleship division commander. The convoy escort work continued then as well.

Serving as escort commander of troop convoys was a great experience—exciting, dangerous, and a great responsibility. In looking back, I shiver to think of the responsibility placed on the shoulders of a young captain, though at the time I took it in stride. Imagine, if you can, being responsible for some twenty-five to thirty merchant vessels, steaming at fifteen knots in nine columns of three ships each. They covered a front of five miles with a screen of some fifteen destroyers spread out ahead. It took ten days to make the crossing, and the incidents that took place within each twenty-four-hour period of those ten days were entirely my responsibility to handle.

The questions dealt with such things as submarine contacts, whether or not to zigzag and how much, what to do with the second ship in column two that was making too much smoke, and how to handle a sudden shutdown of fog. Hardly an hour went by during the day without some decision having to be made and made quickly—without hesitation.

When the weather and visibility were good, it was really quite pleasant. A cloudless sky, a calm sea, a bright, shining sun—it was sometimes difficult to remember a war was on. It was another matter in bad weather, wondering whether or not we could hold course and speed without the convoy falling apart.

And there were undoubtedly stresses on the young soldiers that we were carrying across to an unknown fate in the battle zone. On almost every trip, one or more ships would report having a man jump overboard when the situation got too big for him to handle. There was nothing we could do in those cases but keep going. I hope the men didn't survive too long in the water.

In May 1943 I was promoted to rear admiral and transferred from the *Arkansas* to become Commander Battleship Division Five. The division was made up of the old battleships *Texas*, *New York*, *Arkansas*, and later the *Nevada*. Even in the new capacity, I continued as escort commander, shifting from ship to ship as required. Occasionally, the various ship captains would be designated by Commander in Chief Atlantic Fleet to be escort commander. In those cases I had to find a relief flagship. For some months I flew my flag in the old wooden frigate *Constellation* in Newport, Rhode Island. Sitting in her after cabin of an evening, I sometimes half expected to see a door open and Stephen Decatur himself walk in, in full uniform, and ask, "And just what are *you* doing here?" Then for some weeks my flagship was the new USS *Iowa*—quite a contrast.

One of the things I missed after I had been promoted to admiral was being able to handle a ship myself. A captain handles his ship. He can manipulate the engine order telegraph, if he wishes, and even steer the ship. A flag officer, however, must keep hands off the ship he is riding. He can maneuver the group of ships he commands, but not an individual ship.

There was plenty of satisfaction in the work, whether as skipper or admiral, because of the contribution to the war effort. During the period from 1942 to 1944, when I was involved with fast troop convoys, I claim to have escorted some one million men safely across the Atlantic. Possibly an exaggeration, but not far off.

In the spring of 1944 I was called off escorting convoys and ordered to Belfast Loch, Northern Ireland, to prepare for the invasion of France in June of

The battleship *Texas* in her World War II rig. (*Navy photo in the National Archives: 80-G-233594*)

that year. We went through the motions there to keep the men occupied. Newcastle was a place down the coast, and we'd make believe that was the invasion place. We were furnished with some rubber topographical maps, made to scale, of the area where we would be shooting. They had all the contours. They also had every tree, every fence, every house, every ditch, and every dike on them. We put one of these maps up in a secret room in the *Texas*, at a level that would represent the distance from which our people would see the shoreline, and we let them study it. The German gun emplacements were not on this rubber map but were marked on our paper charts.

During our stay in Belfast I was ordered to London and Portland several times to learn about the plans for Normandy, particularly for my part in that operation. At one such meeting we gathered in an old school building for a conference of all the high-ranking officers who had planned the invasion, together with all the ranking officers of the various services involved. Included were Churchill, Eisenhower, Montgomery, commanders of the U.S. and British air forces, the general officers who had drawn up the plans—everyone who had any part in preparing for this big operation. A German bomb, dropped on that particular building on that day, would certainly have upset things.

For the invasion on June 6 I was designated commander of the gunfire-support group for Omaha Beach, for which I had under me the battleships *Arkansas* and *Texas*, a squadron of destroyers, two British cruisers, and two French cruisers. Omaha Beach shelved sharply upward toward a road, and then cliffs

rose two hundred feet to the countryside. On the far right side of Omaha was a high cliff on which enemy batteries were believed to be located. These were the primary target of the larger naval vessels; the destroyers closer to shore had as their assignment the machine-gun emplacements in the cliffs. The London fire department trained a force of commandos to scale the cliff wall at its highest point, using fire ladders and other scaling equipment.

On the night before the invasion, minesweepers preceded our heavy bombardment group across the English Channel. We anchored in our proper position about 1:00 A.M. to await dawn, the hour when our bombardment was to start. It was an eerie night. The full moon was shielded from us by a cloud layer. Those conditions produced a kind of half-twilight. There wasn't much sleep on board any of the ships. Gunfire and flashes could be heard and seen in the back country, where paratroops were being landed. Passing by us all night were small amphibious craft loaded with men. Some were making for Pointe de Hoc, where commandos were to scale the cliff. Others contained underwater demolition teams who would work on the beach obstructions.

Early dawn finally came, and there before us was the French coast. The bombers made their runs on the beaches, and we could see their bombs explode, the antiaircraft fire directed at them, and the occasional sight of a plane caught in searchlight beams. Now and then a green parachute would drop from the clouds and land in the water. Our time came shortly before six o'clock in the morning. The naval vessels opened up on shore defenses; it was a noisy time and *awesome*. After our allotted time, our fire ceased, and we awaited calls from our fire-control officers sent ashore in the landing parties, but none came. Later we learned that nearly all had been killed.

From our distance offshore we could see men, tanks, guns, and landing craft on the beach, but we were unable to tell friend from foe. At the foot of a cliff was a whole group of men, but I didn't know if they were Germans or ours. Nothing was moving. We knew instinctively that something was wrong. The beach was a most alarming sight. Tanks were burning, ships were burning, and every so often a larger explosion would indicate a hit on an ammunition dump. That was very frustrating, because we had all sorts of gun power but didn't know how to use it.

At about the middle of our sector was a gully up which our men and equipment were to go to get inland. But nothing at all was going up it. A mass of men were huddled at the sea, and nothing moved. I finally obtained permission from Rear Admiral Alan Kirk, our senior naval commander on the scene, to fire a few 14-inch shells from the *Texas* up the gully. The ship fired perhaps half-a-dozen rounds, and they had immediate effect. Soon we could see Germans coming down the gully with their hands up. Then our men, guns, trucks, and so forth began to move up the gulch.

As for the guns on Pointe de Hoc that the commandos planned to silence by scaling the cliffs behind Omaha Beach—they weren't there. Fortunately for us, the Germans had been so beaten down by the air people before D-Day that they had actually taken the guns out. They had them in a lane back some distance from where they had been. I don't know what they were going to do with those guns. Actually, we didn't receive any fire from big guns at Omaha Beach, which was fortunate because we were close and would have been hit. The fire that was directed at us came from machine guns, small mortars, and stuff like that. Splashes came around us. Mines, of course, were a threat.

The next afternoon, June 7, things began to look bad again. Shells were landing among the landing craft on the beach and raising particular hell. At first we couldn't see where the firing was coming from. But finally we spotted smoke rings caused by the firing of the enemy guns. We had a wild time for an hour or so focusing on these rings, and finally the harassing fire stopped. The German machine guns were in a tunnel that ran along the top of the cliffs. When under fire, the crews would duck out of sight, then come out again and man their well-concealed guns when our fire stopped. It took a couple of days to root them all out.

Some two miles inland was a church tower. We got the word that the Germans were probably using it to direct fire onto the beach—fire then at its heaviest. Now, I can't say that they actually were using it for an observation post, but if they weren't, they were dumb,

because it made an excellent one. After several requests we got permission to knock it out. From a gunnery point of view, what followed was a beautiful sight. The first shot from the destroyer assigned the job knocked off the very top of the tower, the second took off the next third, and the third shot took the rest—all in a few seconds. (When I revisited the town in 1960 I found that American contributions had fully restored the church.)

The following days were pretty much of the same order. By this time our landings were secure, and we had established communication with our fire-control observers ashore. Some days were slack; on others we had incessant calls for fire: a town, a crossroad, a concentration of troops or tanks at such and such a point. Several days we gave support fire continuously.

We remained off Omaha Beach for some two weeks, giving gunfire support to the army ashore as requested—and undergoing nightly air attacks. Normally, there is a hum or a buzz in a ship when she is operating. But during those air attacks there was an eerie silence. Everybody just stood still—listening. There was one encouraging sound in the *Texas* during those attacks. The ship had a jamming device to interfere with the enemy radar and buzz bombs. It made a squealing or screeching noise, and that was a reassuring sound when everybody on deck was so quiet.

It was quite evident to me during these attacks that we were in as much danger from friendly ships firing as we were from enemy planes. When firing began, every merchant ship let go with everything she had, and the guns were not always pointed at the enemy airplanes. Shrapnel fell on our decks like snow. So we decided to shift anchorage to a position close to shore, near where a landing field had been built and antiaircraft guns installed. This worked out well; we kept our own guns silent and just sat and watched the show.

I had a couple of mess attendants who served in my flag mess. They didn't have any battle stations, but they wanted to get into the war. So we had them assigned to an antiaircraft gun. I had seen plenty of war by then, so I just went to my emergency cabin and tried to sleep through the darn air attacks. One morning, after the ship had been through a pretty good air attack the night before, a mess attendant brought me my breakfast. He liked to talk, and I could tell that he was just bursting to tell me something. He said, "Admiral, where were you in that air attack last night?"

I said, "I was right here in the cabin."

"That was a pretty bad one, wasn't it?"

I said, "Oh, yes." Actually, I didn't feel very good that morning. I hadn't gotten much sleep.

"Yes, sir. There was a lot of shooting going on."

"Yep."

"We shot down a plane. Did you know that?"

"Is that so?"

A near miss by a German 11-inch projectile throws up a waterspout between the *Arkansas*, foreground, and the *Texas* during the bombardment of Cherbourg on June 25. (*Navy photo in the National Archives: 80-G-244210*)

"Yes."

"Well, that's good."

He waited for me to say something else, and I didn't say anything, so he said, "Do you know who shot down that plane?"

I said, "No. No, I don't. Who did?"

"Me and Blair." Blair was the other mess attendant.

Well, I imagine right to this day he's telling somebody that he and Blair shot down a German airplane. And maybe they did.

On June 25 we were part of a force sent to bombard enemy fortifications at the city of Cherbourg, which our troops had surrounded on the land side. At the time, I didn't believe the operation was necessary, nor do I now. It subjected our ships to an unnecessary risk of damage.

I was in the *Texas*, in charge of a section that also included the *Arkansas* and some destroyers. Rear Admiral Mort Deyo and his ships were on the other side. We approached Cherbourg from the east of up-Channel, where we would find several large batteries at intervals along the shore. We were on our toes, ready for them—only to have our spotter planes report that the batteries were abandoned. It was a beautiful sunny Sunday, with a bright ripple on the water. As we followed our minesweepers toward Cherbourg, we were lulled into a false sense of security. I was on the flag bridge, and I could hear the captain and the exec down below on the ship's bridge. They were chinning about what their mothers had cooked for them when they were home, and so forth.

Suddenly, we saw three tall splashes among the minesweepers ahead of us. Those were followed some thirty seconds later by three more among the destroyers and in another thirty seconds by three more close

aboard ahead of the *Texas*. One splash was under our port bow. The ship's crew later found that projectile unexploded. It was resting in the bunk of a warrant officer's stateroom, just over a magazine for the 14-inch ammunition for the *Texas*'s guns. (Back in England it was defused and kept on board the ship. It can now be seen on board the *Texas* at her permanent berth near Houston.)

The salvos fired at us all landed within three or four minutes, but we could not see where the enemy shore battery was located. Therefore, Captain Charles Baker, commanding officer of the *Texas*, reversed course with the idea of making another try when the battery had been located. This he did, and this time the ship opened fire on what we believed was the site of a three-gun battery of 11-inch guns. (This was the type of gun we had expected at Omaha Beach but had not encountered there.) For the next fifteen minutes we were under heavy fire from this battery, and it was doing some fine shooting. They had us pretty well pinpointed. Having 11-inch shells fired at you is no fun. You can actually see those black specks when they pass over you. They have the most seductive sound—a soft swish, almost a caress. Then, when the salvo hits the water, there is the most ungodly smack you ever heard—sharper than that of your own guns firing.

Well, of course, we knew that the enemy would get us sooner or later—and he did. At about 1:15 in the afternoon, a German shell hit the top of the conning tower and exploded upward, doubling the deck of the captain's bridge back on itself and splattering fragments up through the deck of the flag bridge. The ship's bridge was wrecked. One man was killed, his legs severed. The captain escaped, having just given the order "Right rudder," and then stepping outside the

A sailor begins repair work on the hole made in the side of the *Texas* when she was hit by a dud projectile at Cherbourg. (*Marine Corps photo from the Fred Freeman Collection at the Naval Institute*)

Back in New York, Admiral Bryant and the skipper of the *Texas*, Captain Charles Baker, pose with the dud projectile that lodged in the battleship off Cherbourg. Notice the grooves at the base of the shell, designed to fit into the rifling of the German gun barrel. (*Courtesy Captain Carleton F. Bryant Jr.*)

starboard door to see if he would clear the *Arkansas*, which was following us. The gunnery officer, at his periscope, was knocked unconscious.

We on the flag bridge, about ten feet higher up, were scared to death but unharmed. The war correspondent who was on the flag bridge at the time later asked, "How do you get used to things like that?"

I lied to him and said, "Just our training, I guess." I was glad to know that I had fooled him at the time.

After what seemed hours, I was able to speak to Captain Baker, who had gone to the conning tower to take control of his ship from there. I relayed the order I had just received from the admiral in charge to "Cease exercise and return to port." We did so without further ado. Cherbourg fell to our forces the next day, but I don't believe our venture advanced the surrender one hour!

CARLETON FANTON BRYANT (1892–1987) graduated from the Naval Academy in 1914 and then served in the battleship *Wyoming* for five years, including overseas duty during World War I. Afterward he received postgraduate education in ordnance and gunnery and put that knowledge to use subsequently as fire-control officer of the battleship *Pennsylvania* and gunnery officer of the aircraft carrier *Saratoga*. He was an inspector of ordnance at the shipyard where the *Saratoga* was built. In the early 1930s he had a variety of duties on the China station, including service in gunboats and the destroyer *Stewart*. After ordnance inspection duty at Quincy, Massachusetts, he commanded the gunboat *Charleston* and then served in the Office of Naval Intelligence in Washington. From 1941 to 1943 Bryant was commanding officer of the battleship *Arkansas* during convoy-escort duty across the Atlantic. He continued in convoy escort after being promoted to rear admiral in 1943 and duty as Commander Battleship Division Five. In 1944 he was commander of a gunfire-support group for the invasion of Omaha Beach, the bombardment of Cherbourg, and the invasion of southern France. In 1944–46 he served as Commander Fleet Training Command Atlantic Fleet, then retired in May 1946, having served exactly thirty-six years after joining the navy in May 1910. (*Naval Historical Center: NH 51564*)

A STRANGE PLACE FOR A MARINE

By Irvin Airey

One thing that particularly struck me when I joined the marine detachment of the battleship USS *Arkansas* was that every one of us was the same size—same height, about the same weight, and practically the same shoe size. Talk about uniform! I don't think they stocked more than a couple of sizes for us in the uniform locker. When you went to get a pair of skivvies or something, they wouldn't even ask your size. They'd just throw you a pair and know it would fit. When we lined up for inspection on that old battlewagon, you could look down the row to left and right, and everybody's nose was at the same level as your own. So few marines were in shipboard detachments that the Corps could pretty well pick and choose people who matched.

Kids in navy ships today have no idea how rough it was to serve in one of those old battleships. In 1944 the *Arkansas* was *the* oldest—commissioned in 1912. Before I reported, I went through the Marine Corps sea school in Portsmouth, Virginia. That was the typical preparation for a marine going to the detachment of a navy ship. We had been trained for land warfare, and this was to get us ready to go to sea. Just as I was being detached, a marine at the school gave me a bucket to pack away in my seabag. I said, "What in the hell do I want a bucket for? I'm not going to swab decks in any damn ship."

He said, "Well, you'll need this. No matter what happens, you keep this bucket." Then I reported aboard the *Arkansas* at the Brooklyn Navy Yard. She was in for repairs while between voyages on North Atlantic convoy duty. I got ready to go back to the head, in the stern of the ship, so I could take a shower. I heard people guffawing at me, because there were no showers. Then I noticed that other marines were coming back from the head. They had wooden clogs on their feet and towels around their middles. Each of them was carrying his bucket, bar of soap, and toothbrush.

And that's the way it worked. I would get one bucket of water a day (two in port) that I used for washing, shaving, and brushing my teeth. Someone did put it under a steam jet to heat it for me, but that's all there was. If you wanted to drink some water, you had to stand in line at the scuttlebutt. There were no commodes in the head. You had to sit down over a trough that had salt water flowing through to flush it. When the ship was in rough seas, you learned to squat over the trough rather than sit down; otherwise, you might get splashed on the backside. That was really the old navy.

Shipmates, both Marine Corps and U.S. Navy, pose on the *Arkansas*'s forecastle, under the guns of her forward turret. Irvin Airey is at the far left. (*Courtesy Irvin Airey*)

The *Arkansas*, left, and *Texas* were two of the fleet's oldest battleships in 1944. Here they are shown in their youth, passing through the Gatun Locks of the Panama Canal in July 1919. The camera angle is deceiving. The *Texas* was actually slightly larger than the *Arkansas*. (*Naval Institute Collection*)

Actually, in comparison with the sailors, the Marine Corps detachment on that ship had it made. We had our own sleeping quarters with pipe-frame bunks that folded down from stanchions. The sailors had to sleep in hammocks that were slung between stanchions in their compartments. It was an art to learn to sleep in one of those, and quite a few newly arrived sailors had the painful experience of falling out and dropping several feet to that hard steel deck. The marines also had lockers to store our uniforms and steam irons to press them. The sailors had to live out of their seabags and do their own laundry. Despite all this, the sailors and marines had a good relationship. I didn't see any animosity; we were true shipmates.

The *Arkansas* was so old that I used to kid my wife after the war that occasionally we had had to run up the sails on the ship or to start rowing. It was really antiquated. For one thing, the steel plates were held together by rivets instead of welding. When we got out into rough seas in the North Atlantic on convoy duty, we'd sometimes be awakened from a sound sleep when the ship would start creaking and groaning. If one of the rivet heads popped off, it would sound like a damn gun going off as the loose piece shot out. Then it would ricochet down through a passageway before coming to rest. You'd pull in your head real quick in case one of those things came flying around.

Old as she was, the *Arkansas* had to be pressed into service to support the invasion of France because all the new battleships were over in the Pacific at that time. We went into Ireland, then came around into the English Channel when it was time to go to Normandy. Around ten o'clock on the night of June 5, we went to our battle stations. I was a corporal then, and my station was on the fantail. One of the sergeants made all of us take our M-1 rifles up on deck with us, and we put them in the ammunition lockers while we manned our battle stations. The M-1s were there in case we saw any floating mines; we would try to set them off with rifle fire. All of us in the marine detachment were experienced marksmen, but I don't think many guys wanted that job, because we knew what mines would do. Around three o'clock in the morning we could hear the explosions and the concussion as the minesweepers set off the mines in the approaches to the beach at Omaha. So that was a relief.

My battle station was as gun captain of the crew for one of the 20-millimeter antiaircraft guns. In the darkness we could see flashes from the German antiaircraft guns shooting at American planes heading over the beach. The noise of the engines of those hundreds of airplanes flying over was one big hum. Some were going to France, some were coming back. They were practically intertwined; how in God's name they didn't run into each other, I don't know. Sometimes the darkness would be interrupted temporarily when a plane was hit and turned into a fireball.

It was a chilly, damp night, and I guess I fell asleep about 3:30 A.M. while we were waiting for the landings to begin. I was leaning up against the gun shield with a gun cover pulled around me to try to keep warm. Two guys stayed on the phone lines, ready to wake up those of us who were sleeping when something came up. Someone woke me up around 5:30, just about the time it was starting to get light. I saw that the *Arkansas* was anchored about two miles off Omaha Beach, parallel to the shore. My 20-millimeter mount was on the port side, facing the beach.

Right around dawn—as soon as the Germans could see us—an 88-millimeter gun opened up on us from the beach and fired maybe ten rounds in our direction. They must have been terrible gunners, because there were so many ships out there to shoot at that I don't know how they could have missed hitting something. The shells were close enough that we were getting splattered with shrapnel in our positions on deck. We managed to duck down behind the shield of a 40-millimeter mount back there. The *Arkansas* opened up with her guns and quieted that German 88.

I never was scared that day. It was more a sense of excitement and wondering what the day would be like. I had the feeling that if something bad happened, it was going to happen to somebody else, not to me. If you didn't approach it that way, you'd go nuts. Part of it may have been that we were so young we didn't give a damn. We were living for the next moment—to see what would happen. Now, I did notice some worry lines in the faces of a couple of those older marines we had, the sergeants who had been around for a long time and probably had wives and children back home.

After the day grew brighter and the troops were getting ashore, the German gunfire shifted to them rather than the ships. The soldiers on the beach were catching hell. We couldn't see individual soldiers, but we could certainly see the hail of fire that was coming down from the cliffs in back of Omaha Beach. Our feeling in the crew was that we were there as a kind of backup—a floating, expendable fort. We could cover the retreat if the soldiers had to be pulled off the beach the way the British were rescued at Dunkirk in 1940. The three American battleships at Normandy—the *Arkansas*, *Texas*, and *Nevada*—were among the oldest in the fleet, so we figured the navy had decided it wouldn't lose all that much if we were sunk.

I remember that D-Day was a long, long, long day, with a lot of time up on deck for us. We didn't get to eat regular meals. We ate K rations, which weren't even as good as the C rations that soldiers were getting. Those K rations would give you a sour stomach for a week. The reason for the boxed meals was that the galley in that old ship was topside, and the captain didn't want any fires burning in stoves in case the *Arkansas* was hit.

The 12-inch guns did do some shooting during that long day, and things gradually got quieter as the soldiers ashore got a foothold and began heading inland. We figured we would get pounded once it got dark. Around dusk a Messerschmitt flew out over the ships off the beach. It was in among the various American ships and was quickly shot down by their antiaircraft fire. Who did it, I don't know: the *Arkansas* took credit for it; the *Tuscaloosa* took credit for it; and the *Texas* took credit for it. Everybody took credit for that one aircraft that was shot down. I pulled the trigger on the 20-millimeter and fired off half-a-dozen shots at the damn thing. I don't think I even came close to it; I was only shooting with the rest of them. Tracer bullets were flying around all over the place—quite a spectacle there in the darkness. It reminded me of the sparks thrown up by an acetylene torch.

The next morning, landing craft began bringing casualties aboard from the beach. Many of them were going to the LSTs that were rigged up as hospital ships, but we had medical personnel and facilities that weren't being used for the crew, so some of these wounded soldiers were coming to the *Arkansas*. Sometimes we felt a little sorry for ourselves because of being stuck in such an old ship, especially when a brand-new one like the heavy cruiser *Quincy* sped past while we were just chugging along. On the other hand, when we compared our lives in the *Arkansas* with those of the soldiers on the beach, we felt we were much better off than they were. I remember seeing one wounded soldier brought aboard after he had stepped on a mine about the third day of the invasion. He still had his boot on when he came aboard, but the calf of his leg was gone, and you could see the bone. His leg was amputated on our ship.

After about two weeks at Normandy, the *Arkansas* went to Portsmouth, England, to replenish ammunition. From there we went to join the force bombarding Cherbourg on a Sunday morning, June 25. It was a beautiful sunny day. The water was like a piece of glass. There was really no need for the American ships to shoot up that city, because the U.S. soldiers had advanced far enough on land that they were about to cut it off. I think the navy ships took part just to try to make themselves look good. The Germans let us get in as close as we wanted, then they really caught us. The old *Texas* caught two of their shots. When those projectiles started falling all around our ships, those of us on deck were saying, "Come on, let's shag-ass out of here." We shagged out.

We then went back to England briefly and on into the Mediterranean to prepare for the invasion of southern France. We did some bombardment as part of that landing and later picked up some prisoners of war. We were going to take them to Palermo, Sicily, but they weren't welcome there, so we finally landed them at Oran, North Africa. This was a work battalion, and there were maybe only five Germans in the entire group. The rest of them were Armenians, Yugoslavians, Bohemians—you name it. They were a scroungy-looking lot.

After that we returned to the United States. The ship pulled into Boston for repairs and painting. I went on leave and came back home to Baltimore. One day I went downtown with my mother because she wanted me to meet one of her friends and go to lunch. While we were walking down the street, two army MPs came up to me. "Let's see your papers," one of them demanded. I showed them my leave papers. One of

In a respite between the invasions of Normandy and southern France, the crew of the old *Arkansas* gathers topside at Oran for a USO show. The featured attraction was entertainer Jack Haley, who portrayed Tin Man in *The Wizard of Oz*. (*Navy photo in the National Archives: 80-G-244201*)

them took a close look at the ribbons on my chest. He handed back my papers and asked, "How come you've got a European-North African ribbon with battle stars?"

"I was over there for the invasions at Normandy and southern France," I told him.

"The hell you were over there," he said. "There's no marines over there. It's all army." So I told him about the old *Arkansas* and her marine detachment. But I can't really blame him for being skeptical. In 1944 France really was a strange place for a marine.

IRVIN ALBERT AIREY (1924–) was born and educated in Baltimore, Maryland. He enlisted in the Marine Corps in January 1943 and received boot training at Parris Island, South Carolina. After attending sea school at Portsmouth, Virginia, he reported to the *Arkansas* in March 1943. From operations in the Atlantic and Mediterranean, the ship went to the Pacific to support the invasions of Iwo Jima and Okinawa. Mr. Airey was detached from the ship in August 1945 and discharged from the service that October. After returning to civilian life he worked as a mechanic for various companies, including Cummings Diesel. In 1955 he joined the Baltimore City Police Department and spent ten years as a patrolman, four on foot and six in police cars. In 1965 he became a police detective and remained in that capacity until his retirement in 1980. During his police career he was shot at more than when he was in the Marine Corps. He was decorated for his police service with five bronze stars and two silver stars. Since his retirement, Mr. Airey and his wife have lived in Fallston, Maryland, north of Baltimore. (*Courtesy Irvin Airey*)

One of the biggest reasons for choosing to invade France at Normandy was the element of surprise—hitting the Germans somewhere besides where they expected. A large drawback was the necessity of landing over open beaches rather than in established ports. Cherbourg did offer such a port, and thus the Allied plans called for its capture as quickly as possible. An individual who played a heroic part in that capture was a versatile Coast Guard officer named Quentin Walsh. He had gone to the British Isles initially because of the Coast Guard's role in supervising the merchant marine in wartime. Later he became involved in invasion planning and the question of lining up port facilities. When needed he served with the navy, and once ashore he moved into Cherbourg side by side with the army. There he demonstrated how to win a poker hand—by bluffing.

Another officer who got into the Cherbourg area after having been in Britain previously was Captain George Bauernschmidt of the U.S. Navy's Supply Corps. He had been a line officer and thought like a line officer, but he also perceived the importance of logistics. It wasn't enough to get the fighters to the scene of the fight. They had to be supplied and fed. Bauernschmidt was a keen observer of the scene, one with a wry sense of humor in reporting what he saw in both England and France.

THE CAPTURE OF CHERBOURG

By Captain Quentin R. Walsh, U.S. Coast Guard (Retired)

Initially, I went to England with Commander Alfred C. Richmond as part of the Coast Guard units established to hold hearings and to handle problems concerning U.S. ships and personnel in British ports. I was assigned to Gourock, Scotland, on the River Clyde, serving there from July to September 1943. Then I was ordered to London. Because of the Coast Guard's role in port administration, Admiral Harold Stark had asked Richmond for an officer to deal with matters involved with the capture of ports in France, and I was it. I was originally part of the navy planning and logistics staff, serving under a fine officer named Neil Dietrich. I soon became chief staff officer to Captain Norman Ives, a submariner who was designated as Commander Advanced Bases. I was given security clearance as a "Bigot" and attended meetings at Norfolk House to coordinate plans for the ports on the French coast.

The planning for the invasion of Normandy was completed about the end of January 1944. One of the objectives was the early capture of the port of Cherbourg to supplement the over-the-beach flow of supplies at Omaha and Utah beaches. I wrote the plan for the occupation, clearance, and operation of Cherbourg. This included details of operation and protection against limpet mines. The plan was later expanded to include Le Havre and other captured ports, including Brest, Quiberon Bay, Saint-Malo, and Granville.

One idea was that these ports would be operated by personnel already overseas in England. I opposed that because we needed to keep those people in England to provide continuing support to forces going to France. Instead, I believed that we should bring over navy personnel from the United States and train them for their role in France. Captain Ives and Commodore Howard "Pat" Flanigan of Stark's staff supported my idea, and Seabees were sent over from the United States. They were put into what were known as Drew units and amounted to some twelve hundred men altogether. They were put up at Base Two in January 1944. This was the site of an existing U.S. Navy base at Roseneath, Scotland, on the River Clyde. In fact, it had been used previously for training the men who invaded North Africa in November 1942.

The question came up of what we were going to find in the French ports once they were liberated, because we knew damn well that the Germans would do their best to destroy them. I suggested to Ives that we find out for ourselves what shape the ports were in, rather than depending on information from the army. We could do that by sending in a naval reconnaissance party, because our people would have a better idea what to look for. We could find out what was wrong with a given port and then advise the chain of command. That suggestion was approved.

In April, because of my work on the Cherbourg plan, I was ordered to Base Two. My job was to organize, train, and command a navy reconnaissance unit. We would go along with the army in entering Cherbourg and other ports. We would then determine the condition of the ports, ascertain the extent to which they had been mined, and set up a navy headquarters. In the course of preparation for that mission, I talked with Rear Admiral John Wilkes, who was in charge of amphibious training for the forces going to France. He was one fine, excellent officer—tough and efficient. At one point, before I went to Scotland, he came up to London, and I had a conference with him for about half an hour. He said, "Do you need any more men, supplies, or equipment? We'll get you anything you want, but I don't want any excuses from you when we get over there." The successful performance of the forces he trained and supplied was the best testimony to his effectiveness.

When I reported to Base Two, I told the base commander that I needed three Nissen huts for quarters, about fifty-five men, four motorcycles, two, two-and-a-half-ton trucks, nine Jeeps, a communication truck, and various infantry weapons. I told him I was ordered to carry out a special mission in connection with the upcoming invasion, but I couldn't give him the details because he didn't have the necessary "Bigot" clearance. He and his executive officer, both of whom were naval officers, looked at me as if I had come off the moon. Who the hell was this guy from the Coast

Guard asking for all this stuff? So they said they wouldn't give it to me. Recalling my talk with Admiral Wilkes, I called Commodore Flanigan in London. I don't know what he told the commanding officer at Roseneath, but it certainly changed his attitude. I received cooperation immediately. I still had to insist in order to get brand-new equipment, but eventually I received everything I needed.

About three hundred men from the Seabees responded to my request for volunteers for a special mission. I had been told before leaving London to keep my outfit to a minimum in order to cut down on transportation requirements for getting them to France. This is why we wound up with only fifty-three. Having a large pool to choose from, we got an excellent group. All of them could drive Jeeps and trucks. All had basic training in the use of firearms. Included were divers, bomb disposal men, radio operators, and intelligence specialists. Many could speak French, and a few could speak German. Many of these men had some college education; the enlisted men ranged in age from nineteen to twenty-three. I couldn't have asked for a finer bunch of guys.

I selected Lieutenant Jack Curley, a former marine who had transferred to the Seabees, as executive officer. The communication officer was Naval Reserve Lieutenant George LeVallee. He was a French native who had grown up and been educated in the United States, then had business dealings with people in France. LeVallee proved an invaluable asset in the organization. He had the uncanny ability to look at a Frenchman and know what he was thinking. (One exception came much later, when we entered the French city of Le Havre, which had been devastated by British bombers. We encountered an elderly Frenchman, whom LeVallee greeted with a friendly "Good morning." The old man came over to our Jeep and said, "You kill my friends, you kill my family, you ruin my home, you ruin my city. Then you say 'good morning' to me." He concluded by spitting on our Jeep.")

After the men moved into the Nissen huts at Base Two, we got going on the training, and it was arduous. We started at five in the morning. We ran a mile before breakfast. We had calisthenics; we went through the obstacle course. A small mock village made of canvas and wood gave us the place to practice tactics for house-to-house fighting. We used ranges for firing pistols, rifles, bazookas, and hand grenades. My idea was to make the training so tough that combat would seem easy by comparison.

In the evenings, after the physical training was completed for the day, we crammed in still more with films on such topics as bomb disposal, booby traps, reconnaissance duties, camouflage, and house-to-house fighting. To give us an even better idea how to

perform reconnaissance, I contacted the Third Army and asked for assistance. It came in the form of a colonel from the 28th Division. He brought with him five officers and seven enlisted men, and they trained us in the hills around Base Two and Loch Lomond. They covered reconnaissance, map reading, bazookas, hand grenades, and rough-and-tumble fighting. Except for the use of live ammunition, we got the same training as combat infantrymen. I still have vivid memories of the map reading and tactical problems performed at night in driving rain.

In late May we moved from Scotland to a bivouac area about six miles west of Southampton, England. On May 28, at Breamore, I reported to Major General J. Lawton Collins; he was commander of the army's VII Corps and one superb officer. I told him that the navy had ordered my outfit to land on D-Day over Utah Beach. Then we were to accompany the division that captured Cherbourg and go to work.

When he heard that, General Collins had a staff member pull aside a curtain covering a map of France. He showed me the disposition of all German divisions in the areas of Pas-de-Calais, Normandy, and Brittany. The original plan was to capture Cherbourg around D+6, but he didn't think it could be taken until about D+20. So he revised my orders; my task unit would come ashore a few days after D-Day.

About the same time, at Portland, I reported to Rear Admiral Don Moon, commander of the Utah Beach task force. Unlike Collins, who introduced me to his staff, Moon was working alone in a tiny office, getting into the details himself. He designated me Commander Task Unit 127.2.8 and told me to report to Admiral Wilkes once I got ashore in Normandy.

While in the marshaling area, we shifted into wax-impregnated outer garments so we would have protection against possible gas attack. The army figured that if the Germans used gas, we would have about 70 percent casualties. We remained in these uniforms until early July, when our trucks caught up with us. The result was like walking around in a steam bath all day and in a suit of ice at night. On June 8 we boarded the Liberty ship *James A. Farrell*, along with 250 Royal Marine commandos, U.S. paratroopers, and an assortment of other army personnel and equipment. There must have been at least five hundred men on board the ship for the crossing to France.

We arrived at Utah Beach on June 9 and had everything off-loaded by the following day. We had trouble getting all the vehicles ashore by LCIs because some of them were dumped in holes in the beach and drowned out. We had to wait and move them inland at low water. Some of the men were able to proceed inland immediately with their vehicles. Those of us who remained stayed in foxholes on the beach. We were soaking wet, and the wax-impregnated clothing added

Armored units roll through the ruins of shattered Valognes on the road toward Cherbourg. A Coast Guard combat photographer, moving in with the advancing army units, made this picture. (*U.S. Coast Guard*)

to our misery because it kept our underwear from drying out. The unit finally reassembled at the village of Sainte-Marie-du-Mont. We took casualties when hit by German air attack. While there, we took time to replace the dead batteries in our Jeeps by cannibalizing good ones from Jeeps that were in army gliders that had been wrecked on landing.

Once we were all together, we proceeded north toward Cherbourg, via Montebourg and Valognes. The VII Corps at the time consisted of the 4th Division on the right flank, the 79th Division in the center, the 9th Division on the left, and the 90th Division backing up the line. We had four men to a Jeep, and these Jeeps were combat loaded at all times. Each vehicle had wire-cutting hooks on the front and had sandbags on the floor as protection against land mines. Each man carried a knapsack, a blanket, and half a pup tent. He was equipped with gas mask, trench shovel, dagger, hand grenades, helmet, ammunition, and rifle. Most of the officers carried submachine guns. With four men

and all their equipment in a Jeep, there was little spare room for sleeping. Some slept on the ground, wrapping themselves in blankets and putting the shelter half underneath.

About June 15, on a rainy, windy day, I conferred with Brigadier General Theodore Roosevelt Jr., deputy commander of the 4th Division. I arrived at his headquarters shortly after dawn and found him seated in the map tent, looking at the troop dispositions. I introduced myself and asked him if he recalled me from our previous meeting in 1941. At that time I was navigator of the USS *Joseph T. Dickman*, a Coast Guard–manned transport that was involved in joint amphibious maneuvers at Onslow Bay, North Carolina. Roosevelt, then a colonel, was on board in command of the 26th Infantry. I had some pleasant visits with him at the time. His father, a long-time resident of Oyster Bay, New York, had, of course, been a Republican president early in the century. In 1941, the president was a Democrat and distant relative, Franklin Roosevelt. The colonel summarized the situation by observing, "You know, the Oyster Bay Roosevelts are out of season now."

In 1944, despite his politics and now having become a general, he was still serving his country. During our reunion I caught him by surprise initially, but he recognized me as soon as I took off my helmet. We talked of the days on board the *Joseph T. Dickman*. The visit was so cordial that I think I could have had anything I wanted from the 4th Division. (A few weeks later I had another brief visit with him after Cherbourg was captured. He died shortly after that from a heart attack, evidence that the rigors of combat are for young men.)

On June 19 the big storm hit the Cotentin Peninsula. The wind was of gale force. The rain came down in torrents. The dirt roads, which had been turned to dust by the passing of hundreds of vehicles, became seas of inches-deep mud. The *bocage* country* of Normandy, with its sunken roads and lanes, was a hell of a place to fight a war. The rain and wind would have made a saint uncomfortable. The tents were useless. The sandbags in the Jeeps kept them from draining, so we had to bail them out periodically.

When the storm hit, we were around Montebourg, still about fifteen miles from Cherbourg. On June 22 I took a party of twenty-one men to the small hamlet of Delasse to await the outcome of the surrender ultimatum General Collins had delivered to Cherbourg. The Germans refused. While we were having breakfast on the 23rd, American planes repeatedly strafed the area, which was full of German stragglers, so we scattered. I ran alongside a stone house and threw myself to the ground near a doghouse. In it I found a hen's nest with about a dozen eggs. We hadn't seen fresh eggs for months, so after the planes left we hard-boiled the eggs and divided them up. That afternoon we dropped back to Montebourg, which had been destroyed by fire. As a result of the heat, the statue of Joan of Arc in the town square had been turned a dusty red.

Cherbourg is in a depression formed by Cap de la Hague as a western horn and Pointe de Barfleur as an eastern horn. General Roosevelt had told me that the 79th Division would enter Cherbourg while the 4th Division cleared the resistance in the eastern horn and the 9th did the same to the west. With this information I took Lieutenant LeVallee and four men and reconnoitered well into the 79th Division area, going almost to Fort du Roule. The next morning I was with my constant companions—Seaman Richard Boucher, the Jeep driver, and Yeoman Second Class Edward Perry. We moved out with Company G, 314th Infantry, of the 79th Division. They were going to reinforce a strong point still under fire by the Germans.

As we drove along a country lane, passing through territory already controlled by American forces, we saw some German prisoners of war. They were removing their own dead from the area. Two men pulled on each body, one to a foot. If the dead man had fallen on his back, he was dragged off that way. If he fell face down, he was dragged face down. I wondered at the time what the vaunted German Wehrmacht [armed forces] would have thought of this.

About eleven o'clock that morning we turned onto the Rue de Paris to proceed toward the Cherbourg waterfront. This is where street fighting took place until about eight that night. The railroad yard to the left was an inferno of combat. The machine guns never stopped. American Jeeps with Red Cross markings were going in both directions. Those to the south generally had a wounded man beside the driver, one stretcher across the hood, and another stretcher behind the driver. Dead and wounded from both sides littered the streets. German machine guns were placed at sidewalk level in the basements of buildings that fronted on the street. The Americans would capture the upper part of a building, but then they had to dig the Germans out of the basements. In the meantime, German 88-millimeter guns, in the rear under Fort du Roule, fired into the American troops.

Perry, Boucher, and I were the first U.S. naval personnel to enter Cherbourg. We reached the blazing wrecked waterfront in the eastern section of the port about five in the afternoon of June 26. The Germans still held the western section. By that evening the rest of our task force had arrived, and we found a place to stay in a house at the foot of Rue de Paris, on the waterfront.

Lieutenant General Karl von Schlieben, army commander at Cherbourg, and Rear Admiral Walter Hennecke, the naval commander, surrendered themselves and their staffs on June 26, but they refused to order the rest of the Germans to surrender. As a result, strong pockets of resistance continued throughout the city, and neither Fort du Homet nor Fort Centrale would surrender. A captured German officer told me later that while German troops held back the Americans, German naval personnel under Admiral Hennecke systematically wrecked and booby-trapped the port, sowing additional mines in the harbor. They destroyed the railroad yard in the port, demolished canal gates, blocked waterways with sunken ships, wrecked derricks and booby-trapped them. I soon sent a message back to Rear Admiral Alan Kirk, the overall American naval task force commander, to tell him what a wreck the port of Cherbourg was by then.

Gradually, the Americans took charge of the area. On June 28 the men of my task unit set about doing the survey work for which we had been sent. Even so, we were still subject to enemy fire at times. We installed

* Characterized by thickets and groves of short trees.

Battered almost completely to the ground, the railroad station in Cherbourg provides dramatic evidence of the effects of Allied land and naval bombardments on the city. (*Navy photo in the National Archives: 80-G-231952*)

communications facilities, and we requisitioned garages, billets, and storage facilities. Essentially, we established the U.S. naval headquarters in Cherbourg, and I—as a lieutenant commander—was the senior naval officer present there until Ives arrived the next day.

That same day, June 28, I was with Lieutenant Frank Lauer of the Seabees. He and I led about fifteen men—armed with Thompson submachine guns, grenades, and bazookas—into the Cherbourg arsenal near the waterfront. At the entrance we found about twenty-five American infantrymen disarming a group of German prisoners. We were joined by an American paratrooper and another American soldier who told us there were still strong pockets of resistance in the arsenal. Over the next two hours we killed several snipers and silenced machine guns. We cleaned out about two hundred Germans by using grenades and bazookas against the steel doors of the strong points. Many prisoners were taken near the powerhouse and the E-boat pens, which the Germans had blown up by

detonating piled-up torpedoes. Several E-boats were still burning in their pens when we arrived. The concrete ceilings of the E-boat pens were about eight feet thick, reinforced with steel rods. The walls were about four feet thick.

Later, as we were assessing damage to the waterfront, we surprised an armed German, who took cover as we did, then surrendered. He led us to a bunker, where still more surrendered. One of those prisoners could speak good English. He told us that there were American paratroopers being held as prisoners in nearby Fort du Homet. But he refused to go to the fort, claiming that the commanding officer was a madman who would shoot any man who surrendered. Lauer and I then discussed the possibility of entering the fort under a flag of truce to see if we could get the Germans to surrender. This would be better than assaulting the fort with American troops and delaying the opening of the port. Lauer had been wearing a piece of white parachute as a scarf, so he took that off and attached it to a stick. Crouching underneath a truck, we waved our makeshift flag. Within an hour, a German officer came out of the fort under a white flag.

Lieutenant Lauer's German was poor, and one of the German officers had only a smattering of English, but we were able to communicate that we wanted the German commander to surrender the fort and turn the paratroop prisoners over to us. He refused, saying he had instructions to surrender only on orders of his superior officer. We told him that the American forces were in control of Cherbourg, but he didn't believe it. We haggled back and forth; among other things, we told him that we had eight hundred men in the vicinity of the fort. When he asked for safe conduct for him and his men to the nearest German lines, I told him it was no dice. We would accept only an unconditional surrender. One of the captured paratroopers knew enough German to serve as interpreter. With his help, we eventually got the German commander to agree to surrender if we would separate the officers from the rest of his men. That was part of a regular routine, so the impasse ended. Then the commander brought out a bottle of cognac and poured a drink for each man on

his staff. Lieutenant Lauer and I refused to drink with them.

After that, the fifty-two American paratroopers were released. They had been captives since D-Day, when they had been dropped on Cherbourg by mistake. They told us that the Germans had treated them fine during their confinement. During the U.S. naval bombardment of Cherbourg, they had been taken into the fort for protection. They advised us that the Germans had seen the navy reconnaissance party working its way through the arsenal and several times made efforts to bring machine guns to bear on us. The first thing the paratroopers asked for was cigarettes. The second thing was souvenirs. We told them that the German prisoners had left their pistols, binoculars, and field equipment in a large pile. The last we saw of the paratroopers, they were on their way to ransack the pile of equipment.

By interrogating slave laborers, Free French, and German prisoners, I was able to plot the German minefields in the harbor. Then Lieutenant LeVallee sailed these plots out to the British minesweepers off

German soldiers march through the streets of Cherbourg after being captured. (*U.S. Army: SC-190810-S*)

Lieutenant General Omar Bradley listens as Major General J. Lawton Collins, right, describes the capture of Cherbourg in late June. (*National Archives: SC 191143*)

the port, thus saving hours of time in clearing the minefields. Another interesting thing came out of our interrogation of the prisoners. The Germans said that they hadn't really been bothered by the Allied air raids, because they had enough warning to be able to take cover. But they had been terrified by the naval bombardment on June 25 because the huge projectiles being hurled from offshore were accompanied by a frightening noise, then created large craters in the landscape when they exploded.

There were plenty of dead on both sides at Cherbourg, but one corpse in particular left a deep impression on us. On a final sweep of the Napoleonic fortification near Fort du Homet, we came across the body of a handsome young German officer on a stretcher. His hands were folded across his chest, and a rosary entwined his finger. He looked as if he were asleep. His boots were highly polished. His field gray uniform was immaculate. He wore an iron cross at his collar and another one on his left side. A small purple spot appeared at his left breast. We notified the grave registration unit of his location. As we did so, we wondered how a man who fought for Hitler's Germany could die with a rosary in his hands.

Captain Ives arrived at Cherbourg the afternoon of June 29 and relieved me as senior U.S. naval officer present. As before, I was designated as his chief staff

Navy salvage men at Cherbourg have already slapped U.S. markings on a captured German half-track motorcycle—certainly an all-terrain vehicle. (*Navy photo in the National Archives: 80-G-255619*)

officer. In the ensuing weeks, we got things more and more organized, including setting up a suitable naval headquarters and facilities for transportation and communication. Our harbor entrance control group had located a signal tower at the south entrance to the harbor. The men there set up signal communications with the minesweepers that had the unenviable job of trying to clear the port of mines. I served with Ives until July 15, when Admiral Wilkes came over from England and set up shop as overall commander of ports and bases in France.

One of my early duties in Cherbourg was to establish a headquarters for Admiral Wilkes and his staff. We had commandeered all the buildings on one side of the street that led west out of Place Napoleon. We gathered most of the furnishings from the former offices of the German army and navy commands that had occupied the buildings. We soon put together a nice headquarters, but we had no drapes for the windows. This problem sort of taunted me, so I conferred with Lieutenant LeVallee. He said he would take care of it, and within two days he did. LeVallee went to the German senior officers' brothel in Cherbourg. He got the madame to come to Wilkes's future office and measure the windows. Then she and the women working for her altered the brothel drapes to fit the new location.

LeVallee and I were among the officers who greeted Wilkes and his staff when they arrived in mid-July. We escorted him to his office, and he was agreeably surprised by the furnishings. One of his staff remarked about the drapes, so we said that the ladies of Cherbourg had furnished them. A captain on the staff said he thought the admiral should commend these ladies for their assistance and patriotism. (We didn't say a word about the actual origin of the drapes—not until years later, that is. In the 1950s, I met Admiral Wilkes on the Eastern Shore of Maryland while he was visiting some relatives. I related this incident, and he got quite a laugh out of it.)

Commodore William H. Barton of the Coast Guard soon arrived to become port director. We were beyond being just an advanced base and trying to move toward becoming a working port. Barton requested that I be assigned as his assistant, and I served in that capacity until August 2. Of all the duties performed by any officer during the occupation of Cherbourg, Commodore Barton's task was the most difficult. The personnel assigned to him were inexperienced, to say the least. There were a great many officers who could perform in administrative roles, but damn few who

could perform any operations.

In an extension of the reconnaissance function, Captain Ives departed about August 1 to ascertain the condition of Granville and Saint-Malo in the Brittany area. Ives requested that either Lieutenant LeVallee or I go with his party. Each of us, however, had other assignments. On August 2 Ives and his party were ambushed by a force of approximately six hundred Germans in the vicinity of Dol-de Bretagne [Brittany]. Somebody reported to Ives—without checking—that Saint-Malo had fallen.

So, Ives and his people started down the road in that direction. I think he had about eighty men with him. They came across two soldiers that they thought were German stragglers and captured them. They turned out to be German sentries. While Ives's party was stopped and talking with these sentries on the road, the surrounding area erupted in gunfire. Ives was killed instantly, along with perhaps ten or fifteen men. A number were wounded. The survivors fought there for about an hour. They would have been wiped out except for the fact that a man got out of there on a motorcycle and was able to get reinforcements in the form of light tanks. For operational purposes, the party was annihilated.

As a result, Admiral Wilkes issued orders for me to reform my Task Unit 127.2.8 and gave me about three hundred more men to carry out the reconnaissance of Brittany as far as Brest. I was under army command until Admiral Wilkes ordered me from the Brest area to enter Le Havre with the Canadians on September 12.

As I reflected on the fate of Ives and his party, I realized that he had not been trained in reconnaissance and land tactics. When they got there, he and his men made the mistake of lining the Jeeps up along the sides of the road. Our training in Scotland indicated that Jeeps should alternate and be far enough apart so that the drivers could get them away quickly if they were caught by surprise. We had also learned that you don't move an entire party along together. When approaching a hill, you send out an advance group to make sure no one is waiting on the other side to spring an unpleasant surprise.

Ives and I had spent our entire careers in the naval service, and our experiences had not prepared us for what we encountered once we got to France. My outfit had 25 percent casualties during its operations ashore, and I'm convinced it would have been even worse if we hadn't been so thoroughly trained beforehand in Scotland. For Captain Norman Ives, the lack of training was fatal.

⚜   ⚜   ⚜

QUENTIN ROBERT WALSH (1910–) graduated from the Coast Guard Academy in 1933 and served in the destroyer *Herndon* and cutter *Yamacraw*. In 1937 he began a special assignment on board the whaling factory ship *Ulysses* to observe whaling operations and serve as a Coast Guard observer for the enforcement of the Whaling Treaty Act. He subsequently served in several cutters—the *Cayuga*, *Kickapoo*, *Northland*, *Campbell*—and the navy transport *Joseph T. Dickman*. After service in the Coast Guard Training Station, Groton, Connecticut, he performed the duties outlined in this chapter. He was awarded the Navy Cross for his heroism during the capture of Cherbourg. After his return to the United States, he reported to the staff of the Coast Guard Commandant. In June 1946, because of the respiratory problems he developed as a result of conditions incurred while overseas, he was placed on the retired list for physical disability and moved with his family to Tucson, Arizona. In 1951 he was recalled to active duty during the Korean War and performed a variety of duties at Coast Guard headquarters in Washington, D.C., in the ensuing years. He concluded his active duty in 1960 and moved to Denton, Maryland, where he was active as a schoolteacher and later as a probation and parole officer until his final retirement in 1974. (*Courtesy Captain Quentin R. Walsh*)

THE NON-AMPHIBIOUS SWAN OF CHERBOURG

By Rear Admiral George W. Bauernschmidt, Supply Corps, U.S. Navy (Retired)

In late 1943, after I had been involved for some time in supporting the Allied war effort in North Africa, I was ordered to London and the staff of Admiral Harold R. Stark, Commander U.S. Naval Forces in Europe. I took off from Oran, Algeria, and got as far as Marrakech, Morocco, when my plane was commandeered by a character who had no priority at all. All he had was a name, and his name was Churchill. He had been recovering from pneumonia in the hotel at Marrakech and was leaving for England. To move his whole staff took all of the available airlift for two days.

In due course I hitchhiked to England on a plane that was being ferried there, and my hat is off to the young American boys who made those trips. The plane I was in was a good example. Most of the crew were under twenty-one and had never seen blue water until they took off across the Atlantic. They flew to Brazil, across to the bulge of Africa, then up to Marrakech, and then up to England. We were staggered in altitude and in longitude in our formation so that we wouldn't be a consolidated target if we were attacked by the Germans when we got off the coast of France.

I arrived in London in a traditional fog and soon met Commodore Howard Flanigan, who was my immediate boss on the staff. Flanigan had retired from the navy several years before and had much to do with the management of the 1939–40 World's Fair in New York. Many of his operations were those of a promoter, not those of a logistician or a military planner. He also carried with him the line officer's belief that command was the prerogative exclusively of the line. Since I attempted to persuade him to my point of view, a great amount of friction developed between us, which persisted from then on.

My impression of that staff of London is unquestionably biased, but it is most unfavorable. Admiral Stark appeared to be still suffering from the shock of Pearl Harbor. His deputy was Barry Wilson, a rear admiral, who was an ill man and should have been sent home. Whether the mantle automatically descended on Flanigan or whether Flanigan used his knowledge of Barry Wilson's illness to bulldoze him out of the way, I don't know, but it was quite apparent that the whole show was run by Flanigan.

The staff had created a planning group under Captain Neil Dietrich, a highly intelligent officer. Neil and his group had made what plans were made for the invasion of France. They were not the product of Stark's staff proper. It should be noted that the function of Stark's staff—performed by the planning group—was to provide for the navy's logistic needs for the invasion while the operational plans were the responsibility of Admiral Kirk. This division was not conducive to cooperation. Meanwhile, I was detached as staff supply officer and attached to the planning group.

Two young officers whom I had known in Oran reported to me for duty. They were lieutenants Spencer Hall and Ernest Steinberg. I sent them out to find an apartment for the three of us, which they did, at a long walking distance from our office on Grosvenor Square. Soon after we moved in, I had occasion to send the two of them up to Scotland to visit a supply installation. I was home alone in the apartment when we got one of the heaviest raids of the second blitz of London.

When the raid started, I was in my bunk, and my blackout curtains were parted. I could see a flare, then another, and still another—all in line with me. I thought, "Gee, these people are going to pass right overhead." About that time—whammo—a bomb dropped in the street right in back of our block of flats. It blew me out of bed and apparently knocked me unconscious. When I came to, I was standing beside my bed. I had my shoes on and no socks, my blue uniform over my pajamas, my bathrobe over my blue uniform, my raincoat on, and a flashlight in my hand. I had done

German V-1 rockets, commonly known as "buzz bombs," did devastating damage to London and its environs. (*Imperial War Museum*)

all that in shock. There was a stained-glass window—part of our apartment—that had not blown in. Rather, it had been sucked out by the back draft of the burst, balled up into a jagged mass of lead and broken glass, and slammed through another window. It hit the wall at the pillow of one of these two young officers who were in Scotland.

I checked my apartment for damage and saw there was no gas leak, no water leak. Then, since my apartment was satisfactory, I got in the elevator and went to the top floor. It creaked and groaned. I understood why the next day, when I saw that the guides for the elevator were all bent out of shape. Why the cables didn't snap, I'll never know. But I went up, then came down through the apartment house, checking the various apartments to see if I could help anybody. I was able to help one man who was trapped in his closet, of all places.

I got down in the lobby and saw the most extraordinary sight. Four people had been playing bridge on one of the upper floors when the bomb went off, and you could tell exactly where they had been sitting in relation to the others. One had cuts on the back of his head, one on this side of her face, one on that side of her face, and one had glass fragments in the front of his face. All four were bleeding, and all four were standing in the lobby, still holding their cards, and in the position of a bridge table. They were just standing there stupefied.

Very soon thereafter, I got additional duty on the staff of Rear Admiral John Wilkes, who was Commander Landing Craft and Bases. I found myself in the extraordinary position of writing letters to Wilkes from London and then getting on the train and going to Plymouth and answering them. Then I got on the train and came back to London and took exception to the answer. By this time, spring had come, and as I shuttled back and forth between London and Plymouth, I admired the countryside, which was beautiful. I particularly enjoyed the rhododendron, which seemed to grow in profusion through the woodlands.

As the invasion drew nearer, it finally became apparent that there would be a need for a supply depot on the far shore after the invasion, and Commodore Flanigan directed me to have requisitions prepared to stock the depot. I countered with the suggestion that we order "X triple-B loads." He'd never heard of them, but a "triple-B load" was a load of consumables which experience showed was adequate to support a thousand men for a month. The various depots in the United States had been assembling these and had them ready. Flanigan said this was a lazy Supply Corps officer's approach to logistics, and he'd have none of it. He ordered me again to have the specific requisitions prepared.

Well, this was late in the game, and it took time to make estimates and prepare requisitions for that quantity of material. But in due time the requisitions were prepared and sent off, and the material arrived many weeks after the invasion.

Anticipating the need for the unforeseen on the far shore, I requested and had ordered by Commodore Flanigan two ships from the States. One was a very small semi-passenger ship, and one was a small freighter. I intended that these would be at my disposal for the movement of material back and forth across the

English Channel. As things turned out, I never got to use them. When our ships were bombarding the French, Commodore Flanigan suddenly found he'd made no provision for receiving the empty powder cans and the brass that was generated in huge quantities by the bombardment. So, he took the small freighter and used that to collect the powder cans and the brass and return it to the United States.

Flanigan also took over the other ship, because he found that once the invasion started, large numbers of important people from the United States wanted to have a personal view of the invasion. He personally conducted tours, using this second ship of mine, so I got to use neither of them.

When the invasion of Normandy took place, there were ships off Utah and Omaha beaches that held the staffs of the naval contingents of the assault force and the support forces that accompanied them. I had asked that one or both of the young officers who had loaded the supply ships for the invasion beaches be included in these ships, and requested that I also be included. All three requests were denied with the statement that there was no need for an officer in the Supply Corps in an assault.

That was one of the many manifestations of the line officer's apparent inability to accept the professional Supply Corps officer as an important cog in the military machine. World War II developed the need for logistics to an astonishingly great degree and overran many of the concepts of war which had been in existence before. Logistics were almost on a level with operations, but the line officer was reluctant to admit this fact. He always considered himself as a jack-of-all-trades and a master of all trades, and he considered himself quite able to handle all problems in logistics.

One of the officers who loaded a supply ship was Spencer Hall, one of my London flatmates. He was probably the most eager adventurer that I have ever seen. He would gladly have gone into Normandy on D-1 and actually envied the frogmen who did. He was brokenhearted when he was left behind in London. The effect of the omission of Supply Corps officers from the assault force was almost immediately apparent, because dispatches began coming back to England requesting urgent delivery of materials that actually were in the ships that were with the assault force and had been loaded by our supply officers, but there was nobody there to tell the forces present what was in the ships and in what quantities.

As a consequence, there was a tremendous cross-Channel movement of emergency freight. I landed on Omaha Beach several days after the initial assault and was vastly impressed by what had been accomplished. I was amazed to see that the Seabees and the army engineers had carved roadways up that bank almost immediately behind the attacking waves of soldiers

Temporary memorial to an American soldier killed at Normandy. The circular device in the right center of the photo is a land mine. (*U.S. Coast Guard*)

who took the top of the bluff at bayonet point. The roads were cut out right behind them, and vehicles went on up to the top.

Apparently, the Germans did not expect our assault until July, and they weren't sure by any means that this particular stretch of the Normandy Peninsula was the spot. They did have many ingenious defenses, however. One that particularly interested me was a series of mortar pits, the mortar being centered in the bottom of the pit. Around the top of this pit was painted the scene that you saw when you looked over the top, with ranges to all of the prominent items that you saw marked on this scene. The man operating the mortar needed only to train the mortar to look at a clump of bushes and then read off the range to that clump of bushes and drop his shell in. He was all set.

In going from Omaha to Utah I passed through a small village and saw an utterly fantastic sight. There were still corpses in the streets, there was the sound of German burp guns in the offing, and certainly artillery fire. Yet the main road had been cleared by bulldozers, and down this road, coming toward me, was a woman dressed in a white flannel suit, pushing a baby carriage with a baby in it, dressed as though they were going to its baptism. I can't explain it; I just saw it.

As soon as Cherbourg was taken, I was told to go there and make a French château habitable for Admiral Wilkes and his staff. By then he had been designated Commander Ports and Bases France. This château had been a museum before the war. It had been occupied by a German general and a German admiral

Rear Admiral John Wilkes, shown here with a landing craft at Devonport, England, did a magnificent job of preparing both the army and navy in the techniques of amphibious warfare that would be needed on the far shore. Later he set up shop as Commander U.S. Ports and Bases France. (*Navy photo in the National Archives: 80-G-356303*)

who had installed one modern bathroom and had put their field kitchens outside. The fear that the commandos had raised in the German mind was quite apparent, for completely encircling this château were trenches and military strong points.

I found a sizable amount of rifle ammunition, which included red wooden bullets. They were easily identified by feel because the bullets were waxed. These bullets were designed to disintegrate after going fifty yards. They were there to be used in case commandos got between the trenches and the château. The defending forces could fire at them without endangering the people in the château.

Admiral Wilkes did not impress me as one who demanded personal comforts, but his chief of staff and deputy chief of staff, in my opinion, were overly solicitous for their boss, possibly using his stars to create an environment that they themselves would like. In any event, I had several days of work to make the château more comfortable. During that time I was provided with K rations and lived off of them exclusively. Regrettably, whoever supplied them to me gave me only one type, the kind that had cheese in it rather than meat, and I ate nine or a dozen of those meals in succession.

During this time I was quartered in a building that had been a German officers' quarters in the town of Cherbourg. I returned to this late one night, and as I turned a corner of the street, the sentry standing in front of the quarters challenged me. When I identified myself, he told me to come in running, that there was a man across the street who'd been shooting at him all night. As I ran down the street some thirty or forty yards, the rifleman got off two shots at me. He was a very poor marksman. I got stung by a little flying cement, but that was all. I thought of three possibilities: he was a trapped German, in which event he was a fool to disclose his presence; he was a Vichy Frenchman, unsympathetic to Americans, likewise foolish to disclose his presence; or he was a drunken American. The marksmanship strongly indicated the last.

This leads me to observe that the behavior of the Americans in Normandy left much to be desired. There was some abuse of prisoners and more than a little looting. Later on, after I met some of the local inhabitants, I asked one of them how the Germans had behaved at Cherbourg. He explained to me that the enlisted men had been kept in barracks in town, had been marched out to drill once in the morning, and marched out once in the afternoon for athletics. Other than that, the population scarcely saw them. He said they were very well behaved, and they paid for everything they got. That they paid in printing-press money that they themselves turned out seemed to make no difference.

I then asked what they thought of the Americans, and I got a typically French response. "Ah, the Americans, they are winning the war." In other words, they committed themselves to no remark about the Americans' behavior.

Going back and forth to the château, I had to pass over a hump in the street that was caused by a major-caliber projectile. Presumably, it was fired by the *Nevada*, a battleship in which I had served back in the 1930s. The projectile had hit the ground and then plowed under the street and come to rest under the trolley tracks, which it had raised up about a foot, but it did not explode.

Thinking of that reminds me that I, in driving around, saw a large number of German fortifications with major-caliber guns behind them that had been indescribably demolished. The bombardment from the sea and from the air had burned up the ground around them. In one case, there was a block of concrete which I recall as being fifteen feet high, twenty or twenty-five feet long, and ten feet thick. It had been literally blown out of the ground and thrown over on its side. Presumably, a navy shell had gone under this and touched off the magazine below it.

You could see where there was a salvo over a fortification, a salvo short of the fortification, and then two or three direct salvos on it, and then everything demolished. The destroyers going along the beaches came in at high tide, very close to the shore, and opened fire at almost point-blank range. They completely destroyed pillboxes that were equipped with old French 75-millimeter guns. It was not unusual for me to see two or three direct hits on the pillbox in an area twenty inches in diameter, with the aperture of the gun the center of that bull's-eye in which these shots landed. I remember seeing one gun that was split wide open by a direct hit on the end of the muzzle. The Germans themselves were amazed by the volume and accuracy of the naval gunfire.

After four or five days of very hard work, I got the château equipped and the staff moved in. The chief of staff found the flagstones with which the first floor of the château was paved uncomfortably cold, and so I was ordered to cover them with carpeting. I submitted a requisition to the British for four hundred square yards of carpeting of any color. The British were loath to fill it because their storehouses were very empty, and they passed the requisition up to high American levels for comment. It was bounced back to us for further justification with some rather doubting bits of sarcasm attached. When this was received, the chief of staff told me to cancel *my* silly requisition.

What the Americans did to that place scandalized me, knowing that the Cherbourg château was a museum. The flagstones were worn into deep hollows all over the place, where the footsteps of four centuries had scored them. When we couldn't get carpets to cover them, I was directed to have all the hollows filled in with cement. I'm not a great antiquarian, but I thought that was sacrilege.

About this time I returned to London to pick up a few loose threads in our supply plan and was there on a weekend when the V-1 buzz bombs came over. These were very alarming. On a Sunday, in particular, London is very quiet, and the buzz bombs had a characteristic stuttering sound. They came over singly and spaced rather far apart. As they came over, the stuttering engine would stop, and if you then could count to ten, you were going to survive. It took about ten seconds for the engine to cut off and the bomb to nose over and drop. When they went off, they did quite a lot of damage, but there weren't enough of them to be a serious threat.

They could have been a serious threat if the Germans had recognized their importance and had sent them over in quantities and suddenly. Sending over a few at a time permitted the British to launch a defense, which consisted of having fighters over the Channel and shooting down a number of them. I'm quite sure that had the Germans realized how valuable a weapon they had, they could have provided mobile launching sites and produced them in quantity.

I was at tea one Sunday afternoon when a buzz bomb came over. I witnessed two of the ladies present leave the living room, go into the bedroom, and lie under the bed, teacups still in hand, drinking their tea while the buzz bombs went over. Why people do the things they do under pressure, I don't know.

Back at Cherbourg I was given some papers to deliver to the army commander in back of Saint-Lô, where the army was poised for a breakthrough that occurred a couple of days later. As I drove my Jeep down the highway, I found it blocked by a solid stream of traffic. Had I waited to go along with the traffic, I never would have delivered my message. I went down the middle of the road as fast as I dared go and was twice stopped by MPs who threatened to have me fined for violating the speed laws and not staying in the convoy.

In any event, I got to Saint-Lô and delivered my message, and then came back by the byways. I did this, first, to avoid traffic, but, second, as a sightseer, to have a good chance to look at the Normandy countryside. I also found one of the German buzz-bomb launching sites, which was not too badly damaged. It was a long earthen ramp up which the buzz bomb was started. I couldn't get too close to this because the Germans had it fenced off, but I got close enough to see it.

The Germans hadn't left behind booby traps as such, except in buildings, but they had laid land mines in many places. Wherever they had land mines, they had little yellow-and-black flags flying. They were no more than about six inches long, as I remember them, with a skull and crossbones on them, and in German, French, and English the words "land mine." Now, the advantage of that was that it denied the field to you until you had found the land mines and destroyed them. Also, it made you go through the search for land mines in unmined land, where all they did was stick up the little flags, so that they got double value out of them. The Norman countryside was very prosperous, and the Normans looked well fed and well clothed. The

Le Château de Tourlaville in the environs of Cherbourg was for a time the headquarters for Admiral Wilkes and his staff. (*Courtesy Rear Admiral George W. Bauernschmidt*)

Germans apparently skimmed off the cream from this agricultural and dairying community but left plenty to keep the farmers happy and busy.

One more remark about Normandy. This is only hearsay, but I was told that after Admiral Wilkes's staff left Cherbourg, they moved into a similar château at Calais. It also had in back of it a very large pond, which was the remains of the original moat that had surrounded the château, just as the one in Cherbourg had. At Cherbourg there was a large and stately swan that swam in the pond. The chief of staff felt that the admiral admired the swan, so he sent back to Cherbourg and ordered the swan delivered to Calais.

Two men were told to catch it, but they were unable to. It finally took a whole squad to get the swan. When they caught it, they found it couldn't stand up. It had been waterborne for so many years that land was an unaccustomed environment. The only way that they could think of to ship it up was to put a Seabee pontoon on an army truck, the top of the pontoon having been cut out. The pontoon was half-filled with water and the swan placed in there, and it was trundled up to Calais. All this, with German gunfire still within earshot.

After the swan was shipped, the caretaker of the Cherbourg château missed it. He complained to the mayor of Cherbourg, who complained to a colonel, who went up the ladder of generals to the top in London. Then the word came down the ladder of admirals to Admiral Wilkes, "Return the swan."

So the evolution had to be reversed. The pontoon was taken up to Calais again, filled with water, the swan put in it, and driven back to Cherbourg. There were many misuses of power such as that. War involves a great many decisions, not all of them wise.

GEORGE WILLIAM BAUERNSCHMIDT (1899–) graduated from the Naval Academy in 1922 and served in the battleships *North Dakota* and *New Mexico* before going to submarine school at New London, Connecticut. He then served in the submarine *R-3* and commanded the *R-2*. After a stint as a Naval Academy instructor, he went to American Samoa, where he performed a variety of duties, including chief customs officer. In the early 1930s he served in the hospital ship *Relief*, battleship *Nevada*, and Sixth Naval District before shifting to the Supply Corps because of color blindness. As a supply officer in the late 1930s–early 1940s, Bauernschmidt was in the submarine tender *Beaver*, Naval Research Laboratory, and battleship *New York*. During World War II he was at the Philadelphia Navy Yard; staff of Destroyers Pacific Fleet; Naval Supply Depot, Oran; Admiral Harold Stark's staff; Naval Supply Depot, Mechanicsburg, Pennsylvania; and Naval Supply Depot, Guam. After the war he served in the Bureau of Supplies and Accounts, including duty as assistant chief of the bureau. In the 1950s he commanded the Naval Supply Center, Pearl Harbor, and Naval Supply Depot, Clearfield, Utah. Admiral Bauernschmidt retired from active duty in 1955. He now lives in Annapolis, Maryland. (*Courtesy Rear Admiral George W. Bauernschmidt*)

✤ ✤ ✤

By far the bulk of naval aviation assets were being used in the Pacific in 1944, both in patrol planes and carrier aircraft. Two American escort aircraft carriers, the *Tulagi* and *Kasaan Bay*, were used to supplement British carriers in providing close air support for the landing force in the southern France operation. Aircraft carriers were not needed at Normandy because of the proximity of land-based army planes in the British Isles. Even so, U.S. naval aviation did make a contribution at Normandy in the form of antisubmarine planes. One of the navy fliers involved was Lieutenant Joseph P. Kennedy Jr., brother of future President John F. Kennedy. The following account is from his skipper, Sunshine Jim Reedy.

SUBMARINES AND BUZZ-BOMB LAUNCHERS

By Rear Admiral James R. Reedy, U.S. Navy (Retired)

Because of Admiral Ernie King, I flew land-based bombers out of England rather than carrier fighters in the Pacific during the latter part of World War II. He was, understandably, more concerned about the Army Air Forces than he was about my duty preferences. As head of the navy, he was a little bit teed off about the army doing antisubmarine patrols out of England. He did everything he could to get some navy planes over there instead.

At the time, I was in command of VP-203, a navy patrol squadron flying PBM Mariners out of Norfolk. One day in May of 1943 the wing commander called in several of the squadron skippers. He told us that our squadrons would get B-24 Liberator bombers from the army. We were to fly them to the naval air station at

Admiral Ernest J. King, Commander in Chief U.S. Fleet, meets the Dunkeswell staff in June 1944. King's desire to wrest the ASW mission from the Army Air Forces led to the deployment of Reedy's squadron to England. Reedy, newly promoted to the rank of commander, is at left. (*Navy photo in the National Archives: 80-G-237251*)

North Island, near San Diego, so they could be converted for their new antisubmarine mission.

When I returned to my office after the meeting, I received a set of orders to take command of a fighter squadron already operating in the Pacific. That was quite appealing, because VP-203 was far from combat action. I took the orders to the commodore and said, "Look what I found on my desk when I got back."

He read them and said, "Well, goddamnit, that'll teach you to keep from going to Washington," because I'd been up there a lot, trying to get out into the war. He soon had the orders canceled, and I took the Liberators. I was disappointed by the switch, because nearly every pilot of my general seniority wanted to command a fighter squadron. Back in those days naval aviators rotated among various types of planes rather than specializing as they do now. As it turned out, I had a fine tour of duty in the Liberators. I was shot at and missed, so I can't complain about not being in the war.

The navy designation for the Liberator was PB4Y-1, although it was essentially the same airplane as the B-24. Each plane was modified for antisubmarine work by the addition of a twin .50-caliber machine-gun turret in the nose and an ASG-15 radar in the bomb bay. My new squadron was VB-110, which consisted of twelve airplanes and eighteen crews. Beginning with a nucleus of nine crews from VP-203, we did our workup training at Elizabeth City, North Carolina. The rest of the pilots and crews came from various navy patrol squadrons already in existence. Even though the PB4Ys were big airplanes, their four engines made them pretty lively and fairly maneuverable. I remember that one pilot dove his plane onto a target in training, and he was going so fast that he tore off the back part of the elevators on the tail. He had to come in and make a landing at about 110 knots.

We had to be ready to leave for England at the beginning of September. On the last day of August, I called the commodore and told him I was about to leave with the first three planes. He said, "Have a good trip, Jim. Are you reasonably ready to go?"

This aerial view of the U.S. naval air facility at Dunkeswell, England, in June 1944 shows several PB4Ys perched in their circular spots off the main drag. A hangar is under construction at left. (*Navy photo in the National Archives: 80-G-244295*)

A navy PB4Y-1 attacks a U-boat in the Bay of Biscay. (*Painting by navy combat artist Dwight C. Shepler*)

I said, "Well, we're reasonably ready. I hope we'll get more ready as we go along." Some of those crews didn't have a hell of a lot of training when we arrived in England, but they picked it up pretty fast. The original plan was for us to operate out of St. David's, an airfield in northern Wales, but it was not yet functioning. Instead, we were directed to St. Eval, a Royal Air Force Coastal Command air station near New Quay, Wales, much farther south. The purpose was for us to receive training in what the British laughingly called "fighter affiliation." We were assisted in the "affiliation" by Royal Navy fighter pilots who flew into St. Eval and provided opposition during training missions. I'm afraid that if they had actually been shooting at us, our tour with the RAF Coastal Command would have ended even before it started.

Eventually, we moved into an air station at Dunkeswell, England, and we encountered an awful lot of mud there. By bringing in more than a hundred additional American squadron personnel—including both flight crews and maintenance people—along with our accompanying heavy vehicles, we stirred up the mud pretty thoroughly. Some navy Seabees came in to build showers and living accommodations for us. The British continued to use their long bathtubs. Later, after I had flown nearly thirty missions and become a wing commander, I wound up with a fairly cozy little shack of my own.

Once we began our operations at Dunkeswell we were integrated into the Coastal Command, which taught us a lot we didn't know about antisubmarine patrol. The main thing we learned from the British was how to avoid fighters. I can sum up those lessons easily: not going where the fighters were and keeping our mouths shut while we were out over the Bay of Biscay. (If we did sight a U-boat, the procedure called for our radioman to transmit O-break-A by key, thus telling Coastal Command that we were about to attack.)

Unfortunately, our pilots sometimes learned those lessons about fighters the hard way. We lost two planes one day because one guy just cut loose on the radio. The Germans already had some fighters out there, and the radio direction finders homed in on the gabble that this guy was carrying on. They shot down both of our planes. The experience provided a dramatic object lesson for me to use in warning the surviving members of the squadron about the importance of radio discipline. During the course of our tour over there, we lost six planes and six of the eighteen crews that we started with. One of the six might have been shot down when he went too close to France while returning from a mission. Three planes were lost because of bad weather conditions.

One of the pilots who was shot down when the other fellow opened his mouth was a wonderful kid named Gil Rapp. He was just a really nice fellow, as was his copilot, Orville Moore, so it was difficult to write to their families and tell them the men had been lost. That was a tough chore, of course, whenever I had to do it. We had gone off to war with these men who were sons, brothers, and husbands, and some of them wouldn't be coming back.

Making an attack on a U-boat was a rare exception to the normal pattern of patrolling, which usually turned up nothing. Some of the flights took us damn near to Spain. We depended mostly on celestial navigation to get us out and back safely. We were wary of using any radio aids to navigation because the Germans were bending their beams coming out of France to try to trap our guys.

The average patrol was long and uncomfortable. After ten or eleven hours in those hard seats, your butt got sore. The PBM Mariners that I had flown back in Norfolk had wonderfully comfortable seats. The Liberators were much more Spartan.

When we did manage to get a blip on the radar—an electronic picture or a surfaced submarine or perhaps only a periscope—the tactics called for us to turn and head for it. You were lucky if you were able to make an attack sort of across the submarine's path, about 30 degrees off his course. The idea was to fly right down on the submarine and, just before you got overhead, to let go with the bombs that we carried in the belly of the airplane. We tried to place a pattern of bombs in the water around the submarine. They were set at about a thirty-foot depth to cause the maximum damage to the hull.

The British by then had been fighting the Germans for four years, so they had done a good job of establishing their procedures for these patrols. We just followed the practices they had been using. One of our VB-110 pilots, Lieutenant Norman Rudd, made a textbook attack and got a readily confirmed sinking. He even had pictures of wreckage floating on the surface after the attack.

Lieutenant Jack Munson, the executive officer of the squadron, once made a perfect run on a U-boat in the English Channel. He saw only the periscope, but he had a really good radarman, and this guy had picked up the blip from a considerable distance. He went toward it, and they dropped short. He wasn't able to sink the submarine, but he did bring back one of the best sets of pictures to date of a snorkel in action. He flew right over it.

One of the real keys to our antisubmarine efforts at the time was to force U-boats to the surface to run their diesel engines and to recharge their storage batteries for submerged operations. The snorkel was just then coming on the scene as a means of permitting a submarine to run her engines with the hull still submerged and thus much harder to see.

Around Christmas of 1943 we had an unusual mission: to go down and try to help locate a German freighter that was carrying a lot of contraband into France—either Saint-Nazaire or Brest. She was to be escorted by two German destroyers. All we had to drop on them were depth charges, which were not much good against surface ships. The British had a couple of light cruisers out there, and they caught and sank both the freighter and the destroyers. We flew over a lot of Germans in life rafts on the water after they had abandoned ship. We didn't strafe them, because I didn't think that was the right thing to do. I knew they'd have a hell of a time getting back to the beach anyway because they were a long way from land.

On that flight I came out of a cloud and ran into four German fighter planes, Heinkel 119-Es. They were pretty slow as fighters went, so I figured the PB4Y could outrun them. But they had stingers in the tail that the pilot could fire by looking into his rear-view mirror. We shot one guy down, and that must have alerted them that we were back there. Pretty soon, glowing pink balls came flying at me. I decided to use some discretion and get the hell out of there. All they had to do was dive, come back in a loop, and they would have been right on our tail. I didn't feel like sticking around since I was carrying our normal load of ten or eleven depth charges and an acoustic mine.

We got the one plane with our .50-caliber machine guns. We had two guns in the nose, two in the top turret, and two in the tail. Of course, this was a good deal different than those carrier fighters I might have been flying within the Pacific. There the pilot was all by himself. In the Liberator you had a copilot, and the total crew numbered ten or eleven men, including the ones operating the machine guns. No matter what else the Liberator was, it wasn't a fighter plane.

By the time the Allies were getting ready to invade Normandy in early June, our squadron was well broken in, and we had accumulated a lot of flying hours. The

Joseph P. Kennedy Jr. flew in PB4Y Liberators after receiving his wings as a naval aviator. (*International News*)

night before D-Day we saw thousands of planes going over to bomb France. The day after the landing we were flying antisubmarine missions in the English Channel to make sure the U-boats kept away from our large force of ships and landing craft. The British Coastal Command people were in charge of assigning missions and targets to various squadrons, based on whatever intelligence sources they had. They would tell us to fly out on a certain course, then turn and fly another leg back on another course.

Our normal operating area for months had been down over the Bay of Biscay to intercept U-boats coming out of the French coastal ports. We continued this routine up to D-Day, with the idea of keeping the submarines bottled up south of the English Channel itself. We didn't fly over the Channel before the invasion, because that would have been a dead giveaway of the upcoming landing. The Germans hadn't seen the American patrol flights there before, and we didn't want to alert them that anything was up. The Coastal Command itself had been taking care of any antisubmarine action in the Channel.

Once the invasion was in progress, I had a chance to fly over the Channel and see our fleet. I was struck by what a hell of a lot of ships we had there. I saw a lot of shooting taking place on the beaches, but I didn't fly over France itself, because we were pretty sure that the

In 1914 Patrick N. L. Bellinger, one of the U.S. Navy's earliest aviators, piloted the first navy plane to come under enemy fire. Here, thirty years later, as Commander Air Force Atlantic Fleet, he inspects a radar training unit while touring the Dunkeswell station. Lieutenant Commander Reedy is at right. (*U.S. Navy photo in the National Archives: 80-G-237229*)

Germans had a lot of antiaircraft guns set up.

Right after D-Day I was relieved of command of VB-110 and moved up to become commander of the group made up of four of these squadrons, including one that came up from Africa. I was in that role when the group was called on to send a PB4Y loaded with explosives to attack a V-1 site on the coast of France. The Germans had started using these buzz bombs shortly after the invasion, and they were a real menace to England. The man who wound up making the flight was Lieutenant Joseph P. Kennedy Jr., son of the former ambassador to Great Britain and older brother of the future president, John F. Kennedy.

I had gotten to know Joe well during the time he was flying for me in VP-203 and VB-110. He was a damn good pilot, and he was a fine officer—except a little non-reg. It's tough to put a finger on just how he strayed from the norm. He was always in uniform, for instance, but maybe he would leave his collar open instead of having it buttoned. He was a good guy to have in the squadron. I would say he had the best-trained crew of any of the eighteen. And he was aggressive. I think he would have been more inclined to attack the fighters than I was. I was concerned about the responsibility for the other men in my plane. Perhaps he just had enough self-confidence that he thought he could bring everyone else back safely.

When he had completed the number of missions that constituted a normal combat tour, Joe wanted to stay over in England longer. Part of the reason had to do with the marriage of his sister Kathleen to the Marquis of Hartington. He might have been influenced as well by the fact that he was very much in love with a beautiful girl from Woking, right outside of London. Hank Searls, also a navy PB4Y pilot, wrote a 1969 book about Joe Kennedy Jr. Its title is *The Lost Prince*, and in it he suggests still another reason Joe might have stayed. Joe had heard about his younger brother's PT boat exploits in the Solomons, and Searls implies that the older brother may have wanted to get a medal for himself as a means of preparing for a postwar political career.

I didn't know about that part of it myself, although I do know that he was a courageous man and that he volunteered for this mission of flying against the buzz-bomb launching site. Joe wanted to make himself a hero; nearly everybody over there did.

The scheme called for a war-weary PB4Y to be stripped of its normal interior except for seats for the pilot and copilot. The rest of the plane would be crammed full of high-explosive torpex, and the aircraft would be equipped to fly by remote control. It needed a crew on board to get it airborne, but then the two pilots would arm the explosives, exit through the well for the nose wheel, and parachute to safety. An accompanying plane would then control the Liberator the rest of the way by radio signals and guide it into its target by using a picture transmitted by a television camera in the nose of the plane with the explosives on board. Once it got to the buzz-bomb launching site, which was not vulnerable to normal bombing, the unmanned plane would be dived into the target, blow up, and presumably destroy the launcher.

A Naval Academy classmate of mine named Jimmy Smith was in command of the special attack unit, as the outfit conducting this project was designated. I volunteered to fly the first of these missions because I had been talking with Smith. When Commodore Bill Hamilton, the commander of Fleet Air Wing Seven, heard of it, he said, "You will not go off on flights like that. Your business is to run the group." There wasn't anything I could do about it, so I had to get someone else to fly the mission. As soon as the word went out, Joe Kennedy was the first one to volunteer. His copilot for the mission was Lieutenant Wilford Willy.

They took off on August 12 from an airbase at Fersfield in eastern England. It was the headquarters for these special attack flights. Later, I talked with the men in the control plane that was also airborne for the mission. They said that before Kennedy or Willy ever pulled the handle to arm the explosives in their plane, it blew up in the air. I believe that the explosion might have been caused by a shift of the cargo or perhaps a charge of static electricity that ignited all that torpex. But we really don't know what happened. We didn't find any wreckage from the PB4Y for a long time. I understand that a couple of the engines were found even later in the Wash, a swampy area on the east coast of England.

The result was really shocking to all of us. That was a hell of a blow. We had a memorial service in the little Episcopal church in Dunkeswell. There was nothing to send home except the personal effects of Kennedy and Willy. They had taken a risk and had been the victims of a situation that was inherently dangerous. I admire their courage for being willing to undertake the mission. I wish they could have succeeded.

JAMES ROBERT REEDY (1910–) attended Baldwin-Wallace College for a year before entering the Naval Academy, from which he graduated in 1933. He was not commissioned at the time because of the Great Depression and thus enlisted in the Army Air Corps instead. When permitted by Congress, Reedy rejoined the navy and took flight training. He subsequently served as floatplane pilot in the heavy cruiser *Northampton*. Later assignments included carrier duty, patrol planes, and the NATO staff near Paris. He was in command of Naval Air Station Jacksonville when he was selected for flag rank. His first billet as a rear admiral was Commander Carrier Division Twenty, an ASW group. He then took command of the U.S. Antarctic Support Force. In May 1965 he became Commander Task Force 77, operating the large carriers in support of the Vietnam War. In that billet, which also included command of Carrier Division Five, he flew his flag in the *Coral Sea*, *Independence*, *Kitty Hawk*, and *Constellation*. His last billet prior to retirement in 1968 was on the staff of the Chief of Naval Operations. He now lives in San Antonio, Texas. (*Navy photo in the National Archives: 80-G-237229*)

Initially, the Allies had intended to invade northern and southern France simultaneously in the spring of 1944. When the planners discovered that not enough shipping was available to support two such landings at the same time, the invasion in the south was postponed until August. Thus it was that Rear Admiral Don Moon was freed from the Mediterranean to go command the amphibious task force for Utah Beach at Normandy. In the meantime, unfortunately, occurred the disastrous Exercise Tiger and a chain of events that led ultimately to his death by suicide. The following accounts present different facets of the southern France invasion, including an overview by the Eighth Fleet commander, Admiral Kent Hewitt. He was an experienced amphibious commander in the Mediterranean, going back to the invasion of North Africa in November 1942. The assault on southern France was his crowning triumph. Combat artist Al Murray complements Hewitt's high-level view with an anecdote about a tiny facet of the overall operation.

Admiral Moon's case is given special attention here because he was the only U.S. Navy flag officer known to have killed himself during World War II. (Rear Admiral John Wilcox was lost overboard from the battleship *Washington* in 1942 under mysterious circumstances. There is no way of knowing whether his death was the result of a deliberate act on his part.) Don Moon was a meticulous, highly conscientious officer who wanted things to be right and often preferred to do them himself rather than delegate. Regrettably, this resulted in a tendency to get bogged down in details rather than viewing events from the broader perspective of a flag officer. His sense of duty—along with an expression of scorn from a senior admiral—apparently compelled him to carry personally the burden of loss for the hundreds of men killed off Slapton Sands in late April. What he probably needed most in the summer of 1944 was a chance to get away for a time from the stresses of combat and receive appropriate medical care. But it just wasn't possible to call "time out" in the midst of war, and Admiral Moon never got the break he needed.

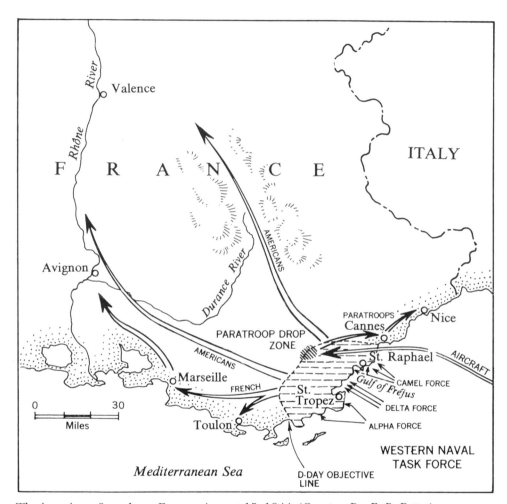

The invasion of southern France, August 15, 1944. (*Courtesy Dr. E. B. Potter*)

A WARM WELCOME IN SOUTHERN FRANCE

By Admiral H. Kent Hewitt, U.S. Navy (Retired)

Some time before we made the move of Eighth Fleet headquarters from Algiers to Casablanca, Admiral Ernest King had been to a conference in London. He came back through Casablanca on June 17, and I flew down to join him and have a conference. We went up to Port Lyautey, Morocco, to look at the airfields, and then we had a chance to discuss further developments in the plans for Operation Anvil. That was the last time I saw

him before we actually carried out the invasion in August.

The plan had been discussed in the Combined Chiefs of Staff first. They wanted, of course, not only the liberation of southern France but to get the port of Marseille and the railroad system up the Rhône Valley, which would be of tremendous value in support of the armies operating in northern France. That was particularly true because the western ports such as Cherbourg

The Allied invasion fleet lies at anchor in the Bay of Naples on August 13, just ready to get under way for the invasion of southern France two days later. Mount Vesuvius towers in the background. (*Painting by navy combat artist Albert K. Murray*)

218

Barrage balloons stand guard overhead as a row of LSTs beached in Italy takes on vehicles to be landed during the invasion of southern France. (*Navy photo in the National Archives: 80-G-59476*)

were much more badly damaged than expected. The Allies weren't able to use them to full capacity for some time. Marseille was almost a lifesaver from that point of view.

General Dwight Eisenhower was adamant as to the importance of the southern France landing. He fought on that thing. But actually we didn't know until the very last whether we were going to be able to carry out that operation or not. It took Franklin D. Roosevelt himself to insist on it.

Winston Churchill did everything possible to change the plan. But once it was decided upon, he went along like a good soldier. He was in Naples when we set sail with our big convoy; he passed in as we were steaming out. He came in a British admiral's barge, and we recognized him. He waved to us and held up his V-for-victory finger signal. He was a very good sport about it. Then he flew over to Corsica and came out in a British cruiser and took a look at us again as we went by. I would like to be able to confirm the story that Sir

Winston renamed the operation from Anvil to Dragoon because he was dragooned into it. Churchill himself said it was renamed because they didn't want to take the risk that the Germans had discovered the meaning of Anvil.

Planning for the operation began in January 1944 in Algiers, very shortly after the invasion at Anzio, Italy. The planning section of my staff and that of Lieutenant General Alexander M. Patch, commanding general of the Seventh Army, were established together in Algiers. A general of the Army Air Forces was also assigned to the planning and stayed with us right along. That is the first time we ever had any air planning at all to go along with the naval and military planning.

Let me add some little human-interest remarks. When we went into Sicily the year before, we strove to get the air officers to join with us in making plans. They never did, and so we put to sea without knowing what the air force plan would be. We made preparations, and Lieutenant General George S. Patton came to me.

On board a Coast Guard–manned attack transport in the Mediterranean, crew members and embarked troops listen to a concert from the band seen at left shortly before the invasion of southern France. (*Coast Guard photo in the National Archives: 26-G-2679*)

We had had naval air support for the landing in Morocco in November 1942, so General Patton said, "Admiral, I wish you'd get one of your navy carriers to back us up on this landing. I can't get that blankety-blank air force to do anything." We were all fighting the same war, but they were interested in long-distance bombing of enemy airfields and things of that sort. Anything like the supporting of a landing or supporting the troops on shore seemed to be a sort of sideshow for them. Later on that condition improved.

I told Patton that I wished just as much as he did that we had some navy air behind us, but that with the land bases so close, I didn't feel I'd be justified in asking for it. And even if I did ask for it, I wouldn't get it, because all our carriers were badly needed in the Pacific at that time.

The landing in southern France was carried out on August 15. I think it was about the twelfth or thirteenth we sailed with the big transports from Naples. The other ships—the smaller landing craft—had to be sent earlier from various places, some of them from Corsica. All these details were worked out very carefully, with the result that everything worked almost perfectly. We didn't know until we actually sailed whether we were really going to carry out the operation or not. We were threatened with having to take the same troops around and land them somewhere in the Bay of Biscay. This wouldn't have been so good. We would have had to replan and reload and do almost everything over.

The troops that were going to make the landing had to be withdrawn from the Italian front a little ahead of time so they could be retrained. There were ten divisions, eventually, including the French army. There were three American divisions and seven French. There was also a British airborne unit—the only British troops that took part in the operation. I don't think it was division strength.

The French—and you couldn't blame them—were extremely eager to be the first to land on their own soil. General Jean de Lattre de Tassigny was insistent about that. He was a very fine man, very pleasant, very volatile. I had to convince him, and General Charles de Gaulle too, that it was hard enough to get soldiers and sailors working together in the same boat in the first place, but with the language barrier it would be absolutely impossible. It would be chaotic. Fortunately, I had my friend Rear Admiral André Lemonnier, head of the French navy, to back me up on that completely. So they agreed to it, finally. As it worked out, the American troops took the beachhead, and then the French army landed in behind them and started inland.

For this operation we had a considerable naval force. We had three of our battleships, several cruisers, and a large number of destroyers. We had British battleships, a number of British cruisers, and a number of British destroyers and minesweepers, as well as the transports and landing craft. We had everything in the French navy that was available.

We had forces divided up among the different assault groups so that each group had its own force—battleships, cruisers, and so on—to call on for gunfire. Thinking things over from the political point of view, we carefully assigned at least one French ship to each of those units because we felt that if some honest citizen

on shore got his house shot up during the operation, we didn't want him to be able to blame the Yankees or the British for it. It might be one of the French ships.

Some of the small craft, the LCTs, had to be moved up ahead of time because they were very slow and they couldn't go too far. The craft were dispatched according to their speeds, rather than by the final force to which they were attached. So the slow ones went first, then the next ones, then finally the fastest ships came. As they approached the general attack area, they split up, and the different craft went to their own assault forces. We had had to do the same thing in Sicily and Salerno, as a matter of fact.

It was all a great responsibility, the coordinating of these movements. I felt the responsibility, naturally. But I always had the feeling we had worked things out as well as we could. I could rely on my very fine staff and on my subordinate naval commanders. I didn't worry. I mean that. I had the attitude that we'd done our best and that everything would be all right.

I'm one of these double-acrostic addicts. It's a great relaxation. But sometimes some of my staff would have a fit because we'd be going into one of these landings and I'd be sitting up on the bridge of the flagship *Catoctin*, ready to take action if anything unexpected came up, working out some of these puzzles. I had to concentrate my mind on that. It took it off other worries.

We met some opposition, particularly on the right, in the Gulf of Fréjus. We were supposed to land first up

LCVPs on the beach at southern France during the invasion. (*Navy photo in the National Archives: 59475*)

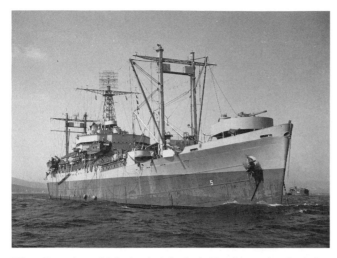

The *Catoctin*, which had Admiral Hewitt embarked for Operation Dragoon, was one of several merchant-type hulls converted for use as amphibious force flagships. They provided ample communications facilities and staff accommodations. (*Navy photo in the National Archives: 80-G-362811*)

toward Cape Geramo at a very steep shelving beach there. Then we were to get some of the army ashore so they could advance along the coast toward Saint-Raphaël, because the big beach was at the head of the gulf, where we really wanted to land most of our forces. But that was flanked, on the shore, by the enemy force at Saint-Raphaël, so we'd try to land farther down the beach.

They landed at eight o'clock in the morning on Green Beach. The other landing was supposed to be made at twelve o'clock at Red Beach. By this time the army was supposed to have been able to flatten those defenses. We made the landing on time. The boats went in, with the scout boats ahead and the slow minesweepers and whatnot. They were immediately taken under fire by the German guns from Saint-Raphaël.

Rear Admiral Spencer Lewis, who had been my chief of staff, had taken over the command of that group after Admiral Moon's death. On his own, he made the decision to hold that landing up and to land those troops on Green Beach, behind where the others were.

The combat information center of the command ship *Catoctin* was crowded on August 15, D-Day for the invasion of southern France. (*Navy photo in the National Archives: 80-G-362857*)

Senior officers on board the flagship *Catoctin* look over a rubber terrain map of the invasion area. *Left to right are:* Lieutenant General A. M. Patch, commanding the Seventh Army, Secretary of the Navy James Forrestal, and Vice Admiral Hewitt. The sailors at upper right are taking it all in. (*Navy photo in the National Archives: 80-G-46368*)

That was very fortunate because there would have been very heavy losses if they'd continued to land.

The orders were to carry out the landing regardless, so when I first heard that it had been held up, I was somewhat annoyed. But when Lewis explained the situation to me, I agreed with him. He'd done absolutely the right thing. Major General John E. Dahlquist, commanding the 36th Division, agreed with Lewis too. He was already ashore and not in position to make that decision himself.

There was some resistance at other points, but it was not too heavy. That was the main thing. Compared with what we'd faced before, it wasn't bad. I think it was more or less a surprise landing. Of course, the Germans were ready for it. They had put up a lot of beach obstacles and the beaches were mined, but they didn't concentrate everything right at that point to meet it. I think they were looking for some landings maybe farther east, along toward Cannes.

We received an amazing welcome, perfectly wonderful, on the part of the French people. I went ashore with General Patch the first day to go around and see what was going on. We took Admiral Lemonnier with us. He had begged to be taken along. He had no part, no command in the operation, but he went about with us. He was the junior, but we all stood aside and said he was to be the first one to land on his own soil. We went around in a Jeep. We had a marvelous reception everywhere. We'd go through a little town and crowds would rush out from cafés with wineglasses and bottles

of wine held up for us to partake of.

I remember the first five or six hundred yards in this Jeep after we landed. We went along on the road toward Saint-Raphaël, and there was a French girl riding a bicycle ahead of us with her skirts ballooning out. We overtook her, and the admiral said something to her. I don't know what he said, but she was so surprised that she promptly fell off her bicycle. We stopped, and she came rushing up to the Jeep and gave the admiral a kiss. That was his first welcome to France.

When the French people there recognized Admiral Lemonnier as one of theirs, they just went wild. They had never been told anything. They didn't know whether France still had a navy. So he got a royal welcome, and as soon as he told the crowd who General Patch and I were, we got an equally warm welcome. It seemed as if everyone was trying to get within arm's reach to shake our hands. Then someone started to sing the "Marseillaise," and the entire crowd joined in, with all of us, of course, standing in salute. It was one of the most spontaneous and most moving incidents I have ever been privileged to witness.

On the day after the invasion, the local schoolmaster at Fréjus is the center of attention. Second from left is Admiral Hewitt; next to him is Secretary Forrestal. At right, with his back turned, is Rear Admiral André Lemonnier, head of the French navy. (*Naval Institute Collection*)

Allied troops move ashore on D-Day, 15 August 1944. (*Army photo in the National Archives: SC 192907*)

HENRY KENT HEWITT (1887–1972) graduated from the Naval Academy in the Class of 1907 and made an around-the-world cruise in the battleship *Missouri* of the Great White Fleet. He was involved in survey and patrol work in the Caribbean, then commanded destroyers during World War I. In the 1920s he had battleship duty, staff service afloat and in OpNav, and taught at the Naval Academy. After taking a Naval War College course, he commanded a destroyer division, served on the Battle Force staff, and again taught at Annapolis. He was commanding officer of the heavy cruiser *Indianapolis* in the mid-1930s. As war approached, Hewitt commanded the Special Service Squadron and Cruiser Division Eight. In November 1942 he commanded the Allied landings at North Africa. In February 1943 he became Commander Eighth Fleet for amphibious landings at Sicily and Salerno, Italy. In 1944 he commanded Allied forces for the invasion of southern France. In 1945 Hewitt investigated the Japanese attack at Pearl Harbor, then at war's end became Commander U.S. Naval Forces in Europe. He subsequently had special duty at the Naval War College and later at the United Nations prior to his retirement in 1949. The destroyer *Hewitt* (DD-966) is named in his honor. (*Portrait by navy combat artist Albert K. Murray*)

THE DEATH OF ADMIRAL MOON

By Captain John A Moreno, U.S. Navy (Retired)

Captain Don Moon evidently made a strong impression when he served on the staff of Admiral Ernest J. King in Washington during the middle part of the war, because he was awarded the assignment of commanding one of the assault forces destined for southern France. Moon, who had been selected for rear admiral, chose Captain Rutledge Tompkins as his chief of staff. I never understood why; the two were entirely different types. Moon was hardworking, hard driving, and humorless; Tompkins was quick and brilliant and had a sardonic sense of humor, but he was not too hardworking. They were not congenial, which was obvious to the entire staff.

It was a small staff, no more than thirty most of the time, and all the senior people were career regulars. For some time I have been the senior surviving member of that group. I was the air officer and assistant planner, based in part on my recent completion of the Army-Navy Staff College in Washington—now the National War College. When I was interviewed for the billet, I told Moon that—based on my experience in the landings in North Africa—one of our major requirements would be for transportation and communications.

Moon, by now wearing the two-star rank of rear admiral, gathered us up, and we headed overseas. Our original headquarters was the invasion training center at Arzeu, Algeria, where we were supposed to plan for the invasion of southern France, which was then expected to be conducted simultaneously with the one at Normandy. After we had been there for only a couple of weeks, we got the word that there was not sufficient sea lift available for the two operations to be conducted at the same time. Sea lift is not as glamorous as aircraft carriers and submarines, but without it the army can't get to the fight. So we pulled out of Arzeu and flew to Dunkeswell Field in England, then to Plymouth. My guess is that Admiral King personally selected Admiral Moon to command the Utah Beach task force for Normandy; it was a prize command.

We received a frosty reception—in more ways than one—on a cold February morning at Dunkeswell. No one greeted us, so we made our way to Plymouth as best we could. There we set up headquarters and billets in a newly completed U.S. naval hospital until the Seabees could raze and rebuild a section of Plymouth that had been completely devastated by German bombing. The British didn't bother to repair or reconstruct the damaged areas; they just filled them with water in case of more raids and fires.

Our headquarters office space was the second floor of what had been a tailor shop—no longer in business. The admiral's working hours were hellishly long: from 7:30 A.M. until one or two the following morning, punctuated by an occasional German air raid. I got tired of that routine, both literally and figuratively, so I began calling it a day at 11:00 P.M. That was not looked on with great favor by Admiral Moon, although we

Don Moon, newly promoted to rear admiral, wears his stars in March 1944 at the amphibious training base in Algiers, North Africa. (*Navy photo in the National Archives: 80-G-250062*)

On board the flagship *Bayfield* during Exercise Tiger, Captain H. G. Moran shows a clipboard to Rear Admiral Don Moon, in the two-star helmet and fur-collared coat. (*Courtesy the family of Rear Admiral Don Moon*)

generally got along well. He was not the kind of person who had a close relationship with anybody on his staff, but of them all, I blush to admit that I probably knew him better than most.

Each morning we would appear in the staff mess for breakfast. Occasionally, visiting officers came in, and it was difficult for them to get to know Admiral Moon. As I said, he had no humor at all. He would turn to the visitor and say, "Well, now, what are you famous for? What do you do?" So, of course, they were most uncomfortable about the whole thing. I will say that Admiral Moon had a very good relationship with Major General J. Lawton Collins, who was on board with us as commander of VII Corps. I think Collins went out of his way to make sure that the relationship worked smoothly.

One of the men we had on board the *Bayfield* was Brigadier General Theodore Roosevelt Jr., son of the former president. In 1944 he was fifty-seven years old and serving as the assistant commander of the 4th Infantry Division. He was a lovable old man—I was then thirty-five—and very much a politician rather than a professional soldier. He had previously been Assistant Secretary of the Navy and Governor of Puerto Rico and the Philippines. We all liked him, because he had a charming personality and was very cultured. He was among the few American general officers ashore during the assault landings on D-Day, and I daresay the oldest man to hit the beach. He died of a heart attack a few weeks after D-Day.

We had several rehearsals prior to the real show at Normandy. The most complete, held the night of April 27–28, was Exercise Tiger, in which two LSTs were sunk by German torpedo boats and a third damaged. An element of the drill that hasn't received much attention is that of friendly fire. The army had fitted

some of its tanks to be waterborne, an idea that didn't work out too well. They were firing as they approached the beach at Slapton Sands, but their guns were not stabilized. As the tanks pitched in the choppy water, they fired their artillery rounds in the middle of friendly soldiers already on the beach. Several of our people were wounded as a result.

The aftermath of the disaster in Exercise Tiger affected Admiral Moon very deeply. As soon as the exercise was over, we received a dispatch from Rear Admiral Alan Kirk in the *Augusta*, ordering Moon to appear on the flagship immediately. I was somewhat surprised when the admiral requested that I accompany him. When we got to the flagship, we were sent to talk with Rear Admiral Arthur Struble, who was Kirk's chief of staff. There was bad blood between them; I believe Struble was resentful that Moon got the assignment to command the task force at Utah Beach. Struble was a year senior to Moon at the Naval Academy, and it's natural for a flag officer to want to be in a command position for an operation such as this. Instead, Struble had a staff job.

When we got aboard the *Augusta*, I knew it was going to be a bad time, so, frankly, I quickly disappeared. I had a friend who was a captain on Kirk's staff, and I dashed down toward his cabin. I hadn't even gotten there before Struble's orderly came along and said, "The admiral would like to see you in his cabin." I went up to the cabin, and the flag lieutenant was waiting there as well.

When the three of us were ready, we went in to see Struble. He was looking out the porthole and initially didn't even turn around to acknowledge our arrival. A British submarine went by with a broom lashed to the periscope, signifying that she had made a clean sweep during her last patrol. Struble remarked, "Well, I see *somebody* did his duty." Then he turned to Moon with the coldest glance I've ever seen and said, in an unfriendly tone of voice, "All right, Moon, tell me what happened." I think that is when Moon really broke down.

In all fairness, we didn't yet know in full detail just what had happened because this was the same day that we had lost the ships and hundreds of men. So Moon was really at a disadvantage in trying to offer an explanation, and he didn't do too well at it. Later, we found out that the British escort commander, who was in a flower-class corvette, didn't fire a shot. And the convoy commander, who was in the lead LST, never issued an order. It was a real breakdown on the part of Moon's subordinates. We discovered, in trying to reconstruct what had gone wrong, that there was no common radio frequency in the communication plan for the escorts to talk to the LST convoy they were guarding. It was a mess.

After we got ashore, Moon told me to get in touch

Rear Admiral Arthur Struble, Admiral Kirk's chief of staff, is in a jovial mood here as he visits with members of a 40-millimeter gun crew on board the flagship *Augusta*. Struble was a good deal less pleasant when interrogating Rear Admiral Don Moon following the disastrous Exercise Tiger. (*Navy photo in the National Archives: 80-G-356314*)

with the staff of the Commander in Chief at Plymouth, who had furnished the British ships for the operation. I was supposed to find out what they had to contribute. I had a friend who was the assistant chief of staff for operations. He was a typical British line officer of the old school. He said, "I think this is a bit too much for us. It has to be handled on a higher level." That was the end of my interview with him. So Moon had to deal directly with Commander in Chief Plymouth.

We just couldn't get too much out of the British, and their contribution to the disaster was certainly significant. They had had a destroyer assigned to protect the convoy, but she had suffered a very minor collision, and even though capable of further operations, was sent back to port for repairs. This was done without any notification to Admiral Moon and without provision of a timely replacement. That destroyer could have been

helpful in combating the German E-boats, which did a splendid job, I must confess, in their attack on the LSTs.

Our flagship for both Normandy and southern France was the USS *Bayfield*, an attack transport that had been converted to that role from her original design as a commercial cargo ship. She had adequate communications facilities but was quite cramped for the flagship role. In addition to the Utah Assault Force staff, she carried the staff of the army's VII Corps commander, the 4th Infantry Division staff, the 82nd Airborne Division ground echelon, an Army Air Forces liaison unit, and a battalion landing team from the 4th Division. Things were very cozy. We greatly envied the Omaha Assault Force in the USS *Ancon* because she had been a commercial passenger-cargo carrier. More to the point, she had been specifically converted for use by the navy as an amphibious force flagship, not a transport. Thus, she had ample accommodations for Rear Admiral John L. Hall's entourage, plus the embarked army staffs.

As the ships of our task force sailed out of Plymouth on our sortie toward Normandy, we passed HMS *Erebus*, an old monitor built for the bombardment of German fortifications in World War I. It seemed that her hour of destiny had finally arrived; she was now going to shell the Germans. She burst out in a display of signal flags, proudly spelling out, "England expects every man to do his duty!" She was too slow for our fast convoys and too fast for the slow ones, so we didn't know where to put her. We finally decided to place her between the two groups, proceeding independently. When H-hour came, she was in position and trained out her one turret, fired one salvo, and then disaster struck. One gun failed to return to battery. She was loaded up with prisoners of war and returned to home waters, her crew completely disconsolate.

As air officer on the staff, one of my jobs was writing up a plan for a smoke screen to cover our troops ashore. Admiral Moon had me redo that plan twenty-five times before he would approve it, although I would have to say it was no better the last time than the first. In any event, the smoke plan was a complete failure. We were required to submit it to the Army Air Forces six days before the landing, even though no one could forecast six days ahead of time what the wind would be on D-Day. Further, the army refused to give us any direct communication with the smoke planes. All communications had to be through Army Air Forces headquarters, which in turn would communicate with the six P-47s assigned to the task. When the time came for them to smoke, they foolishly flew directly over the advancing forces. "They're smoking in the wrong area!" yelled Admiral Moon.

"Not to worry, sir," I replied. "They'll all be shot down by our own forces in just a minute." And that's exactly what happened. We got one of the pilots back aboard the *Bayfield*, shook up but not shot up. The ship's medical officer, a young Public Health Service officer who was a good friend of mine, said, "He's had a great shock. He'd better have a good drink of whiskey."

"Doctor," I said, "I'm shook too."

"Okay," said my friend, "you can have one also."

The physician on Admiral Moon's staff was Commander Ed Lowe, a regular navy doctor who had been a hero on board the stricken cruiser *San Francisco* at Guadalcanal in 1942 and had been awarded a well-deserved Navy Cross. Off Normandy one day I observed a commotion at the gangway. A man had fallen over the side into the chilly waters of the English Channel. Commander Lowe jumped over the side and into the water some twenty feet below to rescue the drowning man. With the administrative confusion that later occurred, I don't think he ever received recognition for his feat, but he certainly should have.

All ships were required to fly kite balloons, much against our will. They accomplished very little. I once asked the operations people at a British airfield if their balloons ever bagged anything. "Oh, yessir," they replied. "Twenty-five of ours and three of theirs!" But we didn't like them because they were visible for miles, showing the Germans exactly where we were. Fortunately, a severe thunderstorm came along on D+3 and destroyed all of them. They made perfect lightning rods and produced a spectacular display.

One of the most unusual items of equipment at Normandy was "Bedbug." The Germans had developed a radio-controlled glide bomb with which they had previously scored a direct hit on the light cruiser *Savannah* off Salerno in the Mediterranean. During an air raid on Plymouth, while we were still there, the British shot down a German bomber that had on board the entire radio-control installation. Within little more than a month, counter-frequency equipment was built and installed in many of our ships, including the *Bayfield*. The warning code word, broadcast on all frequencies, was Bedbug. Sure enough, the Germans did use radio-controlled bombs off Normandy, and Bedbug stopped all of them.

We were off the Normandy beaches for almost two weeks, but the second week was rather quiet after the events of the first. The army moved rapidly inland, and things slowed down a bit. Nonetheless, we were glad when the show was over and we could head back to England to prepare for the next operation, the previously postponed invasion of southern France. Soon we were under way again, reporting to the Mediterranean in late June.

By early August we had finished writing the operation order for southern France, and we were on board the *Bayfield* at Naples as we made final preparations. On the morning of August 5, I went to Salerno to brief the 36th Division on what was coming up. I left the ship about 6:30 in the morning, came back that night about 6:30, and the staff duty officer met me. I said, "Well, I think I'll go in and tell the admiral that everything went off as scheduled."

He said, "Oh, I'm sorry, sir, he's buried."

I said, "What?"

"Yes, he's buried."

He had shot himself that morning and was buried that very same day. This was in a temporary grave ashore. I assume the body has long since been returned to the United States. I believe the order to keep the admiral's death quiet came from higher up, possibly from Admiral King himself. The news reports of the time indicated only that Admiral Moon had died, not where or under what circumstances.

In addition to the shock of the thing, we had a very

real practical problem as well. We were all set to go on the next invasion, and we didn't have a leader. So they dug around frantically to find somebody whose flag we could fly. Vice Admiral Kent Hewitt finally came up with Rear Admiral Spencer Lewis, who was his chief of staff. Hewitt was the overall commander for the upcoming invasion, and I must say that Lewis came to us reluctantly. He had just married a WRN—a British navy woman—and he didn't want to make war; he wanted to make love. He went to sea with us and stipulated that as soon as the touchdown came, I would fly him back from southern France to Naples to be with his bride. Of course, he knew nothing about the specifics of the operation.

When we got into the invasion itself, one facet of it completely failed. We knew that the Germans had a lot of obstacles on the beach to prevent our landing, and we had some radio-controlled LCVPs loaded with explosives so they could knock out the obstacles. So we sent the landing craft in, and—to our horror—the LCVPs turned around and headed right straight for us. The Germans had gotten the control frequency and turned the craft around. Fortunately, as the landing craft returned toward the line of departure, our own people regained control.

One battalion of the 36th Division had made a small landing in the first phase on a road coming into the Fréjus/Saint-Raphaël area, and they were on Red Beach. In the meantime, the whole reinforced division was hung up, and there we were. We couldn't make the landing as originally planned, so the chief of staff, Captain Tompkins, redirected the whole landing onto Green Beach, a very small area which was, at the most, only five hundred yards wide and had only one outlet. Twenty thousand troops were trying to get ashore on this one area. Major General John Dahlquist, a wonderful guy who was in command of the 36th Division, had already gone ashore. So Tompkins said to me, "You notify the division commander that I have redirected the whole landing."

So I went ashore, and the beach was under fire by German 88s by this time. I said, "General, I'm sorry to tell you this, but the landing has failed."

Well, he got a little white along about this time. He said, "Where are the troops?"

I said, "Oh, they're going to be touching down in about half an hour at Green Beach."

So he said, "Show me where," and we jumped in a Jeep and dashed down to the beach where they were coming in. General Dahlquist personally deployed the entire division as they came in.

The next day, the VI Corps commander, Major General Lucian Truscott, said, "Dahlquist, I'll give you five minutes to tell me why you shouldn't be relieved of your command on the field of battle."

Evidently General Dahlquist said the right thing in

Rear Admiral Spencer Lewis left Admiral Hewitt's staff to become Commander Task Force 87, but his heart was elsewhere. (*Navy photo in the National Archives: 80-G-302426*)

those five minutes because he kept his job. I saw him again some years after the war and asked him if he remembered the situation. "I'll never forget it," he said.

I suppose you could give Admiral Lewis the credit for the decision to land the division on a much more hospitable beach than the one planned. That's the navy system—the man at the top gets the credit or the blame for what his subordinates do. But I think the officer who really saw what needed to be done and made it happen was Captain Tompkins, the chief of staff. In any event, it was Tompkins who stayed behind and ran things while Admiral Lewis went back to his British lady.

In the wake of an unhappy experience such as Admiral Moon's death, people are likely to look back and search for clues in an attempt to explain why things happened as they did. What might be called the conventional wisdom was expressed by two authors writing in the 1950s. Samuel Eliot Morison wrote in his history that Admiral Moon was already worn down by the strain of the Utah Beach landings and worried about the planning and rehearsal for the upcoming invasion of southern France. After a series of sleepless nights, Morison wrote, Moon "took his own life, a victim of extreme physical and mental fatigue."

In an article in the *Proceedings* magazine, on the tenth anniversary of the southern France operation, Admiral Hewitt said that Moon had come to him and talked of the unreadiness of his force and had begged to have D-Day postponed. This, of course, fits in with the picture of Admiral Moon as a conscientious and methodical man—someone who wanted all the details in order before proceeding. It fits as well with the idea of combat fatigue after the Normandy operation, but I think at least part of the explanation lies elsewhere.

We did go through a lot in the D-Day phase, but I remember that when we were in Naples, writing up the operation order for southern France, Admiral Moon was a lot more relaxed than he had been in preparing for Normandy. In fact, in the afternoons we would actually take time off from working, and he would go

swimming with us. The Italians had built a beautiful swimming pool for the planned Olympics that didn't take place because of the onset of war. We frequently went there in the afternoons, and I thought it was wonderful that the admiral relaxed that much.

Subsequent to the suicide, I talked with Ed Lowe, the senior medical officer on the staff. He confided in me that he had been trying to treat Admiral Moon for acute depression. In the midst of war, however, there was no opportunity for the admiral to take some time off and be treated in an appropriate setting. Lowe was a very fine guy and certainly a competent doctor, but he wasn't a psychiatrist, and thus I don't think he was able to help very much. Lowe definitely attributed the admiral's feelings of depression to the loss of ships and men during Exercise Tiger. Perhaps it was Admiral Moon's worry over the southern France landings that pushed him over the edge, but the origin was two months earlier. In a way, Admiral Moon was perhaps the last victim of the German E-boat attack that night at Slapton Sands.

JOHN A MORENO (1908–) graduated from the Naval Academy in 1930 and had a varied career prior to his retirement in 1960. He served in the battleships *West Virginia* and *California*; the destroyers *Ellis*, *Breckinridge*, and *Greer*; the survey ship *Nokomis*; as an aviator and ship's officer in the cruisers *Pensacola* and *New Orleans*, and as an aviator in squadrons on board the carriers *Saratoga* and *Lexington*. He commanded Patrol Squadron 92, the seaplane tender *Floyds Bay*, and the carrier *San Jacinto*. Other commands included air stations at Willow Grove, Pennsylvania, and Agana, Guam; Fleet Air Guam; and Naval Air Bases Marianas. Moreno served on amphibious staffs for three wartime landings. Other staff assignments were to the Joint Staff, Joint Chiefs of Staff, Commander in Chief Pacific Fleet Evaluation Group, and the executive office of the Secretary of the Navy. Shore assignments were to the Bureau of Aeronautics and to the Deputy Chief of Naval Operations (Air). He participated in seven campaigns in North Africa, Europe, and the Pacific, and one in Korea. His decorations include the Legion of Merit and two Bronze Stars with Combat V. Captain Moreno is a graduate of the Army-Navy Staff College and has a master's degree from George Washington University. He now lives in Coronado, California. (*Navy photo in the National Archives: 80-G-45136*)

DOG TAGS AND DIRTY BEANS

By Commander Albert K. Murray, U.S. Naval Reserve (Retired)

The landing in southern France was reasonably easy, in my opinion. I went ashore with the third wave in my role as a combat artist, supposedly to cover this thing pictorially as best I could. I soon ran into my boss, Rear Admiral Bertram J. Rodgers, Commander Task Force 85, who was in command of the landing force at the Bay of Bougnon. He asked me, "Well, how are you making out? What do you think of it?"

I said, "Well, I think it's a little bit quiet."

He said, "I'll tell you what you do. There's a special service force, the rangers, down there that are trying to get to a fort that's harassing us badly, right in back of Monaco. You go down there and see what you can dig up in a pictorial way. We've lost all contact with those people."

When I got to this place, it was between Nice and the casino at Monte Carlo. A considerable mountain, Mont Argil, looms there, and about halfway up was an old Roman town with a Roman aqueduct and a fort. It was a medieval fort with a drawbridge over the moat, which was then dry, of course. It had a parapet wall with lance windows in there for archers with bows and arrows. The rangers had been assigned to get the Germans out of that place. They were harassing our troops because they could look over the parapets right into the town of Monaco. There were ten thousand German troops, and we were not allowed to assault them because that was neutral territory. Finally, these special service guys got the Germans out of there about three in the afternoon, and we came in.

I discovered that we were at an elevation of three thousand feet. There was a wonderful view of the whole coast along there, all the way down to Menton on the Italian border and the casino at Monte Carlo and Cape Ferrat and all. I'd been sailing around Cape Ferrat every night with the PT boats that were sent out to give screening coverage for our fleet of considerable size there—the combatant ships, the support units, and the whole works for the invasion.

Down in front of me, in this afternoon sun in August,

was the French light cruiser *Montcalm* having a duel with a 10-inch German cannon in somebody's dry swimming pool on the beach there at Monaco. While I was observing this thing, it was mid-afternoon, and the special service crowd hadn't had anything to eat. We

This painting undoubtedly resulted from Murray's afternoon overlooking the Mediterranean. In the foreground are American soldiers; in the background a cruiser and destroyer provide gunfire support for the army men ashore. (*Painting by navy combat artist Albert K. Murray*)

Shell splashes erupt as army troops come ashore from LCIs during the invasion of southern France. (*Painting by navy combat artist Albert K. Murray*)

had only five gallons of water for a whole company of men. They were trying to get lunch ready, which turned out to be cold beans.

I wasn't interested in lunch at that point because out there, all of a sudden, I saw a big column of black smoke come up off the fantail of the *Montcalm*. I thought the German battery had made a direct hit. So I got out my watercolors and started making some notes of what I was looking at. The *Montcalm* sent a signal to two destroyers down there to come up and make a smoke screen cover. She was only about two miles from the beach at the time of this assault and was trying to get into deeper water. It was like sitting in the number-one box in the opera, where you could see the prompter and both sides of the scenery at the same time. You're right up at the proscenium arch; and that's about where I was, watching this dramatic episode.

These two destroyers responded to the call from the *Montcalm*, the cruiser under attack. Black smoke was pouring out from these destroyers, and I could see tremendous wakes as they were coming up. They were using all the speed they could make to get up there and

surround the *Montcalm* and give her smoke coverage and hide her from the beach. Well, I was so absorbed in what was going on that I was not aware that I was under observation. When the Germans left Mont Argil, they retired to the summit. It was five thousand feet at the summit, and we were at three thousand.

They dragged some of their artillery up there, and the first thing that made me aware of them was a tremendous explosion in the courtyard. I hadn't been aware of any of that because I was so absorbed in what I was looking at. Then there was a second explosion. Then there was a third one, and finally it dawned on me that these things were timed. The fourth one that came in veered to the dugout in the fort.

The only other fellow outside with me was a fire-control officer from one of the destroyers. Ordinarily, way up there, if that fort needed some artillery support from the beach, we would have to go through the chain of command. Then it would take a little bit of doing before the ship would respond to give us the gunnery support that we wanted. They changed the rules so that if you had a fire-control officer who had a direct radio circuit to the gunnery officer on board the ship, he could get it instantly, what we needed.

So they had spotted this German battery up on the summit there, and they wanted fire directed up there, to knock off that attack on us down below, because these explosions were 88-millimeter cannon shells exploding in the courtyard. Fortunately, their fuzes were a little bit long, so they didn't explode on the fort itself. Then, for some reason or other, the gunnery officer disappeared and went back inside the fort, where everybody else was getting ready for their lunch.

It was hot; it was August. My shirt was open; my helmet was over on the grass, and I was dealing with this watercolor business. I'd just bought some wonderful paint called *bleu verdat*. It was a blue-green color that was just right for August weather on the Mediterranean. I was thinking more about that paint than what was really going on. So I leaned over to get that paint and close up the box. One of these fellows called from that dugout entrance out to the terrace where I was, behind these parapets. I was a two-striper in the navy, wearing the same collar insignia as a captain in the army. He yelled over at me, "For God's sake, Captain, don't you realize you're the target out there?"

So I leaned over to shut the paint box to get that *bleu verdat* and then get the hell out of there. Then the next round came; that was five. My dog tags were hanging down from my neck on a chain, and one of the pieces of shrapnel cut a dog tag off. I still have one, but shrapnel got the other one. That's what really alerted me that I was in a hot spot and that I'd better get out of there in a hurry. It was a lucky break, so as quickly as I could, I got back inside the fort. There was complete silence in there until some voice said, "Well, damn you."

I said, "Well, what's the matter?"

They said, "Well, look at us." They were down on their hands and knees, picking up bean after bean, wiping the dirt off of them from all the debris still there after the Germans had left. They had put some planks up on some empty ammunition boxes to make a little table to put the mess kits on for the beans. Then the concussion of these explosions in the moat knocked the table and the ammunition boxes down, and all the beans were now on the floor. But people in that situation can't be choosy, so they were getting ready to eat the beans after wiping the dirt off. I didn't get any because I was the cause of it all.

So, I was spanked by receiving no chow and also having to be apologetic to these guys. If I hadn't been out there, they wouldn't have been in the fix they were in. As I reflected on it, I thought to myself, "Well, I'm really lucky being here at all, under the circumstances."

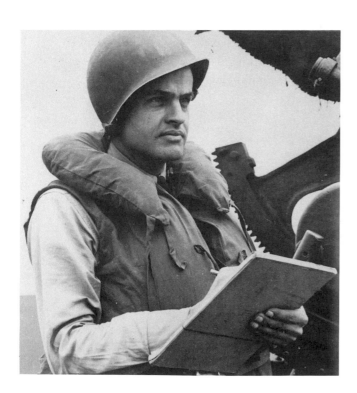

ALBERT KETCHAM MURRAY (1906–1992), a native of Kansas, studied art at Cornell University and Syracuse University. He did additional study in England and France and received special tutelage from the noted portrait artist Wayman E. Adams. By the late 1930s, Mr. Murray was exhibiting his paintings at such prestigious places as the Carnegie Institute and the Corcoran Gallery in Washington, D.C. In March 1942 he was commissioned a lieutenant in the Naval Reserve. Initially a line officer, he was soon switched to the service's new art program. He painted portraits of the members of the navy's General Board and later he did a series of paintings of crew members from the damaged cruiser *Boise*. His combat art career included assignments to the Fourth Fleet in the South Atlantic and the Eighth Fleet in the Mediterranean. After the war Mr. Murray remained on active duty to paint a series of portraits of the navy's top-ranking flag officers in their wartime roles. Later, he resumed his career as a top-notch civilian artist, maintaining a studio in New York City, where he painted leaders of business and industry. He also did a series of portraits of Chiefs of Naval Operations for the Naval Institute. (*Courtesy Dr. Marion C. Gilliland, on behalf of the estate of Albert K. Murray*)

One of the problems of writing history comes in trying to ascertain what really happened. For some events the memories and perceptions vary markedly, and that is the case in the next two accounts. In August 1944 Lieutenant Commander Douglas Fairbanks Jr., a Naval Reserve officer, and Lieutenant Commander John Bulkeley, a career officer in the regular navy, were on board separate ships in a surface action against two German corvettes. Surface gun battles involving naval vessels were rare in the campaign to liberate France, and this one was particularly dramatic.

The versions of the two officers differ principally on one important point—the degree of damage inflicted on the enemy corvettes by two British gunboats under Fairbanks's command. Fairbanks's account is supported by an official action report—submitted shortly after the battle—by Captain Henry C. Johnson, Commander Task Group 80.4, who was in command of the diversionary unit that included the ships of both Fairbanks and Bulkeley. Bulkeley's description of the role of his destroyer, the *Endicott*, is supported by his own official action report, submitted a week after the battle.

When the chronologies of the two reports are put side by side, they do not jibe. Perhaps the differences can be ascribed to record keeping in the heat of battle and the reconstruction of events after the fact. When viewed from a larger perspective, though, a consistent pattern does emerge. Both versions depict the desperate plight of old British gunboats under Fairbanks's command. They had reached the point of being overwhelmed by the newer and better-armed German ships. Fairbanks appealed for help from Bulkeley's *Endicott*. Bulkeley's ship arrived on the scene, fought aggressively, sank the German ships, and saved the old British gunboats from becoming victims themselves.

BEACH JUMPERS DON'T REALLY JUMP

By Captain Douglas Fairbanks Jr., U.S. Naval Reserve (Retired)

Within hours of arriving in London and reporting to U.S. Naval Headquarters, I learned why I was back. Dickie Mountbatten, bless him, had wasted no time in reacting to my written hints about joining other U.S. officers on his Combined Operations staff. The reason for a U.S. presence was to teach our people how the mixed amphibious command worked. Later, the British would help us form a similar setup within our own military establishment. I reported to Dickie at Combined Operations Headquarters in Richmond Terrace, off Whitehall, the next day. He was marvelous to me. He was always to be rather like an older brother in my eyes.

The first week or so I was bounced around from one part of this fascinating outfit to another. I soon met several other Americans, the most senior of whom was a regular navy captain, Elliott Strauss. They were attached as observers to such departments as plans, operations, air, communications, and research and development. The purpose of the organization was to develop amphibious war plans in every detail: weaponry, methods, types of ships and vehicles—everything that might be needed for a successful amphibious invasion of the Continent. Dickie, the chief of Combined Operations, was charged with training, developing, planning, and executing a number of small but daring raids in selected parts of Nazi-held Europe. This would at the same time be a means of experimenting with the newest amphibious craft, vehicles, and equipment and also a way of keeping the enemy worried and on the defensive.

The job at Combined Ops went very well in this summer of 1942. Though Dickie himself was given to "loose talk," he trusted my discretion, and it was exciting to be so near the high inside. When I was moved into the study of camouflage (erroneously thought appropriate because of my knowledge of films, photography, trick shots, and sound effects), I was let in on a new and very secret tactical deception and diversion development.

This project had begun with the building of dummy tanks, armored cars, and wooden replicas of big guns, landing craft, and airplanes. All this evolved into an idea to deceive the enemy by projecting the prerecorded sounds of tanks and landing craft from a hidden distance—behind smoke screens. They were testing the sounds of moving a squadron of armored cars, together with soldiers' voices and related noises. These sounds were to be projected from within a forest or wooded area, for example, to give the enemy the impression of movement by an armored group.

The intention was for the enemy to adjust his local defenses to meet our nonexistent group. The idea, originated by Brigadier Dudley Clarke, had been tried out first in a small way in the North African desert and then enlarged against the Italians in Ethiopia from the sea toward the land. For amphibious purposes a motor torpedo boat projected the sound from behind real fog or a smoke screen. From that small start, the Combined Ops camouflage section began further experiments on a large scale for army use on land. Now they had returned to an amphibious concept, to which I was assigned, in addition to other ways and means of creating deceptions.

Since I was an American officer "under instruction," and destined for naval amphibious operations, apart from some hard physical preparation for the first week or two, I was not obliged to go through such rough training as the commandos from the Royal Marines and the army's infantry up in Inverary, Scotland. Our particular quarters were at the supposedly haunted Achnocarry Castle, near the even more secret base for deception development at Ballantrae. Although the ideas for deception equipment and diversionary planning originated with the Eighth Army in Egypt and evolved further at Richmond Terrace Headquarters, it was at Ballantrae that most of the actual experiments

Thanks to makeup artists and special effects, Fairbanks portrayed twins in the 1941 film *The Corsican Brothers*, his last before entering naval service. The actress is Ruth Warrick, who played the wife of newspaper magnate Charles Foster Kane in the 1941 classic *Citizen Kane*. (*Courtesy Douglas Fairbanks Jr.*)

with visual tactical ruses and camouflage devices were carried out. There were scientific experiments with ways to project sounds over considerable distances—say, of landing craft coming in to shore. Jamming or deceiving radar, constructing masses of landing craft and tanks to be spotted from the air, and overloading and misdirecting radio chatter with false codes were other experiments carried out. The diversionary units, small as they were, had to become, in effect, military decoys.

Over the course of the next two years, we developed the tactical deception techniques. The group came to be known as beach jumpers, a title that gave some indication of our mission without actually giving it away. After the group's origin in Combined Operations, I migrated back to the U.S. Navy so that we could incorporate the methods in our own operations. Because of my status as a reserve officer, relatively junior at that, I was not able to command a beach jumper unit at that point. Our first commander was ineffectual and unbalanced. Fortunately, after we employed our devices and methods in various operations in the Mediter-

ranean, including the invasion of Sicily, we got a new leader who was much better suited to the job.

In the spring of 1944, before leaving Algiers for our newly liberated base at Naples, I had somehow learned about a few of the preliminary strategic deception plans for the future Big Show, the cross-Channel invasion of France. Now I could easily guess that we in the Mediterranean were to be at least a part of the smaller part of two invasions of France—one from the U.K. and one from the south. Very early on the sixth of June the vast fleets of Allies, jammed with soldiers, sailors, marines, weapons, mechanized vehicles, and all, burst ashore on the Coast of Normandy in France not far from where William the Conqueror sailed to conquer England nearly a thousand years earlier. The surprised but desperate enemy defended themselves fiercely, selling every yielded yard for high prices.

Months earlier I had been asked by Captain Bob English, a planner on Vice Admiral Kent Hewitt's staff, whether I wanted orders to go to England and be in on Operation Overlord, with only some nominal adviser-observer duties, or stay in Corsica for Anvil (the code name for the invasion of southern France), where, in addition to heading up the amphibious diversion plans, I would actually take tactical command of a task unit within the old Task Group 80.4. My indecision lasted for seconds only. I saw immediately that for me to join in Overlord was only to be able to say, "I was there." Of course it was tempting, but to be a useless extra observer would not really be satisfying. I wondered briefly if I could do both—fly up for Overlord and, if still in one piece, fly back as soon as possible, do my bit for the invasion and recovery of Elba, and then pick up the planning and rehearsals for the Anvil operation against southern France, due to be launched about eleven weeks later, on August 15. I got no further with that idea as Bob English said, "Too irresponsible! Choose one or the other!"

As soon as I could, after Elba, I set about working out details for our largest diversionary plan so far and for my command of a sizable operational unit. The principal and ultimate strategic aim of Anvil was to relieve enemy pressure on our forces in Normandy: to attempt, after a great amphibious assault, to swing inland to the north and envelop the Nazis in a huge pincer movement.

Actual landings were to be between Fréjus/Saint-Raphaël and Saint-Tropez/Sainte-Maxime. The enemy's dilemma, which Allied planners intended to intensify, would be where to concentrate their main defense. Movement along so much of the Côte d'Azur could be made only on a small coastal road through towns, or one of the other corniches that wound around the high hills behind. Or they could go way inland, circle around, and come out again. The ultimate target of the Anvil landings was the Marseille-Toulon area, and the question for the Germans was how best to defend it.

All our local diversionary plans, coordinated with London's overall deception plans, were intended to suggest at first that we might land in northern Italy, near Genoa. Actually, the main thrust was to be far to the west, in France, between Saint-Raphaël and Bormes-les-Mimosas, behind the Îles d'Hyères.

The first stage of our diversion plan was to land a group of French commandos at a place called La Pointe des Deux Frères, between Cannes and Nice, at about four hours before predawn H-hour. They were to move inland, do some sabotaging, and raise general hell in the area. We at sea were to carry out some desultory coastal bombardment. Then as the main armada, just arrived, was to begin debarking troops, we were to scoot behind them to an area between Marseille and Toulon called Baie de la Ciotat. After darkness the first night we were to pull out all the stops—with some help from the air forces—in our efforts to suggest another major landing right there.

The naval craft assigned to us were an almost

Fairbanks, right, and Lieutenant Jack Watson are shown during the southern France operation, when their specialty was tactical deception. (*Courtesy Douglas Fairbanks Jr.*)

comically patternless force. There were first two small British gunboats, the *Aphis* and the *Scarab*, brought halfway around the world from the Yangtze River in China, mounting just one big 6-inch gun and a few antiaircraft guns apiece, four RN MGBs (motor gunboats), twelve USN PT boats, and one American destroyer, the *Endicott*, commanded by the colorful swaggerer Commander John D. Bulkeley. He had won our highest wartime award, the Congressional Medal of Honor, in recognition of his command of the "They Were Expendable" squadron of PTs that took General Douglas MacArthur, his family, and staff safely out of threatened Japanese clutches in the Philippines to Australia in 1942.

Early on I had located the exact targets of our two gunboats' bombardment. I took care—disgraceful care—to avoid hitting the houses of people I knew. Instead, I pinpointed what I was pretty sure would be empty railroad stations, post offices, beachfront cabins, and the like. With luck in our not-too-accurate marksmanship (from well offshore, in the pitch-black dark, with only two or three radars in my task unit), we *might* hit one or two targets.

Jack Watson of our unit had carefully prerecorded a lot of meaningless chatter between American aircraft pilots to be broadcast by one single air force plane dropping strips of tinfoil as our new device for radar-jamming, called "window." A more sinister but very effective bit of lethal gadgetry was dropping hundreds of dummy paratroops in the hills near Toulon. When I ordered them, I suggested they be made in different sizes—normal, half-size, and very small—so that when they were dropped from a plane, the ground observers' perspective would (at least at first) make it seem as if the large ones were closer and the smaller ones proportionately farther away. On being thrown from the plane, those wrapped-up, rubberized dummies automatically inflated. Then, inspired by ideas from the Far East, I requested that all the dummies be booby-trapped.

Thus on August 14, D-1 of Anvil, the several units of our task group would set out from different ports hours before the main task force, as if going toward Genoa. After one big group made this feint—for the benefit of German radar and spy planes—they would converge in two sections at precisely planned times, all well before midnight.

The collective tension of our group could not have exceeded mine. We received coded messages that the several task forces—a plodding, military-laden argosy—had already left their different ports and were even now converging on their planned rendezvous points prior to the clashing of arms on the southern French beaches. I led one of our ML and PT squadrons to a point where we were to put the first Free French troops ashore in their still-captive country. One of our frogmen swam in

About six hours before D-Day at southern France, a PT boat put ashore a number of French commandos ("froggy frogmen"), who then ran into a mined beach ashore. (*Painting by navy combat artist Albert K. Murray*)

to the beach. After a seeming age of waiting, we picked up his infrared signal light through our special goggles. The light was to direct us to the spot at which we were to send our eager Frenchmen ashore. From there, they were to go rapidly inland to sabotage road, rail, and telephone-telegraph equipment.

The brave young French—or "Froggy-Frogmen" as some called them—eagerly waded ashore. It was too dark to see them, but we heard several severe blasts coming from their direction. We slowly pulled back out to sea, contenting ourselves that the noise indicated our Frenchmen were doing their job quickly and very well. The next night we received the sickening news that the infrared signaler had somehow got himself way off the place where his regimental pals were supposed to come ashore. Instead, we had landed them right on a big, freshly laid mine field. That explained the first explosions we had heard. The losses suffered by that small gallant group were dreadful: more than half. But they did cut a crucial coastal supply road.

Not knowing of this immediately, we turned back out to sea and swung well in front of the main oncoming invasion fleet until we reached the other, or western, side of the assault front. Our task unit chugged closer to our target area: the big Toulon naval base and its environs, in particular the Baie de la Ciotat. Our group's protective destroyer, *Endicott*, carrying our task group commander, Captain H. C. Johnson, deliberately stayed about fifteen or twenty miles away, though ready to dash to our help if necessary.

The main assault landings had already begun, as planned, very early in the morning of August 15, only shortly after we had passed in front of them. It was now between 3:00 and 4:00 A.M. that same morning. We began firing our best salvos into designated targets, and our PTs and very fast ASRCs—air-sea-rescue craft—fired their beach-barrage and heavy-smoke rockets.

This immediately drew a gratifying reaction from shore as the enemy, clearly believing we were a powerful force about to land, opened up on us with heavy but ill-aimed fire. Soon the whole area lit up and then quickly went dark; star shells roared in the sky trying to illuminate us. Searchlights flashed along the coast and inside the Baie, east and west. Twenty- and 40-millimeter shells flew from all directions and burst near us. These were followed by huge flashes from 88-millimeter, 105-millimeter, and 240-millimeter near misses. Some of our craft reported minor damage, but that, "for the moment," they said, was all.

Despite the risk of mines—we knew their general locations—I ordered our gunboats, the MLs, and ASRCs to maneuver as close inshore behind smoke as we dared. Then we started up our sonic and radio tricks. Between 4:00 and 5:00 A.M. we withdrew, hoping to be out of clear sight by the time it was full daylight.

We earnestly hoped that our simulated threats were

The old British gunboat *Aphis* served as Fairbanks's flagship for deception operations in connection with the invasion of southern France. Her antiquated gunnery setup was overmatched by those of the German opponents. (*Imperial War Museum*)

being supported, not only by prerecorded chatter from our aircraft, but also by the "rising up" on a broadcast signal of the much-vaunted French underground, *La Résistance*. We had heard so much about its size and potential for so long. But when it was time to call on them, our Free French liaison officer admitted their number was not so large as predicted, and the best disciplined and organized ones were, alas, the communists. He also told us sadly that the original resistance groups in the Netherlands, Belgium, Denmark, Norway, and Luxembourg were, in proportion to the population, the best and most reliable.

As soon as I could, I transferred my command from our leading PT to the *Aphis*, the senior of the two British gunboats. I did so because its skipper, a reserve lieutenant commander, was an older, very experienced ex-merchant ship's master who knew infinitely more about everything nautical than I ever would. I was still theoretically commanding one small unit—a section only of our bigger task group—but the *Aphis*'s skipper was right there to advise and correct me whenever I made a mistake.

At daybreak on the morning of the fifteenth we could see in the hazy light the other gunboat, *Scarab*, astern of us, and then, tagging along in loose formation, our slightly scattered flotilla of MLs, raiding or landing craft, several of our PTs, and ASRCs. At 5:40 the *Aphis*'s radio crackled and squealed with a call from one of our ASRCs. It had a breakdown, and was now under attack from two big enemy ships and asking for immediate help.

This was a brain-rattling moment. Our intelligence had assured us there were no enemy warships left in Toulon or the Baie de la Ciotat. But, goddamnit, here they were! Two of them! They had already disabled our leading ASRC, equipped with our best secret electronic gear and some rockets. She was now lying dead in the water, partly aflame but still firing defensively as best she could.

I sent a PT to rescue her and ordered both our gunboats to turn about and engage the enemy ships as soon as possible. At first we could see only two small specks about four or five miles away, with flashes from their guns coming at us. At ten minutes past six, precisely, we opened fire on them, still not knowing what kind of ships they were. Earlier, we had radioed the *Endicott*, requesting—nearly *begging*—her to come and help out. In case they cared, we also radioed Admiral Kent Hewitt's HQ ship, the *Catoctin*.

Our returning shots, not well aimed, were wide of their targets, but we pressed on nonetheless. The Germans began to bang away at everyone, so it seemed, in our group. I ordered the MLs to screen us as best they could as we closed first to less than two miles and then down to one.

The big, very old 6-inchers on both our gunboats were getting so hot that our gunnery officer said we must allow a bit more time after what he called, with a smile, our "cannonading" to cool down. The early exchange of fire had indeed been violent, and the *Scarab*, still astern of our port side, noted about fifty straddles and near-misses in those almost endless few minutes. Then the Nazi gunfire became even more intense and accurate. As the leading ship in the group, we were their principal target. We were not close enough to see that the two ships trying to destroy us were both slick and fast. A fresh radio report told us that one of them had just been identified by a U.S. naval air scout as a small, former Italian (now German) destroyer-corvette-type ship, the U-Jäger *Capriolo*, and the other was a large, armed converted yacht, the *Nimet Allah*. Too late, we learned that each mounted three radar-controlled 4-inch guns, plus torpedoes, and were capable of between twenty and thirty knots. We could sometimes, with luck in wind and tides, push our broad-bellied gunboats to about ten knots.

When it became foolhardy to get closer, I signaled a couple of our still-screening small craft to circle around and lay a very thick smoke screen. While that was being done, we led the rest of our little group into the middle of the smoke and made wide circles inside. We were like a couple of ducks leading our little ducklings around and around. The *Aphis*'s skipper and I decided in an exchange of shouts that there was no sense in slugging it out any longer. Both the *Aphis* and the *Scarab* had had their radar shot away. Since our radio was still operating, we sent further frantic word to Captain

Johnson and Commander Bulkeley in the *Endicott*: "For Christ's sake, hurry up! We're in a bloody pickle!"

Since we could no longer fire our big guns except at intervals of a couple of minutes, we fired antiaircraft guns just to make trouble. Most of the electric power on both ships had gone out minutes before. Soon after, we saw the *Scarab*'s radio antennae being shot away, then minutes later, our own went. Compasses too had been struck out, one by one. The great skipper of the *Aphis* was so very calm that he might well have been in a peacetime exercise with harmless firecrackers exploding. I made no bones about being terrified but, as was so often the case, my fright disguised itself with a forced show of high, good spirits. Usually only *I* knew my lighthearted banter was my particular form of hysteria.

With shrapnel bursting around us like steel confetti, we continued to lead our little pack of moving targets in great figure eights. Some of our ships sustained damage but, thank God, none of our people did. Continuing to disguise my terror while still on the *Aphis*'s bridge, and supposedly in command of our task unit, I deliberately kept dropping things on the deck—my helmet, or binoculars, for example—behind the ship's canny captain. This meant, of course, that I would have to bend down and pick up whatever it was in the shameful hope that the next bits of flying metal would hit something or someone besides me!

But where, in God's name (the international object of many different appeals and some blame), was Captain Johnson? And the *Endicott*, with skipper John Bulkeley? Our gunnery officer shouted above the din that our big main battery had now cooled enough to begin firing again. Though our smoke screen had helped hide us somewhat, it couldn't hide us from the enemy's radar. And as the Germans were causing more damage to all of us, there seemed no point in continuing to hide behind the smoke. We had long since lost our bearings and didn't know where the hell we were. The captain and I agreed, when we could hear ourselves shout above the din, that we might as well come out into the clear and shoot at anything until rescue came.

The men were marvelous, beyond praise. They went about their jobs efficiently and shouted jokes at each other. The cooled-off guns were reloaded and more shells were ready to be shoved into the breeches.

The next problem was that we didn't have a clue as to how to get out of our goddamned smoke screen. I wanted, if possible, to get around to the rear of the German ships, thereby hoping to cut off their easy escape to Marseille or Toulon. Suddenly, we saw a thinning of the smoke and headed for it. Once in the clear I saw we were going at right angles across the bows of the two enemy ships, which were still keeping a fair distance from us. I can't say how far away they actually were. They had visibly slowed down and were nearly abreast of each other, still firing, though not, it seemed, as much as before.

Now, by the purest chance, we had come out of our bloody smoke screen and performed the classical naval maneuver of "Crossing the enemy's T," a more or less self-explanatory description of naval choreography. Because they were heading for us, they could only fire with their forward armament. We, on the other hand, were coming across and in front of them and could fire on them from anywhere.

I don't know if I gave the next order to fire or not, but I got the credit for it. I honestly doubt that I was thinking very clearly, though someone was. And with our very first salvo, shooting point-blank at the *Capriolo*, with neither our radar nor targeting devices left, we made a direct hit! The *Scarab* made a very near miss that was said to have damaged the enemy destroyer's plates. To our shocked surprise, the other enemy ship—the old converted armed yacht—seemed to hesitate momentarily, as our first target began visibly to list, as if in the first throes of sinking.

Stunned by our accidental success, we saw great flashes and explosions all around on first one, then the other, enemy ship. By God, again like the old stories of the cavalry to the rescue, our fast guardian tin can, *Endicott*, came pounding in, her several 5-inch guns blazing. Once more, good old dashing John Bulkeley, the "sailor's sailor," did the spectacular thing. First, he finished off our own already near-mortally wounded victim and then proceeded to blast the second one out of the water.

The smaller craft of Task Unit 80.4.1 went busily about picking up as many as they could of the enemy still able to swim in the calm, oily, and very messy water. The gunboats, designed only for river water, had shallow, nearly flat bottoms, with no more than three feet of freeboard, so they joined the rescue party.

The whole of Dragoon went exceedingly well. From scattered parts the invasion fleet had converged and another hell was let loose on schedule and according to plan. The Germans' "Mediterranean Wall" had several holes in it and their coastal defenses were hampered. To thwart them further, our diversionary tactics, though little noticed by historians, were on the largest scale so far and proved very helpful. In fact, it was a fatal two days before the Germans knew for certain where our main thrust would be. We had pinned down another complete enemy division. We were, on the whole, very well satisfied with our sideshow part in the victory.

The Nazis originally had moved in several divisions of infantry and over two hundred big coastal defense guns to protect the falsely threatened Toulon and Baie de la Ciotat area, with almost the same amount to defend the port of Marseille from the sea. (Both were eventually taken from the landward side.) In fact, forty-five more German coast artillery batteries were spread along the Côte d'Azur, some even camouflaged as cabanas. Mine fields on land and in the harbors were all over the place, and sharp-pointed poles were erected in fields to impale paratroopers. (French workers deliberately dug such shallow holes that most fell over at a touch.) When our multisized inflatable rubber parachute dummies were discovered to be booby-trapped, the Berlin radio squealed and protested at the "inhuman, bestial" methods of the "evil" Western Allies!

We knew that they knew we were coming—but they didn't know where. The great pincer movement did work, and the main attack in the north continued, expensively but steadily victoriously.

DOUGLAS ELTON FAIRBANKS JR. (1909–) began his film career in 1923 in a movie called *Stephen Steps Out*. He is perhaps best known for his roles in *The Prisoner of Zenda* (1936) and *Gunga Din* (1939). Altogether, he appeared in more than seventy-five films and produced or coproduced a dozen more. He also had an active career in live theater and television. Prior to World War II, Mr. Fairbanks performed various official and semiofficial government duties at the behest of President Franklin D. Roosevelt and the secretary of state, including a mission to South America. During World War II he served as a reserve officer, including sea duty on board the *Ludlow*, *Mississippi*, *Washington*, *Wasp*, and *Wichita*. He also had a variety of assignments in special operations as part of the beach jumpers. Mr. Fairbanks's civilian services on behalf of the government resumed after the war. He served in a voluntary capacity with various organizations, including the United Nations and CARE, dealing with problems in the postwar world. Mr. Fairbanks, who now lives in New York City, has recounted his career in two memoirs: *Salad Days* (Doubleday, 1988) and *A Hell of a War* (St. Martin's, 1993). This article is an excerpt from the latter. (*Photo by Marion Warren*)

SURFACE ACTION AT POINT-BLANK RANGE

By Vice Admiral John D. Bulkeley, U.S. Navy (Retired)

After I'd been on the line for weeks with the PTs, Captain Harry Sanders, commodore of Destroyer Squadron 18, came over to my boat for a conference. Right off the bat, he told me I was going to relieve the captain of the destroyer *Endicott*. The essence of it was that the destroyer was not performing adequately under her skipper, Commander Wilton S. Heald. The ship had had a collision on May 24 that kept her out of the Normandy operation, and she had a reputation of always being late for whatever task was assigned. She was not, in any material condition, ready for war. Watertight doors were not watertight and not properly adjusted. The damage control organization was loosely run. Sanders was unhappy with the whole situation, so he ordered me to take command of the *Endicott*. I didn't say anything.

On July 17 the commodore had the motor whaleboat take me to the destroyer and said I was to go to the ship's plotting room. He told me to stay there until I heard an announcement saying he had left the *Endicott*. Then I was to go to the bridge, make an announcement that I had taken command of the ship, and get her under way for the Mediterranean. Rear Admiral Arthur Struble, chief of staff to Rear Admiral Alan Kirk, had authorized the action, and the Bureau of Personnel issued the appropriate orders.

When I got to Naples, I met Lieutenant Commander Douglas Fairbanks Jr., who was putting together a scenario for diverting German divisions to Baie de la Ciotat from Saint-Raphaël and Saint-Tropez during the upcoming invasion of southern France. I told Fairbanks that we of the *Endicott* would be able to carry out our part of the plan. So we took aboard Captain

The USS *Endicott* had missed D-Day in Normandy because of a collision in late May. In August she took an active part in supporting the invasion of southern France. (*Naval Institute Collection*)

This German naval headquarters at Baie de la Ciotat shows the effects of the *Endicott*'s shelling. (*Courtesy Vice Admiral John D. Bulkeley*)

Henry C. Johnson, commander of the Special Operations Group, Task Group 80.4, and also Lieutenant Jack Watson, who would undertake a program of communications deception. Johnson was designated the tactical commander for the operation.

During the two nights of the diversion, August 15 and 16, we were involved in radio deception of the enemy, and we also fired some three thousand rounds of gunfire. We were fired on from the beach by a big gun that was very erratic. It missed us by four or five hundred yards, or something like that. We did fire back a couple of times, but it was useless. On those raids into Baie de la Ciotat the *Endicott* was accompanied by a group of PT boats and other vessels. We had already used intelligence photos of the area to pick out our targets. Among them were a German headquarters, a gun position we managed to destroy, the harbor area and its ships, and a breakwater. With our combination of 20-millimeter, 40-millimeter, and 5-inch, we just raised hell.

During those night operations, I fired what I thought the targets were worth, with the result that we were getting fairly low on ammunition by the end of the second night, having fired a total of nearly six hundred rounds of 5-inch. I didn't think we were going to have any other use for the ammunition, so I was perfectly willing to make a hell of a good show. The guns were

definitely hot when we got done shooting the second night. Of the four 5-inch guns on board the *Endicott*, three of them were disabled after all that shooting.

The breech blocks on the guns had overheated, mainly because both the bearings and pinions were made of steel. It was a poor design; those bearings should have been made of hard phosphorous bronze. Later, back in the United States, I showed these bearings to the chief of the Bureau of Ordnance and told him it was no way to build a gun. He wasn't very pleased with me, and I wasn't very pleased with him. The good news is that the bearings were later changed to bronze so they would not freeze during a sustained firing.

Lieutenant Charles Rogers was the gunnery officer, and he ordered that there be no repairs to the 5-inch guns. He didn't want any of the guns fully disassembled, because we might have to use them again. We wanted to wait until we got to Sicily, where we were ordered for repairs to the guns and other items of equipment on board the ship. Early on the morning of August 17, however, I got a radio message from the skipper of an air-sea rescue boat. He said that his boat and two old British gunboats of the diversionary force, the *Aphis* and *Scarab*, were under attack by two German destroyers. I had known this skipper and believed that the call was legitimate. So I cranked up the speed to thirty-six knots with all the burners in the boilers and all superheat on.

Shortly after six in the morning I saw a huge cloud of smoke, and I headed right for it. This was a smoke screen put up by the *Aphis* and *Scarab* in their efforts to escape from the German ships, which were actually the corvettes *Capriolo* and the *Nimet Allah*. They posed a real threat to the British gunboats. While all this was going on, the director operator for the 5-inch guns put his range-finder optics on the British gunboats. Surrounded by their smoke screen, they were running like hell. Retiring was a good tactical move for them at that point, because their fire-control gear was out of commission, and the German ships were after them. All they had was local fire control on the gun mounts themselves. So there was nothing prudent that the gunboats could do besides get the hell out of there.

When the German ships saw us, they immediately cranked on speed and started heading for the port of Toulon, France, so they could get away from us. I moved then to cut them off from heading east. I wanted to corner them, which I did. The range to the enemy ships at that time was probably just over ten thousand yards, but I concluded our guns would be more effective if we were closer, so we went in to about six thousand yards.

In view of the action that was about to take place, we wanted to make certain of the identity of these ships. On the bridge with me was Quartermaster First Class

Soon after the battle, a crew member adorned a bulkhead of the *Endicott* with symbols of the two German ships recently sunk. (*Courtesy Vice Admiral John D. Bulkeley*)

Bethel Dial, who was a very capable petty officer. He had keen eyesight, but he could not make out a German flag on either of these two ships. No one else could either, but I figured they must be hostile if they were firing at the two British ships. As I was preparing to join the action, Captain Johnson turned to me and said, "If you lose your ship, I'll have you court-martialed." That was not exactly a resounding vote of confidence. On the other hand, Johnson didn't interfere in anything I did, so I had a completely free hand to fight the battle my way. I took tactical command by default.

My answer to his cautious warning was to order, "Commence firing," and away we went. We were still having an enormous amount of difficulty with the 5-inch guns, including hand loading because of problems with the hydraulic rammers for loading powder and projectiles. A seaman first class named Pete Barge was the first loader on mount three, and during our night firing he had been ramming the powder and projectiles into the breech by hand because of the malfunction to the mechanical equipment. He was a huge man and a real tough one. The breech block wouldn't automatically snap shut because the friction

between the bearing and the block was so much that it was essentially frozen in an open position. So it was necessary for Barge to use a leather-covered hammer to open the breech block and then to slam the damn thing into position after loading. Because of the problems with the various 5-inch mounts, it took more than three minutes from the time I gave the order until any of the guns was able to fire. Over the sound-powered telephones I kept pleading with the gunnery officer, Rogers, to open fire.

Meanwhile, as we steamed along at thirty-five knots, we were getting within range of the enemy guns. Although I didn't pay too much attention, the German projectiles were starting to straddle the *Endicott*. Then we were hit. One of the German 4.7-inch shells went through the side of the ship, landed in a bunk, and set the bedding on fire. One of the crew members burned his hands in the process of taking the dud projectile up on deck and heaving it overboard. Fortunately, it didn't explode when it came aboard. In addition to that shot, some shrapnel hit us up on the bridge. I caught some of it in the face, and the word went for the exec to come to the bridge and relieve me. When he showed up, I said to him, "Get out of here. No problem at all."

Finally, our 5-inch guns began firing as we continued to close the range on the corvettes. Our fire control was excellent, using the optical range finders. We hammered those ships.

By this time we were near enough to see that the German ships had large crews manning their topside guns. This was getting more and more like the PT-boat tactics I had been accustomed to. We got to within fifteen hundred yards of those ships with the *Endicott*—point-blank range. We were near enough for our light antiaircraft guns—the 20-millimeters and 40-millimeters—to be extremely effective as antipersonnel weapons. We literally just swept the decks of the German ships with the bullets from those guns.

A point of contention about this battle is the question whether either of the German ships had been disabled by the *Aphis* and *Scarab* before the *Endicott* got into it. In my opinion, neither one of them was disabled or slowed down one whit. In fact, the two British gunboats were causing something of a problem. I had to send them a message to cease firing because their shells were so wild that they were landing near us. There was a lot of confusion, as there frequently was in the course of a surface gun action.

The Germans were firing torpedoes at us, but we watched them carefully and managed to evade them. I made some radical course changes, which Captain Johnson didn't like until he found that the torpedoes had been fired at us. We had fired our torpedoes at a range of thirty-two hundred yards, which was much too far away to be effective. Of course, they missed. But

The *Nimet Allah* was one of the two German corvettes sunk by the *Endicott*'s gunfire on August 17. This photo is a copy of one taken from a German prisoner captured by the *Endicott* after the battle. (*Courtesy Vice Admiral John D. Bulkeley*)

that wasn't a problem, because I knew the guns would be the decisive weapons. Off and on, we were able to get more than one 5-inch gun mount working during the battle and scored some disabling hits. Mount three was really the key to the whole thing. With his hand ramming and his leather maul to close the breech, Seaman Barge got off 161 rounds at the Germans. His hands were bruised and burned as a result.

Barge was a manifestation of the type of organization that we had developed in the *Endicott*. The captain can't do everything himself, and that's an important lesson for any skipper. He's got to stay focused on the main problem and let the rest of the men do their jobs. If the ship is organized right, they'll all do what they're supposed to do without getting specific orders and without the skipper keeping track. For instance, when the ship was taking on water after being hit forward by that dud projectile, I said, "Tell the damage control officer to take care of it. I've got other things to do." And that's all it took. They got the dud out, took it up topside, and threw it overboard. I couldn't be distracted from the main business, which was socking those German ships. I stayed on the bridge because I had to be there and alert to the threat of Luftwaffe air action—a threat that was always there.

The result of the gun battle was that we sank both of the German ships (the *Nimet Allah* sank at about 7:15 and the *Capriolo* around 8:30) and saved the British gunboats from an unpleasant fate. Captain Johnson, who had warned me of a court-martial before the action, appeared to be in a state of shock afterward. "You're damn lucky," was all he said. I think it was a combination of aggressiveness and professional skill—rather than luck—that made the difference. Alto-

A radioman in the *Endicott*'s crew drew this sketch of the surface action against the German corvettes. (*Courtesy Vice Admiral John D. Bulkeley*)

German prisoners are collected on the forecastle of the *Endicott* after being rescued from the water. To starboard of the forward 5-inch gun mount is a stack of the cylindrical tanks that held powder charges used in firing the 5-inch guns during the battle. (*Courtesy Vice Admiral John D. Bulkeley*)

gether, about two hundred Germans were killed in this battle. That's quite a few. We picked up 159 prisoners out of the water after we sank their ships. The physical strength of our gunner's mate, Pete Barge, again came into play. I saw him reach down with one big arm and pull a German prisoner out of the water by the nape of his neck.

The *Endicott*'s crew put these Germans on the forecastle, fed them, gave them dry clothing, and guarded them with submachine guns. They were all docile, making no attempt whatsoever to rebel against our treatment. I think the explanation for their reaction was that they were glad to be picked up by Americans and expected to go to the United States.

From the beginning, in a situation like this, you have to show the prisoners that you are in charge. We put the skippers of the two ships down in our wardroom. In our crew were two Jewish sailors, Motor Machinist's Mate Henry Schwartz and Torpedoman's Mate Joe Finkelberg. Schwartz spoke German, and he kept needling these two German captains in their own language. The skippers wanted to be turned over to the British, but I gave them to the French at Toulon. One of the skippers protested something about the Geneva Convention, so I reached for the .45 on my hip, halfway drew it out, and that ended that matter quickly. I understand the French later stripped them naked and made them walk bare-tailed down the center of town.

Our ship's doctor did more than forty operations for the prisoners on our wardroom table. He was assisted by a German medical technician, who was very capable. We had several funerals on board as well for Germans who were killed. Our chaplain presided and we treated these enemy dead with the proper reverence.

Earlier, while the prisoner recovery was going on, we received a message that Douglas Fairbanks wanted to come aboard the *Endicott*. We sent a whaleboat over and picked him up. I want to emphasize that I stayed on the bridge the entire time that the battle was in progress and afterward; I never went below. Sam Rush, the executive officer, went down to the quarterdeck to take charge of the prisoners as they were brought aboard. He saw that they were disarmed and put up on the forecastle under guard. He was very careful about that. When Fairbanks came aboard, Rush called the bridge and said, in jest, "This man says he's Douglas Fairbanks Jr. What do you want to do with him—throw him back in again?"

I said, "No, send him up to the bridge." And he came up, wearing a salt-water-stained battle jacket, a helmet, and a .45-caliber pistol hanging loose from his belt. He looked the picture of a real fighting pirate—in keeping with the swashbuckling image from his films. Captain Johnson and I, who had been up all night on the bridge, were cool and calm. Fairbanks sat down and wrote something.

We few, we happy few, we band of brothers.
For he today that sheds his blood with me
    Shall be my brother; be ne'er so vile,
This day shall gentle his condition.
    And gentlemen in England now abed
Shall think themselves accursed they were not here,
    And hold their manhoods cheap whiles any speaks
That fought with us upon Saint Crispin's Day.

I thought it was terrific and kept the original that he wrote out. I was genuinely impressed that the man could come up with such stirring words off the top of his head. I came to find out later that he was delivering

Left to right are: Lieutenant Commander Douglas Fairbanks Jr., Captain Henry Johnson, and Lieutenant Commander John Bulkeley on board the *Endicott* following the surface battle against German corvettes. (*Courtesy Vice Admiral John D. Bulkeley*)

lines he'd memorized as part of his career in the theater. That quotation was straight out of Shakespeare's *King Henry V*.

A few months after that, when he was back in the United States and away from the battle, Fairbanks wrote me a personal letter. This one was from the man himself—not something from a playwright he was quoting. He recalled the battle against the German corvettes and said that if it hadn't been for the *Endicott*, he and his men would have been goners that day. I'm convinced they would have been.

ADMIRAL BULKELEY'S biographical sketch appears on page 54.

✣   ✣   ✣

Along with the fighting part of the navy, its technical personnel also had a role as Allied forces advanced into Germany. Following not far behind was a naval technical mission seeking to determine what the Germans had accomplished in the way of weapons development, particularly in their quest for an atomic bomb. Commander Albert Mumma, who earlier in his career had done postgraduate work in France, was back on the scene to gather up information that could benefit the Allies both during and after the war. He found that the knowledge and interests of people in the scientific area can transcend national boundaries and those that divide friend from foe. He also found that the German nation was reeling badly by the time he reached it.

THE ALSOS MISSION

By Rear Admiral Albert G. Mumma, U.S. Navy (Retired)

I reported to the old ship model basin at the Washington Navy Yard in 1939. The new model basin at nearby Carderock, Maryland, was still under construction. I was a half-breed; I had been trained as both an engineer and a naval constructor. I had wrangled with the question of whether to follow the line officer path or concentrate on research, and the technical side won. Over the next several years we studied such things as the vibration of battleship propellers, how explosive bubbles damage a ship, and optimum propeller design.

In the spring of 1944 two of us from the model basin and two other naval officers were called upon to be the navy members of a scientific team that was being called the Alsos Mission—*alsos* means "grove" in Greek. (Major General Leslie R. Groves was running the Manhattan Project to develop the atomic bomb for the United States.) We were supposed to go to Europe to find out how far the Germans had gotten with their atomic bomb project, because the United States was scared to death that they might have been way ahead because of their two-year head start.

The leader of our group was Dr. Sam Goudsmit, a Dutchman who had been involved in nuclear physics research for years. The administrative head was Colonel Boris Pash, a hard charger who was "Mr. Yes-I-Can-Do-It." Most of the other members were scientific types: the head of the Bureau of Standards, the chairman of the chemical engineering department at M.I.T. All of us had top-security clearances but were on the fringes of this thing; nobody was actually connected with the building of the real bomb. We were the investigators, and the Manhattan District people were going to be the digesters.

The day Paris was liberated, in late August 1944, the four of us from the navy landed at Orly Airport in Paris. I was familiar with the city, so I drove us straight to the Ambassador Hotel, which had just become the Allied headquarters. Everything was laid out for us. They were going to give us such-and-such type of equipment. We were not to displace any French. They assigned us to a hotel—the *Étoile*—that had been occupied by the Germans. As it turned out, the *Étoile*

was a German cathouse, so we went back to the ambassador for another lodging assignment.

At our new hotel, the *Royal Monseau*, the maître d'hôtel, Antoine, practically hugged us, he was so glad to see us. He had no food to offer, but he turned our C rations and K rations into a six-course dinner. He made prune whip—a fluffy pudding dessert—out of the old prune bars we used to have to eat.

Within the next few days the rest of the scientists arrived. About one-quarter of the total number of those involved with Alsos were scientists; at Paris we filled out with the necessary auxiliary personnel. Sam Goudsmit and several others called on Joliot-Curie, the son-in-law of Madame Marie Curie, whose laboratory had been taken over by the Germans working on chemical matters. A couple of us navy types went down to Bordeaux, where a German destroyer, the *Z-39*, had been captured in dock. We gave a quick look and then turned it over to the British for a more thorough evaluation.

Things were slow until the fall of 1944. The Allies had gotten as far as Strasbourg, where they ran across a large group of scientists that had been assembled by the Germans. These men kept meticulous records of everything they'd done. Our language beagles got in there and found that the Germans had been absolutely unable to build a nuclear bomb. All they had was a graphite pile that was supposed to produce plutonium, and it hadn't been working very well. They also had a heavy-water project up in Norway, but it had been pretty well destroyed by the attack on Narvik.

Not long after that the Alsos group was split up. The Alsos scientists continued to detail the work the Germans had done on nuclear research. The navy members formed what was known as the Naval Technical Mission Europe, with our own separate operation. We had very good logistical support from the army, and as most of our work was done in the British sector, got very good support from the British as well.

We planned to evaluate Dr. Hellmuth Walter's research at Gdynia (near Gdańsk) on high-speed submarines with hydrogen peroxide, which was also used for V-1 launching, as well as the proportioning pumps

The Alsos Mission pauses en route to Bordeaux in September 1944 to get information on a German destroyer abandoned in dry dock. The American flag on the command car is for the benefit of French civilians—to keep them from shooting at the vehicle. Commander Mumma, in field uniform, is at right with his back to the vehicle. (*Courtesy Rear Admiral Albert G. Mumma*)

for the V-2 rocket fuels. Dr. Wernher von Braun was working at Peenemünde. They were very good friends and cooperated with each other completely.

The Americans had previously collaborated with the British and Soviets in every respect relative to a technical exchange. Drs. von Braun and Walter, and their scientific cohorts, had agreed among themselves that they were not going to be captured by the Soviets. In the spring of 1945—when the Ruhr fell, the Americans crossed the Rhine, and the Soviets were advancing from the other direction—Hellmuth Walter abandoned Gdynia and retreated to Kiel. The Soviets pulled a fast one to keep us out of Gdynia, so we canceled any further technical exchanges with them.

An advance group of the Naval Technical Mission left for Bremen. I took off with just a photographer and came up along the Ruhr. I had never seen such devastation. There was not a single window intact. Most of the water lines had been broken. The population

lined up in the street to get water from a single spigot. The Germans had been blowing up bridges all the way to try and prevent the Allies' advance, so the first question we'd ask whenever we came to a fork in the road was, "*Ist die Brücke kaput?*" We met quite a few dead ends.

The first of our group reached Bremen at night and found that British combat troops had gone through that day. I arrived the next day. Those first few nights were pandemonium because as the troops passed through, they released all the slaves—Frenchmen and Lowlanders—that the Germans had working in the shipyards and in area camps. By the second night all these former slaves were drunker than skunks, having found the warehouse where the Germans stored liquor they had stolen from France. I was asleep that second night when I got a call from the senior watch officer. It seems that my photographer had joined in the drinking and was now wandering around town waving his pistol. It became my responsibility to disarm him. Fortunately, he gave up his gun to me peaceably.

At Bremen—not a major target of ours—we visited the shipyards, which were mostly used for commercial shipping. There were some floating cranes and other things that we were interested in, so we cataloged them and got all that information.

When we heard that Hamburg was about to fall, we started for that city. There the devastation was even worse. The Ruhr had been pinpoint-bombed by our Army Air Forces. The British had saturation-bombed Hamburg, and eighty-five thousand people died in the firestorm that consumed almost all of the center of the city. It was the most upsetting thing you can imagine, to see all this devastation and tremendous carnage around you, because they had not had time to clean up after the troops went through. The German civilians were doing the best they could to take care of the survivors, setting up emergency hospitals. This was in April, and it was still pretty damn chilly in northern Germany.

We were a seventy-five-man task force, which included four British officers, four American officers (of which I was in charge), and many Royal Marines. There was a young major in charge of the 30th Assault Unit of the Royal Marines. He was full of beans, and I enjoyed

him tremendously. We had gotten word that Kiel was pretty well opened. The surrender had not taken place, however. We did not know it at the time, but we were supposed to stay a hundred miles back from the Elbe, in accordance with the agreement that the Russians and Americans were not going to touch and fight each other.

Since we didn't know this, we decided to go on up to Kiel, all seventy-five of us. We were self-sufficient; we carried our own gasoline, rations, and guns for protection. When we got to Kiel, we decided that in view of the fact that we were a hundred miles behind German lines, the best thing to do would be to live in the submarine pen. We went in and cleared out the Germans and lived there for the few days we were there.

By this time Hitler was dead in his bunker in Berlin, and Admiral Karl Dönitz had taken over as head of state, transferring his headquarters to Flensburg, up on the Danish border. We knew that the government had pretty well collapsed. In the meantime, this young commander of the 30th Assault Unit decided that there was a very good chance that he might be court-martialed for not knowing that we should not be a hundred miles ahead of the front lines. Fortunately, the Germans hadn't fired on us on our way north, so we

German civilians in Dortmund line up at a water pump after their city has been devastated by war. (*Courtesy Rear Admiral Albert G. Mumma*)

In July 1945, two months after the German surrender, Secretary of the Navy James Forrestal visited Germany for a look at captured technology. Here he and his party stand before a completed U-boat section at Wesermünde. (*Navy photo in the National Archives: 80-G-337783*)

The results of Allied attacks are dramatically evident in this shot of shipyard shops at Bremen, Germany. (*Courtesy Rear Admiral Albert G. Mumma*)

hadn't really been engaged in combat. When we located Hellmuth Walter at the Walter Werke, this major decided to call on the commander of the German forces in Kiel. He went over and negotiated the surrender of the 150,000 Germans in the local garrison to our seventy-five-man task force. So, instead of getting a court-martial, he got a commendation.

At the Walter Werke, Dr. Walter welcomed us—to a degree. The first thing he said to me was, "When are you going to let me get back into operation so we can help you lick the Russians?" Obviously, he saw on which side his bread was buttered. Unfortunately, we had orders that he was not to continue working, but he did tell us quite a lot about his research. There was word that we weren't supposed to fraternize with the enemy, but I knew we weren't going to get anywhere by antagonism, so I gave him some tea. We had plenty of both coffee and tea, and they had very little. The Walters had just had a baby—their fifth child. His wife was a lovely person. She appreciated the tea very much. It helped a great deal in setting up a situation where we could talk.

While he was helpful, Dr. Walter refused to discuss the combustion chambers that were a major part of his hydrogen peroxide propulsion system. He had been personally responsible for setting up the manufacture of this throughout Germany. This propulsion system was also used in the Messerschmitt 163 rocket airplane. So I got the gang together—the senior group of

American and British officers—and we went up to Flensburg in our Jeeps. When we got there we saw this big German command car go by with its top down. I recognized Dönitz as he drove by. The fellow I wanted to talk to was the head of the navy. When we found the navy headquarters, it turned out that the commander in chief of the German navy was on his way to Compiègne to participate in the surrender.

We talked with Admiral Otto Backenkohler, the Vice Chief of Naval Operations. He whistled up the chief of each of the major bureaus that had to do with shipbuilding, torpedoes, and ordnance. The major thing we wanted to know was what they had given to the Japanese, what surprises we could expect. Admiral Backenkohler was a little reluctant at first, but after we began discussing the problems we'd had with the Japanese, he decided that it would be wise to cooperate, even though Germany hadn't surrendered yet. I asked him to sign a release for scientists like Dr. Walter, releasing them from their oath of secrecy. He signed approximately fifty of these so that each person in our group who needed it for debriefing purposes would have one.

All I had to do was pull out this paper and show Hellmuth Walter, and he was quite willing to discuss the combustion chamber. But our enterprising young major had made inquiries and discovered that there was a whole trainload of these chambers on a siding way up in the peninsula. He took a group of Royal

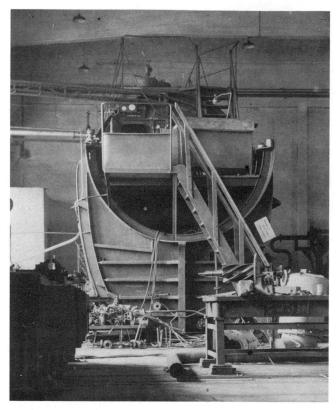

In Hellmuth Walter's workshop, Mumma found a test stand and mockup for a Type 26 U-boat, to be powered at high speed by hydrogen peroxide. (*Courtesy Rear Admiral Albert G. Mumma*)

Marines there, loaded the vehicles onto a train manned by German engineers, and came chugging into Kiel, right on into the Walter Werke. To the front of the train he'd attached a banner reading, "30th Assault Unit Special."

The U.S. Navy chose not to pursue hydrogen peroxide as a method of propelling submarines. Our first priority was a nuclear-propelled submarine, a true vessel of unlimited speed and endurance submerged. The British, however, were interested, so they moved Hellmuth Walter and his submarine setup to Vickers Armstrong in England for further evaluation.

While I was in Flensburg I interrogated the head of the German submarine force. He could not understand how our Bay of Biscay offensive in 1943 had succeeded so well that only 5 percent of all the submarines he had sent out returned. I attributed this to our combined air-sea operations, where we used radar in aircraft as well as in ships so that no German submarine—even one with a snorkel—could sortie without being detected. The Germans had no idea, at first, that we had aircraft radar that small. To them, radar took a whole roomful of equipment.

I asked how extensively they had cooperated with Japan. I learned of a group of German submarines, with their lead ballast replaced with gold, that had been dispatched to Japan. This gold was to be used to enlist additional support from Japan, and to purchase material that was in short supply in Germany. Many of these submarines were sunk on their way to Japan.

From April 1945 until that December, when I came home, I was in London as the assistant naval attaché and was the only engineer on the Commander Naval Forces Europe staff. Life in Britain was bleak; they were still on rationing. I felt so sorry for the British, because it really was an austere situation. And yet I attended several meetings where the British were encouraging—and the Australians wanted—a large migration of British citizens to Australia and New Zealand, but they wouldn't go. England was their home, and they were going to stay in spite of how tough it was. The government had hoped to reduce imports to the U.K. and be able to tighten their belts more, but it did not take place in the numbers they'd hoped for.

Of course, after the defeat of Winston Churchill in July, things got even worse under Clement Attlee, the new Labour Party prime minister, particularly when his new government began to nationalize things. There was a story circulating at that time. Churchill, who was still a member of Parliament, went to the men's room in the House of Commons. As he entered the room, he saw Prime Minister Attlee standing at the first urinal. Churchill went all the way down to the other end to do his business. When he left, he found Attlee waiting outside. Attlee said, "Winston, I know we have our differences on the floor of the House, but I didn't know we were so personally obnoxious to each other that you'd go out of your way to avoid me."

Churchill said, "Clement, you know the trouble with you fellows is that whenever you see anything large and running well, you want to nationalize it."

ALBERT GIRARD MUMMA (1906–) graduated from the Naval Academy in 1926, standing 17th among the 456 members in the class. He served in the cruiser *Seattle*, carrier *Saratoga*, and destroyer *Waters*. He then did postgraduate work in both Annapolis and Paris in the field of naval engineering. After duty in the destroyer *Clark*, he left the unrestricted line to specialize in engineering duty. During World War II he served in the Bureau of Ships and was one of four naval members of the top-secret Alsos Mission. He later served on the staff of Commander U.S. Naval Forces in Europe. Following the war, he was involved in the initial stages of the development of the nuclear submarine. He was later production officer of the San Francisco Naval Shipyard, commanding officer of the David Taylor Model Basin, and commander of the Mare Island Naval Shipyard in Vallejo, California. From 1955 to 1959 Admiral Mumma served as Chief of the Bureau of Ships, overseeing construction of the first nuclear-powered surface ships. From 1959 to 1971 he worked for the Worthington Corporation, serving his last four years as chairman. Admiral Mumma and his wife, Carmen, divide their retirement time between Gladwyne, Pennsylvania, and Lake Wales, Florida. (*Navy photo in the National Archives: 80-G-43278*)

Throughout their entire participation in the European theater, the sea services were to support the landing forces of the army. We have already seen the ways in which that support was provided at the beachheads at Normandy and in the Mediterranean. Here are three accounts describing what became of American soldiers once they moved inland and encountered the Germans at close range.

The three accounts demonstrate that army men, by and large, faced a more hazardous day-to-day existence than did naval personnel. Instead of experiencing moments of danger just during the invasion itself, soldiers had to keep fighting on an extended basis. They saw friends die and pondered their own mortality. Rex Barney, a baseball pitcher before entering the army, found that civilian celebrity was a worthless commodity on the battlefield. Jim Skidmore grieved over fellow soldiers killed when the transport *Leopold-ville* was torpedoed on Christmas Eve within sight of Cherbourg. Bob Lee tried to stay warm and stay alive in the bitter cold and bitter fighting of the Bulge. Each of the three men still has haunting thoughts about those who did not come back.

A DIFFERENT KIND OF UNIFORM

By Rex Barney

I was scared the whole time I was overseas in World War II. Anybody who says he wasn't is a liar. I went through the war with a rosary and an M-1 rifle. I depended more on those beads than the rifle, but I used the M-1 when I had to. And I saw things I never want to see again.

The war had a dramatic effect on my baseball career. Because so many of the prewar ball players were in the service by 1943, I went from high school to the major leagues in the same year. In the spring I was in school in Omaha, Nebraska. At the end of baseball season I was an eighteen-year-old rookie, pitching in Ebbets Field in the blue-and-white uniform of the Brooklyn Dodgers. Before the next season came, my draft board had put me into a different kind of uniform, the khakis of the U.S. Army.

The Dodgers finished the 1943 season in Cincinnati. I went home to Omaha, said hello and goodbye, and reported to Fort Leavenworth, Kansas. My army duty looked like a lark at the start. My pay went from five hundred dollars to twenty-one dollars a month, but, like many athletes, I was assigned to special services to play basketball and baseball on camp teams. They transferred me to Fort Riley, Kansas, and I skipped basic training because the basketball season was about to start. The following spring we put together a pretty good baseball team that included a number of other major league players: Joe Garagiola, Lonnie Frey, Harry Walker, Pete Reiser, Alpha Brazle, Ken Heintzelman, and Frank Crespi. We played my old semipro team in Omaha and other camp teams. One Sunday I arranged for the team to go to Boys Town for mass and to meet Father Flanagan, an exciting day for all of us.

My life of Riley was shattered in the summer of 1944 by the news that I was headed overseas. I went first to Camp Shelby, Mississippi, for processing. That in-

cluded going through a line where they hit you with shots in both arms. If you didn't keep moving, they'd hit you again. From there I found myself back in New York. But this time, instead of a subway to Brooklyn, I was on a troopship to France. It was a converted Italian luxury liner. Fourteen days on a ship crowded with scared young GIs who are trying not to show it is no luxury cruise.

We were part of a twelve-ship convoy, dodging German U-boats all the way over. Four ships did not make it. The ship I was on rocked and rolled constantly, and we were seldom allowed to go up on deck. The food was terrible. There were bunks six high, and everybody prayed for a top one. But we couldn't sleep anyhow; most of us shot craps all night. When you lost all your money, you borrowed from one of the winners and got back in the game. I hated it all.

At Fort Riley I had felt like some kind of a big shot, a former major league ball player. No more. The army is a great leveler. Now I was just another buck private like everybody else. Only an occasional baseball nut from Brooklyn had ever heard of me. I didn't know what I was headed for, but I was pretty sure it was unlikely to have anything to do with baseball. By the time we landed in Le Havre, I had been assigned to a tank reconnaissance group. Never mind that I was six feet, three inches and knew zilch about tanks. The army needed a body for the tank corps and I was it.

It was bitterly cold when we landed. Le Havre was a shambles, flattened by constant German air raids. Debris and bodies floated in the harbor. We could not get to the docks and had to wade ashore in waist-high water, carrying rifles and equipment over our heads. It was cold, dirty, and muddy, with death and destruction everywhere. I don't want to remember it, but I cannot forget it.

I didn't have the vaguest idea what I was doing when I landed, but I learned quickly. It's called Survival 101. I soon discovered that tank reconnaissance means that a line of alternating tanks and Jeeps advances ahead of everybody else until they draw enemy fire. Then they

This chapter is a condensed, modified version of Chapter 8 from *Rex Barney's Thank Youuuu for 50 Years in Baseball from Brooklyn to Baltimore* by Rex Barney with Norman L. Macht; © 1993 by Tidewater Publishers. Used by permission.

Former major league baseball players wear a different kind of uniform as they visit Father Flanagan's Boys Town in August 1944. *Left to right are:* Harry Walker of the Cardinals, Rex Barney of the Dodgers, Father Edward J. Flanagan, Barney's high school coach Skip Palrang, Joe Garagiola of the Cardinals, Pete Reiser of the Dodgers, and Lonnie Frey of the Reds. (*Father Flanagan's Boys' Home*)

radio back to the infantry to tell them where the enemy is. Sound like fun?

But first we had to get the tanks to the front. The first real action I saw was on a cold winter night at the Rhine River. We had to move all the heavy equipment across, but there was a German outpost on top of a hill on the other side. Somebody asked for volunteers to go across and find out what was up there. Dumb-ass me, I figure it's my first night of action—go for it. Eight of us and a sergeant got into two rubber boats, dirt smeared on our faces, carrying rifles, pistols, and grenades, watching chunks of ice floating by as we silently crossed over. We slithered around and up the hill, trying to stay out of sight. An old stone house came into view. Then suddenly we heard noises and guys talking German. The sergeant hollered, "Fire!" and we rose up and opened fire. Just like that, there were six dead Germans.

We slid back down the hill and raced to where we had tied up the boats. Gone. The Germans must have found them and cut them loose. I was a good swimmer, but with all that equipment and the frigid water and hunks of ice hitting me in the head, getting across the river took forever. They dragged us out and took us someplace warm and we slept the whole next day.

I was scared out of my wits, but at least I had gotten that duty out of the way. Some guys who went on later patrols got killed or wounded. We each received a

Bronze Star, which was nice; more important, it earned us five extra points toward our ultimate discharge date, which was based on a point system. That was one thing about the army I had learned fast.

The houses in Germany had walls like forts and made good outposts. We occupied one near a creek and the Germans held one on the other side. We sat there watching each other. Lookout duty was on the second floor in two-man teams—two hours on, two hours off, which meant we never slept. If we saw or heard anything, we shot first and asked questions later.

There was running water in the creek. If you've ever sat near running water on a cold, dark, still night, you'd swear you could hear eight thousand troops marching right up your front walk. One night I was on duty with a big Dodger fan named Jim Eisely. He had an M-1, and I had my M-1 and a rosary and a brilliant idea. We rounded up all the empty tin cans we could find and threw them all over the front yard, so if anybody moved we could hear them.

In the middle of our late-night shift we were startled by a racket like a string of cans being dragged behind a newlyweds' getaway car. We opened fire and raked the place, and everything went quiet. We couldn't wait for sunup to see how many dead guys we got. When the dawn came, we found five stone-dead billy goats in the yard.

The tank had a four-man crew: a driver, who sat deep inside near ground level on the left; a radio operator beside him; a gunner, who sat a few steps higher and operated a .50-caliber machine gun; and the tank commander, a sergeant who stood—never sat—with his head sticking out through the opening. He gave the orders and fired the 75-millimeter cannon. There was no steering wheel; the driver moved two sticks to maneuver. I never drove one; I started as a radio operator and wound up as a tank commander. The inside of a tank is cramped, hot as hell in the summer, and cold as hell in the winter. Many a night we slept in one. It was our home.

The Germans hated our cannon and took off when they heard it. They had an 88-millimeter cannon that we dreaded. Those shells had a distinctive whistle that struck icy fear in us. One night in that outpost where we decimated the billy goats we heard one coming in, and I just knew we were gone. It landed in the backyard and never went off. They also had a bazooka, a one-shot gun that tore a huge hole in a tank and exploded all the ammunition inside. One day I was in the second tank and we rounded a curve in the road and heard this gun go off. The lead tank stopped and we knew right away there was nothing left of anybody in it. We bailed out of ours in a hurry. The commander dove off the top, but it took the driver a few minutes to unstrap himself and get out of there. Hairy moments, those.

The tanks and Jeeps moved forward until they ran into the enemy or it got dark, whichever came first. At night we threw a net over the tank and crawled into a barn with the animals, or an empty farmhouse—any place where it was warm. The whole experience was a rude awakening for me. And I don't mind telling you, I hated it, absolutely despised it. I couldn't wait to get back to the life that was waiting for me.

Later, after I got out of there, I could see what an education it was. If you ever think you're better than anybody else, think about your days in the army, where you'd find maybe the world's richest guy next to some bum who never had a dime, a professor in a foxhole with a guy who couldn't add two and two. I also learned that the guys who were real tough and macho in the States were the sissies and wimps under fire.

The first words of German I learned were, "*Haben Sie Eier?*" (Have you any eggs?). We'd go to a farmhouse looking for an egg; we'd eat it raw, or cook it in our helmets. We took a bath in our helmets if we ever found water. We were filthy dirty; you could scrape the dirt off with a fingernail. Once in a while the Red Cross showed up with five-gallon cans of coffee. I poured some of that in my helmet and shaved with it. I remembered my mother preaching cleanliness and telling me, "You can always go into a gas station restroom and find soap and water," and I laughed.

We ate C rations: little packages of dehydrated something, powdered eggs, some kind of dog meat, and a chocolate bar. That is, when the rations caught up with us. I learned what complete hunger feels like. And if we ever saw a live chicken, it was dead in a hurry.

We were in action for thirty days at a time and then got a few days off to go back, take a shower, get deloused, and eat some decent food.

Some things happened that did not seem funny at the time, but later we could look back and joke about them. Things like near-misses by whistling shells, and billy goat body counts. One day we were crossing the Saar River in Germany. While we waited for the engineer to put down pontoons for the tanks to cross, we emptied a five-gallon gasoline can and filled it with some wine we had requisitioned along the way. I was sitting atop the tank when two war correspondents came up to me.

"Sergeant, you got any water?"

"Sure," I said without thinking. "Right back there. That five-gallon tank on the left."

One of them took a swig and said, "Dear God, this is the greatest water I ever tasted." In twenty minutes they were drunk as skunks. I guess they thought the age of miracles hadn't passed, and I had turned water into wine.

Both sides fired tracer bullets at night; we could see them flashing by. The Germans fired them high and we thought, "Okay, I can get down under that." But they were firing the invisible ones down below at the same time.

Land mines were another menace. We had to clear a path wide enough for the tank treads to get through. We'd round up all the animals we could find—pigs, cows, whatever—and send them across a field to see if they blew up. Otherwise, we were on our hands and knees, crawling gingerly yard by yard and poking bayonets ahead of us. I found some mines that way and saw friends get killed or lose some limbs beside me.

It was constantly wearing. Sometimes I would go to sleep and hope I didn't wake up for three days. I had frostbitten feet from pulling guard duty in subzero weather and was wounded twice. That earned me two Purple Hearts, good for ten points. But nothing major. Once I was dashing behind a barrier and machine-gun fire grazed my leg. Another time the firing was pretty heavy and I was trying to dig a hole in some concrete with my fingernails and got hit in the back with some shrapnel.

I was attached to the 4th and 6th Armored Divisions of the Third Army and had two contacts with General George S. Patton. Once he called a meeting of his tank recon commanders in the town hall of Nancy, France, which the Germans and Americans kept taking and retaking. I drove a captain to the meeting. There were a couple hundred officers there. Patton ranted and raved and cussed and screamed about how the Ger-

Lieutenant General George Patton was aggressive and profane in his leadership of the Third Army eastward to Germany in 1944–45. (*Naval Institute Collection*)

mans were pushing us around. He said, "From this point on, every infantryman who doesn't fire at least a hundred rounds a day at the enemy is as worthless as a prick on the Pope." And I'm thinking: here's this nice Irish Catholic altar boy sitting here listening to this, and what would my mother say?

A recon group was not prepared to take prisoners, and that was fine with Patton. He preferred to shoot them all on the spot. One time we were trying to take some little hill, but we were pinned down by mortar and machine-gun fire from the hilltop. It was midday. A couple of our guys were hit and fell dead beside me. Three or four men got around behind the Germans and captured three of them. They went behind a barn and killed them point-blank. It wasn't tough to watch at the time, but later my stomach turned a few times. I never thought I would see Americans do anything like that. I didn't do it, but I was part of it; I sanctioned it. I don't think I could have fired the shots, but I saw it, and I will never lose that sight in my mind.

We did some nasty things, but I suppose they did the same to our guys. A Jeep always led the recon column, followed by the lead tank, and so on. We crept along very slowly. If we captured a German soldier, we put him on the hood of the lead Jeep with his hands behind his head. Talk about a scared son of a bitch. We didn't want the Germans firing on us, but if they did . . .

I'll tell you, I've seen some scared guys. I used to think: Damn, I'm glad I'm not up there. And if we ever got hold of an officer and put him up there, was that fun. They'd protest that they didn't have to do that, but

when it was explained to them that the alternative was to go behind a barn and get shot, they got up there. They were the bitter, deadly enemy, and we had to think of them that way at all times.

We had no way to take prisoners, but one day we came to a small town, and the whole town surrendered to us, soldiers and everybody, white flags flying everywhere. We had to call the infantry to come and get them.

We were sitting in the tank one night in April 1945 and the radio operator picked up some music on the BBC. I was juking around to the music when suddenly a bulletin came on that President Roosevelt had died. My father had said that Roosevelt was the greatest president who ever lived. And if he said it, I knew it must be true.

I'll never forget the strong stench that filled my nostrils as we got closer to something we did not know we were coming to, and then we went into Buchenwald. Bodies piled up everywhere. Walking skeletons. We didn't expect it, because when you are in the thick of war you don't really know what else is going on in the world. We knew there were prisoner camps and American prisoners of war, but we never knew when or where we would happen onto something. And there was no way to be prepared for this.

They mobbed Jeeps, turning them over, to get at a scrap of bread. We just had to let them go to it; you could not say no. Those who could move wanted to go to the nearest village and kill everybody. We had to

Barney is shown here at Ebbets Field in Brooklyn. After the war he pitched for the Dodgers from 1946 to 1950, posting his top record, 15-13, in 1948. (*Courtesy Los Angeles Dodgers*)

stop them from doing that. Others begged us to let them go home. Just walk home. That might have been eight hundred miles away. I didn't want to see all that, but I think I've become a better person for having seen it.

By now the Germans were in full flight, abandoning the camps. We rolled down the beautiful autobahn, the superhighway, toward Austria. But when the prisoners started telling us stories about the slave laborers from Poland and other countries who had built it, how people who collapsed or died were just buried in the concrete, we didn't know that we ever wanted to ride on it again.

It was all an eye-opener for a naive kid from Omaha.

And then the war was over in Europe, and I was in Vienna, and every day was like New Year's Eve. A kid athlete from Oshkosh and I got hold of a bottle of champagne and killed the bottle. I hadn't been so sick since one day when I swallowed my chewing tobacco while playing baseball.

With Europe liberated, I was liberated from the tank corps and went back to playing basketball. Vienna was divided into French, British, Italian, American, and Russian zones. We had everything; the rest had nothing. People tried to sneak into our zone from every direction, but especially to get away from the Russians. They were mean and rough; I mean animals. If they couldn't rape a girl in the street, they would just as soon shoot her. They drove tanks down into the subway and fired guns into the tunnels, just to destroy it. We took all their money on the black market, selling them food and things we had. I did that, but I'm not proud of it. All we had was scrip money; I had footlockers filled with it, but I couldn't spend it anywhere else.

A lot of servicemen had used the C ration chocolate bars to trade with the German girls. A little piece went a long way. I stayed away from that action because I knew when I got back, Branch Rickey, president of the Dodgers, would be asking me about social diseases.

In Vienna I met a Red Cross girl from Nebraska. We Nebraskans were pretty scarce, so we stuck together. And I'll never forget a nurse named Alice Pierce. It was October 1945 and I met her in a USO Red Cross center. We started talking about the World Series between the Tigers and the Cubs, and she said there was a radio upstairs. We went up there at night and I heard bits of that series, including a Hank Greenberg home run. Bless Alice Pierce. Shows you what I had most on my mind.

REX EDWARD BARNEY (1924–) began his professional baseball career in 1943, appearing in nine games for the Brooklyn Dodgers at the end of the season before entering the army. After the war, he pitched for Brooklyn from 1946 through 1950. His best season was in 1948, when he won fifteen games and pitched a no-hitter against the New York Giants at the Polo Grounds. He pitched in three of the seven games of the 1947 World Series, including starting the fifth game. His overall major league pitching record was 35–31. He was known as one of the hardest throwing pitchers ever, but his big-league tenure was shortened by difficulty in throwing strikes consistently. After ending his career as an active player, he became a sports broadcaster. He was a play-by-play announcer for Mutual Radio's "Game of the Day" program in the mid-1950s and also announced games locally in New York. In the 1960s he began doing radio work in Baltimore. Since the 1970s he has been the stadium public address announcer for the Baltimore Orioles. Mr. Barney, who lives in Baltimore, is host of a popular sports call-in show on one of the city's radio stations. (*Courtesy Rex Barney, via Norman Macht*)

GAMBLING FOR DRAMAMINE

By Lieutenant Colonel James H. Skidmore, U.S. Army Reserve (Retired)

New York presented a multitude of sights and sounds when I arrived there in October 1944. Ships went back and forth, shepherded by the tooting whistles of tugboats; airplanes and squawking seagulls flew overhead; ferryboats made their runs between boroughs; and the towers of Manhattan loomed in the background. I looked in all directions with a sense of wonder. It was a whole new world for a second lieutenant who only a few years earlier had been a farm boy in Missouri. My job now was to serve as a member of an advance party, preparing for soldiers of the 66th Infantry Division to go aboard troop transports and ship out for France.

A small tug of some kind took us out into the harbor, and right in the middle was one of the famous British passenger ships—either the *Queen Mary* or *Queen Elizabeth*—being used as troop transports. As the tugboat approached the liner, I thought that was going to be the ultimate way to go across. We came right up to the side of the ship, and just down at about the waterline we could see an opened door through which men and equipment would be put aboard. We passed

close alongside, but the tugboat never slowed down. Instead, we went on over to a much smaller ship, the USS *General G. O. Squier*, that we would be boarding. Although only about two years old, the navy transport looked like a real junker.

Being tantalized by a queen and then passed off to a commoner was disappointing, but not surprising. By that time I had grown accustomed to the ways of the army, convincing me that there must be some office in the Pentagon that was in charge of irrationality. When I was going through officer training at Fort Benning, Georgia, the year before, one of the instructors was a wild man known as "The Mad Major." He called on me one time to stand up in the bleachers and answer a question. I really didn't care a whole lot, so I answered, "Just beats hell out of me, Sir." It took him aback, and I think that was one reason I got through the whole course.

I was commissioned a second lieutenant in March 1943 and sent to Blanding, Florida, to help form up the new division for combat. But there was no combat for almost a year. Instead, the 66th became a training

The navy transport *General G. O. Squier* was a relatively new ship in 1944 but much harder on her passengers than one of the British Cunard liners would have been. (*Navy photo in the National Archives: 19-N-68707*)

division. Our cadre was augmented with fillers—new men whom we trained and then sent to the various war theaters of the globe. Only after we had done this for the better part of a year did logic set in: those of us trained for combat would be sent overseas to fight. First, all of us were issued little booklets on how to speak the Cantonese dialect of Chinese. Then we were put on a train to New York so we could ship out for Europe. The booklet must have been the idea of that Pentagon office.

As I remember, the trip across the Atlantic took about ten days, because those convoys ran at the rate of the slowest vessel. I don't know how big the convoy was. Whenever I looked out, there were just ships as far as I could see in all directions. I was seasick from the time I got on board ship until the time I got off. My salvation came from a navy chief carpenter's mate named Vincent Andrews; he was one of the boys that I'd gone to school with back home. After we'd been out for a day or two, I finally found him in his workshop. He made a place for me there, then he went down to the navy mess for me. On a regular basis he brought me ice cream and cookies to eat. I've always said that he kept me alive, because I couldn't abide the regular messing conditions the ship had for the troops.

The *General G. O. Squier*, I presume, served good enough food, but the area where the troops had to eat was so enclosed that the odors engulfed everybody in there. I tried that approach the first day or two, and by the time I hit the door to the galley, it was all over. I'd just turn around and go back. I couldn't stand to eat in there. Even though my friend Andrews was providing goodies, I still didn't keep down much of what I ate or drank. In recent years I've been to our division reunions, where I talk to some of these people. They say, "Well, I was just never sick a minute on that ship." Hell, I stood right there by the railing and threw up with them. I know that they're lying.

At that, we officers had it better than the enlisted men. We had bunks in a deck that was fairly high in the ship. Every day, though, we would go down into the berthing compartments to check our people, and they were living in miserable conditions, stacked in bunks that were awfully close together. As I remember, the bunks were made of webbing attached to metal frames, and there were maybe six, seven, or eight bunks in a stack. Not too many men could be up at a time. They had to lie in their bunks and either read or talk, because there weren't enough passageways where they could stand. They were thrown in there like cattle. They had absolutely no privacy whatsoever. And everybody was pretty sick. Because of the congestion, they often didn't make it to the head to vomit. There was a lot of filth on the decks, and the stench was really something awful.

Another problem for the soldiers on board was that we didn't have much to focus on except how bad we felt. We did hold meetings and do a little bit of training on artillery procedures and other things we might encounter over in France, but we weren't in shape for much of that. At times, if I could find a warm spot up on deck, out of everybody's way, I'd lie down there for a while. We spent a lot of time just in bull sessions. Also, the medics passed out Dramamine, or whatever they called seasickness tablets back then. Soon we got to playing blackjack for those tablets instead of money. It was really a cutthroat game, because anybody that could get a pocketful of tablets had it made. That's where I learned to play blackjack.

The soldiers got along well with the navy crew, although there was one interesting incident. Going over in the fall, the ship was carrying a lot of extra rations for the holidays. Someplace down in one of the holds, the army men figured out how to get into another section of the ship where they found the navy's beer supply. They drank up most of that, and that caused a good deal of friction. There were several investigations of that, with the naval officers telling us that we should have known that the troops were in it. After all, when you take several hundred men, they were able to get away with a good deal of beer. The American GI can be very resourceful in these situations. There's not anybody like him in the world for that.

Finally, we got to England, and we officers all assembled on deck. A very proper British officer came aboard and said to us, "Welcome home." Since we were colonists, he welcomed us back. It was a nice touch. It was a bright day, and everything went pretty smoothly as we got off the ship. We set up our people at Lyme Regis, a seaside resort town in southern England. That was where the movie *The French Lieutenant's Woman* was filmed a number of years later. It was a nice area to be in, very picturesque. The British people were civil enough, but part of the time we had the feeling that we weren't all that welcome. Their attitude was that they were fighting the war by themselves, and we were just there.

We got established in Lyme Regis about the middle of November, some six months after the initial landings in Normandy. This was obviously a huge campaign on the Continent, and we had had the feeling month by month that we were just moving progressively forward until our time came. At our headquarters we picked up battle reports on the BBC and the American armed forces radio station. I used that information to keep a map of Europe updated with the lines as we thought them to be. We got virtually no information on war events through official channels.

During those few weeks in England we just didn't have enough area to do large-scale maneuvers, so we did a lot of company exercises: maneuver of platoons

Skidmore and his outfit trained in the vicinity of the quaint old English village of Lyme Regis. (*Courtesy Lieutenant Colonel James H. Skidmore*)

and training with rifles and machine guns. Shooting is like riding a bicycle; you always remember the basics, but it helps to practice often if you want to be really proficient. One afternoon when we were out in the field we got the word that we were going to make the final leg of our journey—to France. The result was pandemonium because people were scattered all over that end of England. The officers in charge told us that we had to be ready to move in three hours, and so the 66th Division started for its loading ports. Part of us went to Weymouth, and part of us went to Southampton. The biggest contingents went aboard the transports *Cheshire* and *Leopoldville*. The latter was an old Belgian passenger ship that had been pressed into service for the war.

On Christmas Eve I was in a group that made a terrible crossing in an LST. It was rough, cold, raining, and very dark—and an LST was even more uncomfortable than a troop transport. When the ship got to Cherbourg that night, we were ordered to get ready to disembark. We were out on deck and saw lots of lights. We thought that it was peculiar for them to be showing so much light in an area like that. We later learned that those were rescue vessels belatedly trying to save the men from the *Leopoldville*. She had been torpedoed off Cherbourg by a German U-boat. The LST ran her bow

up onto a cobblestone ramp at the water's edge and a soldier there told us what happened.

Pretty soon the corpses of our fellow soldiers began coming in. One of the problems was hypothermia. With that cold December weather, the estimate was that a man wouldn't live unless a rescue boat came along and picked him up within fifteen minutes after he got into the water. Our reaction to the whole thing was one of shock. You hear about incidents in other outfits, but you never believe something will happen to you. Earlier in the day, we had all been in England, ready to shove off. Now more than eight hundred men of the 66th Division were dead.

One of the officers from the division, Jacquin Sanders, later wrote a book on the sinking called *A Night Before Christmas*. As Sanders described, the men on board the *Leopoldville* had a really hellish experience, in part because of a failure of communication. Because of the proximity of the port, men were ordered to stay on board and await rescue. But the ship sank before enough small craft could be mobilized to take off the whole crew; too many people ashore were taking things easy because of the holiday. Another difficulty was that the Belgian crew abandoned ship early and left the Americans to their fate. Sanders wrote in his book that the Belgian captain went down with the ship. Maybe so, but for a long time there was a lot of satisfaction in everybody's mind to think that somebody had hanged the son of a bitch.

One of the men who was lost with the *Leopoldville* was Lieutenant Colonel Chris Rumburg, an officer with whom I was well acquainted even though he was commander of a battalion in another regiment. A veteran of the commando raid on Dieppe, France, in 1942, he was a superb leader and probably physically the largest man I ever knew. He was a giant of a man. It was always hard for me to believe that he didn't survive. I thought back to the division's days in Florida when we were undergoing ranger training. The area was in the swamps back there, near an old sawmill, so there was a lot of sawdust. This was hand-to-hand combat with knives and so forth. I was the smallest guy in there, and Rumburg was the biggest. He invariably would come over and use me when he was demonstrating a hold or something. He would throw me across in that sawdust, which wasn't all that soft. Then some joker would say, "Well, I didn't see that." So the colonel would come back over and pick me up and throw me back the other way. So I got to know him very well. He was a tremendous guy, and now he was dead.

The sinking of the *Leopoldville* had another consequence I didn't even realize at the time. Back when I completed high school at Flemington, Missouri, in 1939, we had thirteen in the graduating class. All five boys went into the service during the war and two were killed. One of the eight girls became an army nurse, and by late 1944 she was serving in the Cherbourg area. She saw the 66th Division shoulder patches on the uniforms of the *Leopoldville* casualties. As a result, she wrote a letter to my parents and told them she didn't know whether I was alive or dead, but she knew that the ship had been sunk. It was sometime later before I was able to write home and they learned I was still alive. The delay wasn't at all comforting for them—as they mentioned a time or two after I got home.

After we got off that LST, we had strip maps that showed us where we were supposed to go. We had our vehicles and everything with this advance party. We were to report to an area perhaps ten or twelve miles inland, at which point we would form up and make a convoy, and then proceed on to the division that we were to relieve. Well, when the *Leopoldville* was sunk, everything was thrown into total chaos. The people that were to be there weren't. In the particular group that I was with, we waited a period, and then we just proceeded on our own. We knew about where this unit was, and we just went directly to this division and reported in to the commander there.

For a while the food setup was as confused as the tactical one. When we got on the beach there at Cherbourg it was dark, and everything was mixed up. We had not one bit of ration with us. Someone had dumped a lot of supplies out on the LST ramp, and there was a black man with a machine gun guarding the whole big pile of rations. We asked him if we could get a box of something to take with us, and he said help ourselves. When the sun came up the next morning, we discovered that we had a box of Vienna sausages and a box of canned pears. That was our menu every day for the rest of the week: Vienna sausages and pears.

Another item in short supply was crucial—ammunition—because it hadn't yet been issued. See, nobody has ammunition until you get close to combat, just because of the possibility of accidents. We were to be issued ammunition at our assembly point. But, as I said, when we got to the beach at Cherbourg it was so confused that we didn't even try to assemble there. We went there, but nothing was happening, so we went on to the division. And we drove completely across that area before we found a supply of ammunition. So that was a cause for a good deal of concern.

It took a while to get things organized because of all the chaos that followed the *Leopoldville* incident. Some of our troops got as far away as Belgium and several other places before we got them all back. People were scattered just to hell and breakfast on that thing. The area where we wound up operating was near a little farming village called Fay-de-Bretagne, perhaps sixty miles inland from the port of Saint-Nazaire. I stayed in the battalion headquarters, which were in an old château on the far side of town. There were a lot of buildings there, and a lot of the troops lived in chicken houses and hog houses.

Helmeted U.S. soldiers prepare to go aboard ship for the voyage to France. (*Navy photo in the National Archives: 80-G-231227*)

Lieutenant Skidmore is seated at right in his Jeep as two members of his platoon make a patrol near Pont Château. At left are two Free French soldiers. (*Courtesy Lieutenant Colonel James H. Skidmore*)

Even before that we got a quick sense of our duties. The battalion commander of the unit we were joining said to us, "Well, the best way for you to get acquainted is to go out and just assume position with the men you're to relieve." It was dark and raining, and when we went down this road, I could hear people talking, and their voices were in front of me. The closer I got, the lower the voices were. I don't mean lower in pitch or loudness but closer to the ground. I heard the voices of people squatting down and finally voices coming from down in holes. That made an impression—that we'd finally arrived. We were in an area where we could be hit.

As I soon found out, our mission was to keep large pockets of German soldiers bottled up. When the invasion forces broke out from Normandy, General George Patton and his people pushed a large element of the German army back into pockets against the sea. Some strategist determined that it would be better to hold them where they were than to try to clean them out. This division we joined had been doing it. Before the *Leopoldville* disaster, we had thought we were going to relieve the division at the Bulge in the Ardennes Forest. Whether we were headed here to the Brittany coast or whether we were headed for the Bulge, I don't know. But we ended up in this pocket area where our immediate front contained some 120,000 Germans.

The Germans didn't come out in force, but they had a lot of artillery and a lot of ammunition. The situation was obviously static—reminiscent of World War I. We had to make sure that the Germans were staying in their pockets, because they certainly had the capability to break out if they had wanted to. So we had to maintain constant contact with the enemy, and that involved sending patrols. You had to physically go out and find them. This was one of the jobs that I did, either organizing or going myself.

The Germans had all the advantages when we sent out patrols because we were walking toward them. We had to find them by following paths through farmland that was mined. We frequently didn't know where all the hazards were. Going on those patrols undoubtedly caused the most fear I experienced during the whole campaign. I especially remember the first night patrol, because I just wasn't really prepared for that. All farm kids grew up learning how to shoot. But I hadn't had any experience being shot at, and I didn't like it when it happened.

We went down a country road. There was a creek that seemed to be, at that time, mutually understood as the dividing line between the Germans and Americans. If we didn't go over it, they'd let us alone and vice versa. We got down about that far that night and were shot at. It's a helpless feeling, because the only sensation is the sound of rifle fire, and you don't have any idea what direction the bullets are coming from. And since you've never been there in daylight, you have no idea of the geography and terrain. That was frightening.

Artillery was also a problem. You hear the booming of their guns over and over and know that each explosion means shells headed in your direction. More than anything, you want those guns to get quiet. And even when we weren't patrolling, we could be shot at, so we spent a lot of our time wedged up against hedgerows or in one of the foxholes that were dug all over the country. Whether this was yours or somebody else's, whichever one was close, that was the one that you got in. We put logs over the tops of them for additional protection.

The French people still lived in their homes, and they got caught in the middle of all this cross fire. Our medics and doctors treated any number of civilians in our battalion aid station for fragmentation wounds, gunshots, and other injuries. There just weren't any other medical facilities available. The condition of those French civilians is one of the things that I look back on with sorrow. They had been terribly overridden by the Germans, and then the Americans came along. These French were reduced to eating out of garbage pails around our mess halls. I thought they were the dirtiest, most unkempt people in the world. I was too green to know what they had gone through. They'd just been ground down to nothing. I still am sorry for that attitude I had toward them.

Our holding action in that area was ultimately successful, so that these German troops in Brittany were unable to aid their countrymen being pushed back toward the fatherland. Hostilities ended in May 1945, and we made our way to Saint-Nazaire. The Lorient and Saint-Nazaire pockets were large, large landmasses. At both Lorient and Saint-Nazaire were the submarine pens for U-boats. The ones at Saint-Nazaire were so massive that the French have never tried to tear them down. For example, the concrete on top was thirty feet thick. I went up on top of one. I could see that it had taken a few direct bomb hits, and they had only scooped out a place six inches to a foot deep. The bombs hadn't done any damage whatsoever. At Saint-Nazaire we also saw the large dry dock that British commandos had put out of action with a raid back in March 1942 so that the German battleship *Tirpitz* couldn't use it.

Eventually, we went to Marseille, where the division was disbanded. Many of the 66th troops were sent, as was I, to the 42nd Infantry Division as occupation forces. Then we took a train to the port of Le Havre and boarded a ship for home. I have a picture that I took on board ship just before we left France, and everybody looks very somber. They were all wrapped up in what they saw and what they remembered. We had more seasickness on the way back, and then came that moment of jubilation when we reached New York again. They had all the trains I've ever seen in my life lined up there. They were taking people home to places all over the United States.

The war was over, and we were going home to a multitude of pleasures that we had missed for months and months. For instance, I remember that store-bought bread was a real treat for me. It was so tender and soft it was like biting into angel food cake.

In a sense, I suppose some of the men of the 66th Infantry Division were disappointed to be tied down in that static situation around Fay-de-Bretagne rather than being in the Battle of the Bulge or part of the forces that were heading east to liberate France and go on into Germany. But as we get together for our reunions, we can reflect on the fact that we did what we were ordered to do, and that we are still alive when a lot of others, including hundreds from the *Leopoldville*, are not. I'm satisfied with what we accomplished by our service because it was one part of the big picture.

In recent years I've been back to France and walked along some of those country roads where I crawled in 1945. It still raises the hair on the back of my neck when I remember the sound of a bullet snapping in the night. I've also been to the American cemetery at Normandy. The immensity of it is just hard to visualize. You hear of these casualties, but to know that every one of those crosses is a person makes it very vivid. As I've stood there and looked at those rows upon rows of white markers, I've had a feeling that is difficult to describe. It's not sorrow exactly, but you feel very subdued, very humble, that you're here and they're there. It could easily have been the other way around.

JAMES HARRY SKIDMORE (1921–) graduated from Kemper Military Academy, Boonville, Missouri, in 1941, and was a student at the University of Missouri in Columbia when he was drafted for army service in June 1942. After basic training in California and officer training in Georgia, he was commissioned in March 1943 and assigned to the 66th Infantry Division, in which he served as intelligence and reconnaissance officer. He was a member of the 42nd Infantry Division as part of the occupation force in Austria from October 1945 to April 1946. He was discharged from the service as a captain in June of that year, then resumed his education, graduating from the University of Missouri in 1948. Skidmore then taught in the public schools of Polk County and Hickory County, Missouri, for several years, in addition to operating as a farmer and stock man. He joined the 3/75 8-inch Artillery Battalion of the Army Reserve in 1951 and served until his retirement as a lieutenant colonel in 1971. He continues to operate his farm near Flemington, Missouri. (*Courtesy Lieutenant Colonel James H. Skidmore*)

THREE FACES

By Robert Lee

After lots of training in the United States, I went overseas in the autumn of 1943 as part of a replacement group on board the British liner *Mauretania*. The ship had a British crew and a British menu, including kippers and herring for breakfast. When I reached England, I was assigned to the 635th Antiaircraft Automatic Weapons Battalion, which consisted of four weapons batteries and a headquarters battery. In defending against enemy aircraft, the army used some of the same guns that were aboard navy ships. As a second lieutenant I had a battery that consisted of two platoons, with four units in a platoon: four Bofors 40-millimeter guns and four quadruple .50-caliber machine guns. The guns were mounted on trailers so we could move along with the ground troops. The trailers were towed by six-wheeled two-and-a-half-ton trucks.

When we started operating our weapons in England, we didn't have radar—just mechanical gun directors to control the aiming of the guns. These directors, which stood on tripods, weighed perhaps seven or eight hundred pounds apiece. They were so heavy and bulky that we converted our 40-millimeters to British gunsights. We substituted British gunsights on the Bofors. They gave us better performance and made us a lot more mobile too. In the previous arrangement, the large director behind the 40-millimeter guns created a blind spot that had to be filled by the .50 calibers. Now we had eliminated the blind spot.

We spent the next several months in training in various parts of southern England. With our new gunsights, we did a lot of practice firing at canvas target sleeves towed by American planes. Sometimes our bullets walked up the target cable toward a plane, causing the pilot to make a hasty retreat. Occasionally, we even hit a passing seagull with our .50-calibers. The amazing thing was how many seagulls got through our barrage, which was good for the birds but gave us some concern about the effectiveness of our weapons.

We were at Lyme Regis in June of 1944 as we watched part of the invasion fleet sail for France. I remember seeing streams of American bombers going overhead on their way to the Continent. After a move to Ashford, we started seeing the V-1 buzz bombs

For soldiers who went ashore at Normandy in the weeks following D-Day, the situation on the beach was much less hazardous than it had been on June 6. Once they got inland, however, they faced a still-potent German army. (*Coast Guard photo in the National Archives: 26-G-2412*)

Infantrymen celebrate Christmas of 1944 by opening up gift packages of food. (*Army photo in the National Archives: SC 326564*)

coming over, headed for London. At first we didn't know what they were, and for about two weeks we went practically sleepless. Our mission was to send up a wall of fire for the German rockets to fly into. Eventually, I think we knocked down a couple or three of the V-1s. And the Royal Air Force pilots did their part too. They'd fly up alongside the buzz bombs and tip them off course with their wings.

A few weeks after D-Day we were sent to embarkation ports and climbed into LSTs for the journey across the English Channel and our initiation into combat. We were cooped up on board ship for forty-eight hours, so we spent the time playing poker. Then we were landed on Utah Beach, which was secure by then but still littered with such things as burned-out tanks and the remnants of German 88-millimeter guns. The LSTs sent us and our equipment ashore when the tide was out, so we didn't even get our feet wet. It was no problem at all—quite a contrast to what the assault

forces had experienced not that long before. In fact, the people already on the beach hooted and hollered at us as we arrived in France in full combat gear and camouflage.

We spent a couple of days there de-waterproofing our guns and rolling stock. We had to take off the grease that had been applied liberally to protect metal surfaces against corrosion. Then we were assigned to provide antiaircraft protection for the buildup of an ammunition dump. After that, from time to time, we were assigned to protect various objectives, such as a bridge or a headquarters. We'd had a lot of recognition training, so we knew what the various Allied and German planes looked like. We considered the Heinkel light bomber to be the biggest threat.

When the breakout came that summer, we were attached to an armored division and rode in amongst the tanks on the way to the Brittany peninsula. We were around Brest until the Germans in that area surrendered, and then we convoyed all the way across France to join up with the army elements in Belgium and Luxembourg. We lived in various places: the gun crews made dugouts if they were in one place for any length of time; sometimes we holed up in abandoned farm houses; other times, we were invited to stay by the inhabitants. When we got to Bastogne, Belgium, my battery's headquarters was in a château. A countess and some children still lived there; the count had been seized by the Germans, and we never knew what they did with him. It was a very nice six-week period until the Germans literally kicked us out. Up till then we had come to think that we were unbeatable. In fact, we were overconfident, as the Germans demonstrated in the Battle of the Bulge.

My platoon had been set up near Bastogne, covering the east side of the road between Houffalize and Neufchâteau. Another platoon in our battery covered the west side. We went about twenty miles south, to Neufchâteau, as the 101st Airborne Division was coming in. We were there for a few days shortly before Christmas of 1944, until we were ordered to Libramont-Chevigny, which was inside the Germans' main line of resistance.

I was reluctant to go, but we made it. Armed with two quadruple .50-calibers, we reported to an army colonel who—with a smattering of men from various front-line units, a few tank destroyers, and others—was protecting the town in the event the Germans moved south. With our guns intended to fire against aircraft, we were assigned to keep German infantry from infiltrating the railroad marshaling yards. I think there must have been about a foot of snow on the ground. The temperature got down to about 5 degrees above zero at night. I remember lying on the warm hood of a truck when I was trying to sleep.

We didn't see any ground troops, but shortly after Christmas we were badly bombed. I think it was a single Me-262—the first German jet plane—although I don't know for sure because I was about two hundred yards away with my Jeep and driver. The plane came out of the sun and dropped two 50- or 100-kilogram bombs on one of our quadruple .50s; it was sited in a schoolyard. There were two huge eruptions, and the trailer and guns were destroyed. Three of the men in my platoon died, along with perhaps a dozen others; many more were wounded. The three were Tech 5 Carlisle Klossner, from Wisconsin; Private First Class Irving Kahaner, a boy from Brooklyn; and Private Willis Edwards, who came from a farm in Georgia.

A real tragedy of war is that lots of good people are killed—on both sides—and those of us who survived bear the burden of that memory for the rest of our lives. Many times I've thought back with a sense of guilt that I made it when they didn't. I'd been at that gun position only five minutes before it was hit, and I've wondered if there was something I did—or failed to do—that might have led to what happened. All these years later, I can't remember the names of many of those with whom I served during World War II, but I would still recognize the faces of those three soldiers if they could somehow walk in the door.

ROBERT ERWIN LEE (1918–) grew up in Minneapolis, Minnesota. After entering the army he received training at Fort Meade, Maryland, before heading overseas to be part of an antiaircraft artillery unit. He was discharged from active duty with the army in 1946 as a first lieutenant and returned to civilian life. He then pursued a career as a chemist and later as an animal feeds nutritionist in the feed and fertilizer industry, from which he retired in 1980. Currently, he lives with his wife, Helen, in Bloomington, Minnesota, where he enjoys reading, playing golf, and following sports. He maintains an active interest in military history. (*Courtesy Robert Lee*)

Earlier we read Admiral Ruge's high-level account of the German reaction to the invasion of France, both in the planning and preparation stages and later in attempting to repulse the attack when it came. The following memoir provides another German viewpoint, that of a destroyer officer who for a long time maintained a sense of confidence and then saw his illusions crumble. He makes clear that his allegiance was not to Nazism but instead to his German homeland. It was worth fighting for, even if that meant shedding his naval uniform and going ashore to fight as a soldier. His father, a man in his sixties, had been conscripted into the German army late in the war and sent to the Western Front, where he was captured. For the son, doing anything less than he could for his country was unthinkable. And so it was that the strategies of Hitler, his generals, and his admirals were translated into the desperate circumstances in which individual Germans such as Hans Degelow tried to fight on.

A SENSE OF DUTY TO THE FATHERLAND

By Hans J. Degelow

Although there were relatively few German naval forces in the immediate vicinity of Normandy during the Allied invasion, those that were there put up a stout defense. Not many of the vessels and men survived because they were matched against such overwhelming strength. They had little help: the bulk of the German surface fleet—weak as it had become—was bottled up in the Baltic Sea. Allied air superiority kept those ships from moving to the site of the invasion through either the Skagerrak or the Kiel Canal. Moreover, the perception was that the major threat to Germany would come from the east. The barbarians of the Soviet Union were viewed as much more dangerous than any threat that could come from the west.

In June of 1944 I was on temporary duty away from my ship, the destroyer *Z-30*, which was operating in the fjord at Olso, Norway. I myself was then in torpedo officers' school at Flensburg, which was also the site of the German Naval Academy. It was a six-week course, and I had left the ship about a week prior to the invasion. The German army had decided to recall all the troops that were in Norway and send them to fight against the Soviets. That was seen as the most urgent situation, because the fighting was so difficult there. Those destroyers stationed in Norway provided the escort while the soldiers were being transferred across the Skagerrak, first to Denmark and then to the eastern front.

During this time in the school at Flensburg, I was

Degelow's destroyer, the *Z-30*, has a bone in her teeth as she steams at twenty-five knots in Oslo Fjord, Norway, in May 1944. (*Courtesy Hans J. Degelow*)

living on board a beautiful former cruise ship called the *Patria*. It was the most modern motor ship of those that operated in the German tourist trade to the Caribbean before the war started. Overseas travel was a privilege for the very rich in the 1930s, so we had luxurious accommodations for our schooling. We lived in two-man staterooms, and our surroundings at the time were completely peaceful. If I hadn't come from Norway, it would have been difficult to realize a war was in progress. The *Patria* still had the regular waiters and stewards to take care of us. The only difference from her previous existence was that her peacetime colors had been covered with dull-gray camouflage paint. The ship could have gone out of port at any time and left on a cruise, because she had been maintained in a condition of readiness. All this was quite comfortable for someone such as I, who was twenty years old and had just made lieutenant.

I must admit that the meals were rather plain because of food shortages. We had all the bread we could eat with perhaps a little bit of butter and jam. We had coffee to drink but no sausage with our breakfast. One morning we were sitting down to eat, with the meal all laid out and linen on the tables, when we heard the news that the Allies had just invaded Normandy. Of course, that hit like lightning. But our spirits were still high, because we didn't yet realize how dismal conditions were throughout the country. Our school was such an enclave that we were really in sheltered surroundings. We said, "Oh, that's all right. Let them come in for a while, and then we'll really knock them out." When I think back today on our reaction, it was unbelievably naive.

As I've thought about it since then, there were probably several reasons for our isolation. First of all, navy life tends to be that way. Being on board a ship takes you out of the mainstream of events. Another factor was that we didn't get to see newspapers. What we got was all channeled news that had been censored by the German propaganda organization. We were being fed a type of news that didn't really give us the true facts. It never gave us the whole story. In a way, we were off in a separate world, just as we had been in Norway. You know, give a sailor a ship and a gun and he is not afraid, if he is a good man. He cannot imagine that on the other side, against his little gun, there are a hundred big guns. You only realize that when the enemy starts blasting away at you.

Until the very end of the war, the morale of all the units I was associated with was very high. There was no defeatism or rebelling. Our motivation was patriotism. We were young and confident, and all we knew was what we had been told. In retrospect, we were the abused generation in Germany. We had been trained and educated to fight and die if need be. That is the sad part of it, as all of us see it today. Only afterward did we

Men of the *Z-30* do maintenance work on one of the ship's torpedoes. (*Courtesy Hans J. Degelow*)

learn about what had really gone on in the concentration camps.

It angers me to think that we were made the fodder to advance such a dismal ideology. Nazism was not really an issue at all within the German navy. In fact, calling a fellow navy man a Nazi was the same as calling him by a curse word. In a way, we took a rather snobbish attitude toward the Nazis. Many of the high-ranking party members were from the lower, uneducated classes and had made their way up by means of brutality.

When I finished school at Flensburg, I was given

Degelow poses by his gun mount. The 5.9-inch gun was really more than the destroyer could handle. (*Courtesy Hans J. Degelow*)

The battleship *Tirpitz* steams in a Norwegian fjord in mid-March 1944. Degelow's ship was also there as part of the "fleet in being" designed to tie down Allied naval forces. (*Courtesy Hans J. Degelow*)

leave to go home for a while because the *Z-30* was in a shipyard at Swinemünde to receive boiler repairs and to be fitted with more modern equipment. I had about three weeks at home in Luckenwalde, in what later became East Germany. It was the most enjoyable vacation I had during the entire war. I spent some time with one of my school buddies who was at home because he had been badly shot up in Russia.

One thing I remember from that period is being outside in broad daylight and watching hundreds of British and American bombers fly over in formation on their way to Berlin, which was about thirty miles to the north. On their way home, the bombers sometimes unloaded their leftovers on us. That's how our house once lost half its roof. I must say that seeing those planes fly over made us a little bit leery about our prospects for success in the war.

At the same time, I felt uneasy about being home because I wanted to get back and be with my buddies on board ship. And, of course, I felt a sense of duty. I was strong and energetic, and I was the fighting kind. But I should also say that we Germans were not fanatical in the sense that the Japanese were. There's no comparison. We were ready to die if it had to be, but we would not consciously go on a suicidal mission.

One of the happiest days of my life was when I arrived at Swinemünde, an important German naval base in the Baltic Sea. There I met the *Z-30* after she came in from operations, and I felt I was back home again. The ship got more repairs, and then we went out into the eastern Baltic for extensive weapons practice, including both guns and torpedoes. It reminded me of a peacetime training exercise in that sense, but there

was another factor that was quite different. We could look up and see the vapor trails made by high-flying enemy Flying Fortresses and Liberators as they approached the heart of Germany. We tried counting those vapor trails, but there were so many that we finally gave up. It was humiliating to see so many American bombers headed toward our homeland. But they never bothered our ships. They went about their business, and we went about ours.

At that same time I got my first look at the V-2 rockets in flight, because Peenemünde, where they were built, was not far from Swinemünde. At first we couldn't figure out what these new weapons were. They were top secret, and nobody had told us anything about them. Finally, the word came through that these were tests of some of the new wonder weapons that the Führer's scientists were developing. We saw them go up practically vertically until they disappeared out of sight. Earlier, while on furlough at home, I had seen my first jet plane, an Me-262. It was going fast and was rather quiet; the whole thing was quite amazing, another of our wonder weapons. We didn't realize at that time that shortage of fuel would keep these new weapons from becoming effective.

After our training we were assigned exclusively to escort duty between Norway and Denmark. By this time the situation in Russia had become really desperate for the German army. The transport ships were loaded to the fullest so that as many soldiers as possible could be sent forward. I'm proud to say that we were in full fighting condition, still able to make a top speed of around thirty-six or thirty-seven knots.

We operated almost completely at night, not know-

This torpedo training ship, the *Hugo Zeye*, is shown at Flensburg in the summer of 1944 when she was training Degelow and his classmates. (*Courtesy Hans J. Degelow*)

ing that the British had us under radar surveillance the whole time. Every single night, we came under heavy air attack. The Fourth of July is nothing compared to the fireworks we saw on convoy duty. What we didn't realize was that the British were also air-dropping a network of floating mines that were apparently connected to each other with cables. In the middle of October, during the course of the convoy operations, the *Z-30* hit a mine in Oslo Fjord. It was caught on the propeller guard for several seconds until it finally went off. The explosion damaged the ship and caused heavy loss of life. We went into a shipyard in Oslo, and that essentially ended the war for our destroyer. The stern was badly damaged—nearly broken off, in fact. One of the propeller shafts was badly bent and the other was loose in its bearings.

By then we were feeling demoralized. We didn't yet have the feeling that all was lost, but we did feel that much was lost. We really had little in the way of duty, so we began to live a life of happy complacency. It was a wait-and-see period, but the German propaganda was sufficiently optimistic so that we still had a sense of hope. We nursed the dream that the Führer had still more wonder weapons up his sleeve that he was waiting to unleash on the unsuspecting enemies and finish them off. That was the final straw that we clung to.

Actually, we enjoyed it there in Oslo, and I have to admit that I did fraternize with the Norwegians. I spent the last Christmas of the war with a Norwegian family that were very likely German sympathizers. They were very hospitable, like a home away from home. I still have a warm spot for Norwegians. I learned a bit of the Norwegian language, rode the street cars, and blended in as best I could.

Then I came to my senses at the beginning of 1945, and my feeling of duty to country reasserted itself. I realized that the British, Americans, and French had gotten deep into Germany. They had invaded my homeland. Once again, I volunteered. I left the ship and went from Norway to Denmark by destroyer, which was difficult because of the intense Allied air activity over the Skagerrak. I then hitchhiked back to Germany in order to join the fighting forces of the army. I did it because I loved my fatherland. I have no use for the poor chap who cannot see it that way.

At least I had an *idea* of what I should be doing on land, because our naval officer training had included an intense segment on infantry tactics and weapons. In a post at Glückstadt on the Elbe River, I was equipped with a gray army uniform and an infantry rifle. I had a platoon of perhaps thirty or thirty-five men under my command. My rifle was one of the most modern type, which raised my spirits and made me optimistic again. Little did I realize that the British were essentially in control of the area, and gentlemen's agreements were apparently in force so that the fighting had practically stopped. We were contained within an area but not actually prisoners of war.

After a time, we learned of Hitler's suicide. Then we knew it was the end. We felt a sense of relief when Admiral Karl Dönitz became head of state, because we believed that the country finally had an honest man in charge of the government.

The day we learned of the German surrender, May

8, was a day of extreme sadness for all of us. That was a very emotional thing. The big concern for those of us in charge was that there might be an outbreak of mass suicide. The danger was great, and it did happen in the case of some individuals. I must say that the temptation was great for me as well. We had been humiliated. We had lost all that our nation had fought for during those past six years.

We cried for a while, but, fortunately, it was a warm summer. The sun was bright, we were young, and we were a closely knit group. As we thought about things, we realized that there were many tomorrows ahead of us. I am still enjoying those tomorrows today.

Hans J. Degelow (1923–) joined the German navy in 1941, at the age of seventeen, to pursue an officer's career in naval architecture. In 1942 he was one of twenty-six cadets in training on board the heavy cruiser *Prinz Eugen*. After a midshipman's education at the naval school in Flensburg-Mürwik and training in torpedo weaponry, he was assigned to duty in the destroyer *Z-30* from April 1943 to April 1945. He spent half the time as a midshipman and half as an officer, receiving his commission as Leutnant zur See on April 1, 1944. In 1946 he returned to his hometown of Luckenwalde and narrowly escaped a Soviet roundup of returning officers. He managed to slip through the Iron Curtain to West Germany, where he learned toolmaking. In 1950 he immigrated to the United States, first to work as a tool and die maker, and later to study engineering at the University of Wisconsin in Milwaukee. He has remained in this country ever since, recently retiring as a chief engineer in machine tool and automation design. For the past thirty years Mr. Degelow has lived in Brookfield, Wisconsin, with the philosophy that "the best is yet to come." (*Courtesy Hans J. Degelow*)

Once the fighting moved inland from the Normandy beaches, so also did the American naval command. A multitude of chores remained to be accomplished, both political and military. The navy needed to reestablish relations with its French allies, and it had to prepare for its role in the postwar occupation of a conquered Germany. On a more concrete note, it had to join in mopping up areas still in German hands, and it had to plan for the final push across the Rhine River.

Regular officers, such as Commander Donald MacDonald, were involved in making the plans for the final stages of the war in Europe. As they decided how to move the army into the heart of Germany, in many cases it was up to reserve officers to execute those plans. In consultation with MacDonald, Norris Houghton, a Naval Reserve officer from Princeton, wrote an account in 1945 to describe the process by which a fellow Ivy Leaguer, Lieutenant Commander William Leide of Yale, worked with General George Patton's Third Army. Leide was officially designated Commander Task Unit 122.5.2, one of the several subdivisions of Task Group 122.5. Landing craft had been a key to getting troops ashore in France and other ports; now they were needed one more time.

Finally, a Naval Reserve officer was on hand to facilitate the surrender ceremony when the large Allied effort initiated on D-Day came to a highly successful conclusion. Captain Harry Butcher served as General Eisenhower's "Boswell" during the war, recording from close range the thoughts and actions of the officer who had united the Allied coalition both politically and militarily. The sea services played a large role in facilitating victory in the European theater: transporting the soldiers across the Atlantic and the English Channel and providing logistic support once they were ashore. It was symbolic that an officer in a naval uniform should be present to report on the achievement of total victory.

MOVING INTO GERMANY

By Rear Admiral Donald J. MacDonald, U.S. Navy (Retired)

As soon as the Allies liberated Paris in the summer of 1944, General Eisenhower set up his SHAEF headquarters at nearby Versailles. Rear Admiral Kirk, having completed his duty as Commander Western Naval Task Force for the invasion of Normandy, had been reassigned as Commander U.S. Naval Forces France and naval commander for Eisenhower. The naval headquarters were near the Arc de Triomphe, and we lived out at Saint-Germain. Our task was to work with Eisenhower directly, and the U.S. commander, in order to handle any U.S. naval operations that might be required. This resulted in daily meetings with Eisenhower's staff.

By then, even though Paris had been liberated, there were still pockets of Germans in the Channel Islands and around Bordeaux, in the Gironde region. We had to open the blocked ports of Cherbourg and Le Havre and make plans for the opening of the port of Antwerp, Belgium. Rear Admiral John Wilkes, who had trained the landing craft for Normandy, was now in charge of the ports operation in that area. After things settled down a little bit, I began to work with the French to try to get the French navy back into the picture to take over some of these ports and to help clear out pockets of German soldiers left behind by the Allied advance.

The stimulus for clearing out Germans from the Channel Islands was that they sent out raiding forces to Cherbourg and caused problems. It was a challenge to get rid of the Germans because we couldn't bomb the Channel Islands and risk harming the British subjects still living there. So we had to use a slow process, sending out raids and also trying to intercept the E-boats the Germans sent out at night.

With the Allies on the Continent in force, there was terrific fighting in the north. The British were encountering great difficulty in moving, and Churchill insisted that the Americans not move any faster than the British could keep up with, so that everybody would get to Germany at the same time. By the fall, planning was moving forward on getting the advancing armies into Germany and across the Rhine River. This is where the naval forces had to play quite a part. We assumed that all the Rhine bridges would be destroyed, so we would have to find another means of getting the troops across. I was heavily involved in the planning and had to make frequent trips to General Bradley's Twelfth Army Group headquarters in Luxembourg. We needed to coordinate the requirements for the three different armies that he controlled—the First, Third, and Ninth.

We would go in through the ports of Le Havre and Antwerp, which had been opened with some difficulty. Minesweepers had been active there because of the mines left behind. The task was made even more difficult because the German V-1 rockets were a terrible nuisance for quite a time. The plan called for bringing in two types of landing craft, thirty-six-foot-long LCVPs and the fifty-foot-long LCMs. We had to get the craft and their crews into Le Havre and Antwerp and then move them to join up with the armies. In exploring ways to move the landing craft, it worked out that we could haul them on trailers, the kind used for moving tanks. In order to camouflage the whole operation, we moved the boats at night, and their navy crews all wore army uniforms. I don't know how capable German intelligence was that late in the war, but it seemed the Germans didn't really know what we were doing.

All this planning was being done in the tactical headquarters at Twelfth Army Group. One person Kirk used to take along to what they called the chief of staff meetings while we were in France was his aide, McGeorge Bundy, because Bundy kept him on the right track all the time. About eight of us lived in the same château, and I observed that Bundy was one of the most brilliant men I'd ever run into. We had a flag lieutenant and flag secretary on the staff, but Bundy was the guy that Kirk always took along to the meetings. He was sort of an alter ego to Kirk, and he spoke fluent French. In fact, I even got him to instruct all our officers in French so they could make out a little bit better. After Kirk and Bundy had been to these meetings, planning would boil down to a lower level, and I would get involved with the operations people in Versailles.

We had planned to move forward around Novem-

Looking like fish out of water, a row of LCVPs assigned to the Third Army is overhauled and painted on the parade ground of a French cavalry school. (*Navy photo in the National Archives: 80-G-48605*)

ber, so we could get troops to the other side of the Rhine before winter set in. But we were delayed by the requirement to avoid getting ahead of the British; Eisenhower had to hold back Bradley and Patton. The Allies were also delayed by the Battle of the Bulge in December. We didn't make the actual river crossing until March 1945.

We didn't know exactly where the crossing would be, but we had to get all the equipment moved forward to accommodate the troops and tanks and trucks. We wanted enough of the soldiers to be able to get across on the landing craft that they could hold the far side of the river and enable the engineers to go ahead and build temporary bridges. The navy was involved in that as well, because we had to figure out how to protect the bridges from floating mines and other hazards coming down the river. For that we used protective booms to hold netting that would keep the temporary bridges

clear. We had to swing the booms across above the current. Navy boom people helped out on that operation.

In looking back, I am pleased with the way things went. The landing craft were very useful in the beginning, before the temporary bridges were built. They served essentially as ferryboats and moved a lot of troops very quickly. To a degree, we were prepared for a condition that didn't come about completely, because not all the bridges had been blown up. The one at Remagen was only damaged, and so some of our troops were able to move across there. Having done that, our troops were able to spread up and down the river on the eastern side and facilitate the crossing of those to follow.

One of the other aspects of our advance was the possibility that a lot of Germans would try to escape into Switzerland, across Lake Constance. Since we anticipated this, we were able to put some patrol boats down there, manned by the French. We had to get the boats and equip them with searchlights, guns, and other equipment so they would be able to detect and stop the Germans.

In April we got the French navy further back into the swing. The army had given us a priority task: to open up the Gironde River so it could get urgently needed supplies of railroad ties into the port of Bordeaux. Rear Admiral Joseph Rue was in command of a Free French force that included the battleship *Lorraine*, the cruiser *Duquesne*, and some smaller ships. They also took in some minesweepers to sweep the sea area. We coordinated with the Army Air Forces in bombing the pockets of Germans. I did a lot of the planning work on that operation, and the Chief of Staff of the French navy, Rear Admiral André Lemonnier, was back in command by then. He was a great friend of Admiral

Kirk, and he enjoyed playing tennis—as did Kirk. Admiral Kirk and I played tennis frequently with Admiral Lemonnier and his aide. Admiral Lemonnier played barefooted.

The French were most friendly and were eager to do anything we wanted them to do. I'm sure the basic attitude of the people on Eisenhower's staff was not to pay too much attention to the French navy because they didn't want to be bothered. With that backdrop, I had to sell the idea all the way up, including McGeorge Bundy, Captain Bob English, and Admiral Kirk. English was dead against it. I argued that this operation against the German pockets could be useful in helping restore the spirit and morale of the French navy. Kirk was reluctant because he saw the operation as a waste of time. I got the idea that it wasn't a big enough operation for him. In a way, Kirk loved publicity. He was a real gentleman, but he was egotistical. And if he

Belgian schoolchildren watch as an LCVP, secured to a cradle, is hoisted aboard an army truck. (*Navy photo in the National Archives: 80-G-48604*)

Tank haulers carry LCVPs through the narrow streets of a Belgian village on their way to Germany and the Rhine. (*Navy photo in the National Archives: 80-G-48600*)

let the French run this operation, they—rather than he—would get the credit. I felt it would be valuable precisely because the French would get credit for it, and it was successful in that regard.

While these things were happening, Admiral Kirk's staff started working in conjunction with Vice Admiral Robert Ghormley, who was then prospective Commander U.S. Naval Forces in Germany. I had been Ghormley's aide in London in 1940–41 when we were special naval observers to learn from the Royal Navy's operations in the initial stages of the war. That was before the United States had become an active combatant. Now Ghormley was again in London, preparing for the U.S. Navy's part in the occupation of a soon-to-be-defeated foe. The United States was drafting plans of what would be happening after the surrender: de-Nazification, demilitarization, and possibly de-industrialization. We were working specifically on the disarming of the German navy and dividing it up

among the British, Soviets, and Americans. I didn't think it was right to try to destroy Germany as a nation. Even though we were winning, they had been good opponents. The whole country wasn't made up of murderers.

One of those who shared my views about not destroying Germany was Charles Lindbergh. I had met with him in Washington in the summer of 1944, partly because he had been out in the Pacific with my brother, an army pilot, earlier in the war. Now, in the spring of 1945, Lindbergh showed up in Paris. He was over there in some sort of advisory capacity for the army, probably to tell them what he knew about the Luftwaffe, which he had observed in detail before the war. As a matter of fact, the army really appreciated his help on a lot of things. One of the things that bothered him a great deal was that he couldn't go back to London because of his well-publicized isolationist speeches. At the beginning of the war he had indicated that the Germans were so strong that the British probably couldn't handle them. So even though he was in Paris, he couldn't get a visa for England.

Once the Allied forces had gone into Germany, the surrender was concluded in May. I spent a few months on General Eisenhower's staff and then moved over to become Admiral Ghormley's deputy chief of staff in his new role as American naval commander in defeated Germany. I had been with him at the beginning of the war and rejoined him shortly after the end. The challenges were different, but we still had plenty of them as we looked forward to a postwar world.

DONALD JOHN MACDONALD (1908–) graduated from the Naval Academy in the Class of 1931 and served in the *Hulbert, Truxtun, California,* and *Salinas* during the remainder of the decade before reporting for duty in OpNav and additional service as a White House aide. In 1940 he went to England as a special naval observer. In 1942 he became the first executive officer of the *Fletcher*-class destroyer *O'Bannon*. In January 1943 he became the ship's commanding officer and established a brilliant combat record in the Solomon Islands. For his service on board the *O'Bannon* he was awarded two Navy Crosses, two Legions of Merit, three Silver Stars, and two Bronze Stars. After that he was on the staff of Commander in Chief and later Commander U.S. Naval Forces France and U.S. Naval Forces Germany. After duty in operational intelligence in the Navy Department, MacDonald commanded the presidential yacht *Williamsburg* for Harry S Truman from 1948 to 1951 and later the attack cargo ship *Marquette*. In the 1950s he was a department head at the Naval Academy, commanded Destroyer Squadron 34, and had subsequent duty on the staff of the Chief of Naval Operations before retiring in 1959. Admiral MacDonald lives in Washington, D.C. (*Courtesy Rear Admiral Donald J. MacDonald*)

ACROSS THE RHINE

By Lieutenant Norris Houghton, U.S. Naval Reserve

Toward the first of December the pin in the map in Paris that stood for [Lieutenant Commander William] Leide's unit [en route overland from Le Havre] came to rest in eastern France at Toul, up a few miles above Nancy and a good two hundred miles from the smell of salt water. But Toul is near the Moselle and the Moselle is a lot like the Rhine, so it was a good spot for a training site. The unit was given space in a French army post barrack . . . and the process of conversion began in earnest.

By conversion I mean turning a navy crew into a working unit of an army corps. For this was to be a joint army-navy project in fact as well as on paper. Vice Admiral Alan Kirk, USN, Commander of U.S. Naval Forces in France, who had been their commander in Normandy the summer before, now made these Rhine units into a task group under his present command and then turned them temporarily over to the army. When and where they entered the battle would be for the army commanders, not the navy, to say.

The army gave them khaki uniforms, provided rations from army depots, and had the gray-blue hulls of the LCVPs and LCMs repainted olive drab. If you'd gone through Toul last December you'd never have known the U.S. Navy was there (which was the point—to keep their presence a secret and make them a part of the whole); unless, of course, you went to the barrack itself and, asking for the commanding officer, were told by what you took for a good G.I., "He's not aboard at the moment, sir, but you'll find his yeoman on the second deck."

With the army they also worked out their training program. The navy unit was attached to an Engineer Group, for the engineers build the bridges and a boat is the next thing to a bridge in the army's mind. Together they planned how to get the LCVPs and LCMs loaded on trucks, get them overland to the river, into the water, and functioning to maximum advantage. All these things they experimented on in and around the Moselle. They tried, for example, fifteen different ways of launching the boats off the big flatbed trailers into

the water. (When the time actually came, they improvised a sixteenth and hitherto untried technique!)

Leide thought they'd have but a few weeks of this training, but he didn't count—any more than anyone else—on the German breakthrough in the Ardennes which knocked things off schedule a bit; so the period of training and waiting turned out to be nearer three months than three weeks.

Long periods of inactivity are hard on everyone, including the biographers, so there's not much to tell about the days at Toul; except, perhaps, about that midwinter day when the Moselle suddenly swept with full flood strength over her banks, carried the LCVPs away from their moorings, and over a dam and deposited them, when the flood waters abated, like the Ark on Ararat in the middle of startled farmers' fields. U.S. Navy reconnaissance parties out searching for their boats in the meadows of eastern France were an Alice-in-Wonderland sight indeed.

But finally the Ardennes bulge was flattened and General Patton charged forward across the German

Sailors check in their navy gear in preparation for wearing army uniforms during the journey to the Rhine. (*Navy photo in the National Archives: 80-G-48610*)

This picture, showing the Remagen railroad bridge down in the Rhine, symbolizes the reason navy landing craft were transported overland to Germany. Here an LCVP carries a Jeep upstream. (*Navy photo in the National Archives: 80-G-309015*)

Palatinate. Before anyone had quite caught his breath, there he was on the Rhine. Now Patton is not one to sit still for long. On Monday, March 19, his headquarters ordered transportation sent down to Toul to transport his landlocked navy; on Wednesday it ordered the unit to get under way; on Thursday night the first crossing was made.

It was 160 miles from Toul to Oppenheim and Nierstein in Germany, where Patton planned to make that first crossing: 160 miles of roads fought over and bombed during the days and weeks before, roads now as flooded with Patton's armor and motorized columns as the Moselle had been by its winter rains. Roads that avoided towns and too much traffic had to be chosen, although whenever they had to hit a highway, the combat MPs received radioed instructions from their traffic control posts to let the navy boats sweep through along with the top-priority vehicles.

It took more, though, than the wave of an MP's hand to carry the navy overland to the Rhine. The same problems that had to be faced in getting the boats from Le Havre to Toul raised their heads once more. That was why back roads were chosen. But, at that, villages and narrow bridges could not always be avoided. Corners of houses or their overhanging buttresses had to be knocked off at several too-tortuous street corners of German hamlets. Stone or concrete road markers had to be pulled out like aching teeth from a number of sharp curves. All this took time, and because the closer you came to the Rhine and into country that but three days before had been in German hands, the more uncertain everyone was of obstacles to be found along the newly captured roads. So, the harder it was to negotiate those last miles.

Lieutenant Commander Leide went forward into Germany with his executive officer and the Engineer

Group commander to reconnoitre for suitable sites. He left Toul on Wednesday morning. By mid-afternoon the same day the convoy got under way. Perched up in the boats dodging the treetops and subsisting on K rations rode the boat crews, for there was no time to wait for the proper transportation that had been ordered for the sailors. All that night and through the next day they rumbled along the roads.

Leide, meanwhile, tramping the west bank of the Rhine between Nierstein and Oppenheim, could look across to a flat willow-lined far shore, lying deceptively quiet in the spring sunshine nine hundred feet away. On the near side a line of little Rhenish summer hotels and peak-gabled houses faced the river. He chose one of them to house his crew, and a spot at the edge of town where the boats could be dropped into the water.

The day wore on. H-hour was set for ten o'clock that night. The navy was to start launching its boats at H+4. At ten o'clock the boats hadn't yet arrived. The first wave of infantry was just slipping into the little army rubber assault boats that were to be used for the initial sneak crossing, when Leide sent his "exec" Jeeping down the blacked-out roads to locate the hulls towering in the moonlight, to order half of them held back and to guide the others down to the water.

At H+4 the boats rolled down to the water's edge, making their entrance exactly on cue. There was no chance even to brief the officers who arrived with the boats. In the darkness Leide came up to them. "It's just like the Moselle" was all he had time to say, and they set to work. Everything was quiet. Patton had decided to send his first troops across without artillery preparation or air coverage. The enemy was quiet too. Either he wasn't there at all or else he hadn't caught on to what was happening.

At about 2:30 A.M. the motor of the first LCVP rasped out on the night air. Every twenty minutes or half hour thereafter another would announce its presence in the water by the chug of its engine. It began to sound like a barnyard waking up. Off through the chemical smoke screen, which by now had been laid, a bulldozer was crunching around the bank making a loading site. As each boat hit the water, it made at once for the spot where the troops and vehicles were lined up waiting to get across. At still another spot the engineers had already started a heavy pontoon bridge; you couldn't tell exactly where because of the smoke that covered everything and through which the moon had a hard time penetrating.

When daylight came the Jerries woke up with a noisy start. From behind that willow-lined opposite bank 88[-millimeter shell]s began pouring into the area. They zeroed in on one of the launching sites, but by that time all the boats were in the river. Mortar shells plopped in the water and crunched on the shore. And as though that weren't enough, dive-bombers began to roar in. When one loading site was pinpointed, the boats were moved to another one. Bluejackets learned quickly from G.I.s the value of a foxhole and how to get in to one in no time flat. But for the boys out in midstream there was no place to take shelter, so they just kept going—scooting along in their LCVPs that looked just about as they had in the Plymouth Harbor, but invested with a new sombre dignity (or was it was my imagination), just as their crews seemed to have drawn on some hitherto unsuspected reserve of courage and devotion to duty—as sailors always do.

In spite of everything the Germans could do, all day long men and more men, vehicles and more vehicles poured across the Rhine in the LCMs and LCVPs. It took about six to eight minutes to load one of the craft, get it across and unloaded, put aboard an ambulance or something else coming back, and return. I don't know of a ferry service in history that has worked so hard or so fast. At the end of the first twenty-four hours those two dozen little boats with their own crews totaling less than a hundred had transported fifteen thousand troops and more than one thousand vehicles across the Rhine. The rapid buildup that the army needed and for which it had sought the navy's aid was accomplished.

By the end of that first day the army engineers, who had been working just as hard as the navy, completed a bridge, and the major burden of the traffic that was pressing ever harder could be shifted from the little boats to the heavy pontoon structures. Leide sent part of each crew back to the little hotel to stretch out in their bedrolls and get some sleep. After their thirty-six-hour nonstop dash from France to the Rhine, they had followed up with more than two hundred trips from shore to shore under fire in the next twenty-four hours.

But Jerry saw no reason to let the boys relax. Just as they hit the sack, an 88-millimeter shell came walloping in through the roof. It turned out to be a dud, so they weren't all blown sky-high, but one of the boys happened to be in its path as it came plummeting down through the ceiling; now he has no left hand.

Leide had been told, you remember, to bring only half his boats to Nierstein. The next day he found out why. Patton was going to throw other corps of his racing army across the Rhine at other places; and half the boats that were bivouacked (if boats can bivouac) in the woods not far from Bad Kreuznach were ordered to go to Boppard, the other half to St. Goar and Oberwesel.

I won't talk much about those crossings for they followed pretty well the pattern I've just described, except that if you don't know the Rhine around Boppard and St. Goar, you can't realize what a really remarkable feat it was to get the boats down to the river there. For this is the Siegfried country, the Lorelei country, the castles-on-the-Rhine country. The river

To facilitate the movement of traffic across the Rhine, the army erected floating bridges. Here an LCVP pushes a bridge section into position near Remagen. (*Navy photo in the National Archives: 80-G-309016*)

Navy LCMs ferry tanks across the Rhine on March 24, 1945. (*Navy photo in the National Archives: 80-G-306927*)

flows through a gorge; its banks are almost sheer promontories of rock and crazily perpendicular vineyards. Every ten miles or so a narrow road manages to cut its way twisting and turning down to the river. It was by these roads that General Patton had decided to bring his men and armor and supplies and the boats to get them across the river.

But as the first rays of the morning sun slanted through the pine woods atop the crags of the Rhine's west bank, the navy started its tortuous descent to the "beach." In a few hours it was there. Once again, incredulous GIs exclaimed, "Jeezus, how did those great big navy boats get here?" And they filed aboard, through the fog of smoke, while the artillery pounded above their heads and echoed along the mountaintops that used to echo the cry of the Valkyries: the army and navy together at their last water barrier in Europe—and across it.

CHARLES NORRIS HOUGHTON (1909–) graduated from Princeton University in 1931, then joined the University Players before going to New York City, where he stage-managed and designed a number of Broadway productions. In 1934 he went to Russia on a Guggenheim Foundation fellowship, which led to his book *Moscow Rehearsals*. In 1942 Mr. Houghton was commissioned as a Naval Reserve officer. He was involved in the turnover of the cruiser *Milwaukee* to the Soviets, served on the staff of Vice Admiral Alan Kirk, and was part of the support group for the 1945 Yalta Conference because of his Russian-language ability. After the war he returned to the theater in New York and also had a brief stint in live TV drama at CBS. In the early 1950s Mr. Houghton was instrumental in the founding of the Phoenix Theatre, the spearhead of the off-Broadway not-for-profit theater movement. Mr. Houghton had an academic career as well, teaching at Columbia University and Vassar College before becoming first dean of the division of theater arts and film at the Purchase campus of the State University of New York. In the 1970s he was president of the American Council for the Arts in Education and worked with a panel that produced the acclaimed report *Coming to Our Senses*. He has written six books, including his memoir *Entrances and Exits*, published in 1991 by Limelight Editions. Mr. Houghton lives in New York City. (*Courtesy Norris Houghton*)

SURRENDER

By Captain Harry C. Butcher, U.S. Naval Reserve

About 1:30 this morning I was called to the phone. It was [WAC Major] Ruth Briggs [secretary of Eisenhower's chief of staff, Lieutenant General Walter Bedell Smith]. She said, "The big party is on," that General Ike already had arrived, and that I, as custodian of the fountain pens, should hurry over to the headquarters.

"How could the war be ended without the pens?" she gibed.

At the front door [of the school that was to serve as surrender site] there was a hornet's nest of correspondents waiting to get into the school building. If I had good sense, or had seen them first, I would have driven around the schoolhouse into the courtyard and sneaked into the offices the back way. They had driven up from Paris on the chance that they would be permitted to cover the ceremony, despite the fact that a pool of seventeen already was on hand for the job.

I respected their enterprise, but from the standpoint of scores of correspondents who had stayed in Paris and not driven to Rheims on the understanding that they would not be allowed into the ceremony, there wasn't much that could be done for them, despite my normal desire to be as helpful as possible. Standing on the steps, I hurriedly briefed them on events of the two days and told them I would immediately seek [Brigadier] General [Frank] Allen [of the Public Relations Division] and get him to deal with them direct.

I found General Allen with [Major] General [Harold R.] Bull [operations officer], trying to work out details of the procedure for complying with the order of the Combined Chiefs of Staff that announcement of the end of the campaign was to be made simultaneously at a later date by the governments in Washington, Moscow, and London. I gave General Allen the message, but the harassed General could do little about it.

I was about to miss the big show myself, so I hurried

around to the war room. Beetle [Walter Bedell Smith] arrived, looked over the seating arrangements, spoke briefly as to procedure. He didn't seem to notice the one lonely microphone upon which the whole world was dependent. He blinked in the floodlights, but I felt that now with the proper pool of seventeen correspondents assembled quietly but attentively in the rear, he would not call off the proceedings.

General [Gustav] Jodl [commander of the German army] and Admiral [Hans Georg von] Friedeburg [commander of the German navy], the two principals, arrived, escorted by [Major] General [K. W. D.] Strong and Brigadier [E. J.] Foord. General Strong placed the documents for signature in front of General Smith, before whom I laid the solid-gold fountain pen [one of two pens sent by old friend Kenneth Parker of Parker Pen Company to Eisenhower, with the request they be used for signing the surrender documents]. Beetle spoke briefly to the Germans, which was interpreted for them by Strong. It was merely that the surrender documents awaited signature. Were they ready and prepared to sign? Jodl indicated assent with a slight nod. I already had before him the gold-plated pen. Jodl had two documents to sign, so when he finished the first, I retrieved the gold-plated pen and substituted my own—one given me by [war correspondent] Charlie Daly in Algiers. With this he signed the second document.

Generals Smith, [Russian Major General Ivan] Susloparov, and [French General François] Sevez then signed both documents. At the conclusion of the signing, General Jodl stood at attention, addressed General Smith, and said, in English: "I want to say a word."

Then he lapsed into German, later interpreted as: "General! With this signature the German people and German armed forces are, for better or worse, delivered into the victor's hands. In this war, which has lasted more than five years, both have achieved and suffered more than perhaps any other people in the world. In this hour I can only express the hope that the victor will treat them with generosity."

The official time of the signature on the surrender

Early on the morning of May 7 a tired but happy Eisenhower holds aloft two of the pens used in the signing ceremony. *Left to right are:* Major General of Artillery of the Red Army, Ivan Susloparoff; Lieutenant General Sir F. E. Morgan, Deputy Chief of Staff; Lieutenant General Walter Bedell Smith, Chief of Staff; Captain Harry Butcher, naval aide; General Dwight D. Eisenhower, Supreme Allied Commander; Sir Arthur Tedder, Deputy Supreme Commander; Admiral Sir Harold M. Burrough, Allied Naval Chief. (*Courtesy Dwight D. Eisenhower Library*)

document was 2:41 A.M. British Double Summer Time.

I had three pens, and Ike, if he chose, could now send the gold ones to the president and prime minister, and mine to Mr. Parker. The only trouble was that mine is a Sheaffer.

The delegates arose and the Germans were taken to the room assigned them and the remainder went to General Ike's office. He sternly asked the Germans if they fully understood the terms and whether they were prepared to execute them. This was interpreted by General Strong. The answer was made in the affirmative; the Germans bowed stiffly and left the room.

The photographers wanted more pictures. General Ike called all of us to surround him. Someone asked that he hold the fountain pens. He displayed them in a "V for Victory," the pictures were snapped, and congratulations said all around.

But Ike's work wasn't finished. He still had to make a short newsreel and radio recording. Taking the [British] Air Chief Marshal [Sir Arthur William Tedder] with him to the war room, so both Allies would be shown together, General Ike spoke briefly "from the cuff." He

had to make one retake after I butted in. He had used the word "armistice," and I was apprehensive about this term, which to me connoted all the laxity and unpreparedness of the period between the two wars; I thought it was a bad one to use. Growling and scowling at me, he substituted "surrender."

As we walked back to General Ike's office, Tedder poked me in the ribs and said with a twinkle in his eyes that General Ike could make the best speech in the world and I should mind my own damned business.

Anyway, it wasn't an armistice; it was a complete and unconditional surrender, and that's what we've been fighting for.

From time to time, we had joked as to the kind of heroic language that the Supreme Commander [Eisenhower] might use to tell the Combined Chiefs that the surrender had been achieved. "We have met the enemy and they are ours"; or "Don't give up the ship, we've just begun to fight." But the Supreme Commander dictated a cable to the Combined Chiefs simply: "The Mission of this Allied Force was fulfilled at 0241 local time, May 7, 1945."

HARRY CECIL BUTCHER (1901–1985) grew up in Iowa and graduated in 1924 from Iowa State College with a bachelor's degree in agricultural journalism. In 1926, while working in Washington, D.C., he first met Major Dwight Eisenhower. In 1929 Butcher joined the newly established Columbia Broadcasting System and set up its Washington office. Ten years later he was commissioned as a lieutenant commander in the Naval Reserve. Butcher was a vice president for CBS when he volunteered for active duty in 1942. A few months later Eisenhower asked for him as naval aide, an association that continued through the rest of the war. Butcher's day-by-day wartime diaries formed the basis for his bestselling book, *My Three Years with Eisenhower*, which was published in 1946 and from which this excerpt is taken. After the war Butcher returned to civilian life and moved to Santa Barbara, California. He bought a radio station and a television station and eventually got into the cable TV business. His daughter, Beverly Butcher Byron, recently retired from the U.S. Congress after serving for fourteen years as a representative from the state of Maryland. In that capacity she helped dedicate a memorial in England to those who were lost in Exercise Tiger of April 1944. (*Courtesy Dwight D. Eisenhower Library*)

GLOSSARY

Bigot Security clearance for Operation Overlord

Buzz bomb German V-1 rocket

CIC Combat Information Center

C rations Letter designation for a type of ration

DD tank Duplex-drive amphibious tank

Dan buoy Temporary marker buoy used during mine-sweeping operation to indicate boundaries of swept path, swept area, known hazards, etc.

DUKW Amphibious truck, duck, troop

E-boat German motor torpedo boat

Exercise Tiger Rehearsal conducted in late April 1944 to prepare force that was to land at Utah Beach

Fire control The process and equipment involved in aiming guns to hit their intended targets

Force O The naval task force for Omaha Beach during the invasion of Normandy

Force U The naval task force for Utah Beach during the invasion of Normandy

Gooseberry Artificial breakwater created at Normandy by sinking merchant ships offshore

K rations Letter designation for a type of ration

LCA Landing craft, assault

LCI Landing craft, infantry

LCI(L) Landing craft, infantry (large)

LCM Landing craft, mechanized

LCP Landing craft, personnel

LCT Landing craft, tank

LCVP Landing craft, vehicle and personnel

Limpet mine A type of explosive device attached to a ship's hull

Lobnitz pierhead A metal pier structure attached to vertical pilings so it could move up and down with the tide

LST Landing ship, tank

Minesweeper A type of naval ship used to detect and sweep mines

Mulberry Artificial breakwater created at Normandy by sinking concrete structures offshore

NCDU Naval combat demolition unit

Operation Anvil/Dragoon Code name for the Allied invasion of southern France in August 1944

Operation Neptune Code name for the naval aspects of the invasion of Normandy in June 1944

Operation Overlord Code name for the invasion of Normandy in June 1944

PC Patrol craft

Phoenix Concrete structure deliberately sunk off Normandy to be part of an artificial breakwater

PT Motor torpedo boat

Shore-fire control Personnel ashore who called gunfire spotting information to ships doing the shooting

SOURCES OF ARTICLES

"The Memory of Departed Shipmates," adapted from telephone interviews of Commander Bergner by Paul Stillwell, May 14 and August 2, 1993.

"Disaster at Dieppe, Success at Normandy," adapted from Naval Institute oral history interviews of Admiral Strauss by Paul Stillwell, October 30 and November 10, 1986.

"Strategy and Secrecy," condensed from the chapter titled "Naval Aspects of Normandy in Retrospect" by Mr. Elsey in the book *D-Day: The Normandy Invasion in Retrospect*, published by the University Press of Kansas in 1971. Reprinted by permission of the University Press of Kansas.

"Admiral Stark's Role," adapted from Naval Institute oral history interviews of Admiral Dietrich by Dr. John T. Mason Jr., July 27 and August 9, 1971.

"Admiral Ramsay and I," condensed from the chapter titled "Command from the Flagship *Augusta*" by Admiral Kirk in the book *The Atlantic War Remembered*, published by the Naval Institute Press in 1990. The book chapter was adapted from a Columbia University oral history interview of Admiral Kirk by Dr. John T. Mason Jr. in 1961.

"Ultra Warnings," adapted from a telephone interview of Mr. Bundy by Paul Stillwell, June 24, 1993.

"German Naval Operations on D-Day," condensed from the chapter of the same name by Admiral Ruge in the book *D-Day: The Normandy Invasion in Retrospect*, published by the University Press of Kansas in 1971. Reprinted by permission of the University Press of Kansas.

"Exercise Tiger—Screams of Agony," condensed from an unpublished manuscript written by Dr. Eckstam.

"Stripe Five and You're Out," adapted from a Naval Institute oral history interview of Admiral Richmond by Dr. John T. Mason Jr., November 18, 1975.

"Ike Remembered Me," adapted from an interview of Admiral Bulkeley at Silver Spring, Maryland, by Paul Stillwell, June 30, 1993.

"Close-in Support at Omaha Beach," condensed from the article "Omaha Beach: An Episode of Normandy," by Admiral Sabin, published in the June 1969 issue of *Shipmate*, the monthly magazine of the Naval Academy Alumni Association. Reprinted by permission of the Naval Academy Alumni Association.

"Traffic Cop," adapted from a telephone interview of Captain Crook by Paul Stillwell, November 4, 1993.

"DD Spelled Disaster," adapted from a telephone interview

of Mr. Rockwell by Paul Stillwell, November 6, 1993. Mr. Rockwell also did a detailed oral history about his D-Day experiences for the Eisenhower Center of the University of New Orleans.

"Landing the Big Red One," adapted from an oral history of Mr. Adams by the Eisenhower Center of the University of New Orleans.

"My Only Job Was to Stay Alive," adapted from an interview of Commander Fauks at Glendale, Missouri, by Paul Stillwell, November 17, 1992.

"Surviving the London Blitz—And Meeting a Husband," adapted from an interview of Mrs. Fauks at Glendale, Missouri, by Paul Stillwell, November 17, 1992.

"NOIC Utah," condensed from the article of that title by Commodore Arnold, published in the June 1947 issue of the U.S. Naval Institute *Proceedings*.

"Combat Demolition Unit," adapted from an oral history of Mr. Wakefield by the Eisenhower Center of the University of New Orleans.

"The Best Seat for a Really Big Show," condensed from unpublished manuscripts written by Captain Blackburn.

"Make Love *and* War," condensed from the book *The Ship That Would Not Die* by Admiral Becton and Joseph Morschauser III, published by Prentice-Hall in 1980. Reprinted by permission of Admiral Becton.

"Dread of the Unknown," a slightly modified version of an unpublished manuscript written by Lieutenant Howes.

"Shipwrecked in the Channel," adapted from an interview of General Talbott at Annapolis, Maryland, by Paul Stillwell, May 18, 1993.

"Broken Ship, Broken Body," adapted from a telephone interview of Mr. Branstrator by Paul Stillwell, July 5, 1993.

"Getting the Troops 'Over There,'" adapted from a telephone interview of Mr. Horton by Paul Stillwell, July 3, 1993.

"Sub-Ordinary Seaman," adapted from an oral history of Mr. Freed by the Eisenhower Center of the University of New Orleans.

"Liberty Ship Signalman," adapted from a telephone interview of Mr. Burke by Paul Stillwell, August 5, 1993.

"When Sevens Weren't Lucky," adapted from an interview of Father Kemp at Bowie, Maryland, by Paul Stillwell, May 29, 1993.

"Designing the LST," adapted from a Naval Institute oral history interview of Mr. Niedermair by John T. Mason Jr., December 9, 1975. A similar version appeared in the November 1982 issue of the U.S. Naval Institute *Proceedings*.

"Civilians in Uniform," adapted from a telephone interview of Mr. Trombold by Paul Stillwell, August 15, 1993.

"The Hazards of London (and Normandy)," condensed from an unpublished manuscript written by Commander Pace.

"Mulberries and Gooseberries," condensed from various sections of the book *The Far Shore* by Admiral Ellsberg, published by Dodd, Mead, and Company in 1960. The copyright on the book has expired. This excerpt is published with the assent of the estate of Admiral Ellsberg.

"Battleship Commander," adapted from an unpublished manuscript written by Admiral Bryant and from a radio interview with the admiral. Both sources were supplied by his son, Captain C. F. Bryant Jr., USN (Ret.).

"A Strange Place for a Marine," adapted from an interview of Mr. Airey at Fallston, Maryland, by Paul Stillwell, November 2, 1993.

"The Capture of Cherbourg," adapted from an interview of Captain Walsh near Denton, Maryland, by Paul Stillwell, June 11, 1993. The chapter also draws from Captain Walsh's manuscript memoir, *Little Known Facts of a Well-Known War*, copies of which are on file in the special collections of the Naval Academy library in Annapolis and the history section of Coast Guard headquarters in Washington, D.C.

"The Non-Amphibious Swan of Cherbourg," adapted from Naval Institute oral history interviews of Admiral Bauernschmidt by Dr. John T. Mason Jr., November 4 and 18, 1969.

"Submarines and Buzz-Bomb Launchers," adapted from a telephone interview of Admiral Reedy by Paul Stillwell, June 1, 1993.

"A Warm Welcome in Southern France," condensed from the chapter of the same title by Admiral Hewitt in the book *The Atlantic War Remembered*, published by the Naval Institute Press in 1990. The book chapter was adapted from a Columbia University oral history interview of Admiral Kirk by Dr. John T. Mason Jr. in 1963. Related articles by Admiral Hewitt appeared in the July 1954 and August 1954 issues of the U.S. Naval Institute *Proceedings*.

"The Death of Admiral Moon," condensed from an unpublished manuscript written by Captain Moreno and a telephone interview of Captain Moreno by Paul Stillwell, July 17, 1993.

"Dog Tags and Dirty Beans," adapted from a Naval Institute oral history interview of Commander Murray by Dr. John T. Mason Jr., July 28, 1988. A similar version appeared in the book *The Atlantic War Remembered*, published by the Naval Institute Press in 1990.

"Beach Jumpers Don't Really Jump," condensed from various sections of Captain Fairbanks's book *A Hell of a War*, published by St. Martin's Press in 1993. Reprinted by permission of St. Martin's Press.

"Surface Action at Point-Blank Range," adapted from an interview of Admiral Bulkeley at Silver Spring, Maryland, by Paul Stillwell, August 15, 1993. It also draws on material supplied by Harvey N. Massey, formerly a crew member of the destroyer *Endicott*. Included were the ship's action reports for August 1944, which are also on file in the operational archives branch of the Naval Historical Center, Washington, D.C.

"The Alsos Mission," adapted from Naval Institute oral history interviews of Admiral Mumma by Paul Stillwell, October 3, 1986 and April 20, 1987. A similar version appeared as an article in the summer 1989 issue of *Naval History* magazine.

"A Different Kind of Uniform," condensed and slightly modified from the chapter "A New Uniform" in the book *Rex Barney's Thank Youuuu for 50 Years in Baseball from Brooklyn to Baltimore* by Mr. Barney with Norman L. Macht, published by Tidewater Publishers in 1993. Reprinted by permission of Tidewater Publishers.

"Gambling for Dramamine," adapted from an interview of Colonel Skidmore on his farm near Flemington, Missouri, by Paul Stillwell, November 16, 1992.

"Three Faces," adapted from a telephone interview of Mr. Lee by Paul Stillwell, June 27, 1993.

"A Sense of Duty to the Fatherland," adapted from telephone interviews of Mr. Degelow by Paul Stillwell, April 24 and 27, 1993.

"Moving into Germany," adapted from a Naval Institute oral history interview of Admiral MacDonald by Dr. John T. Mason Jr., September 10, 1974.

"Across the Rhine," condensed from an unpublished manuscript written in 1945 by Lieutenant Houghton. A copy is on file in the operational archives branch, Naval Historical Center, Washington, D.C.

"Surrender!" reprinted from the chapter of the same title in the book by Captain Butcher, *My Three Years with Eisenhower*, published by Simon & Schuster in 1946. Reprinted by permission of Simon & Schuster, Inc.

ACKNOWLEDGMENTS

One afternoon in the autumn of 1992 Mac Greeley, a retired marine who works as a *Proceedings* editor, asked me if I was planning to do anything in conjunction with the fiftieth anniversary of D-Day, then a year and a half in the future. Mac is an idea man, and this was a good idea indeed. His curiosity planted the seed that led to *Assault on Normandy*. I quickly settled on D-Day as an appropriate book topic after I got to thinking about how little had been done to explain the naval and maritime side of the operation. Soon it was a matter of proposing the idea to Tom Epley, then director of the Naval Institute Press. He was enthusiastic, and I began rounding up the individual chapters.

Karla Powell of the Naval Institute's marketing department generously shared a photo album put together by her father, Lieutenant Arthur Kruggel, during World War II. Dr. Eugene Eckstam, one of the contributors to the book, gave me the address of Walter Trombold, a shipmate of Kruggel, and that in turn led to Trombold's chapter. Eckstam has gathered a considerable amount of research on Exercise Tiger and was helpful in a number of ways.

Another who helped me land an interview was Peter Gookin, a very friendly man who works in the Naval Institute's marketing department. He had been in touch with Vice Admiral John Bulkeley about D-Day, and Peter not only persuaded the admiral to be in the book but also suggested useful questions as I prepared for the interview. Both Admiral and Mrs. Bulkeley were gracious in providing a tour of their home, which is an endless source of fascination for someone with an interest in naval history. The admiral generously shared his collection of pictures, and he put me in touch with Harvey Massey, an *Endicott* crew member who supplied useful information about the surface battle off southern France in August 1944.

Norris Shane, an LST sailor who landed at Juno Beach on Normandy, suggested that I get in touch with Hans Bergner of the *LST-282* about his LST experiences. Marti Kaderli of the Admiral Nimitz Foundation gave me Bergner's address and telephone number. The result is the superb article at the beginning of the book. It is truly sad that Commander Bergner did not live to see the publication of the book. His widow, Gladys, kindly donated some of the pictures that illustrate her husband's chapter. Bob Busch, editor of the informative newspaper *LST Scuttlebutt*, presented me with useful background information on LSTs. He performs valuable work on behalf of the U.S. LST Association. Jack Niedermair considerately provided a photo of his father, the designer of the LST.

Former Congressman Beverly Byron furnished biographical material on her father, Captain Harry Butcher. Edward Ellsberg Pollard, grandson and namesake of the late Rear Admiral Ellsberg, researched the copyright status of his grandfather's book and gave me a picture of the noted author/admiral. I am, in turn, grateful to Wally Shugg for telling me how to reach Mr. Pollard.

John and Betty Mason have long been friends and mentors in the discipline of oral history. The training they provided was invaluable because of the large degree to which interviews were used to gather the material in the book. In fact, Jack did a number of the interviews himself, first for Columbia University, later for the Naval Institute. The Masons also granted permission for the use of excerpts from Dr. Mason's book *Atlantic War Remembered*.

Naval artist Tom Freeman suggested I check the oral history collection at the Eisenhower Center of the University of New Orleans. Steve Ambrose and Kathi Jones of the center presented me with a wealth of first-person memoirs to choose from. I wish I had room to include even more of them than I did because the Eisenhower Center is in the forefront of preserving material related to D-Day. Freeman also relayed a suggestion from Tony Lambro that I interview Irvin Airey and thus include a marine in the book. Airey's chapter is a charming addition to the collection and most appropriate to ensure that all the sea services are represented. Lemuel and Diane Shepherd provided photos and clearance to use an excerpt from the oral history of Mrs. Shepherd's father, the late Rear Admiral Neil Dietrich.

George Elsey pointed me toward the book *D-Day: The Normandy Invasion in Retrospect*, which produced two chapters for this book, Elsey's own and that of the late Vice Admiral Friedrich Ruge. While I was looking for that volume, I serendipitously discovered a nearby book on the library shelf, Nigel Lewis's *Exercise Tiger*. That book, in turn, yielded leads for the chapters from Dr. Eckstam and Captain John Moreno. Rear Admiral Donald MacDonald didn't believe his oral history contained enough detail about the Rhine River crossing, so he passed along an account written in 1945 by his friend Norris Houghton; it was just what the book needed. Another tip that led to a chapter was from old friend Joe Brooks, a former fire controlman in the battleship *New Jersey*. At a *New Jersey* reunion, Joe suggested I interview his wife's brother, a priest named Patrick Kemp. It was a great suggestion.

Another useful lead was from Gordon Graham, who put me in touch with Captain Carleton F. Bryant, Jr. Bryant was generous in providing a written memoir by his father, taped copies of radio interviews, and photos. Norman Macht, a baseball research enthusiast who was coauthor of Rex Barney's memoir, helped me round up pictures and good-naturedly permitted slight alterations to the text. Captain Dick Crook, a Naval Institute member, called the office one day to say he had a good D-Day story to tell and that his friend Dean Rockwell had an even better one. Crook was right about both of them, and the result is a fuller appreciation of the traffic off Omaha Beach. Captain George Atterbury supplied a fine photo of Crook's ship.

Ted Dietz, an old friend who has been active in restoring the Liberty ship *John W. Brown* at Baltimore, was persistent in making sure that I included a chapter on his World War II ship, the minesweeper *Tide*. Ted gave me photos and also put me in touch with his former shipmate Bill Branstrator for a dramatic interview. Peter Mersky provided a picture of a rare U.S. naval aviator, one who flew a British Spitfire. Scott Belliveau of the Naval Institute and Bob Scheina, formerly Coast Guard historian, suggested an interview with Captain Quentin Walsh about his role in the capture of Cherbourg.

Herb Gilliland and his sister Marion befriended artist Albert K. Murray in the later years of his life and wound up—along with their mother—administering his estate. I am grateful to Marion for supplying several photos of the artist and applaud the family's continuing efforts to see that Murray's art is remembered. They are at work on a book about his career. Gail Munro of the Navy Combat Art Center in Washington volunteered correspondence from Dwight Shepler, the other principal combat artist whose work is featured in the book. Unfortunately, Shepler did not do an oral history of the sort Murray did.

Two merchant ship experts who graciously donated pictures were Mel Lizotte, a Naval Institute volunteer, and his friend Bill Hultgren. Merchant ship chapters grew out of suggestions from Tim Runyan, editor of *The American Neptune*, and Justin Gleichauf, author of *Unsung Sailors: The Naval Armed Guard in World War II*. Runyan suggested I talk with John Horton, while Gleichauf put me in touch with Pete Burke. Burke is an old sailor who is enthusiastic about preserving the record of the armed guard. He treated me as a friend from the moment I proposed an interview.

Mary Beth Straight of the Naval Institute's photo archive is so busy that she puts the Energizer bunny to shame. She assisted in rounding up many of the pictures in the book, including serving as a link to the National Archives. Further on the photo front, I appreciate the consistently cooperative efforts of Cathy Gilchrist and Cathy Lurz of the Blakeslee Group in Baltimore. The former did the copying of borrowed photos expertly, while the latter was always cheerful in looking after the administrative end. Chuck Haberlein and Ed Finney, two knowledgeable specialists at the Naval Historical Center, guided me through the available D-Day pictures on file at their place. Dale Conley and Sharon Culley of the National Archives were similarly helpful. Kevin Gilbert, a photographer for *Annapolis* magazine, took the picture of me that appears on the jacket. The fine crew of the Naval Historical Center's operational archives branch—Cal Cavalcante, Kathy Lloyd, Mike Walker, and John Hodges—cheerfully made available various documents, including biographies of some of the chapter narrators. Roger Kirk and Deborah Solbert, children of the late Admiral Alan Kirk, generously supplied a photo of their father with McGeorge Bundy.

Linda O'Doughda, formerly a coworker in the Naval Institute's oral history department, is now with the book department. She has done a magnificent job as production editor of *Assault on Normandy*. Always cordial and extremely conscientious, she had the chore of looking after myriad details, seeing where the holes were, ensuring consistency of style, reminding me of deadlines, and making sure all the pieces fit together. She worked closely with Karen White, the designer who set the tone for the attractive page layouts and the dust jacket. Mary Lou Kenney oversaw the editing effort and coordination with design. Susan Artigiani, Linda Cullen, Karla Powell, Beth Lewis, Judy Heise, Maureen Peterson, and Tom Harnish have helped spread the word about the book on behalf of the publisher's marketing department. John Cronin and Eddie Vance, experts in typesetting, paper, binding, and the other physical properties of a book, directed and monitored the production process. It is a pleasure to work with all these professionals of the Naval Institute Press.

Finally, as always, I appreciate the forbearance of my family—wife Karen and sons Joseph, Robert, and James—while I've been cooped up on yet another book project. They not only did without me for long periods of time but also joined me in watching a videotape of the movie *The Longest Day* as I refreshed my memory on what I'd seen in Long Beach, California, on the twenty-fifth anniversary of D-Day.

ABOUT THE AUTHOR

Paul Stillwell joined the staff of the U.S. Naval Institute in 1974 and is now director of the history division, including the oral history program, photo archive, reference library, and photo sales program.

Stillwell has a bachelor's degree in history from Drury College, Springfield, Missouri, and a master's degree in journalism from the University of Missouri-Columbia. From 1962 to 1988 he participated in the Naval Reserve, officially retiring in 1992 with the rank of commander. He served in the tank landing ship *Washoe County* (LST-1165) and the battleship *New Jersey* (BB-62) during the Vietnam War. In early 1988 he was recalled to active duty for a month and sent to the Persian Gulf as a historian to document the U.S. Navy's role during the Iran-Iraq War.

Stillwell is editor or author of several Naval Institute Press books, including *Air Raid: Pearl Harbor!* (1981), *Battleship New Jersey: An Illustrated History* (1986), *Battleship Arizona: An Illustrated History* (1991), *The Golden Thirteen: Recollections of the First Black Naval Officers* (1993), and *Sharks of Steel* (coauthored with Vice Admiral Robert Y. Kauffman, 1993).

INDEX

An italicized number indicates a photograph on that page.

ABC-TV, 40
Abbotsbury, England, 83
Abergavenny, Wales, 119
Acheson, Dean, 12
Adams, Robert E., 72–74, *75*
Aerial reconnaissance: *see* Reconnaissance
Airey, Irvin A., xi, *188*, 189–91, *192*
Alcoholic beverages, 5, 12, 26, 44, 81, 121, 134, 143, *150*, 199–200, 223, 228, 250, 259, 260, 263
Alexandria, Egypt, 171
Algeria, 14, 218–19, 225, 236, 289
Algiers, Algeria, 218–19, 225, 236, 289
Allen, Brigadier General Frank, 289
Alsos Mission, 249
America (U.S. passenger liner), 81
American Bridge Company, 160
Ammunition: for 155-mm. Long Tom guns, 3–5, 26; for 3-inch guns, 129; for 4.7-inch guns, 244; for 5-inch guns, 109–10, 116–17, 243; for 14-inch guns, 25, 185, 206; defective, 181, 185, *186*, 245; for machine guns, 26, 51; resupply of, 26, 37, 176–79, 191; for small arms, 25–26, 79, 206, 265
Amphibious warfare doctrine, 55
Ancon, USS (AGC-4), 17, *18*, *24*, 29, *65*, 67, 121, 227
Anderson, Lieutenant Paul, 103
Andrews, Chief Carpenter's Mate Vincent, 263
Annapolis, Maryland, xi
Antiaircraft guns/gunnery: British, 78, 149, 171, 237; against friendly planes, 10; German, 37, 100–1, 183, 213; on Phoenixes in artificial harbor, *173*, *176*, 177; U.S. Army, 268–70; U.S. merchant ships, 139, *140*, *142*; U.S. Navy, 4, 13, 105, 115, 125, 165, 184–85, 190
Antisubmarine warfare, 14–15, 25, 38, 64, 169, 182, 209, 210, *212*, 213, 254
Antwerp, Belgium, 278
Anvil, Operation: *see* Southern France
Anzio, Italy, 16, 165, 219
Aphis, HMS (British gunboat), 237, *239*, 240, 243–45
Arkansas, USS (BB-33), xi, 69, 181–83, *185*, 186, *188*, *189*, 190, *191*, 192
Arlington National Cemetery, xii
Armed guards, naval, 132, *137*, *142*, 143
Army Air Forces, U.S.: antisubmarine warfare, 210; bombing of Germany, 251, 280; bombing at Normandy, 52, 58–59, 67, 88–89, 98, *103*, 109, 120; deception tactics, 238; fighters, 104, 197, 228; photo reconnaissance, 17; planning, 219–20, 227; transport of paratroopers, 100, 108, *122*, *123*, 126

Army Group B (German), 38
Army-Navy Staff College, Washington, D.C., 225
Arnold, Rear Admiral James E., 86–91, *92*
Arromanches-les-Bains, France, 39
Artificial harbors off Normandy, 10, 12, 24, *143*, *144*, 165, 169–72, *173*, 174–75, *176*, *177*, 178–80
Artillery: *see* German army; Guns
Arzeu, Algeria, 225
Ashanti, HMS (British destroyer), 35
Athlone, Earl of, *16*
Atlantic, Battle of, 15, 131, 138, 144
Atomic Bomb, 248–49
Attlee, Prime Minister Clement, 254
Atwood, Tom, 113
Augusta, USS (CA-31), 25–26, *27*, *29*, *30*, *107*, 226, *227*
Australia, 254
Austria, 261
Avonmouth, England, 144

B-17 Flying Fortress (U.S. bomber), 274
B-24 Liberator (U.S. bomber), 210, 274
B-26 Marauder (U.S. bomber), 103, 109
Backenkohler, Admiral Otto, 253
Bad Kreuznach, Germany, 285
Baker, Captain Charles, 185, *186*
Baldwin, USS (DD-624), 112, *113*–15
Ball, Lieutenant Bill, 105
Ballantrae, Scotland, 235
Baltic Sea, 38–39, 272, 274
Baltimore, Maryland, xi, 26, 191–92
Baltimore Orioles, xi
Banminister, England, 83
Barfleur, France, 101, 108–9, 197
Barge, Seaman Pete, 244–46
Barham, HMS (British battleship), 171
Barneville, France, 172
Barney, Rex, xi, 256–57, *258*, 259, *260*, *261*
Barnstable, England, 150
Barnstable, Massachusetts, 113
Barrage balloons, 49, 85, 145–46, *219*, 228
Barton, Commodore William, 201
Barton, USS (DD-722), 67, 106
Baseball, x–xi, 254, 261
Bastogne, Belgium, 270
Battle of Britain, 7
Battleship Division Five, U.S. Navy, 182
Bauernschmidt, Rear Admiral George W., xi, 193, 203–7, *208*

Bayeux, France, 38

Bayfield, USS (APA-33), *88,* 90–91, 226–28

Beach battalions, U.S. Navy, *78, 79, 80,* 81

Beach jumpers: *see* Deception, tactical

Beach obstacles, 1, 12, *17, 33, 34, 35, 58,* 60, 71–73, 93, *95,*
     109, 122, 223, 229

Becton, Betty, xii

Becton, Rear Admiral F. Julian, xii, 106–10, *111,* 181

Belfast, Northern Ireland, 114, 135, 182–83

Belgium, 35, 239, 265, 270, 280, *281*

Bellinger, Vice Admiral Patrick N. L., *214*

Bénouville, France, 38

Benson, USS (DD-421), 103

Bergner, Commander Hans E., 1–4, *5, 6,* 7

Bergner, Gladys, 5–6

Berkeley, HMS (British destroyer), 10

Berlin, Germany, 251, 274

Bermuda, 108

Bideford, England, 150

Biltmier, Lieutenant Charles, 103

Biscay, Bay of, 35–38, *212,* 213, 220, 254

Bismarck (German battleship), 24, 32, 35

Bizerte, Tunisia, 165

Blackburn, Captain John R., 98–104, *105*

Blanding, Florida, 262

Bleasdale, HMS (British destroyer), 10–11

Bletchley Park, England, 30

Bloomington, Minnesota, xi

Bolitho, George, 149

Bombs/bombing: American, 52, 58–59, 67, 88–89, 93, 98,
     100–2, 109, 212, 251, 274–75; British, 37, 195, 251,
     274–75; German, 4, 10, 21, 37, 52, 78–79, 83, 84–85,
     91, 101, 112, 115, 134, 139, *140,* 166–67, 183, 203–4,
     225, 257, 270; Japanese, 58–59; shelters against, 83–
     84; *see also* V-1 rockets

Boothby, Commodore Isaac, 145–46

Boppard, Germany, 285

Bordeaux, France, 249–50, 278, 280

Bormes-les-Mimosas, France, 237

Boston, Massachusetts, 26, 110, 131–32, 134–35, 161, 191

Boucher, Seaman Richard, 197

Bougnon, Bay of, 231

Boulogne, France, 18, 34–35, 37

Bowie, Maryland, xi

Boxing, 47, 49

Bradley, Lieutenant General Omar N., 25–26, 29, *30,* 31,
     172–73, 176–77, *200,* 278–79

Branstrator, William, 3, 125–28, *129*

Brazil, 203

Brazle, Alpha, 257

Breamore, England, 195

Bremen, Germany, 250–51, *252*

Brest, France, 37, 201, 213, 269

Briggs, Major Ruth, 289

Bristol, England, 134

British army, 2–3, 38, 220–21, 250, 275

British Chiefs of Staff, 14

Brittany, France, 50, 162, 195, 201, 266, 269

Brixham, England, 41–42

Brokaw, Tom, 1

Bronze Star, 258

Brooklyn Army Base, 132

Brooklyn Dodgers, xi, 257, *260,* 261

Brooklyn Navy Yard, 188

Brooklyn, New York, 257, 270

Brown, John Mason, x

Bryant, Rear Admiral Carleton F., 62, 115, 181–85, *186,*
     187

Buchenwald, Germany, 260

Buckley (DE-51)-class U.S. destroyer escorts, 121

Bulge, Battle of, 256, 266–67, 270, 279, 283

Bulkeley, Vice Admiral John D., x, *50,* 51, *52,* 53, *54,* 127–
     28, 234, 237, 240, 242–46, *247*

Bull, Major General Harold R., 289

Bundy, McGeorge, 29–30, *31,* 278, 280

Bureau of Naval Personnel, 242

Bureau of Navigation, U.S. Navy, 182

Bureau of Ordnance, U.S. Navy, 243

Bureau of Ships, U.S. Navy, 154–55

Bureau of Standards, U.S., 249

Burke, Admiral Arleigh A., xi

Burke, Cornelius A., 142–45, *146*

Burma, 24

Burrough, Admiral Sir Harold M., *290*

Butcher, Captain Harry C., 277, 289, *290, 291*

Buzz bombs: *see* V-1 rockets

C-47 Skytrain (U.S. transport plane), 100–1, 108, *121,* 126,
     129

Caen, France, 38, 47, 166

Calais, France, 18, 34, 119, 165, 195, 208

Campbeltown, HMS (British destroyer), 9

Camp Bradford, Little Creek, Virginia, 76

Camp Crook, Omaha, Nebraska, 76

Camp Shelby, Mississippi, 257

Canada, 15, *16*

Canadian air force, 136

Canadian army, 10–11, 201

Cannes, France, 223, 237

Cap de la Hague, France, 101, 197

Cape Dramont, southern France, *4, 5,* 6

Cape Ferrat, southern France, 231

Cape Geramo, southern France, 221

Capriolo (German corvette), 239–40, 243–44, *245,* 246–47

Carderock, Maryland, 249

Cardiff, Wales, 119, 138

Caribbean, 273

Carmick, USS (DD-493), 67

Carr, Lieutenant Ed, 59

Carrington, Commander Walter S., 142

Carusi, Commander Eugene, 13

Casablanca, Morocco, 14, 218

Cascio, Mike, 163

Catoctin, USS (AGC-5), 221, *222–23,* 239

Central Intelligence Agency, 9

Centurion, HMS (British battleship), 170, *171, 172,* 177

Channel Islands, 278

Charles Morgan (U.S. Liberty ship), *139*

Chemical Warfare, 2, 41

Cherbourg, France: Allied approach to and capture of, 1,
     26, 109, 172–73, 176, 178–80, 185–86, 191, 193, 195,
     196, 197–98, 199–200, 201, 205; base for German
     E-boats, 24–25, 35–37, 52–53, 110, 116, 198; devas-

tated by bombardment and sabotage, 197, *198,* 200; naval bombardment of, 26, 54, 101, 181, 185–86, 191, 200, 206; port for handling cargo, 23, 81, 193–94, 218, 256, 264, 265, 278; U.S. naval headquarters at, 200–1, 205–6, *207,* 208; in the vicinity of Normandy landings, 10, 24, 38, 100–1, 108, 119

Cheshire (troop transport), 264

Chicago Cubs, 261

Chicago, Illinois, 160

Christie, Agatha, 47

Churchill, Prime Minister Winston, 7, 9–10, 12, 14, *15, 16,* 20, 24, 51, 154, 168, 183, 203, 219, 254, 278

Cincinnati, Ohio, 257

Ciotat, Baie de la, France, 237–40, 242, *243*

Citizen Kane (movie), 236

Clare, Evelyn, 83, *85*

Clark, Captain Dayton, *170,* 174, 179–80

Clarke, Brigadier Dudley, 235

Clyde River, Scotland, 194

Coast defenses at Normandy, 16, *17*

Coast Guard, U.S.: Academy, New London, Connecticut, 131; eighty-three-foot patrol boats, 40, 46, *48–49,* 136, 139, 177; manning of transports, ix, 47, *72, 73,* 74, 90, 196, *220*; operation of landing craft, *61,* 72–74; port administration, 194, 197–98, 200–1; regulation of merchant marine, *46,* 131, 136, 193–94; reservists, 47–49

Cochrane, Captain Edward L., 154

Codebreaking, 29–31

Colleville-sur-Mer, France, 62, 179

Collins, Major General J. Lawton, 26, 109, 123, 172–73, 195, 197, *200,* 226

Colorado, University of, 160

Combat demolition units, 60–61, 71, 93–96, 109, 183

Combined Chiefs of Staff, 15, 23, 218, 290

Combined Operations, British, 7, 9–10, 235–36

Commandos, ix, *9,* 36, 183, 195, 206, 237, *238,* 265, 267

Commercial ships, ix, 26, 62, 76, 130–46, 166, 182, 212, 227; *see also* Liberty ships

Communications, 1, 29–30, 37, 58, 65, 68, 77, *78,* 79–81, 113, 142, 184, 211, 222, 225–28, 232–33, 238, 243, 264, 284

Concentration camps, 1, 261, 273

Constellation, USS (frigate), 182

Convoys, 24, 41–42, 125, 131–32, 134, 136–39, *142,* 144, 148, 161, 163, 165, 182, 188, 257, 263

Corry, USS (DD-463), 38, 104

Corsica, 219–20, 236

Corsican Brothers, The (movie), *236*

COSSAC (Chief of Staff, Supreme Allied Commander), 11

Costobadie, Lieutenant Commander Ackroyd Norman Palliser, 10

Creasy, Rear Admiral Sir George, 23

Crespi, Frank, 257

Crook, Captain Richard H., 64–65, *66, 67*

Crowe, Admiral William J., xi

Crowther, Lieutenant (junior grade) Allen, 148, *149,* 153

Cunningham, Admiral Sir Andrew, 23

Curie, Joliot, 249

Curie, Marie, 249

Curley, Lieutenant Jack, 195

Currents: *see* Tides and currents at Normandy

Cutter, Captain Slade D., xi

Czechoslovakia, 181

D-Day: historical coverage of, ix–x; meaning of the term, 7–8

Dahlquist, Major General John E., 223, 229

Daly, Charlie, 289

Damage control, 43, 242, 245

Damant, Captain, 171

Darnell, Dr. Matt, 106

Dartmouth College, England, 68

Dartmouth College, U.S., 160

Dartmouth, England, 20, *42,* 50, 86, 149

Dart River, England, 86–87

Davisville, Rhode Island, 136

Decatur, Stephen, 182

Deception, tactical, 235–42

De Gaulle, General Charles, 14, 221

Degelow, Hans J., xi–xii, 271–72, *273,* 274–75, *276*

Delasse, France, 197

Democratic Party, ix

Demolition units: *see* Combat demolition units

Dempsey, Commander Jack, *47,* 76

Denmark, 33, 239, 272, 274–75

Denton, Lieutenant Commander William Jr., *101*

Destroyer Division 36, U.S. Navy, 114

Destroyer Division 119, U.S. Navy, 106

Destroyer Squadron 18, U.S. Navy, 53, 62, 67, 242

Detroit Tigers, 261

Deyo, Rear Admiral Morton, 54, *114,* 185

Dial, Quartermaster First Class Bethel, 243–44

Dieppe, France, 7, 9–10, *11,* 16, 34, 36, 265

Dietrich, Rear Admiral Neil K., 19–21, *22,* 194, 203

Dietz, Electrician's Mate Ted, *126*

Distinguished Service Cross medal, 124

Do-215 (German bomber), 4

Dog Green Beach (Omaha), Normandy, 57

Dol-de-Bretagne, France, 201

Dönitz, Admiral Karl, 251, 253, 275

Donnelly, Jim, 163

Dorling, Rear Admiral J. W. S., 155

Dortmund, Germany, *251*

Doyle, Lieutenant John, 44

Doyle, USS (DD-494), *66,* 67

Dragon, HMS (British cruiser), 39

Dragoon, Operation: *see* Southern France

Drake, Sir Francis, 16

Dravo Corporation, 155, 160

DUKWs (U.S. Army amphibious trucks), 72–73, 80, 145, 173, 178–79

Dunkeswell, England, Naval Air Station, *211, 214,* 225

Dunkirk, France, 7, 14, 190

Duplex-drive tanks, 60–61, 66, 68–71, 226

Duquesne (French cruiser), 280

Durkee, Edward, 5

82nd Airborne Division, U.S. Army, 87, 108, 227

E-boats: departure from Normandy area, 39; similarity to British craft, 46; success in Exercise Tiger, 36, 40, 42–43, 50, 78, 162, 226–27, 230; surface actions against U.S. ships, 52–53, 110–11, 116–17; threat to Allied invasion forces, 24–25, 35–37, *42,* 112, 135, 278

East Acton, England, 83–84
Easy Red Beach (Omaha), Normandy, 64
Ebbets Field, Brooklyn, 257, *260*
Eckstam, Dr. Eugene E., 40–43, *44, 45*
Edwards, Private Willis, 270
Egypt, 170–71
Eighth Army, British, 235
Eighth Fleet, U.S. Navy, 218
Eisely, Jim, 258
Eisenhower, General of the Army Dwight D.: call for PT
     boats in Normandy operation, 50; decision on when
     to land at Normandy, 17, 37; expansion of American
     role at Normandy, 16; relationships with other senior
     commanders, 20, 25, 30, 125, 183; selection as Su-
     preme Allied Commander, 11–12, 16, 24; at SHAEF
     in France, 48, 278–80, 282, 289, *290*; southern
     France operation, 219; victory in North Africa, 15;
     visit to USS *Baldwin, 114, 115*
Elba, 237
Elbe River, 251, 275
Elbing, West Prussia, 35
Elder, Captain, 69–70
Electronic warfare, 211, 228–29, 236
Elizabeth City, North Carolina, 210
Ellsberg, Rear Admiral Edward, x, 169–79, *180*
Elsey, George M., xii, 14–17, *18*
Emmons, USS (DD-457), *66,* 67, *70*
Endicott, USS (DD-495), 234, 237–40, *242,* 243, *244, 245,
     246*
English, Captain Robert, 236–37, 280
English civilians, 83–84, *85,* 149, *150,* 167–68, 254, 263
Erebus, HMS (British monitor), 228
Excelsior (U.S. Army transport), *131,* 132, 134–35
Exercise Tiger: *see* Tiger, Exercise
Exeter, England, 20

1st Special Engineering Brigade, U.S. Army, 90
42nd Infantry Division, U.S. Army, 267
Fairbanks, Captain Douglas E. Jr., 234–35, *236, 237,* 238–
     40, *241,* 246, *247*
Fairchild, Lieutenant (junior grade) Ben, 65, *66,* 67
Falmouth, England, 20, 41, 86, 146, 148–49
Farquharson, Captain, 50–51
Farragut, Idaho, Naval Training Center, 76
Fauks, Barbara Clare, x–xi, 78, 81, 83–84, *85*
Fauks, Lieutenant Commander Paul S., x, 76, *78,* 79, *80,* 81,
     82, 85
Fay-de-Bretagne, France, 265, 267
Fécamp, France, 37
Ferris, Joel Tom, 160
Fersfield, England, 214
Fifth Torpedo Flotilla (German), 35
Finkelberg, Torpedoman's Mate Joe, 246
First Army, U.S., 26, 30, 278
First Infantry Division, U.S. Army, 67, 72–74, 119
Fitch, USS (DD-462), 104
Flanagan, Father Edward J., 257, *258*
Flanigan, Rear Admiral Howard A., 19, *20,* 21, 177, 194–95,
     203–5
Fleet Air Wing Seven, U.S. Navy, 214
Flemington, Missouri, 265
Flensburg, Germany, 251, 253–54, 272–73, 275

Food: C rations, 41, 190, 249, 259, 261, *269*; in England,
     83, 119, 168; in France, 109, 197, 232–33, 265; in
     Germany, 259, 261; K rations, 74, 126, 190, 206, 249,
     285; transport of, to Europe, ix; on various ships, 2,
     51–52, 68, 88, 104–5, 126, 128, 132, 163, 257, 263,
     268, 273
Foord, Brigadier E. J., 289
Force O (Omaha Beach), Normandy, 57, 62, 112
Force U (Utah Beach), Normandy, 41, 68, 86, 88, 225, 227
Ford, Captain John, 53
Forrestal, Secretary of the Navy James, *223, 252*
Fort Benning, Georgia, 262
Fort Centrale, France, 197
Fort de Roule, France, 197
Fort du Homet, France, 197–98, 200
Fort Leavenworth, Kansas, 257
Fort Monmouth, New Jersey, 29
Fort Myer, Virginia, xii
Fort Pierce, Florida, 93
Fort Riley, Kansas, 257
Fort San Marcouf, Cherbourg, France, *38*
Fort Schuyler, New York, 160
Fourth Armored Division, U.S. Army, 259
Fourth Infantry Division, U.S. Army, 1–2, 90, 109, 119,
     122–23, 196–97, 226–27
Fowey, England, 41
Fox Green Beach (Omaha), Normandy, 64, *70*
Foxy 29 (U.S. Navy medical unit), 41
Frankford, USS (DD-497), 53, 67
Fraser, Admiral Sir Bruce, *15*
Freed, Frank, 136
Freed, Richard A., 136–40, *141*
Fréjus, France, 221, 223, 229, 237
French army, 220–21, 238, *266,* 283
French civilians, ix, 5–6, 101, 195, 205–8, 223, 266
French Lieutenant's Woman, The (movie), 263
French navy, 50, 58, 183, 223, 231, 278, 280–81
Freseman, Captain William, 109
Frey, Lonnie, 257, *258*
Friedeburg, Admiral Hans Georg von, 289
Friedman, Dr. William, 29

Gallipoli, 26
Galveston, Texas, 142
Garagiola, Joe, 257, *258*
Gdynia, Germany, 249–50
General G. O. Squier, USS (AP-130), *262,* 263
Geneva Convention, 246
Genoa, Italy, 237–38
George VI, King, x, *18,* 20, 51, *52*
Georges Leygues (French cruiser), 58
German air force: action against U.S. aircraft, 213; attack on
     Dieppe landing force, 10; attacks on beaches at Nor-
     mandy, 13, 30–31, 98, 114; attacks on troops near
     Cherbourg, France, 196; bombing of England, 78,
     83–85, 112, 134, 203–4, 207, 225, 269; bombing of
     ships at Normandy, 79, 91, 102, 104–5, 115, *139,
     140*; controlled all German military aviation, 35; pre-
     ceded German navy, 35; reconnaissance planes, 105,
     151; threat to Americans in Sicily operation, 74; use of
     glide bombs, 4, 115, 228; use of mines, 37, 112

German army: artillery support, 3, 26, 34, 36, 58, 61, 65–67, 70, 72, 89–91, 95, 101–2, 109, 114, 115, 135, 152, 171–72, 190, 205, 222, 229, 231–33, 238, 240–41, 259, 266; defeat in North Africa, 15, 34; defense of Cotentin Peninsula/Cherbourg, 172; defense of southern France, 221–22, 229, 231–33, 238; failure to invade England, 14; fighting after U.S. breakout from Normandy, 258–61, 266, 270, 278, 285; Normandy beach preparations, 33–34; perceptions of George Patton, 24; preceded German navy, 35; prisoners of war, 2–3, 96, *152*, 153, 162, 191, 197–98, *199*, 201, 206, 228, 260; reaction to Allied landing, ix, 59, 109, 114, 236, 271, 273; use of tanks, 2, 80

German civilians, 250, *251*, 253

German navy: defense against Normandy invasion, 16, 33–39, 52–53, 116, 272; disarming of, 281; escort of merchant shipping, 213; as fleet in being, 16, 274; naval academy, xii, 272; prisoners of war, *246*; restricted by Treaty of Versailles, 34–35; success against Exercise Tiger, 16, 36, 50, 78, 162; surface battle off southern France, x, 234, 239–40, 243–44, *245*; World War I, 33, 172; *see also* various ship types and individual ship names

Gerow, Major General Leonard, 61

Gesswein, Albert, 77

Ghormley, Vice Admiral Robert, 281–82

Gibbs and Cox, 155

Gilbert, Lieutenant Lawrence, 1, 4–5

Giraud, Henri, 14

Gironde River, 278, 280

Glasgow, Scotland, 46, 138

Glide bombs, 4, 115, 228

Gliders, ix, 108, *123*, 151, 196

Glückstadt, Germany, 275

Goebbels, Joseph, 172

Gold Beach, Normandy, 55, 86, 109

Golf, 20, 23

Gooseberry breakwaters (for artificial harbors), *143*, *144*, 170–72, 176, *177*

Göring, General Field Marshal Hermann, 35

Goudsmit, Dr. Sam, 249

Gourock, Scotland, 194

Gregory, Pharmacist's Mate First Class Arlo, 44

Guillot, Commander J. C., 1

Grace Steamship Company, 120, 132

Granville, France, 194, 201

Great Lakes, Illinois, Naval Training Station, 41, 159

Green Beach, southern France, 3, *4*, *5*, 6, 222, 229

Green Beach (Utah), Normandy, 89–90, 101, 102

Greenberg, Hank, 261

Greene, Dr. Ralph, 40

Groves, Major General Leslie R., 249

Guadalcanal, 228

Guns: 20-mm., 4, 102, 127, 132, 134, *137*, 138, *142*, 151, 165, 190, 238, 243–44; 37-mm., 53; 40-mm., 4, 87, 102, 104, 116, 127, 190, *227*, 238, 243–44, 268; 75-mm., 206, 259; 88-mm., ix, 58, 62, 65–67, 70, 80, 89–90, 95, *101*, 165, 190, 197, 229, 232, 238, 259, 269, 285; 105-mm., 26, 36, 238; 150-mm., 38; 155-mm. Long Tom, 3, 26; 210-mm., 38; 240-mm., 238; 380-mm., 36; 3-inch, 67, 132, 138; 4-inch, 239; 5-inch, 62, 101–6, 109–10, 116, 132, 138, 240, 243–45, *246*; 5.9-inch, 10, 100, *273*; 6-inch, 237, 239; 8-inch, 26, *101*, 104; 10-inch, 231; 11-inch, 100, 185–86; 12-inch, 190; 13.5-inch, 171–72; 14-inch, 25, 58, *59*, 102, 184; concrete emplacements ashore in France, *36*, *38*, 58, 70, 80, 90, *100*, *102*, 109, 112–13, 172, 206, 207; large-caliber German guns, 3, 16, 25, 33–34, 36, 38, 54, 65, 100, 183–84, 206; machine guns, ix, 3, 26, 36, 52–54, 61–62, 65, 70, 72, 73, 80, 95, 100–2, 109, 115, 121, 124, 184, 196–98, 210, 213, 246, 259–60, 264–65, 268, 270; mortars, 58, 60–62, 71–72, 95, 109, 121, 184, 205, 260, 285; pistols, 67, 121, 195, 200, 246, 258; rifles, 72, 76, 79, 81, 89, 121, 190, 195, 257–58, 264, 275

Haley, Jack, 191

Halifax, Nova Scotia, 148, 161

Hall, Lieutenant Spencer, 203, 205

Hall, Rear Admiral John L., 15, 17, *18*, 20, 52, *57*, 58, 60–62, 67, 121–22, 228

Hamburg, Germany, 251

Hamilton, Commodore William, 214

Harding USS (DD-625), 62

Hartington, Marquis of, 214

Hat Creek (merchant tanker), 76

He-119E (German fighter plane), 213

Heald, Commander Wilton S., 242

Heckman, Signalman George, 4

Hedgehog antisubmarine weapons, 64, 129

Heintzelman, Ken, 257

Henke, Lieutenant Al, 110

Hennecke, Rear Admiral Walter, 197

Hewitt, Admiral H. Kent, 216–22, *223*, *224*, 229–30, 236, 239

Heye, Vice Admiral Hellmuth, 39

Hillsinger, Colonel Loren B., 10

Hitler, Chancellor Adolf, ix, 7, 14, 35, 62, 87, 112, 114, 200, 251, 271, 274–275

Hobson, USS (DD-464), 104

Hoffman, Captain Heinrich, 37

Hollywood, California, 53

Holtzworth, Commander Ernest, 155

Hopkins, Harry, 14

Horton, John L., 131–34, *135*

Hospital ships: *see* Medical care

Houffalize, Belgium, 270

Houghton, Lieutenant Norris, 277

House of Commons, British, 168, 254

Houston, Texas, 185

Howes, Lieutenant Davis C., 112–16, *117*

Hudson River, New York, 161

Huebner, Major General Clarence, 61, 67

Hughes-Hallett, Captain Jock, 10

Hughes, Peter, 3–5

Hugo Zeye (German training ship), *275*

Hydrographic Office (British), 18

India, 9

Indianapolis, USS (CA-35), 52

Industrial production, 14–16, 55, 169

Intelligence, 21, 29–31, 57, 88, 100, 119, 213, 239, 243, 278; *see also* Codebreaking; Reconnaissance

Inverary, Scotland, 235
Iowa, USS (BB-61), 182
Ireland, 114, 135, 182–83
Irish Sea, 134
Iron Duke-class British battleships, 171
Italian navy, 171
Italy, 3, 16, 34, 74, 165, *218,* 219, 221, 228–30, 237–38, 242
Ives, Captain Norman, 194, 198, 200–1

Jacobs, Rear Admiral Randall, *50*
Jamail, Sergeant Abe, 124
James A. Farrell (U.S. Liberty ship), 195
Japanese, 31, 50, 58–59, 76, 132, 237, 253–54, 274
Jeeps, *2,* 71, 138, 161–62, 194–97, 201, 207, 223, 253, 257, 259–60, 285
Jodl, General Gustave, 289
Johnson, Captain Henry C., 234, 238, 240, 242–46, *247*
Joint Chiefs of Staff, U.S., 14–15
Joint War Plans Committee, 15
Joseph T. Dickman, USS (AP-26), 196–97
Ju-88 (German bomber), 102, 112
Ju-290 (German bomber), 101
Juno Beach, Normandy, 47, 55, 109, 165–66
Jutland, Battle of, 16, 24, 51, 171–72

Kahaner, Private First Class, 270
Kansas City, Missouri, 160
Kare, Boatswain's Mate, 86–87, 89–90
Kasaan Bay, USS (CVE-69), 209
Keator, Lieutenant Lyle, 105
Keller, Chief Motor Machinist's Mate Pete, 148
Kelly, Signalman Bill, 107–8
Kemp, Father Patrick W., xi, 148–52, *153*
Kennedy, Kathleen, 214
Kennedy, Lieutenant Joseph P. Jr., xi, 209, *213,* 214
Kennedy, President John F., 30, 209, 214
Key West, Florida, 142
Kiel Canal, Germany, 272
Kiel, Germany, 250–51, 253–54
Kiesel, Lieutenant (junior grade) W. C., *18*
King, Admiral Ernest J., 12, 14–16, 30, 50, *210,* 218, 225, 228
King George VI: *see* George VI, King
King, Prime Minister William MacKenzie, *16*
Kirk, Vice Admiral Alan G.: commander of U.S. Naval Forces France, 278, 280–81, 283; commander of the western naval task force at Normandy, 24–27, *30,* 51, 184, 197, 226, 242, 278; head of U.S. planning section for Normandy, 12, 16, *18,* 20, 23–24, 29–30, 203; relationship with Admiral Bertram Ramsay, 23, *24,* 25–27, *28,* 30; staff of, 23–25, 27, 29–30, *31, 50*
Kleeman, Werner, 1
Klossner, Tech 5 Carlisle, 270
Knox, Secretary of the Navy Frank, *63*
Krüder, Captain Ernst Felix, 36
Kruggel, Ensign Arthur, 160

La Bounty, Captain Selah Montrose, 142
Labour Party, Britain, 254
Lafferty, Seaman Tom, 148
Laffey, USS (DD-724), 106–7, *108,* 109–11, 181
Lake Constance, 279

Lancaster (British bomber), 37
Land's End, England, 35, 38, 119
Lanker, First Lieutenant Albert, 17
Largs, Scotland, 10
Lattre de Tassigny, General Jean de, 221
Lauer, Lieutenant Frank, 198, 199
LCAs, 88
LCIs, 24, 47, 57, *58, 61,* 62, 86, 89, *91,* 121, 147, 177, 195, *232*
LCI(L)-530, 86–89
LCMs, 72, *73,* 89, 173, 178, 278, 283, 285, *287*
LCPs, 93, *94*
LCTs, 37, 60–62, 68–70, 87, 89, 109, 147–50, *151, 161,* 173–74, 178, 221
LCT-528, 148, *149,* 150–51, *152,* 153
LCT-535, 68–71
LCT-707, 89
LCT-713, 68
LCT-777, 150–51
LCT(R)s, *59,* 109
LCVPs, 1, 3, 65–66, 70, 72–73, *74,* 79, *88, 91, 107,* 109, 122, 147, 151, 160–61, *162,* 229, 278, *279, 280, 281,* 283, *284,* 285, *286*
Leahy, Admiral William D., 14
Lee, Helen, xi
Lee, Robert, xi, 256
Le Havre, France, 35–37, 194–95, 201, 257, 267, 278, 283, 284
Leide, Lieutenant Commander William, 277, 283–84
Lemonnier, Rear Admiral André, 221, *223,* 280
Lend-Lease program, 121
Leopoldville (Belgian transport), 256, 264–67
Leschak, Yeoman Mike, 160
Leslie, Clem, *168*
Leslie, David, 168
Leslie, Doris, 168
LeVallee, Lieutenant George, 195, 197, 199–201
Lewis, Nigel, 40
Lewis, Rear Admiral Spencer, 222–23, *229*
Liberty for personnel, 76, 78, 81, 106, 167, 191–92
Liberty ships, 130, *136, 137, 138, 139, 140, 143, 144,* 169, *177,* 195
Libramont, Belgium, 270
Licata, Sicily, 165
Lido Beach, Long Island, 41, 76
Lindbergh, Charles A., xi, 281–82
Little, Admiral Sir Charles, 11
Little Creek, Virginia, 76, 78, 148, 161
Liverpool, England, 78, 134, 143–44
Lobnitz piers, 173, *174, 175,* 178–79
Loch Lomond, Scotland, 195
Logistics, 12, 19, 21, 193–94, 203–5, 249, 277
London, England: British Combined Operations headquarters, 235; English civilians, 83–85, 149; evacuation of children from, 83; firemen, 183; German bombing of, 78, 83, *84,* 85, 166–68, 203–4, 207, 269; liberty in, 78, 81, 167; Norfolk House, 11–12, 15, 23–24, 194; radar coverage of, 119; ship operations, 165–67; site of British government, 289; subways, x, 78, 85; U.S. naval headquarters in, 15, 19, 21, 23, 29, 46, 48–49, 177, 194–95, 203–4, 218, 235, 254, 281
London Treaty, 35

Long Beach, California, ix
Longest Day, The (movie), ix
Long Island (U.S. Coast Guard cutter), 13
Long Island City, New York, 76
Longues, France, 38
Loran, 1, 64
Lorraine (French battleship), 280
Lorient, France, 266
Louis, Joe, 47
Lovat, Lieutenant Colonel Lord, 10
Lowe, Commander Ed, 228, 230
LSTs: carried LCTs on deck, 148, *161*, 162; Coast Guard
    crews on board, 47; design of, 147, *154*, 155, 157; lost
    in England, *166*; lost in Exercise Tiger, 17, 40–44, 50,
    78, 162, 226; lost at Normandy, 37–38, 145, *157*; per-
    sonnel, 159–64; requirements for, at Normandy, 16,
    24; role of, x, 147, 154; southern France operation,
    3–5, *219*; transport of troops and equipment to
    France, 79–81, 86, 91, 144, *152*, *155*, *156*, *157*, *163*,
    165–67, 179, 264, 269
LST-21, USS, *156*
LST-55, USS, 41, *159*, 160, *161*, *162*, *163*, 164
LST-271, USS, 160
LST-281, USS, *3*
LST-282, USS, 1, 2, *3*, *4*, 5–6, 128–29
LST-289, USS, 40, *42*, *43*
LST-312, USS, *166*, 167
LST-372, USS, 79
LST-384, USS, *166*, 167
LST-386, USS, 165–66, *167*, *168*
LST-391, USS, 44
LST-496, USS, *155*
LST-506, USS, *155*
LST-507, USS, 40, *41*, 42–44, 162
LST-515, USS, 44
LST-523, USS, 145
LST-531, USS, 40
LST Flotilla 10, U.S. Navy, 1
LST Group 29, U.S. Navy, 1
Luckenwalde, Germany, 274
Luftwaffe: *see* German air force
Lund, Captain Andy, *145*, 146
Luxembourg, 239, 270, 278
Lyme Regis, England, 263, *264*, 268

MacArthur, General Douglas, 50, 237
McCook, USS (DD-496), 67
MacDonald, Rear Admiral Donald, xi, 277–81, *282*
Manhattan Project, 249
Maps, 8, 56, 64, 98, 183, 195, 217, *223*, 265
Marblehead, USS (CL-12), 132
Marianas Islands, 55
Marine Corps, xi, 55, 93, 188–92
Maritime Administration, U.S., 157
Maritime Training School, New London, Connecticut, 131
Marrakech, Morocco, 203
Marseille, France, 218–19, 237, 240, 267
Marshall, Commander William J., *114*
Marshall, General George C., 11, 15
Massachusetts Institute of Technology, 249
Massawa, Ethiopia, 179
Mather, Captain P. L., *24*

Mauretania (British troop transport), 76, 268
Me-163 (German rocket plane), 253
Me-262 (German jet plane), 270, 274
Medal of Honor, *50*, 237
Medical care: LSTs as hospital ships, 2, *3*, 11, 128, 162, 190;
    physical examinations, 41; treatment following
    wounds, 10–11, 43–44, *48*, 128–29, 162, 190, 246
Menton, France, 231
Merchant Marine: *see* Commercial ships
Meredith, USS (DD-726), 106, 115
Mexico City, Mexico, 160
Michel, Lieutenant Commander Ed, 52
Milford Haven, Wales, 41, 134, 138, 148
Mills, Lieutenant Alfred, *160*, 161–62, 164
Milwaukee, Wisconsin, xi
Mines: air-dropped, 13, 112, 212, 275; on beach obstacles,
    17, *35*, 71, 73; in Cherbourg, 194, 197, 199–200; in
    Egypt, 171; land mines, 33, 60, 109, 196, *205*, 207,
    238, 241, 259, 266; naval mines offshore at Nor-
    mandy, 34–38, 98, 100, 103–4, 120, 125–26, 129,
    134–35, 145, 184, 190; in Sicily, 165; in southern
    France, 223, 238, 241; success against Allied ships,
    37–38, 71, 103–4, 118, 120, 126, 129, 134–35, 165;
    success against German ships, 275
Minesweeping, 15, 21, 38, 52, *53*, *89*, 98, 100, 109, 112,
    114, 125–27, 183, 185, 190, 199–201, 222, 278
Mississippi River, 160–61
Monaco, 231
Mont Argil, southern France, 231–32
Montcalm (French cruiser), 58, 231–32
Montebourg, France, 172–73, 196–97
Monte Carlo, France, 231
Montgomery, Field Marshal Sir Bernard L., 23, 125, 183
Moon, Rear Admiral Don P.: command of Exercise Tiger
    force, 17, *226*, 227; command of Force U, 20, 40, 86,
    88, 91, 105, 123, 195, 216, 225–26, 228, 230; com-
    mand of task force for southern France invasion, *225*,
    228, 230; suicide of, 40, 216, 222, 228–30
Moore, Orville, 212
Moran, Captain H. G., *226*
Moreno, Captain John A, 225–29, *230*
Morgan, Lieutenant General Sir Frederick E., 11–12, 16,
    290
Morison, Samuel Eliot, ix, xii, 15–16, 229
Morocco, 14–15, 203, 218, 220
Morristown, New Jersey, 160
Moscow, Russia, 289
Moselle River, Germany, 283, 285
Motor torpedo boats: *see* E-boats; PT boats
Mountbatten, Admiral Lord Louis, xi, 7, *9*, 10–12, 235
Mount Vesuvius, Italy, *218*
Movies, ix, x, 53, 83, 134, 191, 235, 263
Mulberries (part of artificial harbor): *see* Phoenix
    breakwaters
Mumma, Carmen, xi
Mumma, Rear Admiral Albert G., xi, 248–49, *250*, *251*, *252*,
    253, *254*, *255*
Munson, Lieutenant Jack, 213
Murray, Albert K., 216, 231–32, *233*

90th Infantry Division, U.S. Army, 119, 196
Nancy, France, 259, 283

Naples, Italy, 3, *218*, 219, 228–30, 242

Napoleon, x, 114

Narbrough, HMS (British frigate), 121–22

Narvik, Norway, 249

National Guard, U.S., 162

Naval Academy, U.S, xi, 13, 142, 214, 226

Naval gunfire support, 15, 24–26, 57, 61–62, *66*, 67, *70*, 89, 106, 109, 113, 115, 181, 184, *231*, *232*

Naval reservists, 24, 41, 53, 59, 132, 142, 160, 195, 234, 236, 239, 277

Naval Technical Mission Europe, U.S., 249–54

Navigation, 1, 11, 17, 59, 64–65, 100, 212

Navy Combat Demolition Unit 132, 93

Navy Cross, 4, 228

Nazi Party, 271, 273

Nelson, USS (DD-623), 110

Netherlands, 39, 239

Neufchâteau, Belgium, 270

Nevada, USS (BB-36), 25–26, 58, *59*, 102, 135, 181–82, 190, 206

Newcastle, England, 183

New Jersey, USS (BB-62), ix

New London, Connecticut, 131

New Orleans, Louisiana, 148, 160–161

Newport, Rhode Island, 182

New Quay, Wales, 212

Newspapers, 1

New York City, x, 26, 41, 76, 93, 131–32, 136, 142–43, 149, 160, *161*, 186, 257, 262–63

New York, USS (BB-34), 182

New Zealand, 254

Nice, France, 5, 231, 237

Niedermair, John C., 147, 154–57, *158*

Nierstein, Germany, 285

Nimet Allah (German converted yacht), 239–40, 243–44, *245*, 246–47

Nimitz, Admiral Chester W., 14

Ninth Air Force, U.S. Army Air Forces, *123*

Ninth Army, U.S., 278

Ninth Infantry Division, U.S. Army, 196–97

Ninth Naval District, U.S., 159

Nivens, Coxswain Delba, 73

Norfolk, Virginia, 29, 76, 142, 155, 163, 182, 210, 212

North Africa, 7, 11, 14, 33–34, 120, 142, 191, 194, 203, 216, 225, 235

North Devon, England, 150

North Island, California, Naval Air Station, 210

Norway, 38, 138, 162, 239, 249, *272*, 273–75

Norwegian navy, 37, 50

Noyes, Carl R., 96

101st Airborne Division, U.S. Army, 87, 108

Oban, Scotland, 170

Oberbefehlshaber West (OB West), 34

Oberkommando der Wehrmacht (OKW), 34, 37

O'Brien, USS (DD-725), 106

Obstacles: *see* Beach obstacles

Office of Strategic Services, 9, 50

Ohio River, 160–61

Olathe, Kansas, Naval Air Station, 160

Oliver Wolcott (U.S. Liberty ship), *136*, 137–39

Omaha Beach, Normandy: American bombing of, 59, 101; artificial harbor off beach, *143*, 170–72, 178–80; beach obstacles, 17–18, *58*, 60, 71–73; cliffs behind beach, *60*, 71, 80, 183–84, 190, 205; combat demolition units, 60; consolidation of forces ashore, *156*, 162, 205; difficult landing for Americans, 12, 25–26, 30, 55, 59–62, 66, 72–74, 80, 90, 96, 109, 114, 119, 139; Force O commanded by John Hall, 52, 57–58, 60–62, 67, 228; German gunfire on, ix, 3, 25, 60–62, 65–67, *70*, 72, 74, 80, 171–72, 184–85, 190; objective in American planning, 23; ravaged by storm in mid-June, *172*, 176–79; role of patrol craft, 64–66; support from U.S. naval gunfire, 57–59, 62, *66*, 112, 114, 120, 139, 183–84, 190; tanks in support of, 68–71; wounded and dead, 2, 62, 66, 70, 72–74, 79–80, 96, 139, 176, 190–91

Omaha, Nebraska, 76, 257, 260

Onslow Bay, North Carolina, 196

Oppenheim, Germany, 285

Oran, Algeria, 191, 203

Orkney Islands, 16, 33, 138

Orne River, 23, 34, 38–39

Oslo, Norway, 275

Ostend, Belgium, 35

Oyster Bay, New York, 196–97

P-38 Lightning (U.S. fighter plane), 17, 102

P-47 Thunderbolt (U.S. fighter plane), 228

P-51 Mustang (U.S. fighter plane), 104

Pace, Commander D. Allen, 165–67, *168*

Paddington, England, 149

Page, Jack, 113

Paignton, England, 149

Palermo, Sicily, 191

Palmer, Commander George, 62

Palrang, Skip, *258*

Panama Canal, 164, *189*

Panama City, Florida, 161

Panter, Dr. Ed, 43–44

Paratroopers, ix, 37, 87, 96, 108–9, 123, 126, 151, 195, 198–99, 238, 241

Paris, France, 48, 163, 249, 278, 281–82, 289

Parker, Kenneth, 289

Parliament, British, 9

Pas-de-Calais, France: *see* Calais, France

Pash, Colonel Boris, 249

Patch, Lieutenant General Alexander M., 219, *223*

Patria (German cruise ship), 273

Patton, Lieutenant General George S., 24, 135, 219–20, 259, *260*, 266, 277, 279, 283–85, 287

PB4Y-1 Liberator (U.S. patrol bomber), 210, *211–12*, 213–14

PBM Mariner (U.S. patrol bomber), 210, 212

PC-552, USS, 64, 66

PC-553, USS, 64, *65*, 66–67

PC-1261, USS, 89

Pearl Harbor, attack on, 14, 19, 25, 58–59, 203

Pearson, Commander Meade S., *18*

Peenemünde, Germany, 250, 274

Pentagon, 262

Penzance, England, 149

Perry, Yeoman Second Class Edward, 197

Pheasant, USS (AM-61), *127*
Philadelphia, Pennsylvania, xii, 143
Philippine Islands, 50, 53, 226, 237
Phoenix breakwaters (for artificial harbors), 165, 169–70, *173,* 174–75, *176,* 177–80
Photography, 1, 17, 46–47, 89, 196
Pierce, Alice, 261
Pineau, Captain Roger, xii
Pittsburgh, 155, 159–61
Planning, 7–12, 14–17, 19–20, 23–26, 29, 33, 35, 86, 112–13, 193–94, 203, 216, 225, 228, 235, 277, 281
Plymouth, England, 16, 25, 38, 42, 44, 86, 90, 106, *107,* 116, 149–50, 204, 225, 227–28, 285
Pointe des Deux Freres, France, 237
Pointe du Hoc, Normandy, France, 3, 80, 183–84
Pont Château, France, *266*
Poland, 7
Polish navy, 10
Poole, England, 46, *49*
Portland, England, 18, 26, 44, 50, 68, 112, 183, 195
Portland, Maine, 116
Port Lyautey, Morocco, 218
Port Said, Egypt, 170
Portsmouth, England, 10–11, 26–27, 38, 47, 150, 172, 177, 191
Portsmouth, Virginia, 188
Port Talbot, Wales, 41
Powell, Lieutenant Commander Edgar S., 113, *115*
Prisoners of war: American, 163, 198–99, 260; German, 2–3, 96, *152,* 153, 162, 191, 197–99, 201, 206, 228, *246,* 260
Propaganda, 273, 275
PT boats, 40, 50, *51, 52, 53,* 54, 91, 105, 116, *127,* 128, 214, 237, *238,* 242–43
PT-10, 54
PT-502, 51
PT-504, 51, *52, 53, 127,* 128
PT-521, 54
Puerto Rico, 226
Purple Heart medal, 259
Purrick, Signalman Ted, 107

QH gear, 64
Quebec Conference, 15, *16*
Queen Elizabeth (British troop transport), 161, 262
Queen Elizabeth, HMS (British battleship), 171
Queen Mary (British troop transport), 16, 262
Quiberon Bay, France, 194
Quigley, Chief Motor Machinist's Mate John, 126, 128
Quincy, USS (CA-71), 89, *98,* 99–100, *101,* 102–5, 135, 190
Quistran, France, 23
Quonset Point, Rhode Island, 136, 155

Radar, 10, 36–37, 53, 100, 110, 113–16, 119, 125, 131–32, 184, 210, 212–13, *214,* 236, 238–39, 254, 268, 275
Radio, 30–31, 53, 65–66, 68–69, 109, 114–16, 142, 172, 195, 212, 214, 226, 232–33, 238–41, 243, 259–60, 263, 284, 290
Raeder, Grand Admiral Erich, 35
Ramillies, HMS (British battleship), 37
Ramsay, Admiral Sir Bertram, 12, 16, 23, *24,* 25–27, 30
Rangers, U.S. Army, 3, *60,* 62, 80, 231, 265
Rapp, Gil, 212

Reconnaissance, *17,* 21, 35, 37, 105, 119, 151, 194–95, 197, 199, 201, 213, 257–58, 260, 283
Red Beach, southern France, 222, 229
Red Beach (Utah), Normandy, 90
Red Cross, 44, 259, 261
Reedy, James R., xi, 209, *210,* 211–14, *215*
Reiser, Pete, 257, *258*
Religion, 1, 134, 148–50, 214
Remagen, Germany, 279, *284,* 286
Republican Party, 196
Rescue Flotilla One, U.S. Coast Guard, 47
Rescue at sea, 44, 46, 48–49, 52, 104, 121, 127–28, 139, 145, 228, 240, 264
Research and development, 249–50, 253–54
Reuss, Richard, xii
Rheims, France, 289
Rhine River, ix–x, 250, 258, 277–79, 281, 283, *284,* 285, *286*
Rhino barges, 1, *138, 156*
Rhône River, 218
Rich, USS (DE-695), 52
Richards, Captain Dick, 182
Richmond, Admiral Alfred C., 46–48, *49,* 194
Rickey, Branch, 261
Rickover, Admiral Hyman G., xi
Roberts, Major General John Hamilton, 10
Rockets: American, 58–59, 61, 109, 239; German: *see* V-1 rockets
Rockwell, Dean L., 68–70, *71*
Rodgers, Rear Admiral Bertram J., 231
Rodgers, Richard, xi
Rogers, Lieutenant Charles, 243–44
Rome, Georgia, 52
Rommel, Field Marshal Erwin, 16–17, 32, *33,* 34, 38, 90, 172, 176, 178
Roosevelt, Brigadier General Theodore Jr., *90,* 196–97, 226
Roosevelt, President Franklin D., x, 14–15, *16,* 19, *50,* 196–97, 219, 260
Roosevelt, President Theodore, 196
Roseneath, Scotland, 41, 194–95
Roth, Boatswain's Mate William, 160, *163*
Royal Air Force, 10, 37, 42, 102, 212–13, 251, 269, 275
Royal, Captain Forrest, 155
Royal Marines, 235, 251, 253–54
Royal Navy: bases, 50; Churchill as head of, *15;* college, 149; comparison with German navy, 35; conditions for soldiers embarked in transports, 10; escort for Exercise Tiger, 42, 50, 226–27; hosted U.S. observers in 1940–41, 281; logistic support of U.S. ships, 51; Mediterranean campaign, 170–72; relationship with Admiral Harold Stark, 19–20; role of the Admiralty, 24, 171; support of Dieppe landing, 10, 16; support of Normandy landings, 15–16, 50–51, 86, 120–21, 125, 183, 228; support of southern France landings, 221, 234, 239–40; *see also* various ship types and individual ship names
Rudd, Lieutenant Norman, 212
Rudder, Lieutenant Colonel James, 3
Rue, Rear Admiral Joseph, 280
Ruge, Vice Admiral Friedrich, 16, 32, *33,* 34–38, *39,* 271
Rumburg, Lieutenant Colonel Chris, 265
Rupert, HMS (British frigate), 121–22

Rush, Lieutenant Commander Sam, 246
Russia: as an American ally, 12, 15, 131, 138, 250–51, 281;
    German forces in, 7, 14, 34, 274; Russian army, 2,
    261, 272; threat to western Allies, 12, 253
Ryder, Chief Quartermaster William, 107
Ryder, Commander R. E. D., 9

II Corps, U.S. Army, 29
VI Corps, U.S. Army, 229
VII Corps, U.S. Army, 26, 109, 123, 172–73, 195–96,
    226–27
7th Beach Battalion, U.S. Navy, 78
66th Infantry Division, U.S. Army, 262–67
70th Tank Battalion, U.S. Army, 68
79th Infantry Division, U.S. Army, 196–97
635th Antiaircraft Automatic Weapons Battalion, U.S. Army,
    268
741st Tank Battalion, U.S. Army, 68–70
743rd Tank Battalion, U.S. Army, 68–69
S-142 (German E-boat), 42
Saar River, 259
Sabin, Vice Admiral Lorenzo S., 57–62, 63
Sainte-Marie-du-Mont, France, 196
Sainte-Maxime, France, 237
Sainte-Mère-Église, France, 81, 87, 135
Saint Eval, Royal Air Force station, 212
Saint Germain, France, 278
Saint Goar, Germany, 285
Saint-Laurent-sur-Mer, France, 62, 179
Saint-Lô, France, 179, 207
Saint Louis Cardinals, x
Saint Louis, Missouri, x
Saint-Malo, France, 35, 194, 201
Saint-Nazaire, France, 9, 34, 36, 213, 265–67
Saint-Raphaël, France, 5, 222–23, 229, 237, 242
Saint-Tropez, France, 237, 242
Saipan, Marianas Islands, 55
Salcombe, England, 20, 85
Salerno, Italy, 74, 165, 221, 228
Samson, George, 53
Samuel Chase, USS (APA-26), 64, 72, 73
San Antonio, Texas, xi
Sanders, Captain Harry, 53, 62, 67, 116, 242
Sanders, Jacquin, 264
San Diego, California, 210
San Francisco, California, 76, 81
San Francisco, USS (CA-38), 228
Santa Clara (U.S. passenger liner), 120, 132
Satterlee, USS (DD-626), 67
Savannah, USS (CL-42), 228
Scapa Flow, Orkney Islands, 16, 33
Scarab, HMS (British gunboat), 237, 239–40, 243–45
Schaffer, Melvin, 85
Schelde Estuary, 34
Schmidt, Shipfitter First Class Elmer, 127
Schwartz, Motor Machinist's Mate Henry, 246
Scotland, 3, 10, 41, 46, 138, 170, 194–95, 235
Seabees, 90, 93, 136, 174, 194–95, 198, 205, 208, 212, 225
Sea Lion, Operation, 14
Searls, Hank, 214
Second Canadian Division, 10

Security of information, 17–18, 21, 39, 60–61, 68, 79, 93,
    106, 112, 119, 132, 138, 194, 213, 249
Seine River, 16–18, 23–24, 34, 37, 39, 134
Semmes, Lieutenant Commander James, 67
Senn, Captain Elliott M., 105
Seventh Army, U.S., 219
Severn River, xi
Sevez, General François, 289
SHAEF: see Supreme Headquarters Allied Expeditionary
    Force
Shakespeare, William, 247
Shaw, Lieutenant (junior grade) Harvey, 110
Sherman tanks, 2, 68–69, 137, 156
Ship conversion and repair, 38, 41, 138, 167, 186, 188, 243,
    274–75
Ship design, 147, 154–55, 157, 249
Shore bombardment, naval, 10–11, 16–17, 30, 38, 54, 58,
    59, 93, 102–4, 106, 109, 112, 114–15, 120, 135, 139,
    166, 183, 190–91, 206–7, 221, 237–38, 243; see also
    Naval gunfire support
Sicily, 14–16, 24–25, 29, 72, 74, 133, 142, 165, 191, 219,
    221, 236, 243
Silver Spring, Maryland, x
Simpson, Boatswain's Mate Dick, 150
Sims, Admiral William S., 20
Sixth Armored Division, U.S. Army, 259
Skagerrak, 272, 275
Skidmore, Lieutenant Colonel James H., x, 254, 262–65,
    266, 267
Skidmore, Phyllis, x
Skoda munitions works, Czechoslovakia, 181
Slapton Sands, England, 40–42, 50, 68, 78, 106, 119, 162,
    216, 226, 230
Slim, General William, 24
Smith, Boatswain's Mate Second Class Walter, 128
Smith, Commander James, 214
Smith, Congressman Wint, 162
Smith, Lieutenant General Walter Bedell, 12, 24–25, 289,
    290
Smith, Lieutenant Robert Lee, 59
Solomons campaign, xi, 214, 228
Solomons Island, Maryland, 160–61
Somers, USS (DD-381), 110
Somme River, 34
Sonar, 125
Southampton, England, 2, 25, 68, 195, 264
Southern France: air support, 209; D-Day assault, 3, 221–
    22, 224, 229, 231, 232, 238; planning for invasion, 16,
    216, 218, 221, 225, 228, 230; shore bombardment,
    191, 231, 232, 237–38; tactical deception, 237–42
Southwick Park, England, 11–12
Soviet Union: see Russia
Spain, 212
Spencer, Motor Machinist's Mate David, 126
Spitfire (British fighter plane), 10, 83, 101, 104–5
Stalin, Premier Joseph, 7, 14, 16
Stanford, Commander Albert, 170
Stark, Admiral Harold R., 9, 19, 20, 21, 23, 46, 177, 194,
    203
State Department, 46
Staten Island, New York, 163–64
Steinberg, Lieutenant Ernest, 203

Stimson, Secretary of War Henry, 50
Strasbourg, France, 249
Strategy, 7, 14–15, 237, 271
Strauss, Rear Admiral Elliott B., xi, 9–12, *13,* 235
Strong, Major General K. W. D., 289–90
Struble, Rear Admiral Arthur D., 29, *30,* 50, 226, *227,* 242
Sturgis, South Dakota, 76
Supreme Headquarters Allied Expeditionary Force
    (SHAEF), 47–48
Susan B. Anthony, USS (AP-72), 119, *120,* 121, *122,* 132, 134
Susloparov, Major General Ivan, 289, *290*
Svenner (Norwegian destroyer), 37
Swansea, Wales, 134, 165
Swinemünde, Germany, 274
Switzerland, 279
Sword Beach, Normandy, 38, 55, 109

28th Infantry Division, U.S. Army, 195
29th Infantry Division, U.S. Army, 138
30th Assault Unit, Royal Marines, 251, 254
36th Infantry Division, U.S. Army, 3, 223, 228–29
294th Joint Assault Signal Company, 78
314th Infantry Regiment, U.S. Army, 197
359th Regimental Combat Team, U.S. Army, 119, 123
T-21 (German E-boat), 35
T-24 (German E-boat), 35
T-29 (German E-boat), 35
Tactics, 10, 201, 212, 240, 243–44
Taiwan, 30
Talbott, Lieutenant General Orwin C., xi, 119–23, *124*
Tanks, 2, 21, 26, 53, 60–62, 66, 68–71, 89, *137,* 154, *156,*
    179, 184, 201, 226, 257–60, 269, *287*
Tarawa, Gilbert Islands, 93
Task Force 85, 29, 231
Task Force 87, 229
Task Group 80.4, 234, 236, 243
Task Group 122.5, 277
Task Unit 80.4.1, 240
Task Unit, 122.5.2, 277
Task Unit 127.2.8, 195, 201
Teague, Steward Henry, 110
Tedder, Air Chief Marshal Sir Arthur W., *290*
Teheran Conference, 16
Television, ix, 1, 5, 53, 214
Texas, USS (BB-35), 166, 181–82, *183,* 184, *185, 189,*
    190–91
Thackrey, Captain Lyman, 11–12
Thames River, 165–67
They Were Expendable (movie), 53, 237
Third Army, U.S., 195, 259–60, 277–79
Thomas B. Robertson (U.S. Liberty ship), 145–46
Thompson, USS (DD-627), 67
Tide, USS (AM-125), 52, *125, 126, 127, 128*
Tides and currents at Normandy, 2, 12, 17, 34, 36, 58–59,
    65, 69, 119, 130, 135, 150, 152, 165–67, 173, 269
Tiger, Exercise: book concerning, 40; deaths and injuries,
    40, 43, 66, 216, 226; inquiry in aftermath of, 226–27;
    life belts in, 5, 43; loss of LSTs, 17, 36, 42–43, 50, 78,
    162; media coverage of, 40; rehearsal for Utah Beach
    landing, 40, 86, 226; role of German E-boats in, 36,
    42–43, 226–27, 230
Tirpitz (German battleship), 9, 267, *274*

Tompkins, Captain Rutledge, 225, 229
Torbay, England, 149
Torch, Operation, 14
Torpedoes, 10, 37–39, 42–43, 51, 76, 198, 239, 244, 272,
    273, 274
Torquay, England, 20, 42, 119
Toul, France, 283–85
Toulon, France, 237–40, 243, 246
Training, 15–16, 21, 24, 37, 68, 76, *87,* 93, 131, 136, 138,
    148, 159–61, 188, 194–95, 201, 235, 262–65, 268,
    283
Transportation Corps, U.S. Army, 46, 131
Treasure Island, San Francisco, 76
Treasury Department, 48
Trinidad, 142
Trombold, Lynn Louise, 161
Trombold, Walter, 147, *159,* 160–63, *164*
Truman, President Harry S, xi
Truscott, Major General Lucian K., 229
Tulagi, USS (CVE-72), 209
Tunisia, 15, 165
Turner, Motor Machinist's Mate Second Class Harry, 127
Turner, Ted, 53
Tuscaloosa, USS (CA-37), 102, 104, 190
Twelfth Army Group, U.S. Army, 278

U-335 (German submarine), 171
U-boats, xii, 14–15, 17, 32, 35, 38, 76, 112, 132, 134, 136,
    138, 169, 171, *212,* 213, *252, 254,* 257, 264, 266–67
Ultra, 30–31
Underwater demolition teams: *see* Combat demolition units
Uniforms: afire after bombing, 4; baseball, 257; combat
    demolition units, 93; impregnated to protect against
    chemical warfare, 2, 79, 121, 195–96; insignia, 46, 48,
    51; lost in shipwrecks, 44; sizes of, 188
USO, 191, 261
Utah Beach, Normandy: approach and landing on, 1, 87–
    90, 93, 94–96, 98, 100–3, 109, 121–22, 134–35, 151,
    195; artificial harbor off beach, 152, 170; bombard-
    ment of, 98, 101–5, 109, 114; combat demolition
    units, 93, 95–96, 109; consolidation of forces ashore,
    90–91, 96, 122–24, 144–45, 152, 205, 269; German
    gunfire on, 3, 38, 89–91, 95, 152; German miniature
    tanks, *80,* 81; mines offshore, *89;* planning for sup-
    port requirements, 16, 86; ravaged by storm in mid-
    June, 144, 153; rehearsal for, in England, 40, 87, 119;
    role of patrol craft, 64; smooth operation in compari-
    son with Omaha, 12, 26, 109, 119; wounded and
    dead, 2, 89–90, 95–96, 123

V-1 rockets (buzz bombs), 84, 166–67, 184, *204,* 207, 214,
    249, 268, 278
V-2 rockets, 250, 274
Valiant, HMS (British battleship), 171
Valognes, France, 172–73, *196*
VB-110 (U.S. naval aviation squadron), 210–14
VCS-7 (U.S. naval aviation squadron), 102
Versailles, France, 34, 278
Versailles, Treaty of, 34
Vian, Admiral Sir Philip, 12
Vienna, Austria, 261
Vierville-sur-Mer, France, 57, 62

Vietnam War, ix, 119
Vire River, 34
Visual signaling, 58, 65, *78*, 79–81, 142, 144–45, 201, 228
von Braun, Wernher, 250
von Rundstedt, Field Marshal Gerd, 34
von Schlieben, Lieutenant General Karl, 172, 197
VP-203 (U.S. naval aviation squadron), 210, 214

Wakefield, Orval W., 93–96, *97*
Wakefield, USS (AP-21), 81
Wales, 41, 119, 134, 138, 148, 165, 212
Walke, USS (DD-723), 106
Walker, Harry, 257, *258*
Walsh, Captain Quentin R., x, 46, 193–201, *202*
Walsh, Mary Ann, x
Walter, Dr. Hellmuth, 249–50, 253–54
Warrick, Ruth, *236*
War Shipping Administration, U.S., 136
Warspite, HMS (British battleship), 37
Washington, D.C., xi, 14, 16, 23–24, 30, 50, 68, 154, 182, 210, 225, 249, 289
Washington, USS (BB-56), 216
Watson, Lieutenant Jack, *237*, 238, 243
Weather: beautiful spring in England in 1944, 21, 134, 204; caused one-day delay in invasion at Normandy, 1, 12, 68; fog, 131–32, 182; forecasts, 37, 173, 177; Normandy ravaged by storm in mid-June, 26, 144, 152, 166–67, *172*, 173–75, *176, 177, 178, 179*, 180, 197; rough seas, 69, 137–38, 150, 264; thunder storm, 228
Webber, Lieutenant Gordon, 142–43
Wesermünde, Germany, *252*

Westminster Abbey, London, 168
Weymouth, England, 68, 79, 264
White House, Washington, D.C., 14–15, 30
Wichita, Kansas, 159, 161
Wight, Isle of, 25, 37, 144
Wight, Lieutenant Fred, 18
Wilcox, Rear Admiral John, 216
Wilkes, Rear Admiral John, 16, 27, 86, 194–95, 201, 204–5, *206*, 207–8, 278
William the Conqueror, 12, 236
Williams, Brigadier General Sam, 121–22
Williamsburg, Virginia, 93
William Tyler Page (U.S. Liberty ship), 142–46
Willy, Lieutenant Wilford, 214–15
Wilson, Rear Admiral Barry, 203
Winant, Ambassador John G., 19, *20*
Wizard of Oz, The (movie), 191
Woking, England, 213
World Series, 261
World War I, 7, 15, 19–20, 26, 79, 83, 119, 171, 228, 266
Wright, Harry II, 160
Wyman, Brigadier General Willard, 67

Yangtze River, 237
Yank magazine, 120–21

Z-30 (German destroyer), *272, 273,* 274–75
Z-39 (German destroyer), 249
Zanuck, Darryl, ix
Zimmer, John, 160
Z-plan, 35

The **Naval Institute Press** is the book-publishing arm of the U.S. Naval Institute, a private, nonprofit society for sea service professionals and others who share an interest in naval and maritime affairs. Established in 1873 at the U.S. Naval Academy in Annapolis, Maryland, where its offices remain, today the Naval Institute has more than 100,000 members worldwide.

Members of the Naval Institute receive the influential monthly magazine *Proceedings* and discounts on fine nautical prints and ship and aircraft photos. They also have access to the transcripts of the Institute's Oral History Program and get discounted admission to any of the Institute-sponsored seminars offered around the country.

The Naval Institute also publishes *Naval History* magazine. This colorful bimonthly is filled with entertaining and thought-provoking articles, first-person reminiscences, and dramatic art and photography. Members receive a discount on *Naval History* subscriptions.

The Naval Institute's book-publishing program, begun in 1898 with basic guides to naval practices, has broadened its scope in recent years to include books of more general interest. Now the Naval Institute Press publishes more than seventy titles each year, ranging from how-to books on boating and navigation to battle histories, biographies, ship and aircraft guides, and novels. Institute members receive discounts on the Press's nearly 400 books in print.

For a free catalog describing Naval Institute Press books currently available, and for further information about subscribing to *Naval History* magazine or about joining the U.S. Naval Institute, please write to:

Membership & Communications Department
U.S. Naval Institute
118 Maryland Avenue
Annapolis, Maryland 21402-5035
or call, toll-free, (800) 233-USNI.